ROAD AMERICA

FIVE DECADES OF RACING AT ELKHART LAKE

By: Tom Schultz

Acknowledgements

To my wife Jean who has put up with my hundreds of weekends away from home pursuing my muse of motor racing. Also for not complaining when I took over the family room for a year while writing this book.

To Augie Pabst for the Foreword, encouragement and for help at the track.

To Mr. James Dervin, S.J., my high school English teacher, who taught me how to write for publication as the faculty advisor to the school paper and yearbook.

To Greg Rubenstein of SCCA Pro Racing for technical assistance.

To Jim Haynes and Roger Jaynes of Road America for granting me free rein in the archives of the track.

And to Jim Caspary, John Mietus and Mike Mierzwa, boyhood chums and still close friends, who were my means of transportation to the track for years before I finally bought my own car.
The photographs in this book came principally from the Tom Schultz collection. Additional photographs, especially of the period prior to the mid 1960s, were provided by the Road America Archives, the Sandy Silverberg collection and the Jim Caspary collection. I am grateful to them for their kind assistance.

To Clif Tufte, whose vision, persistence and ability gave us Road America. Had Clif not stepped into the picture when the early street races were stopped, there would be no Road America. Further, without Road America, the first of the purpose built road courses, road racing in America today would not be as good, because it is certain that others would not have taken the risk had Clif not shown the way.

Dust Jacket Design: Llew Kinst
Interior Design: Kemnitz Type and Graphics, Inc.

ISBN 0-929758-19-6

Printed in Hong Kong

Foreword

My career in motorsports has covered several phases over 40 years. During my ten years of major racing in the late '50s and early '60s I considered Road America my home track. My first race there was in 1956 driving a Triumph TR3 and for the next 10 years I competed there more times than I can count in many different cars. It is one of the more challenging tracks in North America, and its combination of tight corners, very fast curves, hills, and rather long straights make it one of the sternest tests of car and driver to be found anywhere.

When I returned to driving in the mid '80s after 18 years at the Pabst Brewing Company it was at Road America. I was reunited with an old friend; the track, though modernized in many respects, still was the challenge that I had remembered. Now that my driving is in the historic arena, I still look forward to tackling the four great miles.

Almost as important to what makes Road America unique is the ambiance. Nowhere else can you watch racing in the beauty of the countryside along with the best brats and corn on the cob money can buy. Further, there is great beer and people watching!

I have been involved with the track for most of its life, not only as a driver, but also as a member of its Board of Directors. I'm proud to be associated with such a legend and giant in American road racing.

I've known Tom Schultz for over a dozen years, meeting him when I was running in the Pro Sports 2000 series and he was covering it for various magazines. Since then I have found him to have an extensive knowledge of all things in racing, and especially anything that ever happened at Road America. This book is a thorough retelling of the Road America story, and after reading it you will know not only the results of virtually every race ever held there, but also about its place in American racing and the forces and movements that have shaped and are continuing to shape racing over the years. I know that you'll enjoy it.

Augie Pabst
Pabst Farms
Oconomowoc, Wisconsin
May, 1997

Introduction

In 1955 I was in grade school and knew very little about racing. The only racing news carried by the local papers generally concerned spectacular crashes. Two events then occurred which, over 40 years later, bring us to this book. First of all, the boy at the next desk brought a copy of *Road & Track* to school and let me read it. This magazine opened up a whole new world of wonderful things to me — sports cars and road racing! Then, some 60 miles north of my home in suburban Milwaukee, a new race track was built. This was Road America, and the newspapers gave it major coverage. I was hooked.

It wasn't until 1958 that I was able to make my first trip to the track. Even though it was just over an hour away, the track was as accessible as the dark side of the moon to a youth too young to drive and whose parents were not at all interested in racing. Fortunately, a friend got his license, got his parents' car and I was at the June Sprints. What wonders my eyes saw that day! People and cars that previously had been just pictures and words in *Road & Track* and *Sports Cars Illustrated* were real, were in front of me and were loud! I was not just hooked, I was reeled in, mounted and displayed. Since that time, I have attended virtually every race at the track, the only exceptions being when I spent several years in the Army, but even then I managed to arrange leave in a timely manner most of the time!

That was many years ago but racing and Road America have remained a passion for me. I can't tell you how many times I have driven the 120 miles round trip to the track and back, but suffice to say I have contributed to some oil company dividends. Now that the track is over 40 years old I thought that the story of who accomplished what on the four miles of asphalt should be told, not only the winners of the feature events, but also of the support races and top SCCA National classes. All the spectator events that thrilled hundreds of thousands over the years are between these covers; if it happened, I would like to think you will read it here. If by chance I have omitted something worthy of note, please accept my apology. The records of the early years are a bit sketchy due to the passage of years, but I believe that I have produced an accurate record of the action on the track.

I have attempted to not only tell what happened on the track, but also to place these events in the bigger context of U.S. road racing. The track has been affected by what has gone on in board rooms, by the rise and fall of various sanctioning bodies, by the coming and going of support series and by the politics of racing. I hope that by reading this book you will be able to see what was happening in American road racing nationwide. It is an exciting sport, exciting things happen and they should be enjoyed.

Most of all the jewel that is Road America should be enjoyed. It now is the *doyenne* of U.S. racing, one of the proudest and most historic venues. We are fortunate to have it and to be able to enjoy it. I certainly do, and I hope that you do also.

Tom Schultz

1950-1954

The war still raged on two fronts in 1944, but the Allies had landed in Europe and were island hopping in the Pacific. The war was not yet won, but the tide had turned in the Allies' favor. A small group of motoring enthusiasts met in Boston to share their love of fine automobiles. They formulated ideas about how to enjoy their cars after the war ended and how to meet others with similar likes. Eventually this small group coalesced into a club and this club took the name Sports Car Club of America (SCCA).

Eventually the war ended and the club expanded. Inevitably, the desire to exercise their cars resulted in racing. The year was 1948 and a young lawyer from upstate New York named Cameron Argetsinger arranged to have sports cars race through the streets and hills of Watkins Glen. It was a seminal event; all road racing in the country today can be traced back to this race. Shortly thereafter, the bug spread to the midwest. The Chicago Region of the SCCA had members who vacationed in the Elkhart Lake area. Enthusiasts being what they are, it did not take long before their forays on the back roads gave rise to an idea; since we are having so much fun, why not get some friends together and race over these roads? This spark of an idea was fanned into flames. The Elkhart Lake Businessmen's Association enlisted and racing came to the Kettle Moraine.

The first Elkhart Lake sports car races took place in July, 1950. The course was 3.35 miles long and used the public highways just northwest of the lake. This first event did not receive much advance publicity; nonetheless, some 5000 spectators showed up to watch. The feature race was won, somewhat fittingly, by Jim Kimberly of nearby Neenah, WI in a Ferrari.

The 1951 race was conducted over a much expanded course. It now was 6.5 miles in length and completely encircled the lake as well as went through the village. Two straights nearly a mile in length led to very high speeds indeed. While 1950 had been mainly a race put on, by and for the enjoyment of racing buddies, the 1951 event was of National importance. Publicity was nationwide and the little town of Elkhart Lake was on the map. A very large crowd turned out to watch John Fitch win in the Cunningham C-4R.

By 1952 the event was huge; it was a happening and the place to be. The races were run in September and estimates at the time pegged the crowd at 100,000. This surely was an exaggeration, but the fact remains that

Start of the under 1500cc race at the 1951 Elkhart Lake road races. A full field of MGs takes the green flag. Note the external cooler between the front wheels of #66.

the area was jammed with people trying to see the races. This year the Cunninghams placed 1-2-3. John Fitch again won, with Phil Walters second and Briggs Cunningham third. Phil Hill was fourth in a Jaguar.

The races may have been very successful and certainly brought a lot of dollars into the local economy, but they were on borrowed time. The entire concept of racing on public roads with just an occasional hay bale between the cars and the spectators simply could not last. The thought of the consequences of a car going through the snow fencing into the massed fans was unbearable. Predictably a law was passed in the state legislature which banned speed contests on public roads. The Elkhart Lake road races were finished — or were they?

Enter Clif Tufte and his vision. Clif was a civil engineer who had spent a good portion of his life building highways. Clif was an energetic backer of the Elkhart Lake road races, but he had the foresight to see that racing on public roads was a phase that would not last. He had the vision to realize that if Elkhart Lake was to retain the popularity and the tremendous boost to the economy that the races brought an alternative to street racing was necessary. As with men of vision, Tufte went beyond merely thinking about it or even proposing it. He went out and did it.

The cars line up for the start of the feature race, 1952. The Cunningham cars are at the front of the field. The old mill building in the background still stands.

The idea of a permanent road racing course was quite novel at this time. Virtually all road racing was being done on the public roads, on airport courses, or on the roads of private estates owned by sportsmen. Nobody was constructing a purpose built road racing track. The fact that it was not being done had no effect on Tufte. As early as 1952, while the street races were still running, Tufte was scouring the countryside around Elkhart Lake, trying to find the necessary blend of space, terrain and availability that would allow him to build his dream. In the spring of 1952 Tufte found a couple farms a few miles south of the town that he felt would do the job. Tufte spent the next two years arranging his support and financing. He had to convince a lot of people that what he was proposing would work. It had not been done before, so his sales job was a big one. But he accomplished it, and in November, 1954, Road America was incorporated and the site was finalized. The vision now was taking shape.

Stock was sold in the corporation. The stock sale was widely based, both in the Elkhart Lake area and in Chicago where the Chicago Region of the SCCA was an enthusiastic backer of the track. The stock sale was such that there were many individual stockholders; there would not be just one or two that could exert control over the corporation. The stockholders had their first meeting in April, 1955 and elected the first slate of officers. Clif Tufte, naturally enough, was elected president, Terret Arndt and Edwin Leverenz vice presidents, Jim Johnson treasurer and Everett Nametz secretary.

The farmland for the track was purchased with a mortgage loan arranged through many local participating banks. Tufte spent countless days walking over the 523 acres that were to be converted from farmland. He had the ability to look at a field, a hill, some valleys and see what it would look like as a race course. His engineering training allowed him to visualize what he wanted it to look like. He finalized the general layout in his head and then paced it out, over the moraines, through the kettles, for four miles. Tufte wanted the track to as closely resemble street racing from which it had sprung as possible. He drove around the neighboring country roads and

selected those curves and corners that appealed to him. He then measured them and had them duplicated in the track. This mimicking of actual roads led to the track's most appropriate name: Road America.

Construction started in April, 1955. This gave the builders a most ambitious schedule, as the SCCA had already granted Chicago Region a National listing for races in September, less than five months distant! Nonetheless, construction progressed at a rapid clip. The summer was hot and dry, which greatly helped. Bulldozers scraped out the path, ancient boulders were uprooted and moved, and the road bed was laid. The gravel bed was anywhere from one to two feet deep, depending upon the engineering requirements. In late summer the asphalt was put down at a width of 27 feet, adequate for the times, but it would have to be widened later. A special mix of asphalt was used, a *hot mix* designed to withstand not only the heat of summer but the heat created by racing speeds and cornering traction. Finally the September race date came. The pagoda at the start/finish line was literally being nailed together the morning of the first practice, but the track was ready. Clif Tufte's dream was a reality. Road America existed and racing entered a new chapter.

Road America was the pacesetter in the transition to permanent courses. The era of street racing ended around 1952-53 and road racing was in a real bind. There were virtually no venues available upon which to race. The end of road racing's short life was a very distinct possibility. The opening of permanent race courses was still a few years away. The rescue of road racing during this critical time came from a very unusual source; the U.S. Air Force Strategic Air Command (SAC). General Curtis LeMay, the architect of the aerial war over both Europe and Japan and the Commanding General of SAC, was a sports car enthusiast. He offered the use of SAC bases as sites for racing. The SCCA would be able to conduct up to a dozen major races on the runways of SAC bases per year, while SAC in return would receive the revenues of the meets which would go into the airmen's service funds at the bases. It worked out nicely for both sides. The arrangement continued for both 1953 and 1954 until Congress got a bit huffy about it. The two years of

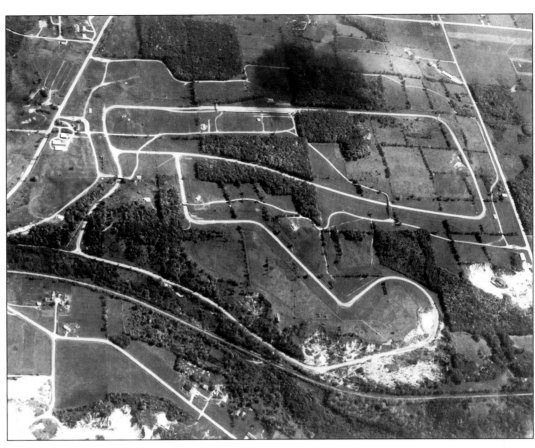

Aerial view of the track (circa 1963) clearly shows the farm fields from which the track was carved.

SAC racing covered the gap between the end of the street racing era and the beginning of the purpose built track era. Without General LeMay there may very well not have been any racing at all. It is not too much of an exaggeration to say that he saved the SCCA and road racing.

The next few years saw many new tracks built: Watkins Glen, Bridgehampton, Marlboro, Virginia International Raceway, Thompson, Lime Rock, Vineland, Savannah-Effingham Motorway, Hilltop Raceway, West Palm Beach Raceway, Mid Ohio, Meadowdale, Lake Garnett, Austin, Continental Divide, Riverside, Laguna Seca, Vaca Valley, Cotati, Willow Springs, Indianapolis Raceway Park and many more. All these were built prior to 1962, and the majority are no longer in existence. It takes promotion, knowledge, good staff, strong support and a loyal fan base to make a race track a success. Clif Tufte and Road America enjoyed all of this. It is significant to note that Road America (RA) is virtually the only track of all that were built in the late '50s and early '60s that is still in business that has never had a change of ownership or a period of inactivity due to a financial crisis.

The track itself is exactly four miles in length. There are approximately 10 actual turns on the course, depending upon how one wants to interpret a turn. It is well known that the official designations of turns differs from what they actually are. This is because in the beginning the track had 14 numbered communications posts around the four miles. It was easier to refer to a location as *corner 14* than *communication post 14* and the usage stuck. Nobody seems to mind.

The track has an elevation variation of 175 feet from the highest point at roughly the starter's platform to the lowest at corner 12. Various sections of the track have acquired picturesque names. The back straight is known as the Moraine Sweep. The section from turn six down to turn eight is the Hurry Downs. The 180 degree sweeping turn 9-10 complex was christened the Carousel (a term that has been used by virtually every track that has a turn of more than 90 degrees). Turn 11 is the infamous Kink, leading into the Kettle Bottoms which run to turn 12. This turn acquired the name Canada Corner a few years after the track opened. Cleaning crews noted a concentration of Canadian beer cans and Canadian tax stamps on film boxes here, hence the name. The track leads out of Canada Corner through Thunder Valley under the bridge at turn 13. This portion of the track goes through a deep ravine and the echo effect makes the name obvious.

The best viewing spot on the course? Everybody has their own favorite place, selected over the years through trial and error. However, year in and year out the largest crowds have seemed to congregate on the slopes of the big hill in the center of the track bounded by turns 5-6, 12, 13, Kettle Bottoms and Thunder Valley. The name of this big hill is Fireman's Hill.

The flavor of the track is made up of many things, not just the marvelous setting and great circuit. The track has had a world-wide reputation from the very start for its food. Without question Road America serves the best track food in the country. The reason for this is that Clif Tufte made the decision before the track even opened that the concession stands would not be run by the track or by an outside vendor, but rather would be run by local church and civic groups. This inspired idea had two consequences; first of all it involved the local community, reinforcing the notion that this was "our" track; secondly, the friendly competition ensured a diverse menu and food from the area (aiding local vendors), cooked before your eyes, the smoky aroma fueling the anticipation: hamburgers, hot dogs, corn-on-the-cob and bratwurst.

Bratwurst. Never, never go to Road America without having the bratwurst! The tasty German sausage is a hallmark of the area and every stand has brats readily available. Once known only locally, the word about bratwurst has spread far and wide as visitors have become believers. There probably is not an entree at any race track that is so associated with a track, as bratwurst is to Road America.

The vision of Clif Tufte had become reality in Road America. Now, let's go racing!

1955

The duel. The first race in September 1955 produced a race-long fight for first between the Ferrari Monza of Phil Hill and the D Jaguar of Sherwood Johnston.

The asphalt was dry, hay bales in place, and it was time for racing! The years of dreaming, the months of planning, the period of construction all paid off the weekend of September 10-11, 1955, as Road America opened. True, the facilities were on the crude side compared to what is the norm today, but for 1955 this was the *state of the art*. No matter that nails were still being pounded into the pagoda, this was it: The best road racing circuit in the country, if not the world. Those connected with RA, from Clif Tufte on down, the competitors, the workers, the drivers, the crews, the spectators, all were here and tickled pink to be part of the inaugural run at Road America.

At this time all road racing of any importance in the United States was run by the Sports Car Club of America (SCCA) with a couple of exceptions. Sebring was an anomaly; it was the only race in the U.S., counting for the world sports car championship and it was promoted by the Automobile Racing Club of Florida (ARCF). It was the only race the ARCF promoted. In California most sports car racing was sanctioned by the California Sports Car Club (Cal Club). Cal Club was a product of the post-war hot rod move-

ment on California's dry lakes. Eventually an evolution produced sports car racing and Cal Club. Whereas the SCCA had been born in the East and spread through the country, Cal Club rarely strayed outside the state of California. They coexisted somewhat uneasily with the SCCA, which had regions in San Francisco, Los Angeles and San Diego. In the early sixties they would merge, giving SCCA sole control of U.S. road racing at that time.

The SCCA had broken road racing down into two categories with several classes in each. The categories were production and modified. Production was as the name indicated and in today's terms would be considered *showroom stock*. Modified was for any production cars that were modified out of the production category and for sports cars built specifically for racing. Classes were based upon engine displacement, as follows:

BM — over 5.0 liters
CM — 3.0 to 5.0 liters
DM — 2.0 to 3.0 liters
EM — 1.5 to 2.0 liters

Trophy presentation after the first race. The trophies were given out at a dinner at Siebken's in Elkhart Lake rather than at the track. Coats and ties were expected attire. From left to right: Jim Kimberly, Sherwood Johnston, Phil Hill and, presenting the Harley Earl Trophy to Hill, Harley Earl.

FM — 1.1 to 1.5 liters
GM — 750cc to 1.1 liters
HM — up to 750cc

Production was similar but with minor variations:

BP — over 5.0 liters
CP — 2.6 to 5.0 liters
DP — 2.0 to 2.6 liters
EP — 1.6 to 2.0 liters
FP — 1.3 to 1.6 liters
GP — 1.0 to 1.3 liters

HP — 750cc to 1.0 liters
IP — 500cc to 750cc
JP — up to 500cc

AP was not used at this time and the sub-HP classes were rarely entered. Class AM was for over 8.0 liters and there were no engines built at this time in that size. These displacement limits were varied from time to time to accommodate new manufacturers, to equalize competition and to recognize the level of participation. In 1960 SCCA would scrap displacement limits for the production category and go to a performance-based classification.

SCCA races were at two levels, National and Regional. Regional races were events put on by local SCCA regions around the country and open to any licensed SCCA competitor. There were probably 75 to 100 of these yearly. National races, on the other hand, were events that awarded points in each class in order to determine the year's champion driver. These were prestige events, awarded to the top tracks and to regions with proven records in race promotion. There were between 12 and 18 Nationals per year. A sanction for a National Championship event was issued to the Chicago Region and to Road America for its inaugural weekend. The concept of national class champions in the SCCA exists to this day although the method of determination underwent change in 1965.

Seven races were scheduled for the inaugural weekend. Saturday had three and Sunday four, with the weekend feature being for the large modified classes. Road America's first race was an eight lap, 32 mile run for G Production cars. GP at this time meant MGs and a large field of TCs, TDs and TFs set the first tires on RA's asphalt. Ralph Durbin had the honor of leading the first lap, but on lap two Roy Heath caught and passed him. Heath then controlled the balance of the race, winning in his MG TC by over half a minute. The race average was 59.6 mph with the fastest laps at the four minute mark. Quite a change from what the following years would bring.

The second race was for CP & DP cars. CP was the domain of the Mercedes-Benz 300SL, a rather startling thought when one considers the car in the context of today's prices. Nonetheless, the Mercedes coupes led the way for the 56 mile race. Paul O'Shea, the country's top Mercedes driver and CP National Champion, led the race virtually start to finish. However, Bud Seaverns got past O'Shea late in the race when faulty brakes took O'Shea down the escape road at turn five. O'Shea returned to the track and ran down Seaverns, taking the lead as the race neared its conclusion. O'Shea won the 14 lap go by just a fraction of a second over Seaverns. Not too far behind in third place was Paul Van Antwerpen in another Mercedes-Benz 300SL. In the DP class Bob Goldich was the winner in a 2.2 Triumph TR2.

The final race on Saturday was a 100 miler for E and F Modified. Two liter Ferraris and Maseratis, Porsche 550 Spyders and Oscas were the main entrants in these classes. In this race Oscas were very strong. Frank Bott took the lead in the second lap and led the rest of the 25 laps. However he had strong competition from Ed Crawford, who was driving a Porsche 550 Spyder, and Briggs Cunningham, who was in another Osca. The first EM car home was the Maserati A6GCS of Ted Boynton. This was the fastest race of the day as Bott averaged 75.7 mph. Tragically, in practice for this race Tom Friedman crashed in his Maserati, suffering severe burns from which he later succumbed.

Sunday was a fine fall day and a good crowd turned out for a splendid time. The first race was for FP cars and was 52 miles long. In this class there simply was no beating the Porsche Speedsters which in reality were fast enough to beat most DP & EP cars. Bob Ballenger in his blue Speedster was too much for the rest as he led a close following Bengt Soderstrom to the finish. Ballenger's winning speed was 67.7 mph.

Race two was the CP event, contested over 56 miles. Jaguar XK-120s and XK-140s were the dominant car. A Jag foursome of Ralph Mason, Chuck Wallace, Ralph Miller and Jim Jeffords separated themselves from the balance of the pack to contest first among themselves. The key occurrence of the race was when the leading Mason spun and was collected by the closely following Wallace, taking both out. This elevated Miller into first with Jeffords following closely but Big Jim could not quite catch Miller who averaged 70.8 mph. Jeffords was second with yet another Jaguar, driven by Tom Newcomer, third.

The third race of the day was for the small modified classes of G and

H. These classes were still much the realm of the special builder with *off the shelf* cars largely being built by such Italian firms as Abarth, Osca and Stanguellini. The English special builders Lotus, Elva and Lola were still a year or two away from taking over the GM class. At any rate this 52 mile race was a two car battle between Rees Makins and Chuck Dietrich. They traded first place a number of times with the Osca 1100 of Makins finally prevailing when Dietrich had to make an unscheduled pit stop in his Lester-MG. Bob Kuhn then moved into second in his Abarth, holding it to the finish. The HM winner was John Mays in a lovely little car of his own construction which he called the Fibresport.

This set the stage for the feature which was 37 laps, 148 miles, for BM, CM and DM cars. This meant Ferrari vs. Maserati vs. Jaguar. Briggs Cunningham had built his own cars for several years, in a glorious but failed attempt to win Le Mans. He ran these cars throughout the U.S. also, where they were very successful, scoring many wins. Now he was closing down his Cunningham effort but replacing it as an entrant of other cars, mainly Jaguars. Sherwood Johnston was his main driver, and he was in a very fast D Jaguar. America's rising star driver was Phil Hill. He had quickly climbed through the ranks of the California racing scene and had recently been drafted by the factory Ferrari sports car team. For RA he was driving George Tilp's Ferrari Monza, a 3.0 liter four cylinder machine best noted for torque if not top speed. Big Bill Spear, a dominant driver in big 4.5 and 4.9 liter Ferraris during the SAC era, was here trying his luck in a new Maserati 300-S. Add in numerous Ferraris, a couple more Maseratis and D Jaguars, sprinkle in some Chrysler and Cadillac engined specials, and it was an interesting field indeed.

The race itself quickly became a two car go as Phil Hill and Sherwood Johnston split away from the rest and raced each other for first. But what a race they did! Lap after lap, turn after turn, the two were together, nose to tail, roaring around as one. Hill led most often during the first 20 laps. Officially, he led all 20, but out on the course there were occasions when Johnston was ahead. Johnston had the slightly faster car, but Hill's cornered better. Johnston could go deeper into the turns with his disc brakes, but Hill was able to accelerate out faster. It was a stand off. Johnston turned the tables in his favor on lap 21, holding Hill at bay for the next ten rounds. Then there were just six to go. Hill ahead. Five to go, Johnston ahead. And so it went, down to the final four miles. As the two white cars wailed past the start/finish line to start their last lap it was Johnston, ahead by four car lengths. Through the lap Hill closed the gap. When they got to Canada Corner, Hill was so close he could reach out and touch the D Jag. They went up through Thunder Valley and then the slight opening Hill was seeking occurred. Johnston ran a bit wide coming through turn 13. Not much, but enough that Hill stuck the Ferrari's nose alongside the Jag. They went through the last turn side by side and came up the hill together, right feet mashing the accelerator flat, every fiber of their being urging the car to go faster, faster, *faster!* As they flashed over the line it was Hill by just a nose! What a fantastic finish to the first weekend in the life of America's new, premier race track. Well behind the first two, but still on the same lap, came Ernie Erickson in his yellow D Jaguar, Gordon Bennett in a Maserati 300-S and Spear in his Maserati. Walter Gray was the BM winner in an Allard, while Johnston was first in CM and Hill in DM. The winning speed was 80.2 mph.

The first race was history. Magazines and newspapers carried the story everywhere and the public knew of this magnificent new creation in Wisconsin. The winter soon took hold, enveloping the track in its mantle of white. In Elkhart Lake Clif Tufte sat at home, not basking in the glow of what had been done, but thinking of tomorrow, of what he would do with his great new track.

6

1956

Clif Tufte's fertile mind was active over the winter. For 1956 he scheduled three weekends, each a major event. From the start Tufte adhered to a plan of promoting major events only. He would steadfastly refuse to promote either minor events or to schedule more than three races a year. His thinking was simple; he felt that one must sell a good product and not overexpose it. He stuck to this philosophy without deviation for the 24 years he promoted at RA. The results speak for themselves. The track exists today and is profitable.

The first race would take place in June and would be an SCCA National. To Tufte major sports car racing was of the endurance variety and he had that in mind for his fall date. For early summer

Lap one of the only NASCAR race at RA, July 1956. The weather was damp, a condition quite foreign to the good old boys from the South. The field is streaming out turn five, ascending the hill towards turn six.

he wanted something different, so that fans could attend two Nationals a year at RA and not see the same format. Hence, he scheduled a slate of shorter races in June. To Tufte anything shorter than several hours in length was a *sprint*. Therefore, these races were christened the *International June Sprints*. Over the next few years the adjective international was dropped as being a bit too unwieldy; the races would be known as the *June Sprints*.

Something different was scheduled for mid-summer. Tufte scheduled a NASCAR race. This was quite a departure, both for the track and for NASCAR. At this time *stock cars* were for ovals and there was a huge gulf between oval trackers and road racers. Nonetheless, a race was scheduled for August 12-13.

The third event of 1956 was the weekend after Labor Day. The race would be an SCCA National, but it would be an endurance format. The feature on Sunday would be a six hour endurance race for the sports racing cars. This was Tufte's answer to the classic enduros at Le Mans and Sebring; Tufte hoped that RA could someday be ranked with them.

Six races were on tap as the first June Sprints were held June 23-24. Three were scheduled for Saturday afternoon with another three on Sunday. The first of the Saturday races was for the FP & GP cars. The fight for first was hot; the Porsche Speedsters of Carl Haas and Bob Ballenger went at it the entire distance with Haas winning by just a whisker. Young Milwaukee car dealer Bill Wuesthoff bested a strong GP field in his Alfa Romeo Giulietta.

Race two was for DP & EP cars. Chuck Wallace made up for his disappointment of the previous September by winning this fairly easily in his

Mercedes-Benz 300SL. The EP winner was Ernie Erickson in an AC Ace-Bristol. The last race of the day was for classes EM & FM. Jack McAfee was one of the top Porsche drivers on the west coast and he showed the folks east of the Rockies why as he scored a comfortable win in his Porsche 550 Spyder. The EM portion of the race was won by Ebby Lunken in a Ferrari 500-TR.

Sunday's first race was for CP. The new Corvette had just received a V-8 engine and was beginning to be taken seriously. In the next couple years they would come to dominate production car racing. The displacement limits between BP and CP would be later changed, so that the Corvette was in its own class. But for 1956 they were still in CP and the Jaguars that had been dominant now had a struggle on their hands. The race was led for most of the distance by the Corvettes of Dick Thompson and Bark Henry. The best production car driver in the Midwest, Jim Jeffords was in his familiar red and black Jaguar XK-140. Jeffords showed why, as he fought for many laps with Henry for second. Two laps from the end Jeffords got past Henry and Thompson pulled off course, his Corvette done. Jeffords now led and was on the verge of scoring a big win when his Jaguar slowed, the strain of the race having caused his engine to overheat. Henry retook first and notched the win.

GM and HM cars ran next. American racers had discovered the English builders of cars in this engine size, and the field had a number of Coopers and Lotuses in it. The three Lotuses of M.R.J. Wyllie, Frank Baptista, and Ralph Miller quickly locked into a duel with the Cooper T-39 of Fred Sclavi.

The freshly painted Pagoda stands as a backdrop to Colonel Easton, the Chief Steward, as he addresses the drivers meeting prior to the six hour race in September 1956.

The win of the six hour endurance race in September 1956 went to Honest John Kilborn, here in Canada Corner. Howard Hively co-drove the Ferrari 375MM.

The first part of the race was a four-way struggle with places changing frequently. As the race progressed, Wyllie and Miller fell back, leaving it to Sclavi and Baptista. Sclavi took the lead and slowly inched away from Baptista to take the win. John Mays was the HM winner again in his Fibresport Special.

The feature for classes BM, CM, and DM was for 38 laps, 152 miles. The top entry was the Briggs Cunningham team which entered four D Jaguars for Sherwood Johnston, John Fitch, new recruit Walt Hansgen and Briggs himself. Three other D Jags were on hand for Ernie Erickson, Jack McAfee, and Lou Brero. Several Ferraris were present, of which the top one was a 121LM for Carroll Shelby. The 121LM was Ferrari's sole attempt at a straight six cylinder car. Three were built for Le Mans in 1955 where none finished. Ferrari ran them a couple more times before deciding that the V-12

cars were the better bet. They were sold and had spotty records thereafter. Shelby, on the other hand, was approaching the peak of his driving career. During 1956 and 1957 he would win many major American races in both Ferraris and Maseratis and would be the SCCA's U.S. champion. As usual, Shelby would be driving in his *Texas Tuxedo*; bib overalls befitting Shelby's self-styled image of *just a poor chicken rancher*. John Kilborn, a Decatur, IL, car dealer had the wherewithal to indulge his racing hobby and selected a 4.5 liter 375MM for today's race. Rich Lyeth also had a 375 Ferrari. The top Maserati present was a beautiful blue 300-S for Phil Stewart. In practice the count of D Jags was reduced by one when Hansgen misjudged a corner and rolled one of the Cunningham cars. Briggs promptly put Hansgen in his own car.

Johnston was on the pole with Fitch alongside, both in Cunningham's D Jags in *American colors*, white with two blue stripes. Row two held the Ferraris of Shelby and Kilborn. However, it was Shelby who got the best start, and at the end of the first lap he had his 4.4 liter six in the lead. Behind him was a snarling pack of D Jags, but one by one they dropped out. McAfee lasted only two laps before retiring to the pits. Then Sherwood Johnston duplicated Hansgen's trick and rolled his D Jag. Not to be outdone, Hansgen went off course, struck some hay bales, and flipped his D Jag end over end. Of the four Cunningham Jaguars, only Fitch did not crash his. However, he was felled by mechanical problems. Cunningham loaded his trucks with smashed Ds, ending an absolutely horrible weekend with three badly damaged racers. Expensive indeed.

Up front Shelby was controlling the race. The 121LM was a difficult beast to drive, but Shelby had its measure. He eased off as the race progressed, never challenged after the Jaguars eliminated themselves. Shelby won the first June Sprints feature, leading Lou Brero in a D Jaguar across the line by six seconds, but Shelby could have stretched that margin at will. Ernie Erickson was third in another D Jag, while John Kilborn and Rich Lyeth followed in 4.5 liter Ferraris. Phil Stewart then came across as the first DM car in his Maserati 300-S. The BM winner, though well behind, was Walt Gray in an Allard.

The second race weekend of 1956 was August 12-13. The event was destined to be the sole appearance of the NASCAR stocks at RA. At this time NASCAR was far from the success that it is today. It was still very much a parochial, southern affair, and the appearance at RA was a rarity as the series virtually never came north of the Mason-Dixon Line. Further, the United States Auto Club (USAC) was the sanctioning body for stock car racing in most of the U.S. and ran four races yearly at the Milwaukee oval track. Nonetheless, Bill France brought the NASCAR circus to town with hopes of not only making a northern beachhead but also of expanding to road courses. There were two races scheduled. Saturday would have a 100 mile event for under 3.5 liter *stock cars*, while Sunday's feature would be 252 miles for the NASCAR Grand National cars, as they were known in the pre-Winston Cup days.

The race on Saturday was a mixture of foreign sedans and small American cars, all qualifying as under 3.5 liter cars. The opening laps were a scramble among Herb Thomas in an English Ford Zephyr, Jerry Walters in a Studebaker, and Bill France Jr. in another Ford Zephyr. Then Paul Goldsmith joined the fray, up from the ninth row of the grid. Goldsmith was in a Jaguar Mk. VII sedan and the 3.4 liter dohc Jag six was just the ticket. Goldsmith moved through to the lead and controlled the pace thereafter, winning at 59.2 mph. Walters, Thomas, and France finished behind him in that order with fifth going to Enoch Staley in a Renault 4CV.

Sunday was not the type of day Clif Tufte wanted. It was very wet and overcast, with rain falling intermittently. The start of the race was delayed almost an hour by a passing storm. The race started on a wet track, although in these days before slick race tires this was not much of a problem, save for those drivers who had never experienced this before! The pole was held by Buck Baker in a Dodge, and Baker led the first five laps. However on lap six he was in the pits and the lead was taken by Tim Flock. He did not have long to enjoy it, though, as Curtis Turner and Marvin Panch were challenging. Both displaced Flock from the front and traded first between them a few times. The combination of a still wet track and the NASCAR drivers unfamiliarity with road racing was producing many spin outs and hay bale bashing. There probably was not a car in the field that was not off course at one time or another.

Marvin Panch was getting a handle of this road racing business and moved into first once again on lap 12. This time he began to stretch his lead, and he held first for the next 100 miles. Then he threw it all away as he went off course in the first turn and left his car mired in a ditch. Speedy Thompson was behind Panch and took advantage to claim first in his Dodge. Thompson was in front from lap 38 until lap 52 when he had a long pit stop to repair body damage which was cutting his tires. Tim Flock then retook first and held it for the remaining 10 laps to win in his Mercury. A second Mercury of Bill Myers was next, then came the Ford of legendary Fireball Roberts, the Chevrolet of Paul Goldsmith and the Ford of Joe Eubanks. The average speed of the race was 71.485 mph, which was not too bad considering the wet track, the distance, and the unsuitability of the cars on a road course.

The weekend had been an interesting experiment but it was not a box office success. The crowd was very small at well under 10,000. It appeared that the fan who would be attracted to RA would come to see sports car racing; if he wanted to see stock cars he would go to the Fair Park circuit in Milwaukee. As a result, NASCAR never returned. In retrospect, the race was 35 years too early!

September 9-10 was the second SCCA National of the year. Clif Tufte indulged his vision of endurance racing by running just two races that weekend, but both were long. Very long. Saturday there would be a 300 mile race for production cars under two liters and modified cars under 1500cc. Sunday's race would be a six hours for cars over those limits.

Jim Kimberly was the heir to the Kimberly-Clark paper fortune. He had indulged his racing appetite for several years with a steady stream of Italian racers, mostly Ferraris. He hailed from nearby Neenah, WI, and was involved at the track since its inception. He was not a spring chicken and his flowing thatch of white hair gave him the appellation *The Silver Fox*. Jim led the opening laps in his Osca MT-4, but Doc Wyllie was right behind him in a Lotus Mk. IX. The Lotus was giving away power, but was probably the best handling car in the race. Wyllie duly reined in Kimberly and took over first. However Kimberly was not to be denied and retook first, thereafter exchanging it with Wyllie several times before Doc's Lotus retired on lap 19 with a broken camshaft in his Coventry-Climax four. The chase was then taken up by the Porsche 550 Spyder of Bob Fergus. Also in the picture was Lance Reventlow, son of Barbara Hutton, the Woolworth heir. Reventlow was driving his Cooper T-39. Kimberly was able to lead more often than not as the mid race pit stops for fuel and driver changes came. Art Bunker took the

lead when Kimberly stopped, but that lasted only three laps until Bunker pitted his Porsche Spyder. Kimberly was relieved by Carroll Shelby and that was the race. Shelby was undoubtedly the best driver in the field and he quickly moved back into first and held it for the duration of the 75 laps.

Finishing behind the Kimberly/Shelby pairing were Fergus and Ray Mason second, Reventlow and Richie Ginther third, Bunker and Dale Duncan fourth, and Jack Manting and M.H. Ward fifth in another Porsche Spyder. The class winners were Kimberly/Shelby in FM, Reventlow/Ginther GM, Herman Behm and Carl Haas HM in a Stanguellini 750, Frank Campbell and Hal Ullrich EP in an Ace-Bristol, Chuck Rickert and Don Kreiplen FP in a Porsche Speedster, and Ralph Durbin and Ken Askew GP in an Alfa Romeo Giulietta. The winning Osca covered the 300 miles at an average speed of 74.44 mph.

Sunday shaped up as another Ferrari vs. Maserati vs. Jaguar race. Briggs Cunningham was back with his fleet of D types and his entry of Jags was augmented by several good privateers. Ferraris abounded but the biggest versions were the 4.5 liter 375MMs of John Kilborn and Rich Lyeth. Phil Stewart had the top Maserati, a 300-S, but it was a DM car as opposed to the CM D Jags and big Ferraris.

The first half of the race belonged to John Fitch. The Cunningham driver took the lead on the first lap and kept his D Jaguar out in front for the first 42 laps. He then pitted and turned the car over to Cunningham. All this time *Honest John* Kilborn was running second, keeping Fitch in sight but never being close enough to actually challenge him. Kilborn passed Cunningham on lap 47 but relinquished it when he stopped for fuel and co-driver Howard Hively on lap 51.

The pale yellow D Jaguar of Ernie Erickson moved into first with Kilborn's stop. The Jag, co-driven by Frank Bott, held the top spot until another flurry of pit stops at the 78 lap mark. Hively retook the lead, but shortly thereafter turned the car back to Kilborn. Yet another D Jaguar had a turn in the lead as Dale Duncan moved Loyal Katskee's black example into first for a few laps. After this it was a fight between Erickson and Kilborn. Erickson kept his D Jag in front of Kilborn from lap 87 on and the race entered the final hour. Cunningham had turned his D Jaguar back to Fitch who took over in fourth. Fitch quickly moved to third behind Erickson and Kilborn.

The race resolution occurred on lap 108. Erickson had raced hard to stay ahead of Kilborn and Fitch and his tires were shot. The left front was down to the canvas and a blowout was just minutes away. Erickson pitted for four fresh tires and the stop was long. He reentered the race in third place but time was running out. Kilborn was in first with Fitch second, lapping faster, but without enough time. The six hours expired as Kilborn completed his 121st lap, covering 484 miles. The Fitch/Cunningham D Jaguar was second, just seven seconds behind after six hours. In third was the Erickson/Bott D Jaguar, while yet another D Jag came home fourth, this driven by Jack Ensley and Gordon Bennett. In fifth was Ted Boynton and Bob Ballenger in a Ferrari 500 TR.

The class winners were Andy Rosenberger and Bob Gary in BM in a Nash-Healey Le Mans, Kilborn/Hively in CM, Rod Carveth and John Barneson DM in an Aston Martin DB3-S, and Boynton/Ballenger in EM. The production class winners were Duke Knowlton and Bill Andrews in CP in a Jaguar XK-140 and Paul O'Shea and Phil Hill DP in a Mercedes-Benz 300-SL.

It was a good race with the second half featuring an almost constant fight for the lead. A seed had been planted and next year Tufte would take the endurance race to a new level of promotion. The track had completed its first full year with two successful sports car meets and one not so successful stock car race. Road America was making its mark.

1957

For 1957 Clif Tufte scheduled two races, both SCCA Nationals. The June Sprints was down for its second running, while the September National would again be an endurance contest. The NASCAR experiment was a one-time affair, as it was not profitable for the track and also was not very popular with the NASCAR crews as they were southern-based and it was a very long tow to Elkhart Lake.

June 22-23 was the weekend of the June Sprints. Four races were scheduled. The first race on Sunday was 48 miles for F and G Production and H Modified. Three Porsche Speedsters battled the entire 12 lap distance, never far enough apart to allow anyone to get comfortable. Don Wester actually led all the way but his mirrors were constantly full. Chuck Rickert and Ray Olson never gave up the chase and the threesome flashed under the flag almost as one. Wester won, while Rickert nipped Olson by the width of his Porsche's front bumper. Al Allin was the GP winner in an Alfa Romeo Giulietta, while Bruce Townsend won HM in a TXP Special.

Race number two was an 80 mile go for E, F and G Modified. This was a showdown between Porsche Spyders and Ferrari 500TRs and Mondials. Lake Underwood was definitely the hot shoe in this class and he showed it by leading all 20 laps to win. Underwood was in a class FM Porsche RS Spyder. Behind him, though, was a ferocious battle. Johnny Von Neumann and Ebby Lunken, both in 2.0 liter Ferraris, and Don Sesslar, in a Porsche RS Spyder, mixed it up constantly. As the race sped towards conclusion the two Ferraris distanced themselves from the Sesslar Porsche. The last lap saw Lunken narrowly squeak past Von Neumann to take second overall and first in the EM class. Frank Baptista was the GM winner in a Lotus 11.

The third race was 60 miles for the production cars in classes C, D and E. Rees Makins had things rather his own way as he led unchallenged in a class CP Mercedes-Benz 300-SL. Behind him Dan Fowler and Bob Kuhn disputed second in a pair of Ace-Bristols with Fowler coming out on top, second overall and first in EP. The DP winner was Warren Cox in an Austin-Healey 100.

This set the stage for the feature race, 152 miles for the modified cars over 2.0 liters and BP. Briggs Cunningham again entered four cars, three D Jaguars for Walt Hansgen, John Fitch and Chuck Wallace, plus his old Cunningham C-6R for himself. Ferraris were a bit thin on the ground with the 4.5 liter 375MM of Rich Lyeth being the biggest. John Kilborn was running a 3.0 Monza this year while Johnny Von Neumann pushed his 2.0 TR onto his trailer and rolled off a 2.5 liter 625LM. The big threat to Cunningham's fleet of D Jags was expected to come from Maserati. The Italian company had

Johnny von Neumann and Chuck Wallace race for position during the 1957 June Sprints, as a lapped Ace-Bristol moves over. No modern guard rail protected the pit crew, who would walk onto the side of the track to signal drivers, apparently oblivious to the danger.

responded to Ferrari's larger engined cars by introducing the 450-S; a 4.5 liter dohc V-8 brute that had already tasted success in the Sebring 12 Hours. Two were entered here; one for Jim Kimberly and the other for Carroll Shelby. Unfortunately, the car destined for Shelby never made it to the track leaving him rideless.

John Fitch had put his Cunningham D Jaguar on the pole and he smoked off into the lead as the green flag fluttered. Walt Hansgen tucked in behind him, followed by Chuck Wallace, making it an early 1-2-3 for the finned, blue-striped white Jaguars. Rich Lyeth was having none of that, though, and moved his several year old Ferrari into the fray, taking third from Wallace. On the fifth lap Hansgen moved ahead of Fitch, and for the balance of the 38 laps the two D Jags circulated in tandem. It may not have been terribly exciting, but it was a crushing display of Cunningham's Jaguar might. Hansgen came home a fairly easy winner, averaging 82.76 mph. Fitch was second, with Lyeth setting the race's fast lap at 84.656 mph in finishing third. Wallace was fourth in the third Cunningham D Jag while Von Neumann took the DM trophy with his fifth place finish. Jim Jeffords had switched to Corvettes this year and was the BP winner in his red example. The BM class was again taken by Andy Rosenberger in the Nash-Healey Le Mans, powered by a Packard V-8.

The fall race was held September 7-8. Tufte shrewdly noted that the six hour race the year before had covered 484 miles. Consequently, Tufte decided to add a few laps and to make the race a distance rather than timed event, and the distance was to be 500 miles. Tufte cashed in on the aura of *500* and thus the Road America 500 was born.

Saturday had two long races for production cars before Sunday's 500. The first was 80 miles for F and G Production and H Modified. Don Wester took the race, leading the entire distance. However, he was pushed hard by Ed Hugus, whose GP Alfa Romeo really had no business challenging Wester's Porsche Carrera. Hugus finished second, an exceptional performance. The HM class was again taken by Bruce Townsend in his TXP.

Race two was 120 miles for the large production cars. It was a two car race as Jim Jeffords and Dick Thompson immediately took their Corvettes well ahead of the rest. In fact, they had lapped the rest of the cars in the field by lap 19 of 30. Unfortunately the prospects of a fight to the wire were dashed when Jeffords dropped out with overheating on lap 23. From then on, Thompson had an easy coast to the win. Dave Causey was the CP winner in a Jaguar XK-140, Trant Jarman took DP in an Austin-Healey and Bob Kuhn was the EP winner in an Ace-Bristol. Thompson averaged 77.19 mph in winning.

A good field of cars was on hand for the 500. Briggs Cunningham again entered three D Jaguars for Walt Hansgen/Phil Forno, John Gordon Bennett/Chuck Wallace, and Russ Boss/Cunningham. Maserati was represented by Jim Kimberly, who had a 450-S and a 200-S for himself and Jack McAfee. A second 450-S was entered by John Edgar for Carroll Shelby, but the Texan chose Edgar's smaller 300-S for the race, apparently thinking that the 3.0 liter six would make up on gas mileage what it lost in speed. Last year's winners of the six hour race, John Kilborn and Howard Hively, were in Kilborn's latest buy, a 3.5 liter 290MM. The biggest paddock buzz surrounded the Ferrari entered by Gene Greenspun. It was a 3.8 liter dohc V-12 315-S, the very car that Piero Taruffi had driven to victory in this year's Mille Miglia. It had been flown to the U.S. from Maranello on Thursday and did not arrive at RA until Saturday morning. Its driver was none other than works driver Phil Hill. George Tilp entered a Mercedes-Benz 300-SL roadster for Paul O'Shea and Dick Thompson. The 300-SL roadster was not yet approved for production racing by the SCCA due to its recent introduction. Consequently, Tilp modified it extensively and ran it in DM. Also in DM was the Aston Martin DB-3S of Rod Carveth, who had George Constantine co-driving. Various and sundry other Ferraris, Jaguars, Porsche Spyders, Lotuses and specials made up the 52 car field.

The field was waved off on a staggered start by class which accounted for Bob Louden leading the first five of 125 laps in a C Jaguar. Then Hal Ullrich took over first in the Excalibur SJ, a supercharged Jaguar powered

one-off entered by Brooks Stevens. However, by lap seven the later starting cars had made their way through the field and Shelby moved into first in the 3.0 Maserati. Phil Hill moved up as well, taking second behind Shelby. Hansgen and Constantine were running third and fourth. Shelby continued to lead until lap 27 when Hill moved the more powerful Ferrari ahead. Up to third by this time was Ed Crawford in a Porsche RS Spyder, rather amazingly ahead of many more powerful cars. Kilborn was running fourth, followed by Constantine, Thompson

Legends – Briggs Cunningham (left) has a pre-race chat with his number one driver, Walt Hansgen, prior to the 1957 June Sprints.

and Bennett. Hansgen had dropped out by this time with terminal engine troubles. McAfee had hardly worked up a sweat, his Kimberly Maserati retiring after only two laps.

The laps wore on with the top three spots remaining static: Hill, Shelby and Crawford. Hill had a lead of over a lap on Shelby, the exact difference changing with the pit stop sequence. The Kilborn/Hively Ferrari ran fourth, then O'Shea, Wallace, Carveth, Jim Kimberly now in Ebby Lunken's 2.0 Ferrari and Boss. The lap count approached 100 with all the passing being done for fourth place and below. Wallace, O'Shea and Kilborn all took turns spending some time in the fourth spot, but none could catch Crawford in third, who was over a lap ahead of them.

A little more than eight minutes longer than six hours had elapsed since the cars were unleashed. Phil Hill's superb Ferrari streaked across the line a convincing winner, both overall and in class CM. Carroll Shelby was second overall and first in class DM in the Maserati 300-S. Third overall and first in class FM was Ed Crawford after an outstanding drive in his 1500cc Porsche RS Spyder. Fourth place finally fell to the Wallace/Gordon Bennett D Jaguar after a race long tussle over the spot. Fifth was taken by the Kilborn/Hively Ferrari, sixth went to the O'Shea/Thompson Mercedes, while seventh was the EM winner, the Ferrari 500TR of Lunken/Kimberly. The trophy for class BM went to John Haas and Bob Rolofson in the *Blunderbird*, a 1955 modified Ford Thunderbird. Dr. M.R.J. Wyllie and his wife Peggy were the GM winners in a Lotus Mk. IX. Hill averaged 81.41 mph in winning, and set the race's fastest lap at 2:49.30. That did not break the lap record, which was held by Shelby, who cut a lap at 2:48.20 in his winning drive in the '56 June Sprints.

1957 had been a very good year. Two excellent race weekends with good crowds in the 30,000 range; this compared with attendance at other tracks, which generally averaged under 10,000. Not only was the track drawing, but it was drawing well, it was profitable, and advance payments were being made on the mortgage. Winter came to the Kettle Moraine, but Clif Tufte was smiling. Matters were indeed going well.

Phil Hill accelerates out of turn 12 into Thunder Valley during his winning, solo drive at the 1957 Road America 500. This very Ferrari 315-S, piloted by Piero Taruffi, had won the Mille Miglia three months prior.

1958

The third full year in the track's history once again saw two major spectator events. The June Sprints continued its growth in stature, while the fall Road America 500 once again drew a large field, including international interest.

The format for the June Sprints was relatively simple. There were four races encompassing all fourteen of the current SCCA National classes. Continuing what was to be a Road America trademark in its early years, the four races all ran to lengths in excess of what was the norm in National racing at other venues. While other tracks typically had preliminary races in the 30 to 50 mile range, and a *feature* of up to 100 miles, Clif Tufte ran distances of up to twice the norm. This met with an enthusiastic response from drivers, as they were able to spend more time on the track doing what they were there for. As a result, entry lists swelled, and Road America attracted far larger fields than other tracks, a situation which continues with the June Sprints to this day.

Saturday was devoted to practice, with qualifying taking the form of four short races to determine the starting order of the Sunday events. These were taken by Chuck Rickert, Don Sesslar, George Reed and Ed Crawford, all of whom would do well on Sunday.

The 48 mile event on Sunday morning for small production and H Modified cars was won by Chuck Rickert, driving a Porsche 356 Carrera. With the four cam race-derived engine, Rickert's car and that of second-placed Don Wester and third-placed Dean Causey easily outran the rest of the field, taking overall and FP honors. Clinton Lindburg was the GP winner in an Alfa Romeo Giulietta, while Ollie Schmidt took the H Modified category in his Crosley-powered Mitchell Special.

Although Porsche Spyders were showing that they could run with the *big boys* for overall honors, this weekend they were restricted to their own event. The under two liter sports racers, classes E, F and G Modified, ran their own 80 mile affair. Don Sesslar took up where he left off Saturday, breaking to an early lead, and holding off the challenge of Bob Donner. Both were driving Porsche 550-RS Spyders, and they lapped every other car in the race. Sesslar averaged 79.03 mph, which due to rain later in the day

The 1958 June Sprints was a Cunningham team demonstration run. Walt Hansgen and Ed Crawford cruised to a one-two finish in Lister Jaguars, playfully swapping the lead. Here Crawford leads Hansgen out of Canada Corner.

was the fastest race speed. Behind the two silver Spyders Chuck Dietrich in an Elva Mk. II and J.C. Kilbourn (similar name, but not the same fellow as John Kilborn who won the 1956 Six Hour) in a Lotus Eleven battled for GM honors with Dietrich prevailing. Five two liter four cylinder Ferraris were in the EM field, and Jack Quackenbush took the class in his 500 Testa Rossa. Already, the nimbleness of the rear engined Porsches was showing its superiority to the nominally bigger engined and higher horsepower, but front engined Ferraris.

Race three was for middle production cars, classes C, D and E. With the BP Corvettes running in the feature, the race promised to be a contest among the many Mercedes-Benz 300SLs that were present. However, there were surprises. At the start, Walt Hansgen, driving a Jaguar XK-150S out of the Cunningham stable, jumped into the lead halfway around the first lap, and was ahead by an astonishing 10 seconds as he crossed the line for the first time. This was a case of driver skill, as the XK-150 was a *boulevard* sports car, hardly a design for the track. Unfortunately, Hansgen's run ended early, as the Jag began gushing clouds of smoke from the engine compartment and retired to the pits. George Reed moved into the lead, driving a pretty Ferrari 250-GT Berlinetta Tour de France, and with Hansgen's absence, ran untroubled to the checker, taking overall and CP honors. Bill Steele finished a fine second overall, first in EP in an AC Ace-Bristol, beating many bigger engined cars. Ralph Durbin was the DP winner in an Austin-Healey.

Rich Lyeth rounding turn six in the Ferrari 375 that he ran for many years. In 1958 he installed a supercharged V-8 and called the car the Hi-Tork Special.

The feature race was a 38-lap, 152-mile affair for B, C, D Modified, and B Production. This was the seventh SCCA National of the year, and so far all had been won by Walt Hansgen. Driving for the Briggs Cunningham team, Hansgen was absolutely dominating the year. After winning the first event of the year in a D Jaguar, Hansgen transferred into the newer Lister-Jaguar. With de Dion rear suspension instead of solid axle, and three years of progress on the drafting board, the Listers were simply newer and faster than the D Jags that Cunningham had employed the previous three years. Add to that the fact that Cunningham used 3.8 liter fuel injected engines in place of the standard 3.4 liter carbureted units, and that he had the renowned Alfred Momo turning the wrenches, an almost unbeatable combination resulted.

Hansgen and Ed Crawford, driving the second Cunningham Lister, took off at the green flag and disappeared into the distance. The only car that was able to keep them in sight in early going was also a Lister. Bark Henry was driving the Chevrolet-engined Kelso Auto Dynamics car, a brutish appearing, flat black painted car that was still going through its new car teething troubles. This showed and the car retired after a few laps in third place. This gave third place to Dan Collins in a class DM Ferrari 250 Testa Rossa, which is where he finished, taking class honors. Hansgen and Crawford played with the race, swapping the lead every few laps, which may have given the announced 35,000 fans a bit of a thrill but in reality, Hansgen as number one was the race winner from the start. A rain shower hit halfway through the event, slowing things considerably, but not keeping the two Cunningham Listers from their appointed rounds. The race average was 74.94 mph.

Fourth overall and first in BP was taken by Jim Jeffords. What was most noteworthy about this was that it was the debut of the Nickey Chevrolet *Purple People Eater*. Driven by Jeffords from nearby Milwaukee, the Corvette was painted a metallic purple and was wrenched by Ron Kaplan, who knew Corvettes as well as anyone in the country. Nickey Chevrolet, a Chicago dealership owned by the Stephani family, was getting into racing and its object was to win the BP SCCA National Championship. The combination of Jeffords' skill and the Nickey/Kaplan preparation led to

what would be a season with a 100% success rate. Jeffords's win this date would be the first of seven straight in SCCA National competition, winning the BP title easily. They went on to Nassau in December, and were triumphant in the Nassau Tourist Trophy Race, a professional event for production-based cars.

Rich Lyeth was fifth, first in BM in his *Hi-Tork Special*, a supercharged Chevy engine now inserted in the Ferrari 375 chassis in which he had finished fifth in the 1956 Sprints. In seventh place, second in DM, was a young man from whom the racing world would hear a lot more. Augie Pabst was moving up from the middle production ranks, and had just purchased a Ferrari 625LM from Jim Johnston, a 2.5 liter four cylinder version of the 1956 Testa Rossa chassis. In his first outing in a pure racing car, Pabst spent most of his time learning, lessons he would put to good effect later.

The weekend of September 6-7 brought all the stars back to the track for the second Road America 500 weekend. Also an SCCA National event, the 500 was for cars in the 'modified' classes B, C, D, E, F and G. The production classes, plus HM, had their events on Saturday.

The first race was for F and G Production and H Modified. The 80 mile event was taken, as in June, by Chuck Rickert. Again driving a Porsche 356 Carrera, Rickert finished two miles ahead of Harry Blanchard, also Carrera mounted. Milwaukee car dealer Ted Baumgartner was the GP winner in an Alfa Romeo Giulietta, while Martin Tanner was the HM winner, driving his own home built Martin T Special.

The large production cars ran a 120 mile race, long enough that some had to make pit stops for fuel. As stated earlier, this was Jim Jeffords' year in BP and this race was no different. Jeffords took the purple Nickey Corvette into the lead early, built it up to a lap, stopped for a minute for fuel, and still won by over three miles over Bill Larson, also in a Corvette. It took Jeffords one hour, 34 minutes to drive the 30 laps. George Reed repeated his June Sprints CP win in the Ferrari 250GT, as did Ralph Durbin in DP. Luke Stear's Ace-Bristol was triumphant in the EP category.

At 10:30 on Sunday morning the green flag waved, and the 500 was on. Starting positions were by class rather than by qualifying times, so the BM cars were released first, some 10 seconds before CM, and so forth. This gave the BM 'Hi-Tork Special' of Rich Lyeth an immediate advantage, and he made full use of it. With the other BM entries trailing behind, soon to be gobbled up by the more sophisticated CM and DM cars, Lyeth kept his foot firmly on the floor, and clung to the lead for 25 laps, 100 miles. Finally the strain told on the supercharged Chevy engine, and it expired on the 26th lap. It was a glorious effort, but now that the *special* was out of the way, it was time for the big boys to play.

The 47 car starting field had the cream rise to the top, and when Lyeth retired from his starting grid aided lead, the race really was on. E.D. Martin was there to take the lead on the 26th lap, his Ferrari 250 Testa Rossa singing on all 12 cylinders. In his mirrors, though, were two blue-striped white cars: the Cunningham Listers. After a few laps Walt Hansgen took his Lister past Martin's Ferrari and into the lead. Observers were forgiven if they experienced that "here we go again" feeling, as the Cunningham Listers had already won eight Nationals this season, and Hansgen had long earlier locked up the CM National Championship. But this time it was not to be. On lap 37, Hansgen's Lister rolled to a stop with a broken rear pinion bearing. It was back to the shop for Alfred Momo, to design some strengthened parts, as Phil Forno, in the second Cunningham Lister stopped on the circuit on lap 41 with an identical failure.

, Martin's Ferrari retook the lead, but now he was being challenged by two other Ferraris. George Reed had dipped into his bag of race cars and pulled out a four year old 375 Plus. He challenged Martin repeatedly, but the car quit on him halfway through the race, Reed rolling to a silent halt on the back straight. The other Ferrari was the one to watch, though. Entered by Luigi Chinetti's North American Racing Team, it was an ex-factory 335-S. A 4.1 liter, four overhead camshaft V-12 powered car, It was the ultimate in front engined Ferrari sports racers. In fact, Phil Hill many years later stated that the 335-S was his all time favorite Ferrari racer. This particular chassis had finished second in the previous year's Mille Miglia, driven by Wolfgang Von Trips in 3.8 liter, 315S form, and Mike Hawthorn/Luigi Musso had finished second with the larger 4.1 liter engine in the season ending 1000 Kms of Caracas. At Elkhart Lake it was driven by Lance Reventlow, taking a one race hiatus from his Scarab effort, and Gaston Andrey, a four time EM National Champion in a 2.0 Ferrari.

Reventlow had taken the opening stint, intending to drive the first half of the race, and then to turn over to Andrey at the car's only refueling stop. Lance had kept the car running to plan, starting slowly, letting the race sort itself out and avoiding early lap entanglements. As the race got into its stride, Reventlow stepped it up, and as the halfway point of the race grew near, passed Jack Quackenbush, in for Martin, for the lead for the first time. Reventlow stopped on lap 57 of 125. By the time the car was refuelled and Andrey returned to the track, Quackenbush was past. Operating on a two stop strategy, the 3.0 Ferrari was trying to make up on weight savings what it lost in power. The strategy had merit, as the two Ferraris were never far apart for the second half of the contest.

Andrey took the lead for good on the 70th lap, but that is not to say that he was home free. Quackenbush, and then Martin again harassed him endlessly, and one little slip by Andrey would have given them the lead. However, on lap 113, with only 12 to go, and only 16 seconds behind, the clutch blew on the 250 Testa Rossa and Martin rolled to a halt. The race was over, Reventlow and Andrey had won. It took them six hours, 18 minutes, 35 seconds for the 500 miles, an average of 79.2 mph.

Finishing four laps behind, but first in DM, was another Ferrari 250 Testa Rossa, this driven by the trio of Jim Johnston, Bud Seaverns, and Ebby Lunken. A pair of Porsche 550 RS Spyders, driven by Dean Causey/Chuck Rickert and Luke Stear/Bob Staples followed, taking FM honors. A Ferrari 500 TR was first in EM, driven by Jim Place and Ken Neill, while Frank Baptista finished a fine sixth overall, driving his Elva Mk. III solo and taking the GM class. In BM, following Lyeth's departure, Jim Jeffords led, getting as high as fourth overall before his Corvette SR-2 broke an axle on lap 108. The SR-2 was one of three built by Chevrolet in 1956-57 as factory sports racers. The SR-2 was essentially a modified Corvette with swoopy bodywork incorporating a headrest and fin. Faster than the production model, it still was not in the same league with pure bred racing cars. However, the fact that Chevrolet had allowed Jeffords to purchase one indicated the respect that he had gained with his achievements on the track. Ultimately BM was taken by Hal Ullrich and Carl Haas driving an Excalibur SJ, the third Excalibur racer built. This incorporated more enveloping bodywork than

Lance Reventlow powers the mighty 4.1 liter Ferrari 335-S through turn 13 during the 1958 Road America 500. Reventlow took a break from campaigning his new Scarab to co-drive the North American Racing Team entered car to victory.

the first two cars, had a finned headrest, and was powered by a super-charged Jaguar XK engine as opposed to the small and tepid Henry J units of the first two.

So ended 1958 at Road America. Elsewhere through, developments were brewing, as the first stages of professionalism were making their presence known in American road racing. The United States Auto Club had taken notice of sports car racing, and in 1958 established its Road Racing Division. In July, at Lime Rock, CT, the first professional sports car race (except Sebring) was held. George Constantine had won in an Aston Martin DBR-2 over a rather motley field of 16 cars. An even smaller field had gathered a month later at Marlboro, MD, for race two, which Constantine also won. SCCA types were hesitant to enter, due mainly to the National headquarters' strict adherence to amateurism. However the small purses of $2500 total could not have been much of an incentive either. This was to change, however.

In October Riverside Raceway in California held the season ending round of the USAC championship. Unlike the previous two, Riverside had many things going for it. Most importantly, the *Los Angeles Times* put its promotional muscle behind the race, promoting the daylights out of it, and putting up an attractive purse. The results were phenomenal. The best entry ever seen for a sports car race in the country was attracted. The top drivers, road racers from the SCCA, oval track drivers from USAC and F-1 drivers such as Phil Hill and Jo Bonnier, entered. A wild and wonderful variety of cars, such as works Ferraris and Porsches, all three Scarabs, Astons, Maseratis, other Ferraris and many Chevy-engined Ferraris, Maseratis and Listers, were present. Most important of all, some *80,000* people showed up, on a hot Sunday in the wind-blown desert, to see sports car racing. The race itself did not disappoint, as the duel between Chuck Daigh, in a Scarab, and Phil Hill, in the factory Ferrari 412MI, was tight and intense until Hill's Ferrari expired late in the race. Daigh triumphed with Dan Gurney second in Frank Arciero's Ferrari 410 Special. (With a second at the round three Watkins Glen Formula Libre race, Gurney won the first USAC Road Racing Championship). While it took a few years for all the ramifications of the Riverside race to work their way through the system, this race at Riverside was a watershed event. It changed the face of U.S. road racing, and things would not be the same again.

1959

For the 1959 season, the program remained essentially the same as the previous year; two SCCA Nationals, the June Sprints and the 500. Again, the menu had a lot of laps, the entries were substantial, and the crowds continued to grow. Competition to the track arose for the first time, as a group of Chicagoans built a 3.27 mile road course, Meadowdale, about 160 miles south of the track near Elgin, Illinois. In 1959 Meadowdale held three USAC pro races, each on a summer holiday weekend. However, the track did not have the promotion that RA did, as well as the physical attractions and spectator friendly atmosphere. As a result, while RA continued to grow, Meadowdale struggled for a decade, running no major events after 1964, before finally folding in 1969.

Bolstered by the success of the Riverside *Times GP*, USAC increased its Road Racing Division championship to 11 events. While those events on the west coast drew very respectable fields, the races in the eastern part of the country continued to struggle, both for entries and spectators. A reason for this is the SCCA's devout stand on professionalism. It was *verboten*. Many did find a way around this, simply by entering the cars under a professional corporation, with the drivers merely being employees. The SCCA permitted this sham for a few years, but later cracked down in 1961, creating a major crisis in the sport. The SCCA's creed was stronger in the east, where all racing was under their umbrella. However in the west, the California Sports Car Club had for years existed as an alternate to the SCCA, and was in fact stronger in the Golden State. Hence, all the top western teams and drivers entered the USAC race-for-pay events, a situation not existing in the east. As a result, the running of three USAC races at Meadowdale had little effect on Elkhart Lake.

The June Sprints began with one event on Saturday, June 20. This was an 80 mile go for large production cars and was won by—who else?—Jim Jeffords in the purple Nickey Corvette. Duke Knowlton won CP in a Jaguar XK-150S, Tim Mayer DP in an Austin-Healey 100-Six, while Harvey Woodward was the EP winner in an Ace-Bristol. During morning practice for this race, Don Wolf struck a deer, demolishing the front of his Corvette. Fortunately Wolf was uninjured, although the same could not be said for the deer. Over the years, despite the best efforts, the occasional deer still bounds through the track property, presenting an additional hazard beyond the expected.

On Sunday, the 60 mile small production event was a duel between the twin Porsche 356 Carreras of Chuck Rickert and Harry Blanchard. This year the flag went to Blanchard first, after the lead had been swapped several times. Chuck Stoddard was the GP winner in an Alfa Romeo, while Ray Heppenstall took HP in a Deutsch-Bonnet coupe. Class JP, rarely used as it was for cars of 500cc or less, actually had a few entries, with Derr Andrlik putt-putting his Berkeley roadster to the flag first.

Fred Windridge scored his only major win in the 1959 June Sprints. He drove the Kelso Auto Dynamics Lister-Chevy in the 140 mile feature.

Classes GM and HM had their own 60 mile run. Allan Ross made the event the U.S. debut of the Lola marque, and it was very successful indeed as Ross romped to the checker first, cutting the first sub-three minute lap for a GM car at 2:58.3. The Lola Mk. I had been cutting a wide swath through English 1100cc racing, regularly trouncing the previously dominant Lotus Elevens and Elvas. Now, with a winning debut in the U.S., it appeared that the tale would be repeated. Ed Walsh was the HM winner in a Cooper-Osca.

For Sunday's 140 mile feature, a stellar field had once again been assembled. The Cunningham team was busy at Le Mans and was missed, but their absence was compensated for by the RA debut of an Aston Martin DBR-2, a Scarab and the Corvette Sting Ray. Add the usual assortment of Ferraris, Jaguars and specials, plus the inclusion of the Porsche Spyders in the feature, and the prospect was for a great race.

George Constantine was the driver of the Aston Martin. One of two DBR-2s built, it was powered by a 4.2 liter dohc 6. Lent by the works to Elisha Walker to run in the U.S., it had won two USAC races in 1958, and was now embarking on what would prove to be a successful SCCA National season. Indeed, the major Nassau Trophy Race in December would be won by Constantine in this car.

Nickey Chevrolet had taken a major step upward. While they were still running a Corvette in BP for Jeffords, they augmented this by purchasing a Scarab. Created in 1958 by Lance Reventlow, the three front engined Scarab sports racers built had been undefeated from mid-1958, their season culminating in victories at the Riverside *Times GP*, and the Nassau Governor's Cup and Nassau Trophy Races. They were unquestionably the top sports

Roger Penske and Harry Blanchard complete the victory lap that wasn't. A scoring failure initially gave them the 1959 500 win. They took the lap, kissed the queen, but had to give the trophy back. They were third.

racers in the country. With Reventlow Automobiles Inc. now concentrating on an ill-fated Formula One program, two of the sports racers were to be sold to private entrants. The first was sold to Nickey in March, with the second going to the nascent Meister Brauser Team in August. The Nickey car was painted in the team's trademark metallic purple with white trim. For a driver the team nominated Jim Jeffords. Success had already been tasted, as Jeffords in the Scarab had dominated the Memorial Day 500 Kilometer USAC race at Meadowdale. In practice, Jeffords showed the Scarab's pace, lapping the four mile layout in the 2:43 range, three full seconds below the existing track record.

The third new car of note present was the Corvette Sting Ray. Entered by Bill Mitchell, General Motor's VP of Design, the car was not a factory entry per se, due to the ban on racing then in force at GM. However, under the red fiberglass bodywork that was a preview of the production Corvettes to come four years later, there was the all-out racing chassis of the Corvette SS. This was the factory's effort to build a world beater. Entered at Sebring in 1957 with much fanfare, the car was a bust. Shortly thereafter, GM pulled the plug on racing and the SS went into the museum. In 1959 Mitchell purchased the 'mule', an identical chassis used for practice. He rebodied it with his own design and gave the car the much needed engineering development the original lacked. John Fitch would be the driver this weekend in place of regular Dick Thompson.

In a surprise, the race did not belong to any of the above highly touted entries. Instead Fred Windridge, an east coast Corvette specialist, dominated the event in the "Kelischev"—the Kelso Auto Dynamics Lister-Chevrolet. His cause was aided mightily by the 11th hour failure of the ring and pinion in the Nickey Scarab. Unable to make the repair in time for the start, the Scarab was sadly pushed back onto the trailer. Constantine gave early chase in the Aston Martin, but its gearbox broke early, leaving the car with only third gear. Constantine persevered however, and brought the hobbled car home in seventh overall, but first in the CM class. Fitch had troubles with the Sting Ray's brakes, finally spinning out of fourth place on lap 19 of 35. Windridge's run to the win may have been untroubled, but that was due to a stroke of luck after Saturday's practice. While the Lister was up on stands having its transmission ratios changed, three cracks were discovered in the de Dion tube. Had they gone undetected, the car would undoubtedly have broken during the race. Windridge averaged 82.47 mph in his winning run.

The real battle in the race was for second place. This year, unlike the previous, classes EM and FM were included in the feature, and this allowed a group of Porsches to show their speed. For 1959 the factory had brought out an entirely new sports racer, the Type 718 RSK. Still powered by a

1500cc dohc flat four, cloaked in a sensual aluminum body, and driven by some of the best drivers around, the RSKs were far faster than one would expect. Three of them broke out ahead of most of the pack and finished 2-3-4 overall, 1-2-3 in class FM. Bob Donner and Don Sesslar traded second place several times. On the last lap Sesslar led Donner, but he had a half spin at turn five, allowing Donner to pass. Finishing fourth behind Donner and Sesslar was the RSK of Roger Penske. Of him much more would be heard in the future...

Alan Connell finished fifth overall, and first in class DM. His Ferrari 250 Testa Rossa had 500cc and eight more cylinders than the 625LM of Augie Pabst, who followed Connell home, both overall and in class. Class EM was taken by Ted Baumgartner, now in a Ferrari 500TR in place of the GP Alfa of the year previous.

On the weekend of September 12-13 the cast reassembled for the running the 500. Everybody from the June Sprints was there, plus a goodly number more. A reported crowd of 37,000 spectators clambered over the hills, enjoying the warmth of a fall sun. It was the perfect way to spend an early fall weekend.

There were only three races on the program this weekend, but they all were *long*. Saturday had two events, a 120 miler for G, H, I Production and H Modified, while the B-through-F Production cars ran to a distance of 160 miles. For drivers used to running 40-50 miles elsewhere, this was definitely an endurance test. Sunday, of course, was 500 miles for all sports racers except HM.

After giving the June Sprints a miss, the Briggs Cunningham team was back. Besides the three Listers entered in the 500, Cunningham also brought an Osca 750 for himself. It did the trick, as Cunningham was a fairly easy winner at the conclusion of the 120 mile first race. Cunningham was elated, for although he had entered scores of winning cars in the last several years, this was the first time he had been to victory circle as a driver in many years. Ed Walsh, Cooper-Osca, was second overall and in class, while Bill Wuesthoff took class GP in his powder blue Alfa Romeo. Art Barsantee was HP winner in an Austin-Healey Sprite, while Paul Richards took IP in a Fiat-Abarth-Zagato 750.

The 160 mile large production race was all Jim Jeffords. Once again in the striking purple Nickey Corvette, Jeffords led all the way. Even a pit stop for fuel did not cost him the lead, as he finished nearly a lap ahead of second placed Chuck Rickert, whose Porsche Carrera took class FP. Everybody else was two or more laps behind Jeffords and Rickert. Jeffords win gave him his second consecutive BP National title. Wayne Burnett took CP in a Mercedes-Benz 300SL, with DP going to Frank Opalka in an Austin-Healey and EP to the Ace-Bristol of Fritz Taylor.

The 500 field was top rate. Cunningham had three Listers, two 1958 models and one 1959 Costin-bodied car. Walt Hansgen, John Fitch, Phil Forno, Ed Crawford, Russ Boss and Cunningham would be the drivers. Two 4.1 Ferraris were present, E.D. Martin with the 335-S that won the year before, and Alan Connell with a newly built version. George Constantine and Paul O'Shea were in the Aston DBR-2. With Nickey having sold the Scarab, Jeffords was down to co-drive the Sting Ray with Dick Thompson. Likewise, Porsche star Bob Holbert left his RSK home and was accompanying Fred Windridge in the Kelso Lister-Chev. Add to this several Porsche RSKs, half a dozen Ferrari 250 Testa Rossas, assorted other Ferraris, Porsche 550-RSs, Lotuses, Elvas and specials, and the field was superb.

The race itself was largely the property of the superbly prepared Cunningham team. Early, Walt Hansgen in the Costin Lister contested the lead with the Connell and Martin 335-S Ferraris, with Constantine dueling Crawford's Lister for fourth. As the race developed, Crawford moved up, Connell and Constantine had long pit stops, and Martin dropped out. When

Hansgen brought his Lister into the pits for mechanical repairs which would take several laps, Alfred Momo decided to switch his driver pairings around. Fitch, due to codrive with Crawford, was put in the Costin Lister Hansgen had vacated, while Hansgen was now deputized into the Crawford Lister, which was running first. As Hansgen began his stint, which was to be the second half of the race, things were looking good. Threats from the Windridge Lister-Chev and Thompson Sting Ray had evaporated with dnfs, while Skip Hudson, now in the Connell Ferrari, was having niggling little problems which prevented the mounting of a full scale challenge. Mix into this the class FM leading Porsche RSK of Roger Penske and Harry Blanchard and the now-O'Shea driven Aston Martin, and the endurance race ran into its final 100 miles, cars now hanging on to the finish, lest the overstressed mechanicals break.

Then, breakage occurred, but not only in the cars. The scoring system, dependent on stop watches and eyesight in the years before electronics and computers, crashed. As the last crucial laps ticked off, timing and scoring was operating by guess. Their initial guess was wrong. The Hansgen Lister, which had led for almost 400 miles, broke a rear axle pinion about a mile from the finish line, on its last lap. With power only going through one rear wheel, the speed dropped drastically and Hansgen limped to the line, expecting to get the checker as the Cunningham lap charts had him comfortably ahead of second placed Hudson. But—scoring had dropped a lap somewhere for both Hansgen and Hudson, and told the flagman that Hansgen was just starting, rather than finishing, the 125th lap. While Walt spent almost six minutes struggling the extra four miles, the checker was thrown at the Penske/Blanchard Porsche RSK, surprising all and sundry, especially Penske and Blanchard. They were not ones to look a gift horse in the mouth, however, and dutifully took the victory lap, the race queen's kisses and the trophy. Meanwhile, protests were flying, and the stewards of the meet and the scorers went into seclusion, methodically going over their lap charts as well as those supplied by several teams. After four and one-half hours, long after the fans had gone home and the champagne had gone stale, they discovered their error. One lap too many. Go get the trophy back from Penske and Blanchard.

Walt Hansgen and Ed Crawford had indeed won the 500. Also with a lap regained, Connell and Hudson were second, while the Penske/Blanchard Porsche was really third, although first in FM. The Cunningham/Forno Lister was fourth, with Constantine/O'Shea fifth in the Aston Martin. Sixth overall, and first in EM, was the Lotus 15 of Pat Piggott and Pete Lovely. Seventh overall, first in BM, was John Staver and Ed Grierson in an Echidna, one of a run of three racers built by the pair and Bill Larson in the frigid climes of far northern Minnesota. Eighth overall and first in DM was a Ferrari 250GT Berlinetta coupe piloted by Bob Bondurant and Bill Sturgis. Art Tweedale and Frank Baptista took GM in an Elva Mk. IV. The winning speed was 82.18 mph, a record for the distance, while Crawford set a new race lap record of 86.486 mph, breaking Carroll Shelby's record which had stood for two years.

In October the track had a first — a non-spectator race. Put on by the Chicago Region SCCA, it was sort of a *super regional*, and over the years the practice of renting the track out to regions, car clubs, manufacturers, and so forth for non-spectator use has ballooned into such proportions that the track now is busy virtually every weekend of the season. For the record, the main race of this weekend was won by John Staver in an Echidna.

Elsewhere, the top SCCA guns of the year were Walt Hansgen and George Constantine, who fought right down to the last race of the year for the SCCA championship. At Daytona, Hansgen ran second behind the winning Connell, while Constantine finished fourth. Advantage Hansgen. The

Briggs Cunningham was one of the first to use a transporter rather than a small trailer to move his multi-car team.

The man who made it work. Clif Tufte enjoys a smoke at the staff Christmas party in December 1959.

USAC Road Racing Championship went to Augie Pabst in only his second season of driving sports racers. Augie had driven his own 2.5 Ferrari (although entered by a *corporation* to circumvent the SCCA's pro ban) to some decent placings in the first half of the season, and then was tapped to drive for the Meister Brauser Team when they purchased the second Scarab from Reventlow in August. While great sport was made of the fact that a Pabst was driving for Meister Brau, the fact is that at that time Augie had no connection with the brewery which bore his name. Pabst promptly won Meadowdale and Vaca Valley in the Scarab, and pocketed the crown. Jeffords had scored two wins in the Nickey Scarab before it all fell apart at mid year. Nickey grew disenchanted with the costs of running the Scarab, and sold it. At the end of the year this car was purchased by Meister Brau, giving it both Scarabs and the prospect of an awesome year to come.

Perhaps the most important development of 1959 was the first World Championship Grand Prix of the United States. Held December 12, 1959, at Sebring, it was the first true formula one championship race in this country. Its long range impact was to go far beyond that of this specific race, which, truth be told, laid a financial egg. The winner of this GP was Bruce McLaren in a Cooper. McLaren also was to have a huge impact on American racing, even bigger than that of the Grand Prix.

1960

The advent of the '60s saw the track add a third event. The first pro sports car race was scheduled for July, as the track added a round of the USAC Road Racing Division. As usual, the June Sprints and 500 continued in their now traditional dates.

The USAC series was reduced to only five events in 1960. Several tracks that had events the year before declined to repeat, no doubt having taken a hit in the wallet. Of the five dates that remained, only Elkhart Lake was east of the Rockies, confirming the east/west split existing in U.S. racing when it came to professionalism.

A major change had occurred in the SCCA's production car classes. The displacement-based class system produced some incongruous results, such as the FP Porsche Carrera being the second fastest car on the track, beaten only by the BP Corvette. Hence, SCCA completely revamped the classes into seven, basing them on performance rather than displacement. As an example, the aforementioned Porsche Carreras were now in class CP. Further, for the first time modifications within limits were allowed. Instead of having to be strictly showroom stock, the engines could now be lightly reworked, different camshafts used, suspensions tweaked and so on. What didn't change was the task of the scrutineers. Now instead of trying to detect modifications, they had to look for illegal modifications, destined to become a never ending struggle.

The SCCA also added a class for 1960 — Formula Junior. FJ had started in Italy a few years before, and was designed to be a training class. The cars were single seater formula machines, powered by engines up to 1100cc with a weight to displacement formula. The engines had to be production-derived and could not have overhead camshafts. Brakes were drum, gearboxes were restricted, and so forth. The class soon became wildly popular and a score of manufacturers were building Juniors. Of long term significance is that the SCCA had now introduced a third category, formula cars, alongside production and modified (sports racers). The National class count increased to 15. In time additional formula classes would be added, then a showroom stock category, then a GT category. The genie was out of the bottle, classes would proliferate (up to 25 in 1996), and as a result, the pool of participants would be spread out over an ever-increasing base. As time would show, this dilution would cause classes to come and go, pro support series to start, prosper for a few years and then fade away. While class growth is inevitable, not all of it was for the best.

The June Sprints comprised six races, recognizing the large entry. The 60 mile large production event introduced the new class structure. George Reed was the overall and BP winner, again driving his familiar Ferrari 250-GT. The absence of the Nickey Corvette was noticeable; Nickey had pulled

The 1960 June Sprints saw two Chevrolet-powered cars stage a thrilling battle for the lead. The Corvette Sting Ray driven by Dick Thompson leads eventual winner Augie Pabst in the Meister Brauser Scarab.

out of racing after the '59 season, and Jim Jeffords was now driving Maseratis for the Camoradi team. Bob Spooner brought the first Corvette home second. Bill Romig was the CP winner in a Porsche Carrera, while Lloyd Barton won DP in a Jaguar XK-150.

The second race on Saturday was the debut of the Formula Juniors. Steve Wendt captured the 40 mile event, driving an Elva-DKW. In the early stages of FJ, the simple but effective DKW three cylinder two stroke motor was the preferred unit. However, as the English tuners wove their magic over the four stroke four cylinder units of Austin and English Ford, this soon changed. Tim Mayer challenged Wendt early, but his Lotus 18 faded to fifth. Bob Major eventually took second in a Stanguellini.

Sunday's first race was 60 miles for class EP. Duncan Black was dominant in the SCCA in this class this year, wisely figuring that the obscure, but powerful, 2.5 liter V-8 Daimler SP-250 was a class sleeper. He was right. He led all the way over Jim Kaser's Alfa Romeo and Bill Flippo's Austin-Healey.

The next race was 60 miles for F, G and H Production. The newly introduced Elva Courier roadster, plastic bodied and MG powered, proved to be the choice in FP. The three Couriers of Pete Ledwith, Ernie Harris and Don Bye dominated, until first Ledwith, and then Bye suffered mechanical difficulties, leaving the win to Harris. Brooks Robinson in a Fiat-Abarth Monza took second, while Phil Seven was first in GP in an Alfa, and Frank Phillips triumphed in HP in a Sprite.

The next race, also 60 miles, was for the G & H Modified cars. Millard Ripley had the only Lola Mk. I in the event and it was enough. Ripley almost threw it away on the first lap, though, spinning out and falling a half minute behind Dr. M.R.J. Wyllie's Lotus 17. However, showing the Lola's class superiority, Ripley caught Wyllie on lap nine and won by 18 seconds. In HP, Ed Walsh and Martin Tanner had a real dogfight, passing the lead several times before Tanner eked out a car length victory in his Martin T Special over Walsh's Cooper-Osca.

The feature event was 140 miles for the big iron. All eyes were on the Meister Brauser Team, on hand with both Scarabs for Augie Pabst and Harry Heuer. Chief competition was to come from the Corvette Sting Ray of Bill Mitchell, now painted silver and driven by Dick Thompson. One *birdcage* Maserati was present for Gaston Andrey, who had won the season's first National at Pensacola and was leading the DM points chase. The Birdcage was a truly exceptional car; it got its nickname from its space frame, operating on the principle that if two tubes were strong, four smaller tubes were stronger, eight were stronger yet, and so forth. The result was a collection of jack straws, ingeniously assembled to give a very stiff chassis. Powered by a 2.9 liter four cylinder engine, the Maserati Tipo 61 would be the Scarab's toughest competition over the year. Add in 12 Porsche Spyders, Listers, Ferraris, Cooper Monacos and Chevrolet engined specials, and it was a good field.

In the morning warm-up, Pabst's Scarab broke a shock mounting. With repairs unable to be completed in time, Pabst hopped into Heuer's car, leaving him to spectate. At the start, Pabst blasted into the lead, with Thompson behind. However, Thompson had some problems with the turn five gravel, allowing Andrey, Roger Penske (Porsche RSK), John Staver (Echidna), Bob Holbert (Porsche RS-60) and eight others to pass him. Thompson fought back, however, and the result was one of the best races seen. By lap five, Thompson was back in second, just seven seconds behind Pabst. By lap seven, Thompson had caught him. From here to lap 28 of the 35 lap race the two cars were never more than a car length or two apart. Lap records tumbled, both setting new marks before Pabst finally threw in a lap at 2:44.4 for a new race record. Thompson got past on laps 12-14, but Pabst regained the lead with a daring out-braking maneuver. Finally, on lap 28 the ignition on the Sting Ray began to act up and the dice was over. Pabst took the overall win, and class BM, averaging 85.54 mph. Thompson had such a lead over third placed Andrey that he held on to second, taking class CM. Andrey was third, first in DM, while Roger Penske was the EM winner and fourth overall in his Porsche RSK Spyder, the engine enlarged to 1600cc to compete in EM. Bill Wuesthoff made the debut of his new Porsche RS-60 Spyder a success, garnering sixth overall and first in FM. It was a very good race indeed.

The weekend of July 30-31, USAC came to Road America. With them came what *Competition Press* called "the best field of top sports cars and top drivers ever gathered in this country". Drivers and teams from the four corners of the country came for the 200 mile professional race. The two Meister Brauser Scarabs were there, four birdcage Maseratis, several Listers, many Porsches, Ferraris, D Jaguars and specials too numerous to mention. Carroll Shelby was the USAC points leader, having won the first two races, Riverside in a Maserati and Continental Divide in Pabst's Scarab, while Pabst was away finishing seventh at Le Mans. For this race Shelby was in Old Yaller II. Despite its mongrel name and appearance, Old Yaller was a thoroughbred. Built by Max Balchowsky in California and powered by a 6.6 liter Buick V-8, the car made up in speed what it lacked in looks. Jim Jeffords was present in the Camoradi Maserati Tipo 61 streamliner. Designed for speed on the long Mulsanne straight, the birdcage had an elongated tail and a windscreen that sloped right down to the nose. Jim Hall brought two Maseratis, one for himself and a second for Bob Schroeder. Hall was a young Texas oilman, a Cal Tech graduate, whose wealth allowed him to purchase the best cars, whose skill would win many races, and

Carroll Shelby hustles Old Yaller II through the kink during the 1960 USAC Road Racing Championship event. This was the only time Shelby drove the famous Max Balchowsky-built car, leading the first 30 laps before mechanical failure side-lined him.

whose engineering expertise would result a few years later in the all-conquering Chaparrals. Many, many other top drivers were present; about the only 'name' missing was that of Walt Hansgen.

Saturday held qualifying and a 100 mile race for Formula Junior cars. Curt Gonstead was the surprise winner, taking his MBM-DKW into the lead early, withstanding a challenge from the Osca of John Haas, and leading Jim Hall's Lotus 18 over the line by 35 seconds. Ron Letellier was third in an Isis, followed by Jay Gould's Stanguellini and Alan Connell's Cooper-DKW.

Record speeds were expected in qualifying, and that is what happened. Augie Pabst took the pole in the Scarab, lapping at 2:41.82, almost three seconds faster than the mark he set a month before. Shelby was second, Jeffords third, Hall fourth and in fifth was a real giant killer—Roger Penske in his Porsche RSK. Penske's lap of 2:47.08 was some five seconds faster than the second under two liter car, Bob Holbert's Porsche RS-60.

The race itself saw Shelby jumping off to an immediate lead over Pabst and Bill Krause's D Jaguar-Chev. Shelby stretched it, seemingly effortlessly, but Pabst was driving to a plan. Meister Brauser team manager Red Byron figured that Old Yaller would not last, and he had Pabst turning lap times that he calculated would both save the car and win the race. Krause was out not too many laps into the 200 miler, with Jeffords, Hall and Loyal Katskee, all in Maserati Tipo 61s, battling with George Constantine in the Kelso Lister-Chev for third. In under two liters, Penske broke early and Holbert was maintaining a comfortable lead over 20 year old Canadian Peter Ryan's Porsche RS-60.

On lap 31 of 50, Byron was proven right. The gearbox in Old Yaller broke and Shelby was out. Pabst now had a healthy lead over the dueling pair of Jeffords and Hall, with Katskee trailing a fair distance behind. Constantine had dropped back to ninth after a pit stop, and Heuer in the second Scarab was next. Just when everyone was beginning to expect another Scarab win, the rear end on Pabst's car broke on lap 38, handing the lead to Jeffords. Hall was immediately behind, but Jeffords now really began to move, and at the end of the 50 laps was almost a minute ahead of Hall. Katskee finished third, Heuer fourth and Skip Hudson drove a virtually brakeless Ferrari 250 Testa Rossa to fifth. Constantine recovered for sixth. Holbert won under two liters over Ryan, with the Jack Ensley/Rodger Ward Porsche RSK third. For his winning drive Jeffords pocketed $3650, a big sum in those days.

The third and final event of 1960 was again the second weekend in September. The Road America 500, again an SCCA National, had four races

A magnificent upset victory. Unheralded Dave Causey and Luke Stear defeat an all-star field to win the 1960 Road America 500 in a Maserati T-61.

on Saturday plus the famous 500 on Sunday. Once again, a fine field of machinery was assembled for one of the country's premier race weekends.

The first race on Saturday was 80 miles for F, G, H Production and H Modified. Ollie Schmidt was the class of the field in his new *special*, a Lola Mk. I powered by a 750cc Osca engine. The English chassis was far superior to the others in the field in qualifying, but in the race he stalled the car at the start and got away last. Martin Tanner led in his Martin T Special, but Schmidt was moving up quickly. He caught Tanner within a few laps, but before he could get past, a lapped car put him in the guard rail. Tanner had the race in hand, until the last lap, that is. A car spun in front of Tanner at turn 5, and Denise McCluggage, driving Briggs Cunningham's Osca 750, was past for the win. This was the first RA win for a woman driver. Harold Zimdars took FP in a Porsche 356, Harlan Besse was the GP winner in an Alfa Romeo, while Dick Stitt was tops in HP in a Fiat-Abarth.

Formula Juniors had an 80 mile race, and it was largely a Cunningham Team show. Walt Hansgen won in a Cooper T-52, Briggs was third in a Lotus 18, while Denise McCluggage finished fourth in a BMC Mk. I. Only Harry Carter's second place in a Lotus 18 prevented a Cunningham 1-2-3 sweep.

A large EP field ran for 60 miles, with E.G. Davis winning in a Daimler SP-250. The final event of the day was 100 miles for large production cars. Bob Johnson, on his way to the National BP title, carried the day in his Corvette, leading George Reed's familiar Ferrari 250GT. In DP Bill Steele won in an Ace-Bristol, while there were no finishers in CP!

The 500 was a lot of should have beens. Many tried, but 500 miles is a long way. At the start, Jim Jeffords broke into an immediate lead. Driving J. Frank Harrison's just out of the box Maserati Tipo 61 with Jim Hall, Jeffords set a scathing pace, piling seconds onto his lead every time around. Their strategy was to run the race as four 125 mile sprints, while virtually all others were planning on a one or two stop race. Hence, the red Maserati was running lighter than the rest, and Jeffords was doing the balance. Everything was going to plan and at the first stop Jeffords had lapped all but the second place Corvette Sting Ray of Dick Thompson. But the exhaust header had broken and the gasses were boiling the brake fluid. Hall ran a few laps, but the brakes were gone and his feet were getting toasted. He pulled the Maserati into the pits and retirement.

At the same time, the master cylinder in the Sting Ray failed and Thompson pitted for repairs. This let a surprise into first—the Porsche RS-60 of Bob Holbert. Co-driving with Roger Penske, Holbert was making the Porsche go much faster than it really ought. Behind Holbert ran Walt Hansgen, driving solo in the Cunningham Jaguar E2A, a one-off prototype that was more of a forecast of the XK-E than a replacement for the D.

Behind Hansgen were Dave Causey, co-driving with Luke Stear in a Maserati Tipo 61; Bill Wuesthoff, in for Augie Pabst in the North American Racing Team's Ferrari 250TR-59/60; Dave Causey's twin brother Dean, sharing a Porsche RSK Spyder with Chuck Rickert; and Bill Kimberly, co-driving Cunningham's 2.0 liter Maserati Tipo 60 with John Fitch.

Pit stops shuffled the order, as these cars all rather amazingly stayed on the same lap hour after hour. More often than not, though, the Holbert/Penske Porsche led, although the pursuers all had some laps in front. Then the gearbox in the Porsche failed, limiting them to just third gear. Sadly, it dropped down through the order. When Dave Causey stopped precisely at half-distance for fuel and a switch to Luke Stear, the pattern was set. The Pabst/Wuesthoff Ferrari stopped twice, as did Hansgen and Fitch/Kimberly in the two Cunningham entries. That was crucial. With pit stops in these times taking three or more minutes, every stop meant a lap-plus. In the late stages of the race, Fitch had a big spin, losing a lot of time. Pabst, back in for Wuesthoff, had an almighty moment in a fierce rain storm that struck during the last final 50 miles. Coming out of Thunder Valley, the Ferrari aquaplaned, went off course and broad jumped a ditch. Pabst now found himself on the outside looking in and had to motor all the way down to turn 14, looking for a way back. Not finding any, he simply backed up, gunned the Ferrari's V-12, floored it and broad jumped the ditch back into the racing arena! But the time lost was crucial and the race was lost, as well.

Not for Causey and Stear though! They ran their race according to plan, and it worked. At the end of Six hours, fourteen minutes and fifty-nine seconds Stear took the checkered flag in the white and blue Birdcage. The margin of victory over second placed Pabst and Wuesthoff was 33 seconds. Third overall and first in CM was Hansgen in the Jaguar, while the Fitch/Kimberly two liter birdcage captured EM. Fifth overall and first in FM was the Causey/Stear Porsche, leading a quartet of Spyders home. The Ernie Erickson/Don Sesslar RS-60 was sixth, followed by the Jack Ensley/John Haas RSK and the Leader Card 550-RS of Bruce Kessler/Buzz Hahn. Class GM went to M.R.J. Wyllie and his wife Peggy, a new Lola Mk. I replacing a long string of Lotuses in their garage. Millard Ripley stepped into this car late in the race when his own Lola experienced difficulties. Ripley was in a tight fight with Charlie Kolb for the National GM title, and with Kolb absent, it was an opportunity to pick up maximum points. As it turned out, his own Lola made it to the finish, co-driven by Allan Ross and Burdette Martin so Ripley was both first and second in class. Just over half of the 44 starters finished.

As the year ended, the SCCA's top driver was Augie Pabst. With five wins in the Meister Brauser Scarab, Pabst was the year's winningest driver. Subsequently, *Competition Press* named him the U.S. Driver of the Year. The last two USAC pro races of the year took place in October in California and they were watershed events. Both the Riverside and Laguna Seca races had newspaper sponsorship, resulting in big fields with several international drivers and large spectator turnouts. Bill Krause won Riverside in a Maserati Tipo 61, while Stirling Moss took Laguna in a Lotus 19. (Incidentally, Pabst was third at Riverside and second at Laguna Seca, both times in the Scarab.) Carroll Shelby was the USAC champ. Two trends came from these two races. First, the concept of big-money, international, end-of-season races grew over the next few years, culminating in the legendary Canadian-American Challenge Cup ("Can-Am") series of 1966-74. Secondly, the Lotus 19 ushered in a new approach; a lightweight, two-seat version of a F-1 car, powered by a rear mounted 2.5 liter Climax four. They were lesser powered, but cornered much faster than the front engined sports racers. The days of the latter were numbered.

1961

I n 1961 the off track political wrangling overshadowed the on track activities. The internal struggle of the SCCA over professionalism vs. amateurism broke out in unrestrained civil war. While allowing SCCA participation in the season-ending Riverside and Laguna Seca pro races, the club placed an outright ban on SCCA driver participation in any other pro race. This crippled the USAC pro season, their events at Indianapolis Raceway Park and Continental Divide drawing only some USAC oval trackers, west coast Cal Club drivers, who never were bothered about such things, and some two dozen SCCA drivers, led by Augie Pabst and Bob Holbert, who defied the ban to race for pay.

As expected, this created a furor. The SCCA suspended the drivers in question. The ACCUS (the FIA's U.S. representative) suspended **all** SCCA drivers from any international competition, including Sebring. Open revolt occurred. The Milwaukee Region defied SCCA National and invited all suspended drivers to compete in its July National event at Meadowdale. There was talk of an alternate sanctioning body. USAC openly courted all drivers to join it. After two months of uproar, cooler minds finally prevailed, and at a late July meeting of the SCCA board, a 180 degree turn was executed. All sanctions were lifted, drivers were free to race for money, and most revolutionary of all, the SCCA hinted broadly that it would go into the pro game sometime in the near future. The knives were put away, the revolt was over. But the effects of it were far reaching indeed. In two years SCCA would be sanctioning pro races, and in three years USAC was out of the road racing game entirely.

The main effect on RA in 1961 was that the track promoted only two races, the June Sprints and the 500. There would be no USAC event. Even though the 1960 race was a success, the prospects for '61 were quite a bit dimmer due to the upcoming war. The next time a pro race would be held at the track would be in 1963, and it would be an SCCA event.

As the season approached, there were several notable changes. The Meister Brau brewery finally woke up to the fact that a Pabst driving a Meister Brauser car was giving publicity to the Milwaukee

The grid for the G and H Production race at the 1961 June Sprints. The starter's bridge and the cross over at the top of the rise were new this year.

Jim Hall on the grid for the 500 in Roger Penske's new Cooper Monaco. Penske at the left is no doubt offering his driver essential advice.

Alfred Momo waves the checker from the back of the winning Maserati I-63 V-12 in the 500. Walt Hansgen is at the wheel and co-driver Augie Pabst sits alongside.

brewery, even though Pabst himself was selling cars in Milwaukee, not beer. Hence, an amicable parting occurred and Augie went off to drive for Briggs Cunningham. Meister Brau sold one of the two Scarabs and it went through three sets of hands before burning to the ground in a garage fire in late 1962. Pabst drove this Scarab to a win at the USAC event at Indianapolis Raceway Park for interim owner Harry Woodnorth in June. Cunningham rotated in another set of new Maseratis, while Roger Penske replaced his Porsche Spyder with a new Maserati Tipo 61. Meanwhile, out in California, Troutman and Barnes, former Reventlow employees, were busy at work building a new front engined Chevy powered sports racer on commission from Jim Hall. This would be the first Chaparral.

Another class was created by the SCCA, A Production. The new short wheelbase Ferrari 250GT Berlinetta had the distinction of being the first member of this class.

On June 17-18 the faithful assembled at RA for the June Sprints. Clif Tufte demonstrated his penchant for the unusual again by making the feature race on Sunday a 300 mile enduro for production classes B through E. Saturday would be three 100 mile events for the smaller cars, while Sunday morning another 100 miler was held, this for the big sports racers.

Bill Kane took the first race in an Alfa Romeo, besting a field of G and H Production cars. He took the lead when early leader Al Weaver took to the escape road at turn five. Race two was for FP & HM, and was a cakewalk for Ollie Schmidt in the Lola-Osca. He won by over 30 seconds from Ed Walsh's Cooper-Osca. Bill Kravas took FP in a Turner. The last event on Saturday was for Formula Juniors, and Chuck Dietrich had an equally easy time. He took his Elva 200 into the lead at the start and cruised, aided by the early departure of his only challenger, Curt Gonstead, also driving an Elva 200. Bob Major was eventually second in an Osca, while Dave Morgan captured third in a Lotus 20. During this race, Hap Sharp took his 2.5 liter F-One Cooper T-53 out for a few exhibition laps. One such lap was done in 2:36.4, eight seconds below the lap record! Since Sharp's run was an *exhibition*, and the car did not fall into any recognized SCCA class, the lap record did not go into the books.

This set the stage for Sunday morning's 100 mile sprint. It may not have been the 'feature' of the weekend per se, but it was by far the best race of the meet, if not the year. The 33,000 fans on hand were treated to 100 miles of absolute side-by-side, nose-to-tail, pass and repass racing by Roger Penske and Jim Hall, both in Maserati Tipo 61s. For good measure,

Hall's teammate, Bob Schroeder, also in a Birdcage, was lurking right behind them, and even took the lead for a lap in the middle of the race. The race was a howler. Penske led laps 1-4, Hall 5, Penske 6-11, Hall 12, Schroeder 13, Hall 14-15, Penske 16-17, Hall 18-20, Penske 21, Hall 22, Penske 23, Hall 24 and Penske 25! Those were just the lead changes at the start/finish line. All around the four mile course the lead was traded, sometimes several times a lap. It truly was probably the most intense, exciting race ever held at the track. The deciding move of the race was in the last turn of the last lap. Penske and Hall came into it side-by-side, but there was a lapped car in Hall's way. He had to lift momentarily to go around, and that was all the break that Penske needed. He took the checker in his red Maserati just a blink before Hall's white example, with Schroeder a couple car lengths further behind. Penske set a new competition lap record at 2:44.1. What a race!

Behind the three dueling Birdcages, Harry Heuer took fourth overall, and first in class BM, in the Meister Brauser Scarab. Hap Sharp had dnf'd in his Cooper-Maserati, a T-49 Monaco powered by a 2.3 liter Maserati four. Ted Baumgartner was out with a broken shoulder after rolling his very pretty blue Ferrari 250 Testa Rossa. Behind Heuer, Peter Ryan, now 21 and legal to race in the SCCA, and Bill Wuesthoff dueled the entire race for class EM honors. Both were in Porsche Spyders, Wuesthoff his familiar silver and blue RS-60, while Ryan was in Milwaukeean Frank Zillner's new white RS-61. Ryan finally prevailed, trailed by Wuesthoff. Fred Gamble was seventh, fourth in DM, in the Maserati Tipo 61 streamliner Jeffords had used to win the year before, now owned by J. Frank Harrison. Tom Payne was the FM winner in his 1500cc Porsche RS-61, while M.R.J. Wyllie copped GM in his Lola.

The 300 mile production enduro had a big field, heavy on Corvettes. Add in a couple Ferrari GTs and the usual assortment of Austin-Healeys, Triumphs, Ace-Bristols, Elva Couriers and the 55 car field resembled the freeway at rush hour. Through all this the Grady Davis-entered Corvette of Don Yenko and Ed Lowther came through victorious. They had led early and they had led late, but in between they had a real fight. Dick Lang chose to drive his Corvette solo, and he powered into the lead on lap 31 of 75. He soon gave it up to the Ferrari 250GT SWB Berlinetta of Charlie Hayes and Carl Haas, until they pitted. Yenko retook the lead, only to be repassed by Lang. He led until lap 69, when, perhaps fatigued by the solo run on a hot day, he spun into the hay bales. Lang recovered, but Yenko was by, and Lang finished second. Hayes and Haas were third in the Ferrari, first in AP, while fourth went to Hap Sharp and Jim Hall, in Sharp's Ferrari 250 California. Tom Terrell and Jim Kaser took fifth in another Corvette. Pierre Mion and Hank Mergner were the class CP winners in an Ace-Bristol, Sheldon Brown and Ernie Erickson took DP in an Alfa Romeo, while Ernie Harris and Lee Wilson came through for the EP honors in an Elva Courier.

The usual weekend after Labor Day saw the cast reassemble for the annual Road America 500 weekend. The schedule called for five races on Saturday, with the 500 having Sunday to itself. With more entries, more time and races were needed, and as a result the distances of the individual Saturday races were less than before. But on the other hand, there were more races, so there certainly was no spectator complaint. Unfortunately, Saturday morning, one of those tragic reminders that the sport is dangerous occurred. Charles Henry rolled a Porsche 356 Speedster in the gravel pit, and succumbed to his injuries.

Three 40 mile and two 60 mile races graced Saturday afternoon. Lynn

Blanchard copped G and H Production in an Alfa Romeo, while Chuck Stoddard did the same in D and E, also Alfa mounted, but a far faster Veloce model. Larry Isenring's Fiat-Abarth took HP while Ernie Harris again was the one to beat in EP in his Elva Courier. The third 40 miler was for Formula Juniors, and it was a race long battle between the Cooper T-56s of Walt Hansgen and Hap Sharp. The lead was exchanged several times before a last lap bobble by Sharp allowed Hansgen to win in the Cunningham Cooper by three seconds, the largest margin of the race. Corvette driver Bob Johnson was third in a Gemini Junior, trailed by the Lotus 20s of Harry Carter and Floyd Aaskov.

The unusual pairing of H Modified and F Production took to the track in a 40 mile race. As was the norm this year, Ollie Schmidt was unbeatable in his Lola-Osca, notching another win on his way to the class championship. Martin Tanner gave him an early tussle with his latest Martin T Special, but a blown engine ended that bid. Second went once again to Ed Walsh's Cooper-Osca. Dick Brakenridge came out on top in FP in a Porsche 356.

The final race on Saturday was 60 miles for the large production cars. Dick Thompson and Bob Johnson were locked in a tight fight for the BP National title, and all eyes were on them. However, in so doing everyone missed Charlie Hayes. Driving his AP Ferrari, Hayes checked out at the start, and that was it for first. Behind him Thompson, Johnson and Dick Lang vigorously contested the class, with Thompson ultimately winning it with Lang next, after Johnson dropped out two laps from the finish. CP went to Pierre Mion's Ace-Bristol.

For the 500, Briggs Cunningham was present with three Maseratis; one 2.0 Tipo 60 and two new 3.0 V-12 rear engined Tipo 63s. Still with the *birdcage* frame philosophy, this was the first attempt by a manufacturer to stuff anything larger than a V-6 into the rear of a sports racer. While it gave prodigious power and speed in a straight line, the idiosyncrasies of making a tail-heavy car corner were still something of a black art. Walt Hansgen/Augie Pabst and Dick Thompson/Bill Kimberly were down to drive the Tipo 63s, while John Fitch and Briggs were in the Tipo 60. In the same vein was the Comstock Racing Team's Sadler Mk. V. This Canadian car was the first to put an American pushrod V-8 into the tail of a sports racer. Since no one built a gearbox for this purpose, car builder Bill Sadler modified a Halibrand quick-change rear end to take a second gear, the result being a two speed box. The results were similar to the V-12 Maserati; great speed, but adventurous cornering. Grant Clark and Peter Ryan were the brave fellows nominated to drive the beast. Roger Penske had purchased a new Cooper Monaco T-57, Cooper's answer to the Lotus 19. An offshoot of their winning T-53 F-1 car, the Monaco was powered by the 2.5 Climax four. Impressed no doubt by what Jim Hall did in the sprints, Penske decided he would rather have Hall with him than against him and had the tall Texan as his co-driver. A second new Cooper T-57 was entered by Hap Sharp, with Sharp intending to try to drive the 500 miles solo. Harry Heuer and Bill Wuesthoff were down to drive the Meister Brauser Scarab, and the North American Racing Team entered a 2.0 Ferrari Dino 206 for Buck Fulp/Skip Hudson. Add to this the usual collection of fast Porsche Spyders and Chevy-engined creations.

The main protagonists were using different strategies. The two Coopers and the Scarab were planning on just one pit stop, at mid distance, having seen how this worked for Causey and Stear the year before. The V-12 Maseratis were too thirsty to try this, so they were down to stop twice. However, that was not apparent as the race began.

Hall, Sharp and Hansgen took off with a rush, seemingly forgetting that this was an endurance race. They left the field at the flag and began a 150 mile long sprint, always very close together, many times exchanging the lead. Hansgen was driving the unruly Maserati faster than it should go, as by rights the two Coopers far superior handling should have made a decided difference. Apparently nobody told Hansgen. Behind them, the Scarab was out early when it lost its oil, and the Fulp Ferrari blew its engine. Clark in the Sadler had to stop on lap four to change the spark plugs, dropping to the back of the pack. Although two laps down, Clark had the car up to 13th place when he turned it over to Ryan. The young Canadian continued the charge, turning the race's fastest lap at 2:47, and setting a new speed trap record at 150 mph. Ryan reached eighth place by lap 51 of 125 when the gearbox, not unsurprisingly, had enough. The second Cunningham Maserati V-12 was having a troubled race, fouling its plugs and having several long stops. The 2.0 Maserati was running much better and late in the race was comfortably in the top 10. When it came time for Fitch to turn it back to Cunningham, Briggs opted to put the faster Dick Thompson behind the wheel, while he subbed for Thompson in the ailing V-12.

As half distance approached, things began to sour for the two Coopers. Hansgen had already stopped to turn over to Pabst, who was charging back from the time lost in the pits. He was lapping faster than the Coopers, but before he could catch them, things began to play into his hands. Both Coopers began to experience severe brake troubles, probably because they were running the same brakes as were on the F-1 cars, but with chassis that were 300 lbs. heavier and with enveloping bodywork. At half distance Sharp retired with the brakes completely gone, while Hall began calling at the pits to attempt to fix not only the brakes, but also a sticking throttle. A very unsettling combination...

Pabst was through into the lead and when he handed the Maser back to Hansgen, it was with a two lap lead. All Hansgen had to do the rest of the way was to stroke it, and that is what he did. Six hours, four minutes, 55.2 seconds after leaving the grid, the Hansgen/Pabst Maserati came home a winner, both overall and in DM. In second was George Reed/Ed Hugus, in the same Ferrari 250TR-59/60 that had finished second the year before. Third overall and first in EM, was the Maserati T-60 driven by Cunningham, Fitch and Thompson. They had risen from eighth when Thompson had taken over at 2/3 distance. The Schiff/Wonder and Lee Hall/Carroll Porsche RS-60s were fourth and fifth, while the RS-61 of Tom Payne and Ed Fuchs took sixth, first in FM. Next was the CM winner, the Costin-bodied Lister-Chevy of Art Huttinger/Pete Harrison. Hall and Penske limped home in eighth, just ahead of the equally limping V-12 Maserati of Thompson/Kimberly/Cunningham. Allan Ross and M.R.J. Wyllie had led GM comfortably in Wyllie's Lola, but when it broke at the 400 mile mark Dick Buedingen and Carl Haas gratefully accepted the class honors in an Elva Mk. V.

For the SCCA, a tumultuous year was over, with the prospect of much bigger things to come. With pro racing now acceptable, just about everyone went out west in October to contest the major Riverside and Laguna Seca races. Showing that rear engined cars now were really the way to go, Cooper Monacos ran 1-2 at Riverside, driven by Jack Brabham and Bruce McLaren, ahead of Jim Hall's new, but already nearly obsolete, Chaparral 1. At Laguna Seca Lotus 19s and Cooper Monacos held the top six places, led by Stirling Moss. Ken Miles picked up points at all four USAC races, including a win at Continental Divide, and was the USAC champion. In the SCCA, the big winner was Roger Penske. He easily won class DM over Walt Hansgen and was the star of the year. The Scarab era was ending, as Heuer, even though he won the BM national title, did not win a National event. The biggest news for American enthusiasts was the winning of the World Championship by Phil Hill, the first American to do so. Of course, Hill was a two-time RA winner.

1962

For 1962, the track again stayed with the program of two SCCA Nationals. At one time, the fall 500 was slated to be an FIA International Championship event for GT cars in the GT2 and GT3 classes. However, after considerable discussion, the championship sanction was dropped, as it was felt that the traditional lineup of SCCA modified classes would have more spectator appeal, and less official confusion, than a race strictly for GT cars.

Off track, the rival USAC pro series had dwindled to five events, of which only the final two, the year-end blockbusters at Riverside and Laguna Seca, would attract decent fields. Corvette came out with a 327ci engine and the SCCA placed this in Class AP, giving some competition to the Ferrari Berlinettas. Classes BM and CM were combined, meaning everything larger than 3.0 liters was in CM. Class FM had its displacement limit increased by 100cc to 1600cc, suddenly dropping all the Porsches with 1.6 liter mills down one class. Not for long, though, as many simply installed 1700cc cylinders, moving back up to EM! The Meister Brauser Team had purchased a new Chaparral 1 for Harry Heuer to drive, resting its race-weary Scarab. The Hall and Heuer Chaparrals would be the only front-engined cars that could compete with the new breed of F-1 based Cooper Monacos and Lotus 19s.

At the June Sprints weekend, the record crowd was treated to quite a display of show cars by General Motors' VP of Styling, Bill Mitchell. An avowed sports car nut and the patron of the Sting Ray racer of 1959-60, Mitchell began a practice of bringing one or more GM showcars to the June

The 1962 June Sprints had a race long duel between Bill Wuesthoff (#77) and Ernie Erickson (#27) for the FM class win. Both were in Porsche RS-60 Spyders.

Sprints, not only to dazzle the fans but also to gauge reaction. This would continue for 20 years. This weekend he brought five cars; the Sting Ray racer, the Manta Ray coupe version, the Corvair SS, the Corvair Sebring Spyder and the Corvair GT. Many frames of film were exposed this weekend! Mitchell was a big booster of the track, and today the bridge at turn 13 is named for him.

As if that were not enough, Mercedes-Benz was present with its one-off 300-SLR coupe. A closed version of the all-conquering 300-SLRs of 1955, the straight-eight powered car did a couple laps driven by John Fitch. Lastly, one of Mickey Thompson's rear-engined, Buick-powered Indy cars, owned by Jim Kimberly, did a demonstration run in the hands of Augie Pabst.

The June Sprints lineup was three races Saturday and three on Sunday.

24

Last season's experiment with the 'feature' being a production car enduro had been quietly dropped, and once again the big sports racers would anchor the program with a 152 mile go on Sunday afternoon. Fans turned out in droves. In fact, a new Saturday attendance record of 21,000 was set, while over 40,000 braved mid 90s temperatures on Sunday.

The first race was 60 miles for small production. This went to Howard Brown's Alfa, after Lynn Blanchard's similar car coughed and died. The 80 mile large production go was won by Dick Thompson in Grady Davis's 327 Corvette. Dick Lang again tried hard, but came up short, finally spinning into retirement. The AP Ferrari Berlinettas of Chuck Dietrich and Doug Thiem took second and third, while the BP winner was another Davis entry, Don Yenko in a 283 Corvette. These two would be the ones to beat in class all year, with Thompson and Yenko ultimately giving Davis two National titles. Pete Ledwith won CP in an amazing little car—a Lotus 7. While the standard Lotus 7 was powered by a pushrod English Ford four, the CP version had a fully tweaked Cosworth on board, and this *Super Seven* would do giant killer duties all season.

The final race on Saturday was 60 miles for Formula Junior. Ted Mayer, who would later achieve much as an owner of McLaren cars and as an engineer for Penske Racing, entered racing as owner/manager of a three car team of new Cooper T-59 Juniors for his brother Tim, Peter Revson and Bill Smith. They were the class of the field all year; Tim Mayer easily won the national crown. In this race, Mayer had early competition from Hap Sharp's Brabham BT-2 before Sharp lost all but fifth gear. Then Mayer eased away to a comfortable win over Floyd Aaskov's Lotus 22 and Bill Smith's Cooper, with Sharp fourth. Augie Pabst was running his first race since suffering serious injuries in a February crash at Daytona. Driving an obsolete Stanguellini FJ, Augie was easing himself back, more intent on becoming fit in the cockpit than hanging it out fully. As it was, Pabst was sixth overall, first in the unofficial front-engined class.

Sunday morning, Martin Tanner took the 60 mile event for FP and HM. Driving a new Martin T-5 Special, Tanner easily won over Glenn Baldwin's Lotus 17 and Guy Bates in the Lola-Osca with which Ollie Schmidt had won the two previous HM National crowns. Shorty Miller was the FP winner in a Turner after an intensely close race with Howard Hanna's D-B and Don Sesslar's Sunbeam Alpine. D and E Production ran for 80 miles with Jay Signore crushing the opposition in an Elva Courier. Eric Mangelson came out on top in EP in an Alfa Romeo.

This set the stage for the feature. It shaped up to be a four car race, the two Cooper Monaco T-57s of Roger Penske and Hap Sharp vs. the two Chaparral 1s of Jim Hall and Harry Heuer. The two Chaparrals led the first two laps, their superior horsepower telling on the straights. However, Penske's immaculate red Cooper was closing, and its handling told the tale on lap three as Penske took the lead. He immediately pulled away, setting a new race lap record of 2:41.3, almost three seconds better than his own record of a year previous. Heuer trailed in second, followed by Sharp, Hall and the Lister-Chevy of Pete Harrison. Alas, on lap 13 the distributor failed and Penske was out.

Meanwhile, a 21 year old Minneapolis stockbroker named Jerry Hansen was having an exciting time. Hansen, who later would gain much fame as SCCA's winningest champion with 27 class titles, had entered racing the previous year in a Corvette. Deciding to hop into the fastest cars right away, Hansen had purchased the ex-Meister Brauser Scarab that Heuer had sold a year previous. On lap two he learned the hard way that the kink could not be taken flat out in a Scarab. He slammed into the guardrail very hard, flipped over it and wound up upside down, hanging by his seat belts. Not realizing that the Scarab was nestled in tree branches some feet above ground, the up until then uninjured Hansen popped the belt release and

tumbled several feet to the ground, breaking his nose in the process! The Scarab was a sorry mess, and most observers thought it was a goner. Rather amazingly, Hansen had the wreck rebuilt and on the grid at the Meadowdale National a month and a half later. Sadly, it never was the same again, and its racing days ended that winter in a garage fire. Rebuilt in 1990, it now is in the Collier collection in Florida.

However, more exciting things were happening up front. After Penske dropped out, Hall put on a charge, passed Sharp and got down to business with Heuer. For several laps the two V-8 powered cars roared around the track in tandem, Hall's white example making every attempt to pass Heuer's metallic blue trimmed in white speedster. On lap 21, Heuer's failing brakes told the tale, and Hall was past. Jim finished the 152 miles with a speed of 87.88 mph, scoring the first of what would be many wins for the Chaparral marque. Heuer took second, with Sharp third, first in DM.

The Bob Holbert and Bob Donner Porsche RS-61 Spyders traded the EM lead a few times before Donner eased ahead, finishing fourth overall in the process. In sixth was Bill Wuesthoff, who took FM in his RS-60 Porsche. Class GM was a shocker of sorts. Ollie Schmidt, whose ingenuity with a Lola-Osca had spread-eagled HM the last two years, debuted a new one-off DeTomaso 1100 sports racer. Driven by unknown Jim Scott, it simply ran away with GM.

Right after Labor Day the annual Road America 500 occurred. Again, the schedule called for five events on Saturday, with the 500 on Sunday. The weather on Saturday was not good, cool with occasional rain that continued all day. Sixty miles for G and H Production was a tight duel between the Alfa Romeos of Lynn Blanchard and Dick Haselton before Blanchard asserted himself. Bob Anderson was the HP winner in a Sprite.

FP and HM also ran for 60 miles, with Martin Tanner prevailing in his Martin T-5 Special ahead of Glenn Baldwin's Lotus 17. Chuck Cantwell won FP in an MGA, but Skip Barber started absolutely last in his Turner, spent the whole race passing cars left and right, and came home second behind Cantwell.

DP and EP ran for 60 miles with Bob Tullius winning in his Triumph TR4. This was the start for Tullius' Group 44 race team, which over the next 25 years would record a dozen National Championships in the production ranks besides being successful in Trans-Am and the IMSA Camel GT series. Chuck Stoddard won DP in an Alfa Romeo Veloce, behind the EP winning Tullius.

In the Formula Junior 40 mile go, Walt Hansgen made it three such September wins in a row as he took the flag ahead of Tim Mayer, both driving Cooper T-59 Juniors, Hansgen's being a Cunningham entry. Floyd Aaskov was third in a Lotus 20, then Dave Morgan's Lotus 22, Suzy Dietrich's Cooper T-59 and Briggs Cunningham's Brabham BT-2. Dietrich had a fright during the race, when Augie Pabst, still playing with the obsolete front engined Stanguellini, had brake failure, hit the back of her Cooper, and went up, up, and over, landing on all four wheels on the track in front of her!

A, B and C Production rounded out the day's activity with an 80 mile race. Doug Thiem took the lead at the start and kept his silver Ferrari SWB Berlinetta ahead of Bob Johnson's Corvette. Johnson chased him hard, but Thiem never made the mistake the more experience Johnson was trying to provoke. Don Yenko was the BP winner in a Corvette, while Ernie Harris triumphed in CP in a Lotus Super 7.

Sunday dawned similar to Saturday, heavy overcast and general gloom. Rain spit occasionally, but the 500 itself was run in the dry. With SCCA's new stance on professionalism, coupled with big money races coming up in a few weeks at Bridgehampton, Mosport, Riverside, Laguna Seca, Puerto Rico and Nassau, the number of 'name' entries was down this weekend.

General Motors VP of Design, Bill Mitchell often brought interesting experimental cars to Road America. In 1962 the Corvair GT coupe was one of them.

Apparently, the thought was why wear your car out over 500 miles for a trophy, when you can race for bucks a few weeks later? Nonetheless, Jim Hall was there with his Chaparral, co-driving with Hap Sharp. Harry Heuer gambled that his old Meister Brauser Scarab would prove to be more durable than the Chaparral, and entered it for himself and Bill Wuesthoff. The Cunningham Team had three cars present, all quite different from each other. Walt Hansgen and Augie Pabst were paired in a Maserati Tipo 151. This was a coupe designed strictly for Le Mans, powered by a front mounted dohc V-8. Cunningham had replaced the original 4.0 unit with one bored out to 5.0 liters. The team was counting on reliability, since the car lacked the outright speed to compete with the Chaparral on lap times. The second Cunningham entry was a Cooper Monaco T-57, fitted with a 2.9 liter Maserati four. Roger Penske and Bill Kimberly were down to drive. Lastly, Briggs himself was in the Maserati Tipo 64. This was one of two built, a 3.0 V-12 successor to the Tipo 63. His co-driver was Paul Richards. Other entries of note were Jerry Hansen/Dick Roe in Hansen's rebuilt Scarab, Alan Connell in a Maserati Tipo 61 with a Ferrari V-12 in place of the Maserati four — painted fluorescent lime green, it carried the notation *Old Blue* on the side, and Dave and Dean Causey in a brand new, just off the boat Lotus 19. Of course, add in the usual Porsche Spyders, older Ferraris and Chevy powered specials.

While most of the teams were using a one stop strategy, Hall and Sharp were planning just the opposite. They were mimicking the plan used by Hall two years earlier, of having the race divided into four 125 mile sprints. At each of the three stops they would not only refuel and change drivers, but would also change the brake pads. Having fitted the Chaparral with quick change brake calipers, they would always be assured of fresh brakes. It was a strategy that would work perfectly.

At the start, Hall checked out, and put in a most dominant drive. He led the first 125 miles, turned it over to Sharp who came out in second behind Heuer's Scarab. At mid distance, both Sharp and Heuer stopped. Hall got back in the car and resumed ahead of Wuesthoff. At the 375 mile mark, Hall gave the car back to Sharp with enough of a lead so that all Sharp had to do was stroke it home. Which he did. The Meister Brauser

strategy of one stop failed; the Scarab's tanks ran dry four laps before midway. When Wuesthoff had to pit again on lap 116 of 125, Heuer took over for the final nine laps. With the Scarab comfortably in second, Heuer inexplicably blew the engine two laps from the end in an attempt to catch Sharp which was never remotely possible. In winning, Hall and Sharp had broken the six hour barrier for the first time, taking five hours, 53 minutes, 1.8 seconds for the 125 rounds.

The Connell Maserati-Ferrari and Hansen Scarab were both out before 100 miles. However this was much farther than Kimberly got in the Cunningham Cooper-Maserati. The gearbox broke on lap two. The other two Cunningham cars fared little better. The Pabst/Hansgen T-151 ran third for quite a while, but retired on lap 92 with a failed wheel bearing. The Tipo 64 ran in the vicinity of fifth place until a rear hub disintegrated on, ironically, lap 64.

These failures cleared the way for a bunch of small engined cars to score well. Second overall and first in EM went to the Porsche RS-61 Spyder of Bob Donner and Don Sesslar. The FM winner was Lee Hall and Glenn Carroll in a Porsche RS-60, placing third overall. Amazingly, fourth through seventh went to 1100cc Class GM cars. These were the Art Tweedale/Frank Baptista Lola Mk. I, Chuck Dietrich driving solo in an Elva Mk. VI, M.R.J. and Peggy Wyllie in a Lola Mk. I and Bob Brown/Skip Scott driving another Elva Mk. VI.

Class DM went to the Dave and Dean Causey's Lotus 19. That they were the only DM car left running, and that they finished last overall doesn't detract from a tale of perseverance. The car burst into flames on the pace lap, and Dean left it there and walked back to the pits. An hour or so later, he went back to the car, discovered a broken oil fitting, put a wooden plug into it and drove it back to the pits. He cleaned it up and started the race. Two hours or so later, with brother Dave behind the wheel, the plug popped out. An oil fire started, Dave parked it and sat down with the corner workers at turn three to watch the rest of the 500. After awhile the crew found out where he was, walked to the corner and told him about the plug. Dave checked, and sure enough, he put a new plug in and restarted. The car eventually completed 75 laps, the absolute minimum to be classified, and won its class!

Both the big west coast pro races were taken by Roger Penske, who ran a modified Cooper T-53 F-1 car called the *Zerex Special*. He also took the Puerto Rico pro race in November. This, coupled with his SCCA DM National championship, clearly made him the U.S. driver of the year, as administered by *Road & Track's Competition Press* magazine. Pedro Rodriguez won Bridgehampton, Masten Gregory won Mosport and Innes Ireland took Nassau, rounding out the end-of-term pro sports car races. Professionalism was here to stay, and in 1963 the SCCA would join the trend.

1963

Many things happened over the off season that would affect racing in 1963. The most significant was that the SCCA fully embraced professionalism, establishing the U.S. Road Racing Championship (USRRC). This was a series of eight races, all offering prize money, with two drivers and two manufacturers championships. Drivers points were awarded equally in the only two classes, over and under two liters. The driver with the most points at season end would be crowned the U.S. Road Racing Champion. A separate race each weekend would be for production category cars, again divided into two groups, over and under two liters, with manufacturers' titles at stake.

Car development proceeded along two distinct lines. The success of the rear-engine Cooper Monaco and Lotus 19 had been noticed, and now the move was on to drop American Chevy and Ford V-8s into the back end of just about any robust chassis available. Further, Kjell Qvale, builder of the BMC Juniors, put the first all

The start of the 1963 June Sprints. Roger Penske and Harry Heuer side by side exiting the Carousel with Don Devine in tow.

American rear engine V-8 sports racer in production, the Genie Mk. VIII. Cooper began producing the T-61 Monaco, delivering them engineless, allowing the purchaser to drop in the powerplant of his choice. Lance Reventlow built one final Scarab, the rear engine Mk. IV. Then there was an intriguing rumor out of Texas that Jim Hall was designing a truly revolutionary Chaparral.

The other school of thought on car design called for diminutive lightweight cars powered by as light and powerful an engine that it could carry. Lotus introduced the 23 and Elva the Mk. VII, both ostensibly 1100cc class GM cars, but both available with an optional 1600cc Lotus developed twin cam English Ford-based four. They would be pocket rockets. Indeed, Chuck Parsons would win the June Laguna Seca USRRC race overall in a Lotus 23. Porsche, meanwhile, saw that its 718 Spyders were in danger of being outpaced in the under two liter category and struck a deal with Elva. About a dozen Elva Mk. VIIs were sent to Stuttgart, where the car was extensively changed from mid-car back, with a 1708cc Porsche dohc four installed. The resulting Elva Porsches would prove to be fast indeed.

Out in California, retired racing great Carroll Shelby had arranged a three way deal with his own company, the Ford Motor Company and AC Cars of England. The result was the Cobra.

The SCCA introduced a new class designed to be entry level, cheap and affordable. Essentially, it was the air cooled VW flat four in a small open wheeler. It was Formula Vee, and it flourishes to this day.

At the track, new covered pits had been erected. Made of wood with

corrugated metal roofs and painted blue, they offered some protection from the sun, if nothing else. With all four sides open, there was little protection from the elements. As time went by, the wooden uprights began to be more of a problem than a help, as it seemed they were always in the way. Ten years later nature settled matters as a big wind storm blew the whole mess down.

The weekend of June 22-23 was a good one at the June Sprints, RA's only SCCA National this year. Wonderfully sunny and pleasant weather saw a new attendance record set, as a reported 43,000 people showed up on Sunday. Saturday's crowd of 13,000 was very respectable too. 285 cars were entered, an SCCA record.

On Saturday, after Bob Shaw took the opening 60 mile race for F, G and H Production in an Alfa Romeo, a 60 miler for Formula Juniors and Formula Vees took place. Augie Pabst led early, driving a Brabham BT-2 he had purchased from Cunningham, until the engine quit. Then Cliff Phillips and Jim Haynes, both in Lotus 22s, fought it out with Haynes prevailing (Jim Haynes, twenty-odd years later would return to Road America as track president and general manager). Phillips dropped out with an engine fire, giving second to Jim LeMahieu's Lotus 18. Third overall in a very noteworthy drive in an obsolete car was Bob Birmingham, in the ex-Pabst Stanguellini. Formula Vee saw Mak Kronn and Bill Wuesthoff fight wheel to wheel with Kronn winning by less than a second.

The final Saturday race was 80 miles for A, B and C Production. Two Cobras were present with Bob Johnson and Bob Brown running away with

The Cobras come to town. Carroll Shelby's big rig carries four of the snakes to the 1963 500.

the race. They were over 20 seconds ahead of the first Corvette, third placed Dick Thompson, at the finish.

Sunday began with an incredible 62 cars in just two classes, D and E Production, running for 80 miles. The Triumph TR4s of Bob Tullius, Dana Kellner and Jim Spencer ran at the front, with each having a turn in the lead. Eventually Tullius in the Group 44 entry won, with Spencer second. Don Sesslar was the EP winner in a Sunbeam Alpine.

Classes GM and HM had their own 60 mile race just prior to the feature. M.R.J. Wyllie, driving his familiar Lola Mk. I, took the lead on lap two from Chuck Dietrich's Bobsy Mk. II and led the duration of the 15 laps. Don Wolf was third in an Elva Mk. VI. In HM, Martin Tanner kept his winning streak alive in his Martin T-5 Special. Second again was old sparring partner Ed Walsh, now in a new car. He had dropped a Saab engine in a Lotus 23 chassis, finally retiring his 1955 vintage Cooper.

The 160 mile feature for C-through-F Modified had a fine field. Meister Brauser had not only the Chaparral 1 for Harry Heuer, but also the Scarab for 23 year old Don Devine. The youngster earlier in the season had proven the wisdom of the choice, as he had won the Virginia Raceway National. Hap Sharp was present with another Chaparral, his partner Jim Hall not present as Hall was spending the season in Europe driving Formula One. A third Chaparral was also present, as Jerry Hansen had replaced his Scarab with the same car that Hall and Sharp had used to win the previous fall's 500. A new, major racing team, the Mecom Racing Team, entered two cars. Formed by Houston oilman John Mecom, the Mecom team would be a major player in U.S. racing for the next four years, their success culminating in a win in the 1966 Indy 500. Roger Penske had sold his cars to Mecom, and was entered in the re-engineered Cooper Zerex Special. Augie Pabst was in the second Mecom entry, a 2.0 Lotus 19 running in EM. Grady Davis, besides entering AP Corvettes for Dick Thompson, also had a class CM Corvette Grand Sport for him to drive. The Grand Sports were designed to be Cobra-beaters, being pure race space frame cars clothed in production-like coupe bodies. Unfortunately, after only five were built, GM's top brass found out about what was happening at Chevrolet and pulled the plug.

The early part of the race was a Mecom demonstration. Penske led in the 2.7 Climax four powered Zerex, with Pabst following. Heuer and Sharp were next in their Chaparrals until Sharp lost it in turn 13 on lap four, flipping end over end, fortunately without injury. Hansen also retired his Chaparral, with mechanical difficulties. Pabst retired from second on lap 10

with a broken brake caliper, and Heuer moved into position to challenge Penske, who responded with some very fast times, setting a new race lap record at 2:39.3. Heuer moved ahead for a few laps, but Penske reasserted himself, only to have the engine expire on lap 25. From that point forward, Heuer was in charge, bringing his Meister Brauser entry home for the third Chaparral win in a row at RA.

Behind Heuer, teammate Devine proved that there still was life in the old Scarab. He fought for a while with Thompson's Grand Sport, then moved into a second place he would hold to the end for a Meister Brau one-two. Thompson finished third, with Ed Hammill fourth in an old Cooper Monaco T-49 (once the property of Rodger Ward, who ran it with a small aluminum Buick V-8) into which he had dropped a Ford V-8. Bill Wuesthoff took fifth in his Porsche RS-60, winning class EM. Doug Thiem was next, still driving a Ferrari, but a rare two liter V-6 SP-206 in place of the AP Berlinetta he had the year previous. Lee Hall was the FM winner in his Porsche RS-60. Heuer had averaged 86.85 mph for the 40 laps.

The fall 500 was part of the new USRRC. Consequently, the lineup of events was changed, since no National points were involved. Three races were held on Saturday for those cars that were not eligible for the money race on Sunday.

The first of these was a 40 mile Formula Junior and Vee event. Augie Pabst ran his Brabham BT-2, now under Mecom colors, to an easy victory over Homer Rader's Lotus 27 and Suzy Dietrich's Lotus 20. His fastest lap was 2:41.2; simply astounding considering that it was an 1100cc pushrod Ford powered machine, and that it would be faster than the fastest lap of the next day's 500! Formula Vee was a race long dice between the Formcar Vees of Mak Kronn, Les Behm, Larrie Isenring and Bill Wuesthoff. Kronn came out on top.

A 60 mile event for small production and HM cars saw Ed Walsh at last get to the line first. His Lotus 23-Saab finally giving him the necessary go power, Walsh led Al Cervenka's Dolphin-Climax to the flag.

The top event on Saturday's schedule was another product of Clif Tufte's fertile mind. This was the *Badger 200*, a 50 lap affair for large production cars. Anticipated to be a Cobra vs. Corvette race, it produced yet another easy Cobra win. Tom Payne and R.E.L. Hayes led the Corvettes of Roy Kumnick, Ralph Salyer and Gene Cormany for the first several laps. On the sixth lap Payne and Kumnick had to make pit stops, leaving Hayes with a big lead, which he was able to keep to the finish. Payne battled back through the field to finish second, with the Salyer/Clusseruth Corvette third, followed by the Montgomery/Skogmo Cobra. In fifth was the story of the race; Jim Spencer slew giants left and right as he dispatched all manner of bigger and supposedly faster cars with his Triumph TR4. Hayes averaged 81.51 mph for the 200 miles.

The 500 was the seventh of eight USRRC events. Coming in, three drivers still had a mathematical chance. Bob Holbert led the standings, having scored two wins so far in a Porsche RS-61, Pensacola and Watkins Glen. In both instances he co-drove with Ken Miles, who was second in the points. The discrepancy is because Holbert finished higher in the shorter events where each drove solo. The third driver with a shot was Don Wester. Also driving a Porsche RS-61, Wester had no overall wins, but due to the equal points scoring for both over and under two liters he had accumulated enough class points to still be in the running.

The entry was top notch. Shelby American had entered three Cobras, two in the manufacturers' GT category for Bob Bondurant/Dave MacDonald and Bob Johnson/Lew Spencer, while the third was fitted with an oil cooler, thus making it *non-production* and placing it in the modified ranks eligible for drivers' points. It was to be driven by Holbert and Miles. Mecom entered a Ferrari GTO in the GT category to be driven by Roger Penske and Augie Pabst. Cunningham had three lightweight Jaguar XKEs present, also all in the GT category. The driver pairings were Walt Hansgen/Paul Richards, John Fitch/Bill Kimberly and Briggs Cunningham/Dick Thompson. With all the hot machinery back in their garages, it was a bit unfortunate that Mecom and Cunningham both opted for what fans considered the lesser category.

The new Elva Porsche made its pro debut, with two cars present. Ollie Schmidt had the faster of the two, and Bill Wuesthoff was down to drive, the intention being that he was going to do the 500 miles solo. The other belonged to long time Porsche-pusher Ernie Erickson. Meister Brauser entered both their cars, the Chaparral for Harry Heuer and Scarab for Don Yenko, with Don Devine down to co-drive whichever one was still running at half distance – not too much optimism there. The Causeys had their Lotus 19, Doug Thiem and Tom Terrell were in the Ferrari SP-206, the usual herd of Porsches were there, now sharing space in the under two liter category with several new Lotus 23s and Elva Mk. VIIs with the twin cam option. Last year's winner Hap Sharp was co-driving a Lotus 23 with Dave Morgan. Stir in the usual older Ferraris and Specials, and it was a full field. Unfortunately it was without Bud Gates and his brand new Genie Mk. VIII. On the way to Elkhart Lake, the trailer carrying the Chevy V-8 powered car overturned, damaging the car beyond immediate repair.

Ken Miles qualified on the pole in the Cobra, but Wuesthoff was right alongside. It was unthinkable that the Elva Porsche could keep up, but as the race started, the unthinkable became fact. Miles, Wuesthoff and Chuck Cassell in a Porsche RS-60 took off and opened up an immediate lead over the others. Two calamities had occurred on the pace lap; Wester had the gearbox break in his Porsche, ruining his title hopes, and Heuer had the shift lever come off in his hand, necessitating a long pit stop. Heuer resumed a lap down, while Wester went in search of another ride, finally finding it in Erickson's Elva Porsche.

As the race settled down, Miles led in the Cobra, followed by Wuesthoff and Cassell. Heuer had recovered to fourth, followed by George Reed in his old Ferrari TR (now powered by a 7.0 liter NASCAR Ford engine), Yenko, Curt Gonstead in a Lotus 23 and the first of the GT entries, Pabst in the Mecom Ferrari GTO. The two GT Cobras were picking their way through the field, and in the race's second hour, Spencer caught Pabst. Attrition set in as Heuer's gearbox broke shortly after he passed Cassell for third. The Pabst GTO began to drop back with a slipping clutch. After a spate of pit stops, the Yenko Scarab, which had yet to pit, was leading, followed by Holbert, in for Miles in the Cobra, Wuesthoff and Don Sesslar, in for Cassell. The Scarab, which incredibly had won the previous USRRC event held two weeks earlier at Continental Divide in a one-off 'nostalgia' ride for Augie Pabst, held on to the lead from lap 47 through 64 until Yenko had to pit for fuel and to change over to Devine. Unfortunately, Devine had no time to enjoy the ride, as the Scarab's engine erupted in a plume of smoke just one lap later.

The race now settled down to a duel between the Miles/Holbert Cobra and Wuesthoff's Elva Porsche. The Cobra was a bit faster, but it had to stop more frequently for fuel, and was decidedly harder on its brakes. The Cassell/Sesslar Porsche trailed in third, followed by the two GT category Cobras. As the miles reeled off, Wuesthoff realized that he would not be able to go all the way. He signaled for a relief driver at his next stop, and who should show up helmet in hand but Augie Pabst. Having turned his Ferrari over to Penske at half distance, Pabst thought he was through for the day.

Carroll Shelby enjoys the over two liter class win in the 500. Bob Holbert and Ken Miles were second over all in the Cobra, finishing on the same lap as the winning Elva Porsche of Wuesthoff and Pabst.

But when his friend and fellow Milwaukee car dealer Wuesthoff asked for help, Pabst was there. At the 84 lap, 336 mile mark, Wuesthoff came in and Pabst took over. This was also their last pit stop, while the threatening Cobra would have to stop once, if not twice, more. This was crucial.

Pabst, not having even sat in this car before, took a couple laps to acclimate himself. In fact, he spun off just three turns after having taken over, still accustomed to driving the completely different handling front engine Ferrari. Nonetheless, once Augie figured out what all the switches and knobs did, he settled down to a consistent lap time that would ensure victory. He gave up three seconds per lap to the Cobra, now again being driven by Miles, but every time the Cobra stopped, it lost a lap. Hence, things went as planned and Pabst brought the Elva Porsche home a winner, the first time an under two liter car had won the 500. Miles and Holbert were second, which was enough to win the inaugural USRRC title for Holbert. Cobra had, of course, won the GT championship. Cassell and Sesslar were third, followed by the GT category winner, the MacDonald/Bondurant Cobra. In fifth was the amazing 1100cc Bobsy, driven solo by Chuck Dietrich. This was the second year in a row that Dietrich had finished fifth driving a class GM car by himself! The Spencer/Johnson Cobra was sixth, placing all three works Cobras in the top six. Following the Thiem/Terrell Ferrari was the Pabst/Penske Ferrari, giving Pabst both first overall and eighth overall, third in GT. All three Cunningham Jaguars finished, but they simply did not have the pace of the Cobras or the GTO.

The USRRC season ended two weeks later, with an event at Mid Ohio won overall by Miles in the Cobra. Then it was on to the fall pro races and USAC's last gasp. The Riverside and Laguna Seca events, both won by Dave MacDonald in Shelby's Cooper-Ford, marked the end of USAC's road racing division. The next year, all major U.S. races would be sanctioned by SCCA, whether amateur or professional. It was a different time indeed.

Sixty miles south of Road America a new road racing circuit was opened. This was Lynndale Farms Raceway, located near Pewaukee, WI. It was a 2.5 mile road circuit that provided good viewing vistas. However, the track never was a serious competitor to RA. It promoted just club events and the occasional SCCA National, and not too well at that. After only three full seasons it was turned into a housing development.

1964

With the success of Formula Junior there was pressure to expand the formula classes. With the advent of the twin cam 1600 Ford engine, many wanted to drop it into their Junior, thus making a much faster car. SCCA acceded to these requests, and for 1964 expanded the Formula category into three classes; A for over 1600cc, B for 1600cc and C for essentially what was Formula Junior, 1100cc. Formula B quickly became popular, while Formula A had a slow gestation, but four years later blossomed into what became known as Formula 5000.

SCCA had completely taken over road racing in the country by this time. USAC had folded its tent and gone back to the ovals. The USRRC series expanded to 10 events, and SCCA now sanctioned all the fall free-standing pro races in the U.S., plus the Daytona and Sebring world championship sports car events in the spring, and the Grand Prix of the U.S. in October.

The advent of professional SCCA racing had the somewhat unintended side effect of siphoning entries from the 'modified' classes of National racing. With a nationwide series of money as well as points paying races, not to mention the burgeoning fall pro races, there was less incentive to spend the money to trailer around the country just for cups. As a consequence, the Divisional racing program gained in prominence. The country was divided into six geographic areas and points were awarded in classes for each division. This produced year end divisional champions. Exhibiting foresight, *Sports Car Graphic* magazine sponsored a year end extravaganza at Riverside, where it brought together the top six in each class from each division for a *runoff*. It proved to be very successful and popular and tended to overshadow the actual SCCA National Championship series. So much so, in fact, that 1964 was the last year for the *Nationals* as they had been known for 15 years. In 1965 SCCA adopted the runoff format, with National class championships determined by the winner of the runoff. This system exists to this day.

While other Nationals around the country saw their entries dwindle over the years, not only due to the change in format, but also to the dilution effect of the creation of new classes and series, RA continued to flourish. The June Sprints, while not attracting the stellar fields in the modified ranks as in the late '50s and early '60s, continued to feature full fields. Indeed, as the years went by, the entry for the June Sprints rose and stayed in the 400+ range.

Roger Penske leads the 1964 500 in the Chaparral 2 until brake problems cost them many laps.

The schedule for 1964 was the same as 1963; the June Sprints as an SCCA National, and the 500 as an USRRC series race. Again, the Badger 200 for production cars would accompany the 500.

The June Sprints on June 20-21 attracted over 40,000 fans once again. A slate of six races were offered, two on Saturday and four on Sunday. The two Saturday races, 40 miles each, were for small production and for Formula cars. Don Sesslar again was victorious in the first event, taking his Sunbeam Alpine to the checker both overall and in class FP. The Formula event saw Hap Sharp again give a demonstration with his 1960 F-1 Cooper T-53, lapping at 2:33.5, breaking the lap record *unofficially* as he had done in 1961. However, since he was running unofficially, the checker went to Cliff Phillips, Lotus 22 Junior. Les Behm and Al Hultgren followed in BMC Juniors, while Ray Caldwell took FV in an Autodynamics.

Sunday had three 80 mile events for medium production, large production and small sports racers. The feature, for C, D and E Modified, was for 160 miles. Jim Spencer took his Triumph TR4 to the first checker, with Bob Johnson and Dan Gerber running to a Cobra 1-2 in the large production event. Jerry Hansen, now in a Cobra, gave chase and set the fastest lap of the race before his snake retired. Corvette honor was salvaged somewhat by Don Yenko's win in BP. Charlie Barnes won overall and GM in a car new to the area, a Merlyn Mk. VI. A second Merlyn, piloted by Lynn Kysar, finished right behind Barnes. In HM, the status quo was reestablished, as Martin Tanner bested Ed Walsh.

Several interesting new cars were present for the feature. Hap Sharp gave the midwest its first look at the new Chaparral 2. Its Chevy V-8 was mounted in the rear of a plastic monocoque chassis. The plastic torque boxes were glued together and the suspension components and engine were glued into place. The concept of a plastic monocoque would not be copied until 17 years later, with the McLaren MP-4 F-1 car. Now, of course, all F-1 and Indy cars as well as many sports cars and even some road cars, utilize carbon fiber tubs, a concept from the mind of Jim Hall. The car was aerodynamically very advanced, and Jim Hall would easily win the U.S. Road Racing Championship in such a car this year. There were two Cheetahs present, for Ralph Salyer and Bud Clusseruth. The Cheetah was originally conceived as a road car to compete with the Corvette. As so often happens, plans go awry, and just a limited number were produced. As a result, the cars that were produced had to run in class CM. They were front engined, Chevy V-8 powered coupes, with the motor located virtually amidships. This put the driver between the rear wheels. It made for great acceleration and speed, but somewhat suspect handling. Down in Illinois, Bob McKee was producing a line of rear-engine American V-8

A very mixed multi-class field files through Thunder Valley in the 1964 500.

powered sports racers. The first one, driven by Dick Doane, was present this weekend. The Mecom Racing Team had two cars present. Walt Hansgen, now driving for Mecom with the retirement of Briggs Cunningham, was in the Lotus 19, which had a small block aluminum Olds V-8 in place of the previous 2.0 Climax four. Augie Pabst was in the other, which was the Lola Mk. VI, better known as the Lola GT. One of three built, it was a rear engine, Chevy V-8 powered coupe built around an aluminum monocoque tub. The car's main significance is that it led directly to both the famous Ford GT-40 as well as the Lola T-70 sports racer. Roy Kumnick was driving the Tero-entered Cooper-Ford that was driven by Ed Hammill the year before. The irony of Kumnick's entry is that while the Cooper was powered by a Ford engine, it was entered and prepped by Tero *Corvette*, an Illinois Chevy shop! The previous years had always seen the field filled out by a number of Porsches. Things were changing, though, as classes E and F Mod were dominated by Lotuses and Elvas.

Disappointment struck on the pace lap as Sharp retired the Chaparral 2 with a broken oil line. At the green the Mecom cars of Pabst and Hansgen sprinted out to an immediate lead, and it looked as if it were to be a 1-2 for the neat metallic blue cars. Behind them were Kumnick, Salyer, Bud Gates in a Genie Mk. VIII and Doane in the blue McKee. Alas for Texas, Hansgen dropped out of first when his Lotus broke, and then Pabst started a series of pit stops with overheating.

Kumnick steadily drew away from Salyer, while the 1600cc Elva Mk. VIIs of Don Wolf and Mike Hall battled their way up to third. Gates and Doane dnf'd, while Pabst was in and out of the pits. On one of the occasions when the Lola kept its water for a few laps Pabst set a new race lap record of 2:34.2. Salyer meanwhile had pulverized the trap speed mark, being clocked at 173 mph!

As they entered the last lap, Kumnick had things in hand. He led Salyer by two miles. But then, incredibly, at turn 14, the last turn, Kumnick's Cooper-Ford threw a rod in the engine and coasted to a smoky halt. Kumnick could only look on in anguish as Salyer sped by to take the checkered flag first. Wolf and Hall were second and third overall, first and second in FM. In fourth Lee Hall took class EM in his new Elva Porsche. Bill Wuesthoff was fifth in a Porsche 904 coupe, while Ernie Erickson wound up sixth, Elva Porsche mounted. Pabst struggled home a game seventh.

By the time the fall 500 rolled around, Jim Hall had put the USRRC title in his pocket. His Chaparrals were easily the best cars around, and development during the year had added a lightweight aluminum block Chevy V-8 and a revolutionary (for a racing car) automatic transmission to the mix.

The Saturday preliminaries started with a 40 mile Formula race. Augie Pabst again won in his Brabham BT-2 Junior, with Cliff Phillips second. In the FV portion, Harold Zimdars came out on top of a dice with the Formcar of Jerry Hansen. Zimdars was in an Autodynamics. Dick Jacobs won the 60 mile small car run, his Jackal HM leading Al Cervenka's Dolphin home.

The Badger 200 had a new car to challenge the Cobras and Corvettes. The prototype Sunbeam Tiger was present, stuffed full of Ford V-8 power, and Ken Miles behind the wheel. Dan Gerber and George Montgomery ran at the head of the field from the start, their 289ci engines and race proven chassis too much for the 260ci Tiger. Nonetheless, Miles drove furiously, keeping the car in a comfortable third. As the laps rolled by, Montgomery spun out of contention, and Gerber had to make a 55 second stop for fuel. His lead was such, though, that Miles, who was driving non-stop, could not make up the gap. Gerber won, with Miles second, David Ott third in a Corvette and Montgomery fourth.

Walt Hansgen in a Ferrari 275-LM streaks under the checkered flag to win the 500.

For the 500, the favorite would have to be the Chaparral. Hall had entered one Chaparral 2 and a Corvette Grand Sport for the threesome of himself, Hap Sharp and Roger Penske. Mecom also had two cars present, the Lola GT coupe for Augie Pabst and a Ferrari 275-LM (a rear engine 3.3 liter V-12 endurance racer coupe) for Walt Hansgen; both were slated to go solo. Shelby again had three Cobras on hand, all in the GT category. The driver pairings were Miles/Ron Bucknum, Skip Scott/John Morton and Bob Johnson/Ed Leslie. Elva Porsches were present in force, led by a three car entry from Ollie Schmidt for John Cannon/Charlie Hayes, Ralph Treischman/Hayes and Bob Markley/Hayes. That's right, Hayes was entered in all three cars, as he still had a shot at the under two liter USRRC title, and was maximizing his chances. The U-2 leader, Bill Wuesthoff, would co-drive his Elva Porsche with Joe Buzzetta. Dick Doane had his McKee on hand, while Jerry Hansen had replaced his Chaparral 1 with the second McKee built. Gary Wilson did have a Chaparral 1 here, the car that Sharp rolled at the Sprints a year previous. The Causey twins had dropped a Ford V-8 into their Lotus 19, Charlie Cox had a similar engine in his Cooper Monaco T-61, while George Wintersteen had a Chevy V-8 in his Cooper T-61. Bud Gates and Don Skogmo entered Genie Mk. VIIIs. Team Lotus sent over two Lotus Cortina sedans to compete in the U-2 GT category. American Dave Clark drove along with Englishmen Chris Craft and the irrepressible David Hobbs, making his first of countless RA appearances. Add in the usual assortment of Cobras, Porsches, Elvas, Lotus 23s and the like, and it was a very good field, 63 strong!

As expected, Hall took the lead at the start, the Chaparral just too much car for the rest. Gates ran second, Doane followed in third, then Miles, Penske in the Grand Sport, Causey and the rest. Pabst had gotten away to a slow start, but was picking his way up through the field from 25th. Pabst was flying, and moved up to second shortly after Hall turned the leading Chaparral over to Sharp. Hall had set a new race lap record at 2:32.3 during his stint. Unfortunately, the Chaparral began to falter with brake problems, and Pabst dropped out with broken suspension. Doane should have had the lead, but his McKee, now driven by Dick Thompson, had the gears disappear one by one. This left the Morton/Scott Cobra up front, with Hansgen closing. At the first of its two pit stops, Pabst replaced Hansgen in the Ferrari, and set out after the Cobra. As Pabst closed, Shelby countered by moving Miles over from his ailing snake. He and Pabst fought it out for several laps, but eventually Augie eased away. From lap 60 on, the Mecom Ferrari would not relinquish the lead, coming home first ahead of the Morton/Scott/Miles Cobra, which easily won GT. The Penske/Hall/Sharp Corvette Grand Sport took third, while Wuesthoff and Buzzetta were the class of the U-2 field, finishing fourth overall and first in class. For Wuesthoff, this clinched the U-2 USRRC title. The father-son team of Lee and Mike Hall were fifth in an Elva Porsche, while Bob Spooner and Roy Kumnick were sixth in the Cooper-Ford which had let Kumnick down in such a heartbreaking fashion at the Sprints. Kumnick was no doubt ruminating over the fact that the car would last 500 miles now, but not 160 miles in June.

The fall pro races went from strength to strength. Pedro Rodriguez won Mosport in a Ferrari, Hansgen took Bridgehampton in the Mecom Scarab Mk. IV, Parnelli Jones was victorious in the Riverside *L.A. Times GP* in Shelby's Cooper-Ford King Cobra, and Roger Penske took Laguna Seca and both big Nassau races in a Chaparral 2. Despite being the dominant car this year, in 1965 Chaparral would be far more successful.

1965

The program at the track for 1965 was similar to the two previous years. The June Sprints were now a divisional event, even though all the SCCA divisional races were referred to as *Nationals*. However, adding prestige to this year's Sprints was the designation of the 160 mile feature as the *President's Cup*. This was a trophy originally awarded by President Dwight Eisenhower to the winner of the 1954 race at Andrews AFB just outside Washington. After a few years it fell into disuse, but was revived for this meet. Of late it has been awarded to a driver at the SCCA's Championship Runoffs based upon a vote. The September race again was the 500 for the USRRC, supplemented by the Badger 200 on Saturday.

The June Sprints got off to a terrible start, as Minneapolis driver Anthony Brooke Kinnard lost his life during the first race. He suffered fatal head and neck injuries when his MG Midget overturned. Kinnard was the first driver to die in actual competition at Elkhart Lake, Friedman and Henry being lost during practice.

Needless to say, this put a damper on things, and Saturday's races were run in a desultory manner. Bryan Fuerstenau won the F, G and H Production event in a Group 44 Triumph TR3, leading Dan Carmichael's Sunbeam Alpine across the line. Carmichael was a newcomer to racing, following an Air Force career during which he was an Ace pilot in W.W.II. He was 47 years old at the time, and 30 years later won the SCCA's Formula Atlantic Championship — at the age of 77! Dick Drexler took GP and Fred Salo HP.

The Formula race was another win for Augie Pabst, as his familiar Brabham BT-2 FJ led Larry Skeel's Cooper home. Formula Vee went to Rick Kohler's Bobsy Vanguard. The D and E Production event was the property of Allan Barker in an Austin-Healey. Ron McConkey was second overall and first in DP in a 10 year old Jaguar XK 140. Larry Dent took third in a Lotus Elite.

The 500 pace lap. Walt Hansgen on the pole in the Mecom Racing Team Lola T-70 with Jim Hall alongside in the winning Chaparral. A large field of sports racers follows as they approach turn 7.

Sunday was also a miserable day, but for another reason. It rained. The entire day's events were conducted in the wet, and yet the crowd count pushed the 40,000 mark. Rain or shine, the true race fan was lured by the Elkhart Lake mystique. The buns may be a little soggy, but the bratwurst still tastes just as great.

The big production go was run over a distance of 120 miles, which would require the V-8 cars to stop for fuel. George Montgomery had the latest Cobra produced by Shelby, a larger chassis version powered by a 7.0 liter Ford V-8. The Cobra 427 was much faster than the previous 289 version—a real blasting package. John Martin, later to spend several years in Indy Cars as a privateer, had a hot Corvette, and did not know that he was supposed to be behind the Cobras. He took the lead at the start and held it for many laps, with Jim Mederer snapping at his heels in a 289 Cobra. Montgomery lay third, getting the feel of his new car. Martin made his fuel stop on lap 22 of 30, allowing Mederer to take over. Then he had to stop, and Montgomery led until his late race stop on lap 27. It would be a sprint for the finish, just three laps away. Mederer grabbed the lead, with Martin right behind. Then on lap 29, with one to go, Mederer spun, and Martin had to come to an almost complete stop to avoid him. That was all Montgomery needed, as he boomed by for the win.

In BP Don Yenko planned to run the entire 120 miles non-stop, gambling on his 283 Corvette getting the necessary mileage. It almost worked. On the last lap the Corvette coughed, gasped, and coasted to a silent halt. Tom Yeager in a Shelby Mustang GT350 was there to give him a friendly wave as he drove by on his way to the BP checker.

After Reed Andrews won the G and H Mod event in an Elva MK. VI, it was time for the feature President's Cup race. The conditions by now were appalling, with the rain coming down in sheets. Consequently, the 160 mile distance was halved to 80 miles and hardly anyone complained; even 80 miles would take over an hour to run. It was a measure of the importance given the June Sprints that Jim Hall brought two Chaparral 2s to the event, for himself and partner Hap Sharp. This would be the only non-professional race the Chaparrals would run in 1965. They were cleaning house this season, having won all but one USRRC held so far, and had trounced the field at the World Championship 12 Hours of Sebring. Arrayed against them were a fine entry of Genies, Cheetahs, Cooper- and Lotus-Fords, plus various Elvas, Lotuses, Porsches, Elva Porsches and specials. The ex-Meister Brauser Chaparral 1 was on hand, being driven by Augie Pabst as a stop gap measure until his new McLaren sports racer arrived from England.

As the race began, the rain was at its strongest. Hall, who had qualified on the pole, took it easy, and Dave Causey jumped into the lead in his Lotus 19-Ford. Pabst was second in the old front engine Chaparral, with Hall third. Sharp was already out in the other Chaparral 2, getting caught up in a three way accident with Ernie Erickson's Elva Porsche and Glen Lyall's SCD-Chevy special. Both Erickson and Lyall got upside down, but with no injuries.

Pabst held onto second until lap nine, when he spun off course and stalled in a water hazard. The rain was letting up, and Hall felt that it was time to get down to business, as the race was but 20 laps long. He pulled up on Causey's Lotus, and on lap 11 passed him and pulled away for the win. Causey finished second, while Ralph Salyer was third. Ironically, Salyer had peeled the top off his Cheetah earlier, due to intense heat in the cockpit. Today he could have used the roof. Bud Gates was fourth in a Genie-Chevy, Charlie Cox fifth in a Cooper-Ford and Don Skogmo sixth in a Genie-Ford. Ralph Trieschman won EM in an Elva Porsche with Brooke Doran first in FM in an Elva Mk. VII. Class DM only four years previous had been the class with the most cars and usually produced the race winner. With the swing to large American V-8s, the class now was virtually extinct. Indeed, Doc Dee was the DM winner, finishing just about last overall in a 10 year old Maserati 300-S. Hall's winning speed in the wet-dry conditions was 73.238 mph, the slowest in years.

The 500 weekend had been moved forward one week to Labor Day weekend. The second weekend in September, where the 500 had resided since it began, was also the opening weekend of the NFL season, and, after all, this was Packer territory. In Wisconsin, it was folly to buck the Pack.

The 500 would be a showdown. Jim Hall and George Follmer were locked in a battle for the U.S. Road Racing Championship. As mentioned earlier, the SCCA had chosen to award equal points for both over and under two liters, with the champion being he who had most points, regardless of how he did in the overall picture. As a result, Hall, who had five overall wins plus a third in eight races run so far, trailed George Follmer for the title. Follmer, driving a Lotus 23 into which he had inserted a 2.0 Porsche 904 engine, had but one overall win, but did score the maximum points in class five times plus two seconds. Follmer's two runner-up scores were the difference over Hall coming into Elkhart, the last USRRC of the year. Simply

put, for Hall to take the crown, he had to win with Follmer no higher than third in class.

Saturday's preliminaries, including the Badger 200, were run in a continuation of June's weather. It was wet. Rain soaked all three events, making things uncomfortable for racer and fan alike. The all-formula race was taken by Dick Eisenmann, who spun at turn five the first lap, but recovered to take the lead on lap six. Eisenmann was in a Cooper T-59 Junior into which he had inserted a 1.6 liter Alfa Romeo four, and running as a F-B entry. F-C went to Alan Hultgren who just held off Cliff Phillips' Lotus 22. Hultgren was in a BMC Mk. II. The FV class was taken by Tom Tufts in an Autodynamics. The fact that Tufts was fourth overall indicates that the weather affected most drivers, many negatively, but in Tufts' case, positively.

The Badger 200 started with 36 cars and ended with 26. That only 10 cars dropped out tells us that most drivers were very cautious indeed, tiptoeing around the rain slicked course. David Ott proved to be the best mudder on the day, taking his rather dated 283ci BP Corvette into the early lead over George Montgomery's 427 Cobra. By lap nine Ott led by a rather amazing 23 seconds. But, unfortunately for Ott, the rain began to ease. This allowed Montgomery to get more of the 427's awesome power onto the track, and he began to eat into Ott's lead. On lap 19 the inevitable happened, and Montgomery powered past Ott on the straight, not to be headed again. As the 50 laps ended, Montgomery led Ott for first, with Bob Spooner third in a Sunbeam Tiger, followed by the Corvettes of Paul Canary and Frank Reimann.

For the 500 both Hall and Follmer were hedging their bets. A driver could win points as long as he drove for at least 35 laps in any one car. Hence, if one car broke, a driver could jump into another, and as long as he finished and drove at least 35 laps, score points in the second car. Consequently, Hall entered two Chaparral 2s, listing himself as a driver in both roadrunners. Hap Sharp, Ron Hissom and Bruce Jennings made up the rest of the Chaparral pilots. Follmer had entered his own Lotus-Porsche, Earl Jones co-driving, and was listed as the co-driver in Joe Buzzetta's Elva Porsche. The Chaparral Team came into Elkhart Lake on a roll; they had won all but the first USRRC of the season, and had won seven straight.

There were other entries of note. Lola and McLaren had gone into production with new sports racers, rear engine cars designed to handle Detroit V-8s. The rear engine revolution started five years earlier had now come to completion, and future developments would be in the area of aerodynamics and engines. Lola was building its own cars, while Bruce McLaren had farmed out the construction of the cars which carried his name to Elva. In the U.S. Mecom was the Lola distributor, while former driver Carl Haas held the Elva franchise. Mecom entered a Ford powered T-70 for Walt Hansgen and Mark Donohue. Two McLaren M1As (also known as McLaren Elva Mk. I) were here. Ralph Salyer had an Oldsmobile engine in his car, while Bud Gates had replaced his Genie with a Chevy-powered McLaren. The Essex Wire Team entered a Ford GT-40 coupe for Skip Scott and Augie Pabst and their Cobra 427 for Ed Lowther and Dick Thompson. McKees were in the hands of Mike Hall (a 427ci Ford in his) and Jerry Hansen. Ford V-8s powered the Lotus 19 of the Causeys and the Cooper of Charlie Cox. Bill Cooper brought his new Ferrari 275-P, while Bob Grossman and Dick Holquist were in a 275-LM. Shelby entered two Cobras, both 289s in the GT category, for Tom Payne/Bob Johnson and Johnson/Don Sesslar. In addition, there were a host of other Cobras, Porsches, Lotuses and Elvas, including four Elva Porsches.

On race day the rain went and a bright, sunny day prevailed. Walt Hansgen took the lead from the 56 other starters going into turn one on the first of 125 laps. But by the time the first four miles were completed, Hall was in front. In fact, his Chaparral would lead every lap of the race, a domination that would never be duplicated in the RA 500. On lap 23, Hall circulated in 2:28.8, a new race lap record. Hall drove the first third of the race before giving way to Sharp, who in turn handed off to Hissom for the last third. The dominance of the Chaparral was utter and complete. The second Chaparral, started by Sharp, got off to a much slower start, and it took him until lap 20 to claim second. This car would not be out of second for the duration. Jennings drove the middle portion, with Jim Hall driving the last third, as insurance in case the lead car broke.

A casual victory circle. Hap Sharp is interviewed while Jim Hall signs autographs after winning the 500 — a far cry from the hat dance and champagne spraying of today.

Behind Hall on lap 10 came Hansgen, Scott, Sharp, Hansen, Salyer, M. Hall and Thompson. On lap 16, however, the first red flag in RA's history flew as a frightening accident occurred coming out of the Carousel. Clint Lindburg lost control of his Elva Mk. V, flipped, came down on top of Jack Ensley's Apache Special, and burst into flames. With the track blocked, the race was stopped. Bud Clusseruth was first on the scene, leaping out of his Cheetah, and heroically pulling Lindburg from his flaming car. Lindburg received superficial burns, while Ensley had a broken arm. Proving the claim that it's more dangerous on the highway than on the race track, the ambulance in which they were being transported to the Sheboygan hospital was involved in a traffic accident. Fortunately, no further injuries occurred.

After a lengthy delay to clean matters up, the race was restarted. The Chaparrals continued on their appointed rounds. The Mecom Lola, now driven by Donohue, ran third and threatened the second Chaparral, now driven by Jennings. But on lap 44 Donohue was in the pits, and the Lola's threat was ended, the victim of broken suspension. Behind the two white cars Jerry Hansen was holding third and Skip Scott fourth. Both had based their strategy on making one pit stop, but when the Chaparrals both made their first stops without giving up the lead, the handwriting was on the wall. In any event, Hansen pitted on lap 52 with engine problems and was out. Then, shortly after Pabst had taken over the GT-40, the ring and pinion broke. The Salyer/Mitchell McLaren ran third, but a lengthy pit stop with a dead battery dropped them many laps off the pace.

What of Follmer? He was doing quite well, actually. Early on, Gerry Bruihl led U-2 in his Lotus 23-2.0 Climax, with Buzzetta second and Follmer third. This only lasted for a dozen laps or so, when the mechanical gremlins began to attack Bruihl's car. Buzzetta went into the lead, with

Follmer second. On lap 43 Follmer turned his car over to Earl Jones, and a few laps later relieved Buzzetta in the leading Elva Porsche. Follmer was now first *and* second in class, and the die was cast, save mechanical problems.

On lap 99 Follmer gave the Elva Porsche back to Buzzetta, then replaced Jones in his own Lotus-Porsche. Mechanical problems did strike, Buzzetta dropping out with a blown clutch on lap 103, but Follmer was still first. That is where he finished, first in class, fourth overall. The title was his.

The Hall/Sharp/Hissom and Sharp/Jennings/Hall Chaparrals finished side by side, one lap apart. Five laps behind was the third place Lowther/Thompson Cobra, then Follmer/Jones, Salyer/Mitchell and the first GT car, the Cobra of Johnson/Payne. The Denise McCluggage/Bill Kimberly Elva Porsche took second in U-2, while Sesslar/Johnson were second in GT. It took the lead Chaparral 5 hours, 35 minutes, 6 seconds, a speed of 89.526 mph.

Follmer had won the title with 66 points to Hall's 59. The fact that Follmer had one overall win to Hall's six did not sit well in many circles, and for 1966 the SCCA quietly dropped the equal points for both over and under two liters provision. That came too late for Hall, who admits to this day to be disgruntled over it, and considers himself the '65 champion. An argument that probably never will be resolved to everyone's satisfaction.

With the conclusion of the USRRC season, the big fall pro races were left. This was largely a Chaparral feast, as Hall won Kent and Mosport while Sharp took Bridgehampton, Riverside, Las Vegas and Nassau. Only Hansgen's win in a Mecom Lola at Laguna Seca prevented a clean sweep. As it was, in 1965 Chaparrals were entered in 22 races and won 16 of them. Quite a record indeed.

1966

Big changes were afoot in U.S. racing. The SCCA, for so long a staunch foe of professionalism, was now embracing race-for-bucks in a big way. This year saw the club unveil two new professional series, while adding four classes to the amateur ranks.

Sedans were in for 1966. The introduction of the Ford Mustang and Plymouth Barracuda, coupled with the soon to come Chevrolet Camaro and Mercury Cougar, created an entire new market. Add to that the existing sports sedans from Alfa Romeo, Lotus Cortina, BMW and others, and the result was inevitable. SCCA introduced a sedan category to club racing, with four classes arranged by engine displacement. In addition, an eight race professional series, dubbed the Trans-American Sedan Championship, would debut at Sebring in March. That series, popularly known as the Trans-Am, has had peaks and valleys over the past 30 years, but it is still going, the country's longest continuously running pro series.

Up the hill during the June Sprints. Charlie Hayes in a McLaren Elva Mk. II leads Ralph Salyer's McKee Mk. VI. Both dropped out, with the win going to Mak Kronn in a similar McKee

The other new series grew out of the fall pro races. Coming after the regular seasons were over, both here and abroad, these free-standing events regularly drew the cream of U.S. racing, as well as a number of international entrants. For 1966 the tracks at St. Jovite, Bridgehampton, Mosport, Laguna Seca, Riverside and Stardust (Las Vegas) banded together for a six races in eight weeks extravaganza known as the Canadian-American Challenge Cup. This of course is the fabled Can-Am, a series that blazed like a comet across the skies of racing, captivating all in its *anything goes* formula. All good things come to an end, and the Can-Am collapsed after the 1974 season, done in perhaps by its own excesses; but to this day it is remembered as the greatest series that ever was.

At Road America, two bridges were added, spanning the track at the top of the hill on the main straight, and the other crossing the back straight. This eliminated an over one mile hike to get from one side of the track to the other at the S/F line. The pits themselves were given a guardrail to separate them from the track proper. To enter the pits the cars had to veer right just under the new bridge in order to pass on the pit side of the rail.

The June Sprints, most unfortunately, saw another fatality as James M. Hartman from Chicago, flipped his Triumph TR3 at turn 14 during practice, sustaining injuries to which he succumbed while enroute to the hospital.

Three races were held on Saturday, the first of which was for D and E Production, and was taken by Jerry Thompson in a Yenko Stinger. This was a two door Corvair coupe which had been heavily breathed upon by Don Yenko's speed shop. It could be said that the Stinger was to Corvair what the GT350 was to Mustang. The SCCA subsequently approved it as a sports car in class DP. The big production race was a Cobra runaway, with Tom Payne leading the snakes of Jack Hurt and Richard Roe across the line in the 100 mile go. BP was more of a battle, with Alan Barker bringing his Corvette home first after a good tussle with Dan Gerber's Mustang GT350. The last race on Saturday was a Formula affair where Larry Skeels in a Cooper and Cliff Phillips in a Lotus 27 traded the top spot several times before Skeels prevailed. The two 1600cc FB cars were followed by the FC winner, James Beltnick in a Lotus 20. FV also saw the lead contested heavily, with Jim Clarke edging Chet Freeman. Both were driving Bobsy Vanguards.

Sunday, a warm and sunny day, started with the small production race, taken by Richard Hull in a Volvo P1800. Following that was a first for RA, a sedan race. The honor of being the first sedan winner fell to Tom Yeager in a Ford Mustang. Yeager, who was a force on the Trans-Am circuit this season with two wins, led all the way, but Scott Harvey in a Plymouth Barracuda was never far behind. Third overall and first in SB was Horst Kwech in an Alfa Romeo GTA, while the Mini-Coopers of Robert Hindson and Robert Zimmermann took SC and SD respectively, although with differing displacements.

G and H Modified then ran for 80 miles and Tom Tufts scored what could be described as an upset victory. Tufts, in a Lotus Eleven, a supposedly obsolete, front-engined, 10 year old car, had no business at all running up with the much newer Lotus 23s and Elvas. But he not only ran with them, he was leading them. Ralph Scott's Elva Mk. VII took second in class, while Bill Mitchell came out on top in H with a Bobsy-Sunbeam.

This set the stage for the 160 mile feature. Three new McKee Mk. VI sports racers were entered, one with Chevrolet power for Mak Kronn, and two with Oldsmobile V-8s for Ralph Salyer and Bud Clusseruth. Jerry Hansen had replaced his McKee Mk. II with the Wolverine, a Chevy V-8 powered special. Two of the new Porsche 906 coupes, using the new 2.0 liter flat six, were entered for Ralph Treischman and Lee Hall. Topping the entry were two new McLarens, M1Bs (McLaren-Elva Mk. IIs) for Charlie Hayes and Charlie Cox. Hayes was contesting the entire USRRC circuit, and stopped off at the June Sprints enroute from Bridgehampton to Laguna Seca, where he would win, at the request of his sponsor, Nickey Chevrolet of Chicago. While not running cars as it had several years previous, Nickey was now sponsoring them. A footnote was the last RA appearance of a front engine Chaparral 1, as Dick Eisenmann was driving the ex-Meister Brauser car, now owned by Pabst Motors.

Hansen had qualified on the pole, just 0.4 second off Hall's lap record. Kronn and Salyer followed. At the start, Kronn jumped into the lead, with Cox moving past Hansen. For Hansen, it was a short race, as the Wolverine started smoking on lap two and retired on lap three with a broken oil seal. Salyer moved up and challenged Cox, while Kronn pulled away at a second a lap. Salyer eventually got ahead of Cox and started cutting into Kronn's lead. Behind this threesome came Clusseruth, Dick Durant in his old but amazing front-engine Durant Special and Treischman in the Porsche 906. Unfortunately, Hayes was already out by this time, retiring on lap two, also with a broken oil seal.

This order lasted until Salyer was forced into the pits with overheating. Cox now had a clear track ahead of him, and he showed heretofore unseen speed as he began to close on Kronn. Indeed, Cox took his new McLaren around the track with a lap of 2:28.4, breaking the lap record set by Jim Hall the previous fall in a Chaparral 2! Alas, it was not to last, as on lap 35 Cox went into turn 12 too hard, ran off course, flipped and had the car catch fire, gutting it. Cox escaped with minor burns. That left Kronn free to lope to the finish, averaging 93.716 mph, breaking Hall's 1962 record of 87.89 mph.

Finishing second behind Kronn was Ralph Treischman, winning EM. Third was Roy Kumnick in the Tero Cooper-Ford, while fourth went to Dean Causey's Elva Mk. VII. Lee Hall took fifth and Ernie Erickson came home sixth overall, first in FM, the latter in his familiar pale yellow Elva Porsche.

The recent stretch of bad weather continued on the 500 weekend. Both Friday and Saturday had on-and-off rain, while Sunday, while dry, was very windy. Most sadly, once again tragedy struck, as Don Skogmo, a fixture at RA since its start, lost his life in practice. His fresh out of the box Lola T-70 lost traction in the wet while cresting the hill at pit start, and the car went broadside into the end of the new pit lane guardrail. Poor Skogmo didn't have a chance.

Saturday again had two support races, plus the Badger 200. John Wetherbee took the small bore event in a Jabro HM, while Cliff Phillips was victorious in the Formula event in his Lotus 27. The Badger 200 had a strange look about it, as no competitive Cobras were present. This opened the door to Dave Ott's Corvette, who won after putting down a strong challenge from the Mustang GT350 of Terry Kohler. Ott led early, then Kohler passed him and opened up a half minute lead. When Kohler pitted, Jerry Dunbar's Corvette took the lead until his stop, when he gave it back to Kohler. Scott Harvey took over the point in his Plymouth Barracuda when Kohler stopped again. Harvey led Dunbar and Ott, but then Dunbar went out with overheating and Harvey made another fuel stop. Ott was in first and he led easily to the finish. Harvey was second, David Pabst third in a GT350, while Kohler took fourth and the Cobra of John Addison was fifth.

The lineup for the 500 was good, but many top cars did not appear, preferring to save their machines for the Can-Am series, which began the following week at Ste. Jovite. The USRRC point standings were led by Chuck Parsons with 26, followed by Buck Fulp with 22, Skip Hudson with 17, and Lothar Motschenbacher and John Cannon with 15. With nine points for a win, Parsons, Fulp and Hudson were still in the chase. The season had been spread out, no driver dominating. Of the previous seven races, only Fulp had more than one win, having scored at Riverside and Watkins Glen. Single wins had been recorded by Cannon, Hayes, Jerry Grant, Mark Donohue and Motschenbacher. Parsons had parlayed three seconds and two thirds into the points lead.

Even though several *big guns* were missing, the field still was top rate. McLarens were entered for Parsons, Hayes/Earl Jones, Motschenbacher, Brooke Doran/Carl Haas and Bud Gates. Lola T-70s were in the hands of Fulp and Hudson. There were McKees for Mak Kronn, Ralph Salyer and Roy Kumnick. A Ford GT-40 was piloted by Dick Thompson/Ed Lowther. Genies were assigned to Bob Harris (owned by *Bonanza's* Dan Blocker) and Jerry Rosbach/Jack Baker. Fred Pipin was in the Tero Cooper-Ford, while Dave Causey had his usual Lotus 19-Ford. Add in a Lotus 30, five Porsche 906s, a Ferrari 206-S and the usual under two liter Elvas and Lotuses, and we were ready to go.

Parsons had arranged for a back up ride in Kronn's McKee, while mutual aid pacts were in place between Fulp and Kolb's Ferrari, and Hudson with Motschenbacher. In the end, none were used.

Charlie Hayes took the pole with a record-shattering time of 2:26.20. Fulp was alongside him, while Parsons and Kronn were on the second row. Charlie Kolb was the fastest under two liter car at 2:38.8 in the Schroeder Racing Team Ferrari 206-S. He was a full second faster than the first Porsche 906, driven by Joe Buzzetta.

Hayes took full advantage of his pole, taking the lead at the start and stretching it out. After 10 laps, Hayes led Parsons, Kronn, Fulp, Hudson, Salyer, Gates, Motschenbacher, Thompson, Doran, Buzzetta, Kolb and Kumnick. Motschenbacher then got the bit between his teeth and started to pick off the cars ahead of him. By lap 17, he had moved into second behind Hayes. Shortly thereafter, Kolb broke a brake caliper, and the way was clear for Porsche in U-2.

On lap 34 Lothar's challenge received a setback, as he had to make an extended pit stop to repair a broken shifter. Meanwhile, Salyer retired his McKee at turn 13, only to have Kronn lose control of his McKee while lapping a car and plow into the parked car. Scratch two McKees, as well as

Around turn 14 in the 500, Denise McCluggage's Ferrari 275 GTB about to be lapped by Chuck Parsons in a McLaren Elva Mk. II. Bill Cooper's just lapped Ferrari 275P follows.

Chuck Parsons complete his victory lap, having driven the 500 solo. He took the lead on the penultimate lap, clinching the 1966 U.S. Road Racing Championship in the process.

Parsons' backup.

Fulp took up the charge from Motschenbacher, closed on the leading Hayes, and when Hayes pitted on lap 44, Fulp became only the second driver to lead the race. However, Fulp had only four laps to enjoy the point, as he pitted on lap 48, never to reemerge, as the Lola had broken the shift linkage. Now it was down to just Parsons and Hudson for the title.

Things were looking up for Parsons, as he took the lead upon Fulp's retirement. When he pitted, he decided to go solo, even though Kronn was standing by. Parsons said he felt good, and he was familiar with the car, while Kronn was not. Parsons pitted for three minutes on lap 65, giving the lead to Earl Jones, in for Hayes. The order now was Jones, Parsons, Hudson, Gunther Klass in Buzzetta's 906, Chuck Dietrich in Ralph Treischman's 906 and Motschenbacher.

As the race wound down to the finish, Hayes took over the leading McLaren for the final stint. However, he was back in the pits shortly thereafter, and added five quarts of oil to the Chevy V-8. This gave the lead to Parsons. Hayes reentered the track and really began to motor, setting a new race lap record at 2:28.1. On lap 95, he regained the lead from Parsons. With six laps to go, Hayes had an eight second lead over Parsons, but trouble was brewing. Smoke began to billow out of the McLaren's engine compartment, and Parsons began closing. On the penultimate lap, Parsons closed up behind Hayes and passed him on the inside at corner 14, entering the last lap. Hayes stayed with the red McLaren of Parsons, even trying a last ditch pass. But it was not to be, as Parsons took the checkered flag just one-half car length ahead of Hayes after 500 miles of racing! What a finish!

Parsons had averaged 92.879 mph in winning, taking 5 hours, 23 minutes 20 seconds. He also, of course, was the 1966 U.S. Road Racing Champion, finishing with 35 points to the 22 of Fulp. The Hayes/Jones McLaren was second, while solo drives netted third for Skip Hudson in the Team Meridian Lola and fourth for Lothar Motschenbacher's McLaren, sponsored for this race by Nickey, as was Hayes and the Genie of Bob Harris. Fifth overall and first under two liters was the first of a string of four Porsche 906s, the Joe Buzzetta/Gunther Klass car. The next three 906s were Dietrich/Treischman, Mike Fischer/Pete Lovely and Lee Hall/Mike Hall.

While the USRRC season was over, the Can-Am was just beginning. John Surtees won the first Can-Am crown with wins at Ste. Jovite, Riverside and Stardust in his works Lola T-70, while Dan Gurney took Bridgehampton in the All American Racers Lola, Mark Donohue won Mosport in the Lola of newly-formed Penske Racing, and Phil Hill was victorious at Laguna Seca in the radical new high-winged Chaparral 2E. Parsons took the pro, but not Can-Am, race at Kent, and Donohue rounded out the year with victory at the Nassau Trophy race. The Can-Am was here and racing would revel in it for the next several years.

1967

Fred Pipin sits in the Tero Cooper-Ford in victory circle after his surprise win in the 1967 June Springs. He was never a factor in the race, but benefited from the high rate of attrition in the 160 mile event.

ig happenings were afoot at RA as 1967 dawned. For the first time since 1960, there would be three race weekends at the track. The 500 weekend was moved from Labor Day to July, making way for the big one: the Can-Am! The track at Ste. Jovite, Canada, relinquished its date due to money troubles, and Clif Tufte snapped it up. The RA date would lead off the six race Can-Am series, and the excitement level was understandably high.

In view of Don Skogmo's tragic accident, the pit entrance was reconfigured. The guard rail was extended to the walkover bridge and new asphalt was laid, putting the pit entrance at the bottom of the main straight hill. This gave an unobstructed view to the drivers pulling into the pits as well as allowing a gradual veering off of the race surface, negating the abrupt jog of the year before. An improvement that was heartily endorsed by all.

Another change, much appreciated by competitors, was the building of three metal garages next to the track HQ building (the *farmhouse*) on Highway 67. This meant that tech inspection would now be on premises, as opposed to down the road at the Sheboygan County Municipal Garage.

One small change had occurred in SCCA club racing. The category that had been known as *Modified* since the early 1950s was renamed *Sports*

Racing to more accurately reflect the nature of the cars competing. On the professional side, SCCA created another pro series, this a five race set for Formula B and C cars. Along with the Can-Am, Trans-Am, and USRRC, the club that at one time abhorred professionalism now had four pro series.

The June Sprints took place the weekend of June 17-18, with a familiar format. Another familiar visitor was rain. Morning rain had delayed matters considerably, and the first race, scheduled to start at 2:45, did not get underway until almost 4:30. The D and E Production event was taken by Gil Littell's Jaguar XK 120 after early leader Jim Dittemore was knocked out of the race by an errant car he was lapping. The big production cars and sedans ran for 100 miles, and it was a cruise for Ed Lowther's 427 Cobra. The final race of the day, for Formula Vee, was taken by Pete Revere in a Bobsy. If the cars had headlights, they would have been on.

Sunday fortunately was fair and dry. Race one was for small production and HSR (formerly HM). With Martin Tanner now retired, the way was clear for long time protagonist Ed Walsh to claim the 60 miler in his Bobsy-Saab. HP and C and D Sedans was a Mini-Cooper benefit. The tiny English bombs dominated, with Bob Kimes winning from Don Schmitt and Art Sutphin. The third 60 mile race of the day was for Formula cars. Dick Eisenmann, driving Ike Uihlein's Lotus 27 scored an easy victory over Dave Dours' Cooper FB car.

Action in turn 6. Lee Hall, Porsche 906; Bill Cooper, Ferrari 275-P; and Skip Barber, McLaren Elva Mk. III during the 500. Barber eventually finished third.

Lap one of Road America's first Can-Am. A fraction of the Group 7 field thunders up the hill to turn 6 to the delight of the record crowd.

The feature race of the weekend was for C through G Sports Racing. One obvious byproduct of the USRRC and Can-Am series was the rapidly decreasing number of top flight sports racers at National meets. Compared to previous years, the number of top cars present was rather thin. However, four McKees were entered; Mk. VIs for Ralph Salyer, Bud Clusseruth and Charlie Hayes, and a new Mk. VII for Skip Hudson. Two McLaren Elva Mk IIIs were here. Jerry Hansen had replaced his Wolverine with one, and Carl Haas had entered another for Chuck Parsons. The Haas car was running the USRRC, but Parsons had just been signed to replace Masten Gregory, with whom Haas had a falling out. Consequently, Haas was running Parsons in the Sprints in order to familiarize him with the car and the team.

As the cars lined up on the grid, Hayes was missing. Dissatisfied with his car, he declined to participate. Nonetheless, pole sitter Hansen streaked off into the lead, followed by Parsons. Salyer failed to complete the first lap, going off course and bending his car rather severely. The two white McLarens led easily until lap nine, when Hansen retired when the clutch packed up. Then it was Parsons in the lead, but his gearbox broke on lap 12. Skip Hudson now had the race under control. He stretched his lead effortlessly, and on lap 37 of 40 he led by over two laps from second place Fred Pipin. Pipin, a virtual unknown, was driving what was called the *Tero Special*, which was in fact nothing but the rebodied Cooper-Ford that had been running here for years. In fact, it was the same car in which Roy Kumnick lost the 1964 Sprints at the last corner. For this car it was payback time. The gearbox on Hudson's McKee seized and he was out. Everyone waited patiently for Pipin to make up the two laps that he was down to Hudson. Finally, five minutes after Hudson had pulled to the side of the track, Pipin officially passed him for the lead. He led the final two laps to the finish.

Behind shock winner Pipin's Tero Cooper-Ford came Bud Clusseruth's McKee. Bud had given up his chance of victory early in the race. Seeing buddy Salyer's car a mess in the ditch, Clusseruth had pitted out of concern, and did not rejoin the race until he got word that Salyer was OK. Third went to Jerry Rosbach in a Genie Mk. VIII. ESR went to Hank Candler's Lotus 23, FSR to Leonard Pickering's Bobsy-Alfa, and GSR was the property of the Heba Mk. 2 special of Quin Calhoun.

The weekend of July 29-30 saw the USRRC return to Elkhart Lake with

the 11th running of the Road America 500. However, with the advent of the Can-Am, the entry list for RA was severely affected. Many entrants decided not to put 500 miles of wear on the cars they would be using for big bucks just six weeks later. In addition, Mark Donohue had won five of the six previous USRRCs in Roger Penske's Lola, and already had the title tucked safely in his pocket. As a result, only 21 cars showed up, of which only 14 were over two liters. Of these seven were McLarens, two were McKees and one was a Lola. The other four were field-fillers, including a 10 year old Lister-Chevy! While 21 cars would be very thin around the four mile course, the 14 that would be running at the end would be thinner still.

The day before the 500 was the usual support slate, headed by the Badger 200. Jerry Nelson won the small bore event in an Elva Mk. VII, while Jack Eiteljorg came out on top in the Formula event. The Badger 200 was just a two car show. Richard Messersmith led for the first half in a 427 Cobra before he spun off. That gave the lead to Warren Fairbanks, who was in a 289 Cobra, and he scored an easy two minute victory over Dave Ott's Corvette. As in the 500, these support races were getting to be thin on entry.

While 21 cars started the 500, in reality only three mattered. In qualifying, Chuck Parsons turned the first 100 mph lap at Road America, taking his Carl Haas entered McLaren Elva Mk. III around the four miles in 2:22.8, a speed of 100.83 mph. Jerry Hansen was alongside Parsons, and he too had been over 100 mph, at 2:23.2, 100.02 mph. For this race Parsons and Hansen were running as a team, with Parsons slated to drive the first third of the race in his car before giving way to Skip Scott. Parsons would then drive awhile in Hansen's car before turning it back to him, and would then relieve Scott in his original car. After Parsons' solo win the year previous, this plan seemed rather simple. The only threat to the two Haas-managed cars came from the McLaren Elva Mk. III entered by Dana Chevrolet. Peter Revson was the regular driver, and he would be aided in this race by Lothar Motschenbacher. This would be the strongest driver pairing present. Other McLarens present were for Jerry Entin/Sam Posey, Don Morin/Skip Barber, Brooke Doran and George Alderman. Ed Lowther was co-driving with Bob Nagel in Bob's new McKee Mk. VII, while Ralph Salyer had his Cro-Sal McKee Mk. VI for himself and Bill Mitchell. The sole Lola present was the T-70 of Brian O'Neill.

The race was a bit of a dud. Hansen took off at the start, and except for five laps when Revson pushed ahead, led until his fuel stop at one third distance. Parsons turned his second place car over to Scott, and took over Hansen's machine. An unplanned pit stop for oil put Scott into the lead, and that is just how the race ran out. Parsons/Scott won in 5:23:42.8, a speed of 92.67 mph. Hansen/Parsons were second, with Morin/Barber third in a McLaren 1-2-3. Fourth, and first in U-2, was the Porsche 906 of Joe Buzzetta and Scooter Patrick. Mak Kronn and Chuck Dietrich were next in Ike Uihlein's new Porsche 906.

The Revson/Motschenbacher McLaren lasted 42 laps before going out with electrical problems. However, before retiring Revson had the honor of turning the first 100 mph lap in competition, setting the race lap record at 2:22.9, 100.559 mph. The two McKees were out just a little after the 100 mile mark, Nagel with oil failure and Mitchell with a spin. The Dick Dagiel/Guy Wooley Lister-Chevy finished in 13th place, 152 miles behind the winner. It was that kind of race.

Finally, it was time for the Can-Am. Labor Day weekend set records everywhere one looked. Best field, fastest speeds, largest crowd. It was indeed a glorious weekend. The Can-Am concept was very simple: two seat, envelope-bodied sports racers with a bottom displacement limit of 2.5 liters. That's it. No top engine limit. No aerodynamic restrictions. No limit on type of engine, number of cylinders, or material used. The only rule in the Can-Am was that there were no rules. This giving of complete freedom to designers produced some truly weird and wonderful cars in the years ahead. It was an era remembered today as being truly golden. These were times to be enjoyed.

On Saturday, the only race was a 200 mile affair for under two liter sports racers. Peter Revson's younger brother Doug, who had competed in this class for a few years, had tragically lost his life a month earlier in a F-3 race in Denmark. In his memory, Peter quickly arranged a five race series for U-2 cars, to run at most Can-Ams, with the winner receiving the Doug Revson Trophy. For the RA event, 17 cars started the race, with five Porsche 906s naturally attracting the most attention. Whereas 21 cars at the recent 500 made the track look bare at times, 17 running 200 miles had a similar effect. Fred Baker took the lead in his 906, with Joe Buzzetta giving chase. Mak Kronn, Porsche 906; Gerry Bruihl, Lotus 23-2.0 Climax; and Hank Candler, Lotus 23-BMW followed. Buzzetta was hampered by a fault in the engine, which did not allow more than 8000 revs. Later, he would run out of fuel and then, finally stop with electrical failure. It was not his day, but it was Baker's. He would lead virtually unchallenged to take the win by half a minute over Mak Kronn. Bruihl was third and Cliff Phillips fourth in another 906.

This set the stage for the Can-Am. Who was there? Denis Hulme, Bruce McLaren, John Surtees, Jim Hall, George Follmer, Dan Gurney, Lothar Motschenbacher, Peter Revson, Mark Donohue, Chuck Parsons, Skip Scott, Charlie Hayes, Jerry Hansen, Don Morin, Sam Posey, Skip Barber, John Cannon, Frank Matich, Bill Eve, Roger McCluskey, John Cordts, Ludwig Heimrath, Brooke Doran, Brett Lunger, Jerry Grant, Bud Morley, Jerry Entin, Bob Nagel, Gary Wilson, Richard Brown, Ross Greenville and Ron Courtney, that's who!

The cars? McLaren and Hulme were in the brand new, factory McLaren M6As. Hall had the high winged, 427 aluminum Chevy powered Chaparral 2G. Penske had two Lola T-70s for Donohue and Follmer. Dana Chevrolet had two new Lolas for Motschenbacher and Revson. Posey was debuting the Caldwell D-7, a high winged car built in Massachusetts. In all, there were 18 McLarens and nine Lola T-70s running. Such a collection of talent and machinery had never before been seen at the track.

In qualifying, no less than *19* cars broke the lap record! Fastest of all was Bruce McLaren who toured the four miles in 2:12.6, a speed of 108.594 mph. This was over *10 seconds* faster than the previous lap record. A combination of factors contributed to this amazing jump in speed; top drivers, the very latest in cars and tires. Perhaps tires accounted for the biggest portion of the jump, as Goodyear had come to the track with a new sticky compound tire, designed to go on wider rims than heretofore seen. Indeed, the first Firestone runner, Follmer, was three seconds slower than McLaren.

The story of the race, though, was the McLaren M6A. The first monocoque McLaren sports racer, it was powered by a 6.0 Chevy V-8 and had a wind-cheating wedge shaped body. Add to that extensive testing over the summer and two top rank Formula One drivers and the result was an unbeatable combination. This was the dawn of the *Bruce and Denny Show*.

The McLaren dominance was immediately apparent. From the front row of the grid, Hulme and McLaren whistled away into an easy lead. In their wake were some very surprised and disillusioned competition! Behind Hulme and McLaren, Dan Gurney ran third in the AAR Lola T-70, powered by a 5.7 Ford V-8 with special Gurney-Weslake heads. The Penske Lolas of Donohue and Follmer were next, trailed by Chuck Parsons in the 500-winning McLaren Elva, Surtees in the *works* Lola T-70, Hall's winged Chaparral, Revson's T-70, Scott in another tube framed McLaren Elva and Sam Posey's Caldwell.

For fans of Dan Gurney disappointment was in store, as the dark blue Lola dropped back with impending gearbox failure. Surtees was on the move, however, and he picked off those in front of him one by one, and moved into third place behind the McLarens. This soon became second, as Bruce McLaren pulled off course at turn 12 on lap six when the engine ran out of oil. However, Hulme was out front and flying, and nobody was going to catch him.

Later, Follmer spun, then had a lengthy stop with a broken radiator. Parsons had his gearbox break, Surtees continued after hitting a dog (!), Hall had handling problems after a coming-together with another car, and Revson broke the rear suspension. Up front, though, Hulme led easily over Surtees, Donohue, Hall and Hayes.

As the race reached its conclusion, John Cordts blew the engine big time in his McLaren Elva, dropping the contents of the sump in turn five, and spinning like a dervish in the mess. Surtees was right behind and could not avoid the oil. In a flash, his Lola was also rotating at great speed, and a wide eyed Donohue slid to the inside to avoid both Cordts and Surtees. Donohue was now second, with Surtees recovering before Hall came around to preserve third. Bad luck struck for Charlie Hayes, who dropped out of fifth with a duff alternator in Ralph Salyer's McKee.

Hulme stroked home the winner, averaging 104.454 mph, over four mph faster than the previous lap record!. He also set the new one mark standard at 2:14.9, 106.746 mph. Donohue was second, followed by Surtees, Hall, Skip Scott and Jerry Hansen, the latter two in McLaren Elva Mk. IIIs. A record crowd of over 51,000 jammed the roads for hours after the race, the displeasure of the traffic leavened by the memory of a really fine day at the races.

Hulme went on to win the next two Can-Ams at Bridgehampton and Mosport, while McLaren triumphed at Riverside and Laguna Seca. Finally, at the sixth and last event, the McLaren streak was broken as Surtees won in a Lola at Stardust. The Can-Am title went to McLaren, who placed better than Hulme when not winning. Hulme, of course, was second. As consolation, if it can be termed that, Denis Hulme won the 1967 World Championship. The SCCA's Trans-Am title went to Ford as the manufacturer, with Jerry Titus recognized as the best driver. Jerry Hansen purchased a Lola T-70 from Penske and won his first National Championship at Daytona in the SCCA Runoffs.

1968

The track again went with a three weekend schedule for 1968. They would be the June Sprints, the Badger 200/RA 500 and the Can-Am weekends. Two changes were that the Badger 200 would be part of an exciting new pro series, and there would be no Saturday support race on the Can-Am weekend. This would be the first time that RA did not have racing on Saturday. Public reaction was such that it would be a long time before a bare Saturday would again be on the schedule.

Off season, the SCCA made some news. The fledgling FB pro series of 1967 was vastly expanded and became a major series in its own right. What made it fly was the expansion of the series to include a new Formula A, which was for single-seaters powered by American pushrod V-8s of up to five liters displacement. This new series, dubbed Formula Continental, had eight events in its first year, and had manufacturers scrambling to build cars for it. Later, of course, Formula A came to be known as Formula 5000 and it had its heyday in the early to mid-1970s.

Jerry Hansen leads all the way to win the first Formula 5000 race at RA, the Badger 200. The reliable tube-frame Lola T-140 was the car of choice this year, taking the first four places.

The other change was on the club level where the Sports Racing classes were consolidated. The new class structure and names were A Sports Racing (ASR) for over two liters, BSR two liters, CSR 1300cc and DSR 850cc. In view of entry distribution the previous year or two, this made sense.

In mid-June the SCCA's club racers reassembled at Elkhart Lake for the June Sprints. This year's format had three races on Saturday with five on Sunday. The weather was good and over 25,000 fans spread over the hills, enjoying brats, beer and race cars.

EP, B and C Sedans began the show with a 60 mile race won by Fred Baker in a Porsche 911. Curiously enough, the Porsche 911 was classified as a sedan, due to the two small jump seats. This piece of illogic persisted for two years before reality intruded. A Morgan, of all cars, was second in the hands of Bob Stanford, winning EP. The Mini-Cooper of Ron Mulacek took CS.

The second race on Saturday was 100 miles for A - D Production and A Sedan. The Cobra era was ending, and the new for '68 Corvettes, with 427 engines, were the cars to have in AP. Two big Corvette teams ruled AP in SCCA's National ranks, the Owens-Corning sponsored pair of Tony DeLorenzo and Jerry Thompson, while out of Oklahoma came two DX backed cars for Brad Booker and Don Yenko. Yenko led the first part of the

race, but had a tire go flat after 10 laps. Then DeLorenzo took over until the finish. Thompson was second while John McComb was third, first in AS in a Ford Mustang. Group 44 took two classes, Bob Tullius CP in a Triumph TR 250, while John Kelly's older TR4 carried DP.

Formula Vee had grown so much that they had a race of their own. The car to have this year was the Zink, and the 60 mile event was a Zink 1-2-3, for Vern Clairborn, Bill Greer and Harry Ingle.

Sunday kicked off with Formula cars running 60 miles. This was the RA debut for the new FA cars, and Stew McMillan took the race in an Eisert after Jerry Hansen's new Lola T-140 dropped out with a blown head gasket. Chuck Dietrich took second overall and first in FB with a McLaren M4, while Tom Gelb was the FC winner in his ex-Pabst Brabham BT-2 FJ.

Bob Sharp took the small production race in a Datsun, with Group 44 taking its third cup of the weekend as Mike Downs won GP in a Triumph Spitfire. Rod Larson's Sprite took the HP, DS race with Bill Schley first in DS in a Fiat-Abarth. The C and D SR race was an upset, as the small DSR Ocelot-Saab of Ron Dennis won overall. It was no fluke, as Dennis led most of the way, a fair achievement for such a small engined machine.

This set the stage for the feature, run over 120 miles. The addition of classes was having the effect of necessitating more races, with the result being fewer laps per race in order to get them all in. The 120 miles was the shortest scheduled distance yet for a June Sprints feature. This year the Sprints were at last going to be the property of Jerry Hansen. He had led each of the two previous years, only to drop out. This year he finished, and he won. Driving an ex-Penske Lola T-70, Hansen was never headed as he led all 120 miles. He came home 58 seconds ahead of the second place car, the McLaren Elva Mk. III of Ron Courtney. Third was the similar McLaren Elva of Leonard Janke. Fred Baker, winner of the previous fall's Doug Revson Trophy 200 miler, was fourth overall and first in BSR in the same Porsche 906. Hansen averaged 96.597 mph and turned in the day's fast lap at 100.962 mph.

A month later the track welcomed spectators back with a double-header weekend. On Saturday, the Badger 200 would be a round of the new Continental Championship featuring the new Formula 5000 cars, while Sunday would be the Road America 500, again a round of the USRRC.

Besides the switch from production cars to formula cars, the Badger 200 was run to a distance of 200 kilometers, not miles. This would translate to 120 miles, the maximum distance these cars could run without refueling. Fourteen of the new Formula A cars were present, six of them Lola T-140s. Lola had been first into production with a car for this formula, a relatively simple space frame affair with a 5.0 Chevy stuffed in the tail. It was relatively crude compared to all that would follow, but it was available, it was cheap and it sold. Jerry Hansen, John Gunn, Bob Brown, Hank Candler, David Pabst and Brian O'Neill would be in the Lolas. The best FA chassis was the Eagle, a sophisticated monocoque car benefiting greatly from the engineering crossover from the Formula One and Indy projects. The Smothers Brothers had caught the racing bug at this time, and they entered the sole Eagle present for Lou Sell, who had won both previous races this year at Continental Divide and War Bonnet Park. There were two Eiserts present, plus two McKee Mk. VIIIs. The balance of the field was made up of various cars that would have short lives, including a McLaren Elva converted to an open wheel car. Since FB & FC were also part of the championship, running for class awards, some 24 of them filled out the field nicely.

In qualifying Hansen was the fastest, clocking 2:19.5. Next to him on the front row was Sell in the Eagle. Mak Kronn had Ike Uihlein's McKee on row two along with Candler's Lola. The fastest FB car was Chuck Dietrich's McLaren M4 at 2:32.9. Hansen carried his superiority over the race itself, as he took off like a rocket, and simply led all the way. His cause was aided by the difficulties that befell his closest pursuers. Kronn, Sell, Candler, Brown and Steve Durst in a Vulcan followed. Sell had passed Kronn, but on lap seven retired the Eagle with overheating. Kronn lasted but a couple laps more, when he lost his McKee at turn five and rather comprehensively rearranged it against the guardrail. Kurt Reinold in the other McKee ran third for a while, but his engine failed on lap 23 of 30. When all was said and done, Candler had bested O'Neill after a long duel to take second, followed by O'Neill, Gunn, Durst and Pabst.

In FB, Dietrich prevailed as expected, but he was chased by Mike Hiss, Martin Sellers, Bill Brack, Tom Tufts and R.B. Negley. Second finally went to Negley, with Brack third, both in Lotus 41s. Dick Smothers finished eighth in FB. FC went to Tom Gelb's old Brabham Junior, which was 11th overall.

This race would be a minor setback to Sell, as he proceeded to win five of the eight events in this inaugural season to become the SCCA's first Formula 5000 champion. The other two races went to George Wintersteen, also in an Eagle.

The next day was the 500. As opposed to the year before, a substantial field of 34 cars was present, headed by the Penske and Haas entries. Mark Donohue had won four of the previous seven rounds, but he had not put the

Tyler Alexander works on the new McLaren M8A while Bruce McLaren and Roger Penske chat in the Garage before the Can-Am race. The M8A featured the aluminum 427 Chevy V-8, easily recognizable by the large velocity stacks.

title away yet. Donohue was driving the Penske Sunoco McLaren M6A, the car that Bruce had driven to the Can-Am title the previous fall. The engine was an aluminum block 7.0 liter Chevy V-8, and it provided awesome power indeed. For the 500, Jerry Hansen would co-drive. Carl Haas was now the U.S. Lola distributor and he entered two T-70s for the driver pairings Chuck Parsons/Sam Posey and Posey/Skip Scott. They, as most entries, were powered by 6.0 liter cast iron versions of the Chevy small block V-8. Scott had won two USRRCs so far, and was chasing Donohue in the points battle. The new McKee Mk. X debuted, owned and entered by Ralph Salyer's Cro-Sal operation for Charlie Hayes and Charles Gibson. The Mk. X was very much a wedge-shaped car, looking for all the world like a giant door stop. Those who followed the movies saw Paul Newman capture the "Redburne 200" with this car in the movie *Winning*. All in all, the field featured seven McLarens, nine Lola T-70s, two McKees, three Porsche 906s, plus a smattering of other interesting cars.

In qualifying there was no denying the power of the 427 Chevy. Donohue took the pole at 2:15.9, with the Scott/Posey Lola second, fully four seconds behind. Hayes was third in the McKee, while the second Haas Lola took fourth. The fastest under two liter qualifier was Horst Kroll in the Kelly-Porsche, a Lotus 23-like special built in Canada by Wayne Kelly, who would co-drive.

The race itself was rather prosaic. As expected, Donohue motored away at the start. By the time he turned the blue McLaren over to Hansen at one-third distance, he had lapped the field. Hansen in turn continued to extend the lead. But not all was right with the big Chevy. Smoke began to puff out the exhausts on the overrun, and the puffs became a cloud before long. Finally, on lap 56 Hansen went down the escape road at turn five and switched off the engine, all the oil gone.

Scott's race in the first Haas Lola did not last long. On lap 11 a piston blew and the orange Simoniz car was parked. Haas then designated Scott as co-driver in the second Lola started by Parsons, since both were in the points race. As it was, Scott had lasted one lap longer than Hayes, who had the oil filter blow off the big Oldsmobile engine in the McKee on lap 10. Parsons, relieved by Scott, held second behind the Donohue/Hansen car until it left, then led the balance of the 125 laps. Their cause was complicated, however, by excessive oil usage, as the Lola smoked incessantly, and had

Jim Hall struggles with the Chaparral 2G, running rain tires on a dry track. These much narrower tires accentuate the tacked on fender flares for the much wider dry condition slicks.

to stop twice in the last 25 laps for replenishment.

Scott and Parsons came home winners, the second in a row for the pairing, and the third on the trot for Parsons. Bob Nagel and Ed Lowther were second in a McKee Mk. VII, six laps behind, while Brian O/Neill and Geoff Stevens brought a Lola T-70 home third. First in U-2, seventh overall, was the Porsche 906 of Cliff Phillips/Al Cervanka. Parsons and Scott averaged 94.730 mph, their pace understandably slowed by oil problems and a large lead.

This result knotted the USRRC point standings with one race left. At the Mid-Ohio finale three weeks later, Donohue would win the race and the championship.

Road America kicked off the six race Can-Am season with a 200 mile event on September 1st. The McLaren team, after dominating the previous year's series, came back with a car which was a big step up. The new McLaren M8A was built to take the 7.0 liter aluminum Chevy V-8, which was mounted on the rear bulkhead as a stress bearing member. The big orange machines clearly were the ones to beat, driven again by Bruce McLaren and Denis Hulme. Last year's M6A had been put into production as the '68 customer car and was designated M6B. Five of these were present led by the Penske entry for Mark Donohue, also 427 powered. Carroll Shelby entered an M6B for Peter Revson, this powered by a 7.0 aluminum Ford V-8, an engine which Ford denied existed! Lothar Motschenbacher had a 6.2 Ford in his M6B, while 6.0 Chevys powered the similar cars of Joakim Bonnier and Richard Brown. Penske had sold the M6A in which Donohue had won the USRRC to Jerry Hansen, who was running it with a 6.0 Chevy.

Lola's answer to the McLarens was the T-160. As ugly as the T-70 had been pretty, the car was behind schedule and only two were present. Carl Haas had a 7.0 Chevy version for Chuck Parsons, while Brett Lunger was in the Autodynamics car. Seven T-70s were present, headed by the 5.0 dohc Indy Ford engined car entered by George Bignotti for Mario Andretti. Skip Scott was forced into his Haas car, his T-160 not ready. Ron Bucknum, former Honda F-1 driver, had a 427 Chevy in the Agapiou Brothers car.

Other significant entries were a revised Chaparral 2G for Jim Hall, a Ferrari 350P4 of the North American Racing Team for Pedro Rodriguez, the McKee Mk. X for Charlie Hayes and the sole Caldwell D7 for Sam Posey. In all 29 cars made the show.

McLaren and Hulme immediately made it apparent that this year could be a repeat of the prior year. They took the front row in qualifying, with Bruce turning a lap at a record 2:09.8, 110.940 mph. Hall and Donohue were on row two, followed by Motschenbacher and Parsons, Revson and Andretti, Hayes and Rodriguez, Bucknum and Hansen, and so forth. The first four cars were faster than last year's best qualifying time.

Race day was wet. A steady rain fell most of the day, fortunately letting up halfway through the race. This sent most teams scurrying for the best rain tire setup, although Motschenbacher decided to start on slicks and see if he could pull off an upset if the track dried early.

On the first lap, Hulme and McLaren not unexpectedly zoomed off into the lead. Donohue created some excitement, certainly for those immediately following him, when he spun all by himself in the Carousel. Amazingly, nobody hit him and he got underway after dropping to 18th place. Andretti and Revson followed the two orange McLarens, with the field behind them taking on strange shapes as drivers moved up or fell back, depending upon their comfort level in the wet. Rain got in the injectors of Hall's Chaparral and Rodriguez's Ferrari. Hall had a lengthy pit stop to dry things out, while Rodriguez's red car was done for the day. Motschenbacher was dropping steadily back, the track too wet for slicks, while young Canadian department store heir George Eaton was reveling in the conditions. Driving a two year old McLaren Elva with a small block Ford, Eaton moved up to fourth in the early going, putting many bigger engined cars (and bigger name drivers) to shame. Indeed, even when the rain stopped at half distance and the track began to dry, Eaton still ran as high as seventh. Unfortunately, the throttle linkage broke two laps from the end, costing him one place.

Donohue was moving back up through the field and by the 15th lap was in fourth behind Andretti. He closed up onto Mario's tail, and then, on lap 48, the Indy Ford blew in a very big way. A huge cloud of smoke ushered a gallon of oil all over the front of Donohue's trailing M6B, but it was the sight of a connecting rod coming straight at him that impressed Donohue the most. Fortunately, the con rod was flying low and went straight through the McLaren's radiator. Exit Andretti, almost exit Donohue. The end of the race was close enough that Donohue could bring the overheating car home third behind the winning Hulme and second place McLaren.

Peter Revson brought the Shelby-entered McLaren-Ford home fourth, with Jim Hall recovering for fifth in the Chaparral. Motschenbacher had dropped as far down as 19th in the wet, but set the fastest lap of the day on the drying track at 2:16.0 to finish sixth. Hayes, Eaton, John Cordts in a McLaren Elva Mk. III and Posey filled out the top ten.

Due to Sunday morning's rain, the crowd count was down from 1967's record, but 41,000 still made the scene. While wet, they still enjoyed watching the most powerful racers in the world at work.

Hulme went on to win three of the six Can-Ams and took the championship. McLaren took one, Donohue triumphed at Bridgehampton and John Cannon pulled off the big upset by taking a small block three year old McLaren Elva Mk. III to victory at Laguna Seca in monsoon like conditions.

1968, however, was Mark Donohue's year. Besides winning the USRRC and one Can-Am, he also absolutely dominated the Trans-Am series, winning 10 of 13 events in a Penske Camaro. Overall, he won 16 major races and two championships. As if that were not enough, Penske entered him in a late season Indy car race with an eye on 1969.

1969

The SCCA picture underwent several changes in 1969. In the top levels, the tension between those who wanted to revert to a strictly amateur club and those who supported the professional growth broke out into warfare once again. The result this time was the departure of the long-time SCCA Executive Director, John Bishop, who was perceived as being on the side of the amateur backers. Ironically, Bishop went on to found the International Motor Sports Association (IMSA), which sanctioned nothing but professional events. Tracy Bird became the new SCCA Executive Director, with Jim Kaser heading up a pro division.

It is within this division that some major changes occurred. The USRRC was proving redundant, being run with the same cars as the Can-Am, but

John Cannon in the Eagle leads Peter Gethin's semi-works McLaren M10 in the first heat of the F-5000 race, eventually won by Cannon.

without the Can-Am's status, purses and J-Wax sponsorship. The result was that the USRRC was rolled into the Can-Am, which expanded from six to eleven events. To fill the gap felt by many tracks at the loss of a race date, the Continental Series was expanded, with more dates and a much higher profile. The Formula B and C portion of the Continental was split into a separate series, as the F-5000 cars were now being built in sufficient quantities to fill a field on their own.

Another new class appeared in the amateur ranks. Formula Ford had been born in England a few years earlier, and now it reached our shores. In many ways it was an update of Formula Junior. Designed as an inexpensive training series, the cars were tube framed, narrow tired single seaters powered by a 1600cc English Ford pushrod four. Over the years it proved to be immensely popular and was the SCCA's largest class for years.

June 14-15 saw the June Sprints attract a huge two day crowd numbering 60,000. This was bucking a nationwide trend when it came to SCCA National racing. With the growth of professional racing, tracks were promoting professional weekends strongly. National level racing was decreasing in

popularity, due to the fact that the name drivers were *graduating* to the pro ranks. Promotability was decreased, fields declined, spectators were harder to attract and many nationals went to a non-spectator basis. However, the June Sprints did not go down this path and to this day, continues to draw the biggest fields and more spectators than any other SCCA National. Having said that, the June Sprints would never achieve the levels of the late 1950s/early 1960s. Its status had changed from one of the major events of the year, to the major amateur event of the year.

Eight races comprised the 1969 Sprints. All were 60 milers, except the big production event on Saturday, which ran for 80 miles, and the sports racing feature on Sunday, which was 100 miles. The production car main was an Owens-Corning walkover. Tony DeLorenzo and Jerry Thompson loped away to an easy win in their twin red and silver Corvettes. Third placed Dick Durant was over a minute behind in his BP Corvette. The Formula car event saw Dick DeJarld come home first in a McKee Mk. XII Formula A. The strung out field had Tom Gelb second overall and first in FB in a Chevron, while Jim Clarke was a rather startling third overall in his Formula Ford Lotus 61.

The early days were rustic indeed. This is the public facility that stood for years at turn 7.

Jerry Hansen, having finally won the Sprints the year before, now began to make it a habit. Driving the ex-Bignotti Lola T-160, he led all 100 miles of the feature. Brooke Doran gave chase early, but only lasted 11 of the 25 laps before he was involved in an accident, eliminating his Lola T-160. Dave Causey, now in the ex-McLaren/Penske/Hansen McLaren M6A, ran about a half minute behind before he too spun off course on lap 16. The Lola T-160 of Jack Hinkle, a Wichita banker and oilman, finished about a lap behind Hansen. The closest battle of the race was in BSR, where Joe Jann took the win over Merv Rosen, who pulled a big gaffe. Rosen, driving a Porsche 906, thought that the Elva Porsche of Jann was a lap down, and he waved him by in the race's last mile. Rosen didn't realize his error until he pulled up to the flagstand to pick up a checker for a victory lap, only to discover that Jann had been there and gone!

On the weekend that Neil Armstrong first touched foot on the moon, the Formula A/5000 cars returned for the Road America 500. With the demise of the USRRC, Clif Tufte wanted to retain the Road America 500 as an event. This presented a problem, since no series at that time lent itself to the 500 mile format. Tufte, however, was nothing if not imaginative, and he devised a three heat, 500 kilometer format. Since the F-5000 cars were essentially sprint vehicles, with a maximum range of just over 100 miles, Tufte would run them in three 100 mile heats, with the scoring done on aggregate. That 300 miles was 12 short of 500 kilometers was of little concern, everyone agreeing that at whatever length, it would be an endurance run for this type of machine.

The day before the 500, the Badger 200 was run once again, this time in its old format of 200 miles for production cars. Alas, time had marched on and the once important race was now greeted with apathy by the entrants. With neither money nor points at stake, only 14 cars of widely varying capabilities ran. Bill Morrison and Chuck Wielosinski won the lackluster affair in a Corvette. This was the last Badger 200.

Sunday morning the 100 mile Formula B and C pro event was run. Mike Eyerly was the man to beat this year, and coming into RA he had won four of the first five events. Driving a Brabham BT-18 Eyerly fought off an early threat from the Chevron of Dick Smothers and the Lotus 59 of Fred Stevenson to win his fifth straight event. Smothers ran second until lap 13 of 25 when his engine blew a head gasket. Stevenson was delayed by a coming-together with the Titan of Earl Jones, but he recovered to take an eventual second place. Steve Brownstein was third in a Chevron, Jones fourth and

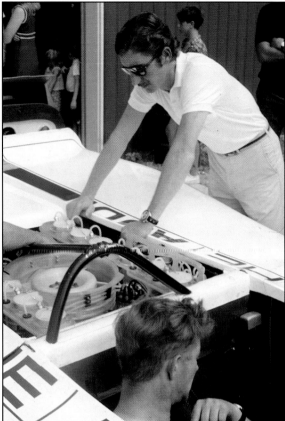

Switzerland's Jo Siffert looks at the flat 12 engine of the works Porsche 917-8 prior to the Can-Am race. Siffert would be a dnf come race day.

Tom Gelb fifth, also Chevron mounted. In the FC category, Denny Lokmer came out on top proving that there still was some life left in the ex-Gelb/ex-Pabst Brabham BT-2.

Reflecting the burgeoning popularity of F-5000, 30 cars ran the 500. McLaren had joined the fray, and its M10 was arguably the best chassis. Five were on hand, including the U.S. debut of the English Church Farm-entered, semi-works car for Peter Gethin, who was the runaway leader in the British F-5000 series. Others were for Jerry Hansen, George Eaton, Sam Posey and John Cordts. John Surtees had joined Brabham, Gurney and McLaren in building his own race cars, and his first effort, the TS-5, had two examples on hand, one being works entered for David Hobbs. John Cannon and Tony Adamowicz had year-old Eagles, but they were still very potent, as they had won four of the first five events. Stir in a good assortment of Lola T-140 and T-142s, some McKees, a Lotus and a Cooper, and it was a strong field indeed.

Peter Gethin, in the works McLaren, had taken the pole at 2:14.6, 106.984 mph. Cannon was alongside, with Hansen and Hobbs in row two, Eaton and Adamowicz in row three. As the first heat began under warm and sunny skies, Cannon took the lead, but behind him a big accident took out Hansen, Chuck Dietrich's Hogan Racing Lola and Kurt Reinold's McKee Mk. XII. Hansen spun, Dietrich T-boned him and Reinold hit the wreckage. Hansen was upside down, pinned in his car, but Reinold somehow righted the car and pulled him out. Fortunately, there were no injuries.

Cannon led the first 13 of 25 laps before Gethin got past. Gethin then opened up a 20 second lead going into the last lap, only to have it go sour. The McLaren's ignition shorted out, and Gethin rolled to a silent stop as a surprised Cannon breezed past to take the heat win. Eaton was second, Gethin third after managing to restart the engine, Adamowicz fourth, Cordts

Marilyn Motschenbacher and Bob Bondurant look on as Lothar Motschenbacher and his mechanics examine the broken flywheel on his McLaren M8B.

the first several laps before excessive bottoming wore a hole in his sump, spreading oil on the track. Hinkle spun out on the oil, Hansen retired to the pits, and Hinkle resumed, assuming that Hansen was long gone. He did not know that Hansen was out until he took the checkered flag, surprised to find himself first. While 58 year old Hinkle won, 60+ year old Orly Thornsjo was second in a Lola T-160. Clif Apel took third in a McLaren M6B. Bobby Rinzler won BSR in a Chevron B-16, while Gene Harrington won AS in a Camaro.

July doubleheader weekend saw two pro races each on Saturday and Sunday. The first day was formula, while Sunday was Trans-Am. Both series had spun their smaller siblings off into separate support series. The Formula B cars ran an 80 mile preliminary to the L&M Series feature, while the Under 2.0 liter sedans had their own 100 mile prelim to the Trans-Am.

Coming into the RA Formula B round, the series had belonged to Mike Eyerly. Driving a Chevron B17 for the Fred Opert Team, Eyerly had won all six rounds run so far. His Opert teammate, Alan Lader, was second in the standings. This day, however, the streak was broken. Jacques Couture led all the way in a Lotus 69, putting a minor speed bump in Eyerly's run to the season title. Eyerly ran second, but he was hindered by a bent front wing, sustained in early race contact, as well as an engine that would not pull maximum revs. Skip Walther diced early with Eyerly, but his challenge for second ended on lap 12 of 20 with a dead battery. Lader came home third in a Brabham BT-29, while Steve Brownstein took fourth in his Chevron B15. Forty-two cars started the race, of which eight were entered by the Opert Team! Twenty-eight finished, with Couture's winning speed being 98.869 mph. Eyerly turned the fastest lap at 2:23.9, 100.069 mph, the first time a FB car topped 100 mph.

Although Couture was to win the next race, the Eyerly express was not to be stopped. Mike easily won the FB title with eight wins. Lader was second, having scored one win, while Couture took third. Fourth place in the season standings, incidentally, was Nick Craw, who in 1983 would take over the presidency of the SCCA.

The L&M Continental 5000 cars ran 100 miles in the Saturday feature. Thirty-five cars made for a full field indeed, with many examples of the latest Lola, McLaren, Surtees and Lotus cars present. John Cannon came into the race leading the points, having won two of the first six events. He was driving a McLaren M10 for Hogan-Starr Racing. Ron Grable, in a Lola T-190 for Shamrock Racing, was his closest competitor, also having notched two wins. Gus Hutchison had won the other two races in his Brabham BT-26A Formula 1 car, but had switched to a Lola T-190 for the rest of the season. Last year's sensation, David Hobbs, was joining the series at RA in a Team Surtees TS-5, having spent the first half of the year racing in Europe.

In qualifying, Cannon was the class of the field. He captured the pole at 2:12.9, significantly faster than Hobbs, who was on the outside of row one with 2:14.6. Row two was Grable and Eppie Wietzes, McLaren M10. Row three comprised Hutchison and George Follmer, in the Falconer Lotus 70.

At the start, Hobbs got the jump on Cannon and led the pack into turn

Lap 46 of 50, Hulme and Gethin on their way to a presumed 1-2 finish during the 1970 Can-Am.

one. He held onto the lead, with Cannon, Follmer, Grable, Wietzes, Hutchison, Spence Stoddard in a Lola T-190 and Bill Brack's Lotus 70 following. TV star Dick Smothers was already in trouble with ignition problems and retired his Lotus 70 after only one lap. After a few laps Grable had discovered that his brakes were not all they should be, as he spun back to sixth. Then Brack and George Wintersteen, also in a Lotus 70, demoted him two more places.

By half distance, Cannon was closing on Hobbs, Hutchison had spun out of the race, and Grable was acclimating himself to his brake problems and began moving back up. Cannon harried Hobbs for a couple laps and got past going into turn five on lap 14 of 25. The order now was Cannon, Hobbs, Follmer, Wietzes, Grable, Wintersteen and Brack. Hobbs mounted a charge in the closing laps. On the last lap, he almost pulled it off, catching Cannon in the final turn, and drag racing him to the finish line. Cannon held on though and took the win by a car length. Follmer, Wietzes, Grable and Brack filled out the top six. Twenty-seven cars finished the race with Cannon averaging 106.901 mph; Hobbs took the fastest lap at 2:12.9, 108.352 mph.

While Cannon held on to win the Championship, he was not to win another race the rest of the year. In the last six races, Hobbs won two, Follmer won two and Mark Donohue, running just the last three races in a Penske-entered Lola T-190, won two of them. Hutchison finished second in points, with Hobbs third.

The 100 mile Under 2.0 Liter sedan event ran Sunday morning and Horst Kwech led start to finish in an Alfa Romeo GTA. Peter Schuster gave chase in a BMW 2002Ti, but lacked the straightaway speed to effectively challenge Kwech. He finished four seconds behind. Harry Theodoracopulos, Kwech's teammate, ran third until spinning off, ceding the place to the BMW of Russ Norburn. It was an Alfa year in this category, with Kwech winning three of the 11 rounds and other Alfa victories being scored by Bert Everett (3), Lee Midgley (2) and Gaston Andrey (1). The other two wins

went to BMW.

The Trans-Am in 1970 was enjoying a truly vintage year. Virtually all the Detroit pony car makers were running factory supported teams and the competition was fierce. After having won two straight titles for Camaro, Penske had switched to American Motors and was running two Javelins for Mark Donohue and Peter Revson. Jim Hall's Chaparral Team had replaced Penske as the Chevrolet entrant, running two cars for Hall and Ed Leslie. Ford was represented by the two Bud Moore Mustangs of Parnelli Jones and George Follmer. T/G Racing ran a Pontiac Firebird for Jerry Titus, the 1967 Trans-Am champion. Dan Gurney's All American Racers had the Plymouth contract and ran a Barracuda for Swede Savage with Gurney occasionally driving a second car around his Formula 1 and Can-Am commitments. Autodynamics, builder of FF, FV and abortive Can-Am and F-5000 cars, had the Dodge deal to run a Challenger for Sam Posey.

Most sadly, in practice Jerry Titus had steering failure and crashed headlong into the bridge abutment at turn 13. He suffered severe head and internal injuries from which the popular and versatile former editor of *Sports Car Graphic* magazine would succumb two weeks later.

A field of 36 cars ran on Sunday. The two works Mustangs of Follmer and Jones headed the grid, Follmer turning the pole lap at 2:31.0. Leslie and Savage were on row two, while Posey and Donohue shared the third row, followed by Hall and Revson. At the first turn, Jones, Follmer and Leslie came together disputing the turf, with the resulting damage eliminating Follmer and Leslie. Jones kept going in the lead, while Savage pitted to repair some minor damage. Posey and Donohue followed Jones. Posey took Jones for the lead on lap two, followed by Donohue, Revson and Savage, making up time fast.

On lap 10, Penske strategy came into play. With all cars planning on two stops in the 200 miles the window was in the area of laps 16-18 and 34-36. However, Roger brought Donohue in early, giving him fuel, and bringing him back out, down several places, but not only out of sequence but also away from the snarling mass up front. This allowed Donohue to lap faster alone than in traffic and it was a telling point.

Jones pitted with two flat tires, putting Savage into second with the Javelins of Revson and Donohue third and fourth and Milt Minter fifth in the independent '69 Camaro of Roy Woods American Racing Associates. When the field all came in for their first pit stops, who but Donohue should breeze into the lead, comfortably ahead of Posey and Savage. Revson had retired the second Javelin by this time, a drive shaft having broken. Later, Posey would spin twice, handing second to Savage.

On lap 30 Donohue made his second and last stop. Savage took over the lead for two laps, but Donohue had come out of the pits right behind him and soon retook the lead. When Savage and the rest pitted, Donohue was home free and came home an easy winner, giving AMC its second ever Trans-Am win. Savage finished second, followed by Posey, Hall, Jones and Minter. Donohue averaged 91.839 for the 200 miles.

The 11 race Trans-Am series title went to Ford, with Parnelli Jones taking the driver's prize. Jones would win five events, with Donohue taking three, and one each going to Follmer, Minter and Vic Elford, who replaced Jim Hall in the Chaparral Camaro. Hall retired as a driver, the legs he injured in a Can-Am crash at the end of 1968 not up to the strain. AMC took second in the manufacturers' race, with Chevrolet, Dodge and Plymouth following. Pontiac had no top six finishes, never recovering from the loss of Titus.

The fall Can-Am race had been moved forward one week, and was now on the last weekend in August. The 200 mile Can-Am was on Sunday, of course, and Clif Tufte scheduled a non-championship 80 mile Formula B race on Saturday to entertain the crowd. That race was a one-two for the Fred Opert entries of Mike Eyerly and Alan Lader. They traded the lead between themselves a few times before Eyerly won in a Chevron B17. Lader drove a Brabham BT-29 to second, with Matt Spitzley and Randy Lewis third and fourth, both in Brabhams. Opert himself took fifth in a Chevron.

One sad change in the Can-Am this season was the absence of Bruce McLaren. The universally popular driver/constructor/entrant/engineer had tragically lost his life in a test crash before the season began. The strength of the organization that he built was affirmed by the fact that Teddy Mayer, who took over the running of the team, and Denny Hulme were not only able to hold it together, but kept winning. Coming into the RA round, the works McLarens had won 18 straight Can-Ams including, of course, all five so far that season. Dan Gurney had won the first two races, at Mosport and Ste. Jovite, before he had to bow out due to a sponsor conflict. He was replaced by Peter Gethin. Hulme had won at Watkins Glen, Edmonton and Mid Ohio coming into RA.

While the McLaren team was running new M8D models, last year's M8Bs had been sold to Lothar Motschenbacher and Oscar Koveleski. This season's customer car was the M8C, and one was on hand for Roger McCaig. To this add two M12 and five M6Bs and 12 McLarens were in the 31 car field.

Carl Haas had entered the latest Lola, the T-220, for Peter Revson. Eleven other Lolas, ranging from several year old T-70s to T-160s, T-163s and one T-165 were also present. Tony Dean had the only Porsche, the same 908 Spyder in which he had finished fifth the previous year. The sole Ferrari was the North American Racing Team 512-S for Pedro Rodriguez. The car, designed for the classic endurance races, was out of place in the sprint format of Can-Am racing. BRM had built their first Can-Am car, the P-154, for George Eaton. The Agapiou Brothers were trying once again with the ungainly Ford G7A, being driven this weekend by John Cannon. Add in a couple old McKees and that was the field.

As could be expected, Denis Hulme was the class of the field. His 465ci aluminum Chevy powered M8D took the pole at 2:10.6, 110.260 mph. The four second difference from the year previous can be attributed to the lack of high wings acting directly on the rear suspension. Now most cars had low wings affixed directly to the chassis. While still giving bags of downforce, this setup gave considerably less than before.

Revson was alongside Hulme on row one, while Motschenbacher had his ex-works M8B in third. David Hobbs put out a great effort placing the T/G Racing McLaren M12 fourth on the grid, subbing for the sadly missing Jerry Titus. Bob Bondurant was fifth in the Smith-Oeser Racing Lola T-163B, the one-off late 1969 development of the T-163. Gethin was next, then Gary Wilson in a Lola T-163, Dean, Chuck Parsons in the Doug Shierson Racing Lola T-163 and Vic Elford, performing very well indeed in Vic Nelli's obsolete Lola T-70. The first five cars were all powered by the large 465ci (7.6 liter) Chevys, while Bondurant and most of the rest had the *small* 427ci Chevys. Sunday morning Eaton did a few slow laps in the late-arriving BRM before parking it with unrepairable engine problems. Scratch one challenger.

Peter Revson led the first lap in the L&M Lola, but on lap two both Hulme and Gethin blew past. Effectively, the race for first was over, the McLarens once again being overwhelmingly superior. Hobbs had already pitted with body damage, taking him out of the top runners. On lap four Hulme decided to let Gethin have some fun, and waved him past. Behind the two orange M8Ds came Revson, Motschenbacher, Bob Brown in the ex-Gurney *McLeagle* M6B, Wilson, Elford, Rodriguez and Parsons.

At the end of 12 laps, Hulme apparently thought that Gethin had enough fun, and retook the lead. Revson dropped out around this time with a broken halfshaft, while Motschenbacher held down third. Brown, Dave Causey in a Lola T-163 and Bondurant followed. On lap 25 Motschenbacher was out. SCCA's results sheet attributed his retirement to *suspension failure*. True enough, but what wasn't mentioned was that the broken suspension had thrown the McLaren M8B violently off course at the Carousel, where it destroyed itself in the trees. Lothar was fortunate indeed to escape with minor injuries.

Matters remained static until lap 37 of 50 when Hulme suddenly spun in turn five, stalling the engine. Corner workers hustled to the scene and gave him a push start, getting Hulme underway still in second. Only Brown was still on the lead lap with them. Since Hulme was the team leader, Gethin obeyed slow down orders from Teddy Mayer and let him past into the lead on lap 45. Things remained this way for the duration, with Hulme and Gethin giving photographers the side-by-side 1-2 shot at the flag.

But no! The SCCA Can-Am rules forbade push starts and Hulme was out! Though Mayer worked himself into a frenzy protesting, it was to no avail; the rule book held. Hulme was not scored past the 37th lap. Peter Gethin was the winner, much to his surprise. Bondurant was second, Causey third, Wilson fourth, Dean again fifth in the three liter Porsche and Brown sixth after having lost what would have been second three laps from the end due to a flat tire.

If this race was a setback for Hulme, the next one at Road Atlanta would be a bigger shocker. A series of accidents and mechanical breakdowns removed Hulme, Gethin, Revson and Eaton all from the lead; Tony Dean won in his diminutive Porsche 908, breaking McLaren's winning streak at 19. That was a temporary setback, though, as Hulme won the last three Can-Ams at Donnybrooke, Laguna Seca and Riverside to easily win his second Can-Am championship. Motschenbacher hastily replaced his destroyed M8B with first his last year's M12 then a new M8C to continue gathering points for second in the standings. Gethin was third after his mid-season start. In all Hulme won six races, Gurney two and Gethin one as McLaren won nine of the ten events. Business as usual!

51

1971

F-5000 racers travel through Thunder Valley. Jim Dittemore, David Hobbs and Jerry Hansen would all taste the lead.

As racing entered 1971, the growth of the sport saw the creation of a new class of race car and the inception of two new professional series. The SCCA in conjunction with Volkswagen created Super Vee. Whereas Formula Vee was based on the 1300cc VW engine in a chassis utilizing VW's antiquated suspension system, Super Vee was for 1600cc engines in a modern race car chassis. Naturally, a professional series immediately followed, sponsored by Volkswagen and christened the VW Gold Cup. The other new pro series was the formalizing of what had been the under two liter portion of the Trans-Am. After having run concurrently with the Trans-Am cars for the first several years, the sheer volume of entries saw some tracks run the U-2s as a separate race. This year the SCCA created the Two-Five Challenge, a separate pro series for sedans under 2.5 liters.

Over at IMSA, John Bishop was running some low key pro races for Formula Fords, small sedans, and as the headliner, GT sports cars. Little note was taken at this time, but in future years big things would come from it.

Road America again scheduled three big weekends; the June Sprints, the Trans-Am/Formula 5000 and the Can-Am. The three other SCCA pro series, Formula B, the Two-Five Challenge and the VW Gold Cup, would all run in support roles.

A crowd of 52,000 people assembled the weekend of June 19-20 for the annual June Sprints. 18,000 showed up on Saturday despite heavy fog and dripping skies, while 34,000 found the weather much better on Sunday. In addition, over 400 cars entered the eight race program. The main event on Saturday was an 80 mile race for A-D Production. Big Corvettes abounded, and the National AP champion, John Greenwood, took an immediate lead over Ron Weaver. This lasted for half the race until almost simultaneously Greenwood and Weaver both dropped out with engine failure. This put Jerry Hansen into the lead in his Corvette, and Hansen led to the finish despite spinning three times due to tires that never

quite came *on*. Allan Barker and Jeff Miller brought their Corvettes home second and third.

Sunday morning's all Formula race was a win for Kurt Reinold in a McKee Mk. XII. Jim Dunkel had replaced his older McKee with a Lola T-190, but he still could not catch Reinold. Taking third overall and first in FB was Chuck Dietrich in a Brabham BT-35. Howie Fairbanks, also Brabham mounted, won FC while Gordon Smiley was the FF winner in a Merlyn.

After Bill Niemeyer won the C and D SR event in his Elva for the second year in a row it was time for the weekend's feature race. This was 100 miles for A and B SR and AS. Once again it would be a contest between Jerry Hansen and Jack Hinkle. This year Hansen was in the ex-Revson Lola T-220, while Hinkle had the same Lola T-165 in which he had won the year previous. However, the race itself did not live up to its promise. Hansen was simply too much. He qualified on the pole, took off at the start and proceeded to lap the field in taking an easy win. Hinkle came in second, with Pete Harrison third overall and first in BSR in a Lola T-212. Dick Kantrud won AS in a Camaro.

At year's end, Hansen attempted to improve upon his *double* at the Sprints by running in three classes in the SCCA National Championship Runoffs at Road Atlanta. He almost did it, winning ASR in the Lola T-220, FA in a Lola T-192, but falling short in AP in his Corvette, taking third place.

The Saturday of the July weekend was reserved for a 200 mile Trans-Am go. Following the halcyon days of 1970, this season was a bit of a comedown. All factories except American Motors had pulled out of the Trans-Am, leaving Penske to run one Javelin for Mark Donohue. Bud Moore had kept his team intact from 1970, but now was running two Ford Mustangs without factory support. Nonetheless, the cars driven by George Follmer and Peter Gregg were the stiffest competition to Donohue. Roy Woods had purchased the two 1970 Javelins from Penske, recloaked them in 1971 bodywork and with help from Penske ran them for Peter Revson and himself. At RA this weekend, he turned the wheel of his mount over to Vic Elford. The rest of the 35 car field was made up of independents and local club racers.

In qualifying Donohue had not unsurprisingly taken the pole, but Elford, in his first outing in a Javelin, was right beside him. Follmer had qualified third, but that did not prevent him from grabbing second from Elford going into turn one. Donohue led, but Follmer was right behind, clearly the only competition to the flying Javelin. Follmer ran in second until lap 14 when he had a tire go down. He lost eight places, coming back on track in tenth. At that, he was much better off than Revson, whose Javelin was out at the start with a failed oil pump.

With Follmer's problem, Elford took over second, but he was so far behind Donohue that his only hope was that Mark would encounter mechanical problems. Unfortunately for *Quick Vic*, it was his car that had troubles, and the Javelin dropped out of second on lap 30 with a failed oil pump. Second place then fell to Follmer, who had made a great recovery, and had clawed his way through the field. Once having reached second, however, Follmer's progress stalled, as Donohue was a lap ahead.

Two hours, five minutes after he took the green, Donohue brought the Penske Sunoco Javelin home in first place. Follmer was second, with Jerry Thompson third, Peter Gregg fourth, Tony DeLorenzo fifth and Warren Tope sixth, all in 1970 Ford Mustangs. Donohue averaged 92.119 mph.

For Donohue, the Trans-Am season was a breeze. He won seven of the 10 races, with Follmer winning the other three, two in the Bud Moore Mustang and one in a Roy Woods Javelin. AMC took the Manufacturers' title, winning eight of the ten rounds.

On Sunday morning the Two-Five Challenge ran for 75 minutes. The prospect would be for an Alfa Romeo vs. Datsun battle. Alfa, represented by several entrants all running GTAs, had won three of the first five events. Datsun was making its first foray into sedan racing, and Pete Brock had assembled a top-notch effort. Two Datsun 510 sedans were on hand, for John Morton and Mike Downs. Morton had won two races so far.

Morton started from the pole, but Horst Kwech took the lead in an Alfa. Unfortunately, his time at the front only lasted one lap, as he rolled into the pits on lap two with a flat tire. For many laps thereafter, Morton and Downs ran 1-2, but on lap 15 the windshield on Downs' car shattered. He had to make a stop to have new glass installed, and that put Bert Everett's Alfa GTA into second. Morton covered 27 laps in the 75 minutes, taking the win over Everett. Kwech recovered to take third, with Lee Midgley fourth in another GTA. The BMW 2002 of Don Pike took fifth. Datsun went on to take the season manufacturers' crown.

The L&M Continental 5000 Championship race was run to a new format. SCCA had decreed that all rounds would be contested over two heats, with the overall positions being scored on aggregate. Hence, the RA round would be run in two 24 lap, 96 mile heats. David Hobbs and Sam Posey were the story of the year, not only fighting over first place on the track, but carrying on a verbal feud that made some great fodder for the journalists. That the ribbing and insults between the two were all a put-on, a huge inside joke between the two, did nothing to reduce pre-race hype, which actually did a lot to promote the series. Hobbs was driving a McLaren M10 for Carl Hogan's team, while Posey was in a new Surtees TS-8 for the Champ-Carr outfit. In the previous four races, Hobbs had won two, Posey one and Frank Matich one. Hobbs and Posey were one-two in the standings.

In qualifying Posey put it together and took the pole at 2:11.007,

Jackie Stewart did not win the 1971 RA Can-Am, but everyone knew he was there. This was during Stewart's *Mod Scot* period.

109.924 mph. Sitting outside the front row was a surprise only in that he was not a series regular. Jerry Hansen had recently taken delivery of a Lola T-192 and was eight-tenths of a second behind Posey. Row two was Hobbs and Jim Dittemore in the Kastner-Brophy Lola T-192, while row three held Ron Grable in a one-off chassis called an American Mk. I and Eppie Wietzes in a McLaren M18. In all, 30 cars qualified for the race.

Heat one began in a light rain, with most cars still on dry tires and praying that the rain would pass. Hansen took the lead going into the first turn, and at the end of the first lap led Posey, Dittemore, Hobbs, Wietzes and the rest. The first major change came on lap five when both Posey and Hobbs spun on oil, dropping back. Wietzes now chased Hansen, trying several times to get past, but unable to pull it off. Hobbs had dropped back to 11th, but was regaining ground rapidly, moving back into third on lap 11. The top three stayed as such until the final laps of the heat. Hobbs took second from Wietzes on lap 21, but could not catch Hansen, who won the heat by four seconds over Hobbs. Wietzes was third, Dittemore fourth, Posey back up to fifth and Brett Lunger sixth in a Lola T-192. Even with the rain, Hansen averaged 104.515 mph in claiming the win.

The cars lined up for heat two in the order in which they had finished the first 96 mile go. The heat got off to a bit of a rocky start when the pace car dnf'd at turn 12(!), but that did not prevent Hansen from nabbing first going into turn one. Hobbs, Wietzes, Dittemore, and the rest followed. Posey had an early end to his afternoon when his Surtees broke the brake master cylinder on lap four. On lap seven, Hansen missed a shift, and Hobbs went past for his first lead of the day. It did not last long, however, as Dittemore surprised both Hobbs and Hansen a lap later. Dittemore led until lap 12, when Hobbs was able to counterattack and regain the lead. This time Hobbs intended to make it stick, and he began to pull out a lead. Dittemore ran second and Wietzes third, having passed Hansen, whose Lola was beginning to experience gearbox problems. On lap 19 Dittemore blew his engine, so Wietzes followed Hobbs home in second, with Hansen third, followed by Evan Noyes in a McLaren M18, the Lotus 70 of Bill Brack and Gregg Young in a Formula One Surtees TS-7. Although the track was dryer, the speed was not much faster, 106.446 mph.

On aggregate, the second and first places of David Hobbs gave him the overall victory. Jerry Hansen was second, followed by Eppie Wietzes, Evan Noyes, Gregg Young and, in sixth, the four year old Eagle of John Gunn. Hobbs went on to win the next two races and took the series championship. He had five wins in the eight races held. Matich, Posey and Lunger won the other three.

The last weekend in August the Can-Am series returned for round six of ten. Running in support were rounds of the FB Championship and the FSV Gold Cup. Saturday's race was the last of the season for the FB cars, and the title was still up in the air. Two drivers, Alan Lader and Bert Hawthorne, were in the showdown. Lader, as the year before, was driving for Fred Opert, in a Brabham BT-35. Hawthorne was driving a Tui. Hawthorne had the upper hand early in the race. He had to finish ahead of Lader by at least two places, and he was leading the 80 mile event. Bill Gubelman was running second in a March 712, while Lader was in third. Then it all went wrong going into Canada Corner. Hawthorne lost the brakes on his car and took a wild, bucking ride down the escape road, virtually wrecking the car and shaking himself up considerably. Gubelman briefly led until Lader passed and then spun out on lap 14. Lader took the win 14 seconds ahead of Nick Craw in a Brabham, Fred Stevenson's Lotus and the Brabham of Mike Hall. Lader wrapped up the crown with Hawthorne second and Craw third.

Sunday morning saw the first FSV Gold Cup race at RA. Bill Scott, who was to win the inaugural series championship, had a fairly easy race as he won comfortably. Scott was driving a Royale FSV. Tom Reddy led the first lap in a Lola T-250 until passed by Scott, then held second for the duration. The Zeitler of John Magee was third, ahead of the Zink of Harry Ingle.

Coming into the RA round, Peter Revson was leading the Can-Am standings. Driving a works McLaren M8F alongside Denis Hulme, Revson had won two of the five events so far. Hulme had taken one. The M8F was the final iteration of the great M8 line of McLaren Can-Am cars. One of last year's M8D cars was on hand, having been sold to Lothar Motschenbacher who was third in points. This year's customer car was the M8E and three were on hand. Motschenbacher entered one for Gregg Young, Roy Woods had Vic Elford in his, and Bob Brown was driving his own. Oscar Koveleski had Tony Adamowicz in his M8B, and there were several older M6Bs on the grounds.

Against this McLaren strength, Carl Haas shot the works. Lola built an entirely new car, the T-260. To drive it, Haas hired none other than two time World Champion Jackie Stewart. As it turned out, the T-260 could be classified as a bit of a dog, and it was only through Stewart's skill that it had won two races so far. The Lola customer car was the T-222, a development of last year's works T-220. Two were present for Hiroshi Kazato and Dave Causey. Other Lolas in the field were all rather tired older cars, including a very elderly T-70 with a small 5.7 engine for none other than Don Devine, back after an eight year layoff.

The American Shadow effort made its first RA appearance with a Mk. II for Jackie Oliver. Not as small as the previous year's abortive Mk. I *roller skate* that had scared the dickens out of George Follmer and Vic Elford among others, the Mk. II was still noticeably smaller than the other cars. Porsche reappeared with a factory effort, a new 917-10 Spyder for Jo Siffert. Whereas the 917-8 of two years previous had been based on the endurance racing coupe chassis, the 917-10 was a new design, much tidier and compact. The main limiting factor on its potential was the 5.0 flat 12 engine, which gave away bags of power to the big Chevy V-8s. This year all the top teams were running 494ci (8.1 liter) versions of the aluminum block Chevy engine. Breathing through great intake trumpets sticking high out of the rear deck and exhausting through pipes the size of furnace ducting, these were awesome indeed.

Speeds were advancing once again after a year's drop due to rule changes. Hulme dutifully took the pole at 2:06.662, 113.688 mph. Oliver gave the best showing yet for a Shadow in qualifying second, albeit 2.3 seconds slower than Hulme. Stewart, dissatisfied with the handling of his L&M sponsored Lola, was third on the grid with Motschenbacher alongside. Row

Peter Revson talks with Stirling Moss in the Mercedes pace car during his victory lap after the Can-Am race. Revson's last to first performance was one of five victories that year.

three comprised Elford and Siffert, with Kazato and Adamowicz in row four. What of Revson? He was in California, qualifying for the Ontario 500 Indy car race, and missed qualifying altogether. He would start the Can-Am from the last row, with no time. In all, a relatively small field of 23 cars would start.

As the race started, Hulme blasted off into an immediate lead and Revson started picking off the backmarkers. Hulme led, followed by Stewart, Oliver, Elford, Siffert, Motschenbacher and so on. By lap eight of 50 Revson was all the way up to third place and breathing down Stewart's neck. Stewart, however, saved him the trouble of passing when he dropped out on lap 11 with overheating, disappointing the crowd of 42,000. It looked to be another McLaren 1-2, as Hulme and Revson cruised around, well ahead of the rest.

Then, on lap 17 Hulme glided silently out of the woods at turn five, went straight down the escape road and parked the big orange machine. Getting out, he looked underneath at the puddle of oil that was quickly forming, shrugged and walked away. The crankshaft had broken in half. Revson thundered by, and the race was his.

Elford now ran second, with Motschenbacher third and Siffert fourth. As the race neared conclusion, Siffert took a place when Motschenbacher had a quick spin, and then took second from Elford when the Englishman's tires began to go off. The race ran out with Revson winning, followed by Siffert, Elford, Motschenbacher, Kazato and Causey in the top six.

Two thirds of the way through the race, a McLaren M6B driven by Stanley Szarkowicz went out of control on the rise before the pits, spinning across the grass and pit entry road before flipping over the fence into a spectator area. Miraculously, only three people were hit, and they all suffered minor injuries. It could have been a lot worse.

Revson went on to win five of the ten Can-Ams, to three for Hulme and two for Stewart to take the championship. It was McLaren's fifth in a row, but a portent of the future was Siffert's second place finishes at Mid Ohio and RA. Back in Stuttgart, a *much* improved version was under development.

Of immense pride to the track was the observation by Jackie Stewart that RA was one of the best tracks in the world and that it should be the home of the United States Grand Prix.

1972

In 1972 IMSA began to rattle the cage of the SCCA as the country's main provider of road racing. It began with the announcement that Camel cigarettes would be sponsoring their main series, to be known as the *Camel GT*. Tracks began signing up to run these events, staged at this time for production-type sports cars and dominated by Corvettes, Porsche 911s and Porsche 914/6s. With Camel beating the drums, and drivers attracted by the type of racing offered, IMSA began a period of growth that would come to dominate road racing in the 1980s and into the 1990s. While SCCA led the way at this time with their multiple offerings of major series, this was not to last, and the balance would shift.

Road America, in the meantime, was continuing to draw very well with its lineup of three weekends featuring the entire SCCA lineup. Besides, the Chicago Region of the SCCA was so closely connected to the track that any suggestion of an IMSA weekend was quickly dismissed. One development at the track this year, though with no public ramifications, was the addition of a non-spectator regional race. The Chicago Region negotiated a date in September on which they staged this race. Up until then, with the exception of a one-off regional in 1959, only National and higher licensed drivers had the opportunity to race at RA. This closed race allowed the regional license holder to experience RA.

The June Sprints again saw over 400 entries perform in front of over 30,000 fans. Jerry Hansen attempted to win three different races on the weekend with a Corvette in AP, a Lola T-300 in FA and the Lola T-220 in ASR.

As the year previous, Group 44 was again a force at the Sprints, winning three classes. Brian Fuerstenau took overall as well as DP in the D and EP, BS event in a Triumph GT6. John Kelly came home first in the F and GP, CS race in a Triumph Spitfire, while John McComb was the CP winner in a Triumph TR6. Turner Woodard won the DSR event in a Bobsy-Saab, while Mike Landrum took FF in a Winkelmann and Ted Schroeder won FV in a Lynx. Second in Vee was Dave Weitzenhof, who would be a frequent Sprints class winner over the next 20+ years.

In the big Formula race, Hansen easily led the first few laps before he had to make a pit stop with a misfiring engine. After the loose spark plug wire was reattached, Hansen was one and one-half laps in arrears, and that was just too much to make up in 60 miles. Mike Hall won the race in his FB Brabham BT-35, followed by Jim Harrell in a Lola T-240 FB and James King in a FB March 722. Hansen recovered enough ground to finish fifth overall and first in FA.

He had better luck in the A-C Prod, AS 60 miler. He led easily, taking his Corvette to the checker ahead of Charlie Kemp's Corvette. Allan Barker won BP, also in a Corvette, while the AS win went to the Camaro of Tuck Thomas.

That was the extent of good luck for Hansen, though. In the sports racing feature he leapt into a comfortable early lead as expected, but soon the

Bert Everett lifts a wheel as he takes turn 8 in the Alfa Romeo GTA during the Trans-Am Two-Five Challenge.

big Chevy in his Lola T-220 began to bang and bark. He pitted halfway through the 100 mile race, but there was nothing immediate his crew could do about the electrical fault that was causing the severe misfire. Hansen went back out to salvage what he could, but the car would not perform. This opened the door wide for Pete Harrison, who went right through. The Atlanta driver took the win in a BSR Lola T-290 while Bill Barber was second in a BSR Chevron B21. In his last race RA director Bill Cooper came home third overall and first in ASR. Cooper was driving the Ferrari 350-P4 that Rodriguez had driven in the '68 Can-Am.

Hansen may have been short in the luck department at the June Sprints, but he made up for it at the SCCA's National Championship Runoffs at Road Atlanta in November. He bagged *three* titles, in ASR, FA and AP, a feat never matched before or since.

July rolled around, and that meant the Trans-Am/F-5000 weekend. This year, the Trans-Am was held on Saturday, with the Two-Five Challenge Sunday morning, followed by the L&M Continental F-5000 race. As last year, the L&M race was being run in two heats, scored overall on aggregate.

The Trans-Am in 1972 was now totally bereft of factory support. AMC was still backing Penske, but had switched their attention from the Trans-Am to NASCAR. The top team in the Trans-Am was the Roy Woods Racing outfit, which was running two AMC Javelins for George Follmer and Woods. The rest of the competitors were all independents in pony cars of varying vintages. Only seven races comprised the series this year, and Follmer had won four of the five preceding Elkhart. The other win had gone to the Pontiac Firebird of Milt Minter.

Follmer took the pole in qualifying, with Warren Tope alongside in a Mustang. Row two consisted of the Javelins of Bill Collins and Woods, while the third row held the Camaros of Warren Agor and Gene Harrington. In all, 42 cars started the race, a full field indeed. Follmer was the expected early leader, with Tope next, then a scramble involving Collins, Harrington, Minter, Agor and Steve Bradley's Camaro. Tope closed the gap, and took the lead on lap 10 when Follmer briefly went off course. George charged back and retook the point when Tope had to pit for a flat tire. Minter was now second, with Woods, Agor and Collins leading Tope. Warren was on that day and regained second place by lap 18 of 50.

The second round of pit stops for fuel did little to change matters, and Follmer appeared to be in total control; but it was not to be. Shortly after his last stop, the engine in Follmer's Javelin began to act up. After a couple futile pit stops, Follmer called it a day. Tope was now in charge, and he held the lead to the finish, his first Trans-Am victory. Minter was second, followed by Collins and Harrington, the only three cars on the same lap with Tope.

Having scored a win, Tope repeated in the next Trans-Am. But the 1972 Trans-Am championship was securely in the hands of George Follmer, with the Manufacturers' title going to AMC.

Sunday morning's Two-Five Challenge event saw 18 cars grid for a 75 minute go. Pete Brock's Datsun team had won four of the first five events this year, building upon the championship they had won last year. For RA Brock was running three cars, for John Morton, Mike Downs and *guest driver,* Sam Posey. Against these Datsuns was a fleet of Alfa Romeo GTAs, headed by Horst Kwech, who had won the previous round in the Herb Wetson/Pepsi car. The Brock Datsuns swept the grid, qualifying Morton-Posey-Downs 1-2-3. Kwech, Bert Everett and Harry Theodorocopulos followed, all in Alfas.

Kwech pulled a surprise at the start, going around the outside of the Datsuns in turn two to take the lead. He enjoyed the fruits of his astounding move for only two laps before Morton got by. The race then settled down to Morton, Kwech, Posey, Downs, Everett, Theodorocopulos, Richard Hull in a Toyota and Lee Midgley's Alfa. Posey had only seven laps to enjoy his ride, however, as he dropped out with a broken rocker arm. Everett dropped back with a leaking differential as Downs, driving his best race of the year, moved past Kwech for second. Midgley and Hull battled mightily for many laps before Hull got an advantage. Up front, though, Morton was not to be denied, and he came home the winner, leading teammate Downs across the line. Hull and Midgley came next, Kwech having dropped back to fifth on the last lap when his engine ran out of oil. Morton's win was another link in what was to be his second straight Two-Five title, as well as for Datsun.

This set the stage for the L&M Continental 5000 race. RA was the fourth of eight races scheduled, and Graham McRae held the points lead, having won two of the first three events. The other win was scored by David Hobbs. McRae, a New Zealander, was driving a McRae GM-1. This was a car that was known earlier in the year as a Leda LT-20, the first F-5000 effort of a small English race car builder. McRae had recently bought the company, renamed it after himself and gone into production for customer sales. Evan Noyes was present with one. The chassis most in evidence, though, was the Lola T-300. Based upon a reinforced F-2/FB Lola T-240 tub with a 5.0 Chevy V-8, the car appeared short and stubby, but it was fast. The top Lola team present was that of Carl Hogan, who was running two for Hobbs and Brett Lunger. Other T-300s of note present were for Eppie Wietzes, Jerry Hansen, John Gunn, Bob Muir, Gus Hutchison, Horst Kwech and others. Sam Posey was in the Champ-Carr Surtees TS-11, while his last year's TS-8 was driven by Rocky Moran. John Cannon had a March 725, a one-off based on a March 722 F-2 chassis. Sid Taylor, a top entrant in British racing, brought two cars over, a Chevron B24 for Brian Redman and a McLaren M10 for Derek Bell. Two McLaren M18s were present, for Lothar Motschenbacher and Alan Lader. Lotus was represented by two 70s, the Roy Woods Racing car for George Follmer and a Pete Brock Racing version for John Morton. But the sleeper in the field of 30 cars was the Formula 1 March 711 of Skip Barber. The rules allowed F-1 cars, and occasionally one did appear. Barber had F-1 experience, having driven this car in several GPs, both in North America and in Europe.

In qualifying, Barber confirmed the potential. He screamed the little 3.0

The Penske turbocharged Porsche 917-10 is unloaded in the garage area for technical inspection. Knowledgeable fans quickly learned that this was the place to see the cars up close.

Ford Cosworth powered car around the four miles at 2:08.610 to take the pole. Jerry Hansen was alongside him, followed by Cannon, Hobbs, Redman, Posey, Wietzes, Gunn and the rest. The stage was set for the first of the two 96 mile heats.

Hansen got the jump on Barber and led the pack in heat one. Hobbs ran third for only two laps when the engine in the Hogan Lola blew. Simultaneously, Barber passed Hansen for first and then Redman also got by Hansen. On lap seven, Barber's engine started smoking, and he shut it off, thus elevating Redman into the lead. However, on lap 14 the Chevron's suspension broke, and John Gunn moved into the seemingly jinxed lead position. He was trailed by McRae, Hansen, Posey, Muir, Motschenbacher and Bell. Sure enough, on lap 17 of 24 the engine in Gunn's Lola broke, and McRae became the fifth leader of the heat. This he held to the end, with Posey, Bell, Motschenbacher, Lunger and Morton filling out the top six.

Twenty-three survivors took the green for the second heat. Posey led McRae, Motschenbacher, Bell and the rest. Lothar started drifting back through the field and then his day came to an end when Lader hit him in the rear and vaulted over his McLaren, putting both cars out. McRae had passed Posey on lap three with Bell following. Barber, meanwhile, had started 21st after his first heat problems and was rocketing back up through the field. On lap 13 he completed a rather amazing comeback when he took McRae for first. Posey was running in third, then Muir, Wietzes, Kwech and Bell. Barber was on form and led to the finish, winning heat two. McRae was second, then Muir, Wietzes, Posey and Bell.

Overall, Graham McRae was the winner, his third of the year, in his STP McRae GM-1. Posey was second, Bell third, Muir fourth, Lunger fifth and in sixth, after a dnf in heat one, was Skip Barber. McRae's average speed for the combined 192 miles was 107.911 mph.

Wietzes won the next race, at Donnybrooke, MN, then Lunger took two, before Redman ended this season at Riverside with a win in the Chevron. McRae was the season champion.

On the Can-Am weekend of August 25-27 the weather did not fully cooperate. An all day downpour on Saturday saw no one go out to qualify, and the FB Championship race was almost washed out. Sunday, while no rain was falling, was far from dry. All of Road America, except the few asphalt roads, was a quagmire. Cars were stuck everywhere, the roads were blocked and unless one had a sturdy blanket picnicking was a muddy adventure. After the Can-Am the track mobilized a fleet of nearby farmers to pull cars out with their tractors. But, what the heck, there were races to watch!

Saturday's FB pro race was very wet. Chuck Sarich, in the Quicksilver Racing March 72B, appeared to be the only driver who was the least bit

Brazilian F-1 driver Carlos Pace gets comfortable in the Shadow Mk. III as team leader Jackie Oliver looks on. Though fast, the car was fragile, and neither Pace nor Oliver finished.

comfortable in the rain. He swam away with the race, able to lap four seconds a round faster than anyone else. In the four previous races this year, Sarich had placed second each time, and was leading the point standings. He wanted a win, though, and there was no touching him. After 80 miles he led Gordon Smiley in a Merlyn, Maurice McCaig in a Brabham BT-35, Tom Outcault in a March 72B, Carl Liebich in a Chevron B18 and Mike Hall in a Brabham BT-35 across the line. This would be Sarich's only win, but he continued rolling up the points and took the season's FB Championship. For good measure, he also won the club FB title at the SCCA's National Championship Runoffs in November.

Sunday morning the Volkswagen Super Vee Gold Cup ran for 60 miles. Bill Scott was the winner in a Royale RP14, coming up from third. Gregor Kronegard and Tom Reddy, both in Lola T-252s, led early, but Reddy later fell out and Kronegard finished second behind Scott. Elliot Forbes-Robinson was third in a Lola, while Bob Lazier finished fourth in a Zink ahead of Tom Davey's Lola. Scott would go on to win the season's title.

The Can-Am had a new look to it. Porsche had done its homework over the winter and had created a McLaren-beater. The car was the Porsche 917-10K Spyder. A development of last year's 917-10, it was powered by a twin-turbocharged version of the 5.0 flat 12 engine. Putting out an estimated 1000hp and cloaked in a new aerodynamic body, the car would be tough to beat. Porsche had retained Penske Racing to develop and run the car in the Can-Am with sponsorship from L&M. Original driver Mark Donohue was out of commission, having torn up his knee and ankle in a pre-season testing crash. Not to worry. Penske immediately put George Follmer in the car and set off to win races. Coming into RA, the Can-Am had run four races, with Denis Hulme winning the first and third runs in a McLaren M20, while Follmer took the second and fourth outings.

The McLaren M20, a side radiatored, ultimate iteration of the McLaren sports racer, was hard pressed to keep up with the Porsche. Hulme had won two races while the Porsche was getting debugged, but it was becoming harder. The second M20 was being driven by Peter Revson. Both of last year's M8Fs had been purchased by Gregg Young, who was running them for himself and French F-1 Tyrrell driver Francois Cevert. Lothar Motschenbacher was temporarily out due to burns suffered in a F-5000 mishap the week before. This was the first Can-Am he would miss, having started every one ever held, the only driver to do so. He put Brett Lunger in his M8D. The other ex-works M8D was entered by Overhauser Racing for John Cordts. The McLaren production car this year was the M8FP. Roger McCaig had the only one present. Warren Agor was in Oscar Koveleski's M8B, while other McLarens present were a variety of M8Es, M8Cs, M12s and even one M6B and one old McLaren Elva.

Lola had built a one-off T-310 as its weapon this year. Entered as usual by Carl Haas, the Steed sponsored car was driven by David Hobbs. One of last year's T-260s was present, run by privateer Tom Heyser. A few T-222s and T-163s completed the Lola entry. Shadow had built two new Mk. III cars, now approaching full size after years of roller skate-like cars. The black, UOP sponsored cars were driven by Jackie Oliver and Brazilian F-1 driver Carlos Pace. The North American Racing Team was back again, something they seemed to do every other year, with the Ferrari 712M. Based on the 512M Le Mans racer, it had open cockpit bodywork and was powered by the biggest engine Ferrari ever made, a 7.0 liter V-12. Jean-Pierre Jarier was the driver.

Two more Porsches rounded out the interesting cars in the 34 car field. These were both 917-10s with the early season bodywork, since replaced on the Penske entry. Brumos Porsche entered a pale blue car for Peter Gregg with a non-turbo flat 12, while the Vasek Polak entry for Milt Minter was powered by the turbo unit.

Qualifying ran on Friday without Revson and Follmer, who were off at Ontario qualifying for a USAC race. When they returned on Saturday they found the track awash, and were only able to post times that relegated them far down the grid. Hulme had taken the pole in his M20 with a sparkling time of 2:04.562, 115.605 mph, the fastest lap yet turned at the track. Cevert was alongside in Hulme's last year's car at 2:07.552. Row two held the Porsches of Minter and Gregg, while Oliver and Hobbs were on the third row. Follmer was down in the seventh row, while Revson was down in 25th place. Thirty-three cars would take the green flag. The first few laps would be interesting.

Hulme took advantage of the situation to blast into an early lead, followed by Cevert and Oliver. Follmer was charging through the field and was in fourth place by the fifth lap! Revson was moving up smartly also, but had to come from quite a ways further back. Follmer knocked off Oliver and Cevert, turning a new race lap record of 2:07.264 in so doing. By lap eight the now second place Follmer was gaining on Hulme. The speed of the turbo Porsche was truly awesome.

On the twelfth lap the question of how long Hulme would lead was answered. Follmer did not catch him, although he certainly would have, but a duff magneto caused the M20 to coast down the Moraine Sweep and come to a halt. Follmer now led and was pulling steadily away from Cevert, Oliver and Minter, with Revson now in fifth. On lap 21 the clutch in Revson's M20 failed, and both of the orange works McLarens were through. So, as it turned out, was their dominance of the Can-Am.

Attrition was affecting more than the M20s. Oliver's Shadow lost its exhaust system, Hobbs' Lola lost its final drive, and Minter's Porsche had its gearbox quit. On lap 38 Follmer completed lapping the field, thoroughly in charge. He ran out the 50 laps amusing himself as to how many times he could lap certain backmarkers. Francois Cevert came home second in his year-old M8F, while Peter Gregg brought the Brumos Porsche home third. Jarier was fourth in the Ferrari while Young completed a fine day for his team by finishing fifth in his second M8F. Gary Wilson rounded out the top six in a McLaren M8E.

At the next Can-Am, at Donnybrooke, lightning struck and neither the Porsches nor the McLarens finished. Francois Cevert took the surprise win. That was not to happen again, as Donohue came back to win at Edmonton, while Follmer finished the season with back to back wins at Laguna Seca and Riverside. The Penske Porsches had won six of the nine Can-Ams and Follmer was easily the champion. In fact, Follmer had a banner year, as he also was the Trans-Am king, the only driver to win two major titles in the same year.

1973

Mark Donohue in the paddock with the Penske Lola T-330 powered by an AMC engine. The top heavy AMC engine was never competitive and Donohue's efforts were concentrated on the Porsche Can-Am effort.

The first alteration to the track occurred for this season. The cars had grown considerably wider than when the track was built, due largely to the ever-increasing tire size. As a result, a six foot strip of asphalt was laid all around the track, giving more racing room. As far as schedule was concerned, the same three weekend format was followed.

Off track, IMSA continued to make major inroads on the road racing scene. The Camel sponsored GT series was growing rapidly, attracting promoter and entrant attention. Indeed, the prestigious endurance races at Daytona and Sebring, under SCCA sanction for the previous decade, switched to IMSA, becoming part of the Camel GT series in addition to their status as world sports car championship events. In reaction to all this, SCCA made the first major change to Trans-Am specifications, opening the series up to sports and GT cars. This mimicking of the IMSA Camel GT format in retrospect was a mistake, as copying another series instead of carving out one's own niche usually does not result in success. In addition, SCCA axed the Two-Five Challenge, disenfranchising a whole group of racers, many of

whom subsequently gravitated to IMSA. As if that were not enough, SCCA inexplicably cancelled the Formula B series, sending that group of competitors up to Canada, where the Player's-sponsored Formula Atlantic (nee B) series was thriving. In sponsorship news, L&M upped the ante in F-5000 and the series was now known simply as the *L&M Championship*. On the other hand, J-Wax had departed, and the Can-Am now was without a title sponsor.

In club racing, SCCA created a new category, joining sports racing, production, sedans, and formula. This was for Showroom Stock cars which, interestingly enough, is what the production category was in the 1950s. Two classes were in this category, Showroom Stock Sedan (SSS) and Showroom Stock Sports Car (SSSC).

The usual slate of races ran in mid-June for the June Sprints. Of particular note was the win by 63 year old Harvey Templeton in the Formula Vee event. Templeton was driving a Shadowfax, a car built in his own shops. The small production and sedan event saw two leaders drop out in the last lap, leaving a somewhat astonished Don Schmitt to take the win in an MG

The start of the 1973 F-5000 race. David Hobbs, Brian Redman, Eppie Wietzes and Joey Scheckter stream through turn 12.

Midget. Ted Schumacher seemed to have things under control until his Spitfire stopped with one lap to go. That put Bob Hubbard's Midget in first, but he coasted to a stop at the top of the hill, within sight of the S/F line. All he could do was watch forlornly as the checker fluttered for Schmitt.

Saturday's *feature* race was for big production cars. Bill Jobe pulled a surprise as he won the 60 mile event in a *small* BP Corvette, beating all the larger 427 Corvettes. Joe Pirrotta was second overall, first in AP, in a 454ci Corvette. Earlier, Ron Dennis had continued his recent dominance of the small sports racing field by taking his Ocelot-Suzuki from the pole to a huge lead. Alas, a flat tire cost him two laps, and the win went to Don Ramsey in a Pegasus.

For the formula race, Jerry Hansen was in a two year old Lola T-192, having sold his T-300 from the previous year. Nonetheless, he led the 60 mile race from start to finish, winning overall and FA by a half dozen seconds over the Lola T-300 of Tuck Thomas. The FB class was taken by Tom Klausler in a Brabham BT-38, while Jim Lloyd's Brabham BT-28 was tops in FC.

The 100 mile feature for sports racers in classes A, B, and C saw Hansen trying something different. He had sold his Lola T-220 to Dan Kampo, and had just taken delivery of a new Lola T-292. However, this car was a 2.0 liter class BSR machine, and it would be giving away tons of displacement to the large ASR cars. Jack Hinkle was on the pole with his big Lola T-165, but Hansen had qualified second fastest, beating out many far more powerful cars. In the race itself, Hinkle led start to finish, Hansen ran second, leading Clif Apel's McLaren M6B, Orly Thornsjo in a McLaren M12, and Wayne Nelson's McLaren M8FP, all powered by big block Chevys. Two laps from the end, Hansen had to pit due to fuel starvation. After a quick fix, he rejoined the race to finish third overall, first in BSR, behind Hinkle

and Apel. Thornsjo took fourth, while Jim Trueman, owner and founder of Red Roof Inns, was fifth overall and first in CSR in a Bobsy SR-5.

The end of July brought the Trans-Am and Formula 5000 cars back to the Kettle Moraine. The Trans-Am was scheduled for 78 laps, 312 miles. Clif Tufte wanted to run the event at the shorter 200 mile distance as in the past, feeling that such a format would not only be easier on the drivers, but would be far more understandable and exciting for the fans. However, SCCA decreed the longer distance, and that was that. Despite the fact that 312 miles equaled 500 kilometers, Tufte declined to use the "Road America 500" title for it.

Under the new eligibility rules, the field had a heavy proportion of Corvettes and Porsche 911 RSRs joining the Camaros and Mustangs. Unlike the heyday of the series just a couple years prior, there was no factory involvement to be seen. All were privateers. Warren Ago put his Camaro on the pole, with John Greenwood's Corvette alongside. Carl Shaffer, Camaro; Jerry Thompson, Corvette; and Paul Nichter, Camaro, came next before the first Porsches, the RSRs of Peter Gregg and Al Holbert. In all, 40 cars gridded.

Agor led the first few laps, but then Greenwood moved past on lap six. Not giving the spectators much room for confusion, Greenwood led the rest of the way, with only Agor on the same lap at the finish. Holbert, Elliott Forbes-Robinson, and Milt Minter filled the next three places in Porsches, while John Buffum finished sixth in an English Ford Escort Twin Cam. In reality, it was not much of a race.

The Trans-Am ran only six races this year. Peter Gregg won the title with one win and several high placings. Greenwood was the only multiple winner, taking two of the six.

On Sunday, a bright and cheery day, the Formula 5000 cars ran three

59

A Porsche parade into Hurry Downs on lap one of the Can-Am. Mark Donohue, Jody Scheckter, George Follmer and Hurley Haywood, all in turbo Porsches, leads Scooter Patrick's McLaren M8F.

times. Reacting to wide spread fan displeasure to the two heat format of the previous two years, SCCA revised the setup, and got it right. From now on, the Formula 5000 cars would have the field split in half based upon qualifying times. Qualifiers 1-3-5-7 and so on would run in an 80 mile heat, while the 2-4-6-8-etc. qualifiers would run a second 80 mile heat. The top ten finishers from each heat would move into the 100 mile finale, gridded in the order of heat finish, the fastest heat occupying the inside grid row, while the other heat occupied the outside row. In addition, four *promoter's options* would be added to the back of the grid, thus covering such contingencies as a 'name' blowing in a heat. In all there would be 24 starters. This format proved to be very popular with all concerned.

Lola had debuted the T-330 to replace last year's T-300. A vastly improved car, many were sold. McLaren had stopped building Can-Am and F-5000 cars, concentrating just on F-1 and Indy cars. Chevron, March, Trojan, and McRae all sold small numbers of cars, but the Lola was the car to have. Carl Haas, the Lola importer, had switched his attention to F-5000 after Lola pulled out of Can-Am car building. Further, Haas had lured Jim Hall out of retirement to be his partner. Besides his considerable engineering skills, Hall also brought to the partnership the superb facilities of Chaparral Cars, including the Rattlesnake Raceway test track, in Midland, Texas. To drive their Steed-sponsored T-330, which was considerably modified by Hall from the standard version, they hired the immensely talented Brian Redman.

Many other Lolas were on hand. Hogan Racing entered two cars, sponsored by Haggar slacks, for David Hobbs and Brett Lunger. Penske Racing had a T-330 for Mark Donohue, powered by an AMC engine. A worthy experiment, it was largely unsuccessful because the AMC engine not only was heavier, but also sat higher in the chassis, thus upsetting the han-

dling relative to the Chevy powered cars. Bob Lazier was in the Oftedahl car, while Roy Woods Racing entered a sharp looking Carling Black Label example for Tony Adamowicz. In all, 19 Lolas were entered.

There was one Trojan present, but it was formidable. Trojan, an English company that had taken over Elva some years earlier, had built the customer McLarens. Now that McLaren had discontinued that side of its business, Trojan built its own cars to try to fill the gap in its ledger. Jolly Brit Sid Taylor was running one on each side of the Atlantic, and for the L&M Series had young South African phenom Jody Scheckter behind the wheel. Three March 73A cars were present, for John Gunn, Gus Hutchison, and Larry McNeil. Two Chevron B24s were to be driven by Bob Brown and Peter Gethin, the latter in Doug Shierson's car. McRae GM-1s were on the ground for Graham McRae, Vern Schuppan, Jon Woodner, Evan Noyes, and Gordon Meffert. Add in two Matichs, some older McLarens, Lotuses, and Surtees, and it was a very promising field of 44 cars.

A crowd of 31,000 plus was on hand for Sunday's two heats and a final. Jody Scheckter had qualified fastest, turning a lap at 2:04.926, almost four seconds faster than a F-5000 car had ever gone previously. In all, seven cars beat the old F-5000 mark as Scheckter was followed by Redman, Lunger, Hobbs, Gethin, Wietzes and Adamowicz. Last year's champion McRae was eighth, with Mark Donohue ninth.

Heat one appeared to be all Scheckter. The Trojan driver zipped away, building a lead of over 10 seconds after only four laps. Hobbs, Wietzes, and Adamowicz followed. Scheckter continued to pull away until lap 16 of 20, when his car began handling erratically. A tire was going down. The subsequent pit stop cost him three places, and he finished the heat fourth behind Hobbs, Wietzes, and Adamowicz.

In the second heat, Brian Redman dominated as Scheckter had in the first, but with the big difference being that Redman finished without any problems. Hence, he took the heat win in the Haas/Hall Lola, with Lunger second after a race long dispute with third finisher Gethin. Hutchison came home fourth followed by Muir and McRae.

That set the stage for the 100 mile feature. David Hobbs got a huge jump at the start, but Redman reeled him in on the second lap, passing for the lead. Shortly thereafter, Hobbs had the throttle stick wide open on the Lola, and he took a wild ride down the escape road, losing a dozen positions in the process. Scheckter had moved up smartly from his eighth place grid position, and was now in second, closely followed by Wietzes. Adamowicz was out early with broken suspension, while the efforts of Gethin and Lunger would also fall by the wayside with engine troubles.

Redman held onto the lead, Scheckter shadowing him closely. But Scheckter also had to keep an eye in his mirrors, as Wietzes was closing up. Indeed, on several occasions Wietzes was to get alongside Scheckter's white Trojan, but he was always able to repel the attack. Donohue was running fourth after Lunger's departure, with Hobbs regaining ground after his off course adventure. As the race wound its way toward conclusion, the threesome of Redman, Scheckter, and Wietzes circulated in close company, any bobble sure to change the order. But nobody wavered, and Brian Redman won the event from Scheckter, with Wietzes finishing a close third. Hobbs had recovered all the way to fourth place, while Bob Brown was fifth in his Chevron, Donohue having stopped on the last lap when his engine died and was susequently credited with sixth place. During the race Lunger set a new race lap record at 2:06.8.

This win broke Scheckter's four race winning streak and started a similar run by Redman. In the nine race L&M Series, Redman won five races and Scheckter four. However, Jody took the championship on points, the two races Redman missed while driving for Ferrari in Europe costing him the crucial points.

The late August Can-Am weekend had two support races. On Saturday, the Formula B cars ran for 80 miles. Although the U.S. FB series had ended after 1972, Clif Tufte thought enough of the 1600cc racers to continue to run them at RA as a non-championship event in spite of that. A good number of those running the Canadian Players series came, and it was Bill Brack winning in a Lotus 69. Brack would be the Canadian champion not only this year, but also in 1974 and 1975. Bertil Roos, who would win this year's Super Vee Gold Cup title, was second, while Mike Hall was the first *local* home, both in Brabham BT-40s.

Sunday morning was the provence of the FSV Gold Cup. It was the best race of the weekend as the lead changed hands constantly. Nineteen cars ran for fifteen laps, with pole sitter Roos the early leader. Fred Phillips in a Tui, Frank Maka and Bob Wheelock in Lolas and Bob Lazier in a Royale mixed in, and these five swapped the lead on almost every lap. Finally, on the last lap Maka led through the final turn but Wheelock won the drag race to the stripe, winning by a whisker. Maka finished second, followed by Lazier and Phillips.

The Can-Am race had undergone a format change. In an attempt to *juice* the show, the SCCA decreed that the Can-Am races would now be run in two heats, rather than one 200 mile race. The first heat was to be a qualifying heat for the final. To say that this was an ill-advised move would be polite. Besides confusing all present this also led to a situation where high attrition in the first heat would mean that the final, which was classified as the actual Can-Am race, would begin with a meager field. Instead of improving the show, it actually contributed to the pronounced fall off in attendance that the series would see.

At RA, the format was a 100 mile heat, paying one-third of the purse with the 100 mile Can-Am race itself following, paying the other two-thirds of the purse, plus points.

This year, if one did not have a turbo Porsche, there was no real reason to show up. To make a long story short, the Panzer Porsches won all eight of this year's events. The first two races were won by Charlie Kemp and George Follmer. They were driving for Bobby Rinzler, who had purchased both Penske Porsche 917-10K Spyders at the end of the 1972 season. The two car team was sponsored by RC Cola. Vasek Polak and Brumos Porsche also entered 917-10K Spyders, with Jody Scheckter driving for Polak and Hurley Haywood for Brumos. Polak also entered a non-turbo Porsche 917-10 Spyder for Steve Durst. But the top Porsche belonged to Penske. Mark Donohue was in the Sunoco-sponsored 917-30KL Spyder, which was fastest of all. In race trim the turbocharged flat 12 put out 1100hp, while for qualifying the boost was screwed up to give an astounding 1400hp. Not surprisingly, Donohue would be the 1973 Can-Am Champion.

Against these Porsches a small, brave, but outclassed field did battle. Roy Woods Racing ran a Carling Black Label McLaren M20 for David Hobbs. Commander Motor Homes bought both ex-works McLaren M8Fs from Gregg Young and was running them this weekend for Bob Brown and Danny Hopkins. Herb Caplan's U.S. Racing had another M8F for Scooter Patrick, while Lothar Motschenbacher had Derek Bell in his M8F. Two Shadows were entered, one for regular driver Jackie Oliver, while the other was for the new F-1 sensation, James Hunt. The Shadows were DN2s, a completely new design from the previous cars. Oliver had a turbocharged Chevy V-8 in his, while Hunt had a normally aspirated version. Also in the "if you can't lick 'em, join 'em" category was Gary Wilson, who had a turbo Chevy in his McLaren M8E. The rest of the small 23 car field was, frankly, made up of field fillers.

In qualifying Donohue showed what he had. He turned the first ever under two minute lap, a startling 1:57.518, 122.534 mph. This was fully three seconds faster than Scheckter, and eleven seconds faster than the first non-Porsche! Now consider this: it would not be until 1982 that anyone else would turn a lap under two minutes, and Donohue's mark would not be eclipsed until 1984—fully eleven years later!

Sunday morning found Hobbs missing, unable to make air connections back from California, where he was qualifying for the Ontario 500 in Roy Woods' Eagle. Hence, Derek Bell switched from Motschenbacher's M8F into the Woods M20, while Steve Durst, on foot after his Polak Porsche blew its only engine in the morning warmup, jumped into Lothar's car. Neither switch would affect the outcome of the race.

The qualifying heat, run to the absurd distance of 100 miles, was a Porsche sweep. Five turbo Porsches, a one-through-five finish in the order Donohue, Scheckter, Follmer, Haywood, Kemp. Patrick, Hunt, and Brown followed.

For the 100 mile feature, only 16 cars gridded. Among the non-starters were Oliver, Hunt, Durst, and Bell. With Kemp, Haywood, and others dropping out during the race, only 11 cars finished. A far cry from just a few years earlier.

The race itself was predictable: Donohue start to finish. Scheckter and Follmer followed in their Porsches, while Patrick took fourth, winning the unofficial *atmo* category. Brown trailed in fifth while Bob Nagel finished sixth in a Lola T-260. Donohue set a new race lap record at 2:04.374, but if pushed could have dropped it much lower. He wasn't pushed.

Donohue went on to win the rest of the season's Can-Ams. With six wins he was the easy champion. After winning the season finale at Riverside, he announced his retirement. A year later he was to be lured out of retirement to drive the Penske Formula One car only to lose his life in August, 1975, following a practice crash at the Austrian Grand Prix.

1974

A dark and damp June Sprints 1974. Jerry Hansen in his 2-liter Lola T-292 leads Dick DeAtley's Special into turn three.

For 1974, the Can-Am declined precipitously, the F-5000 series continued strong despite the loss of L&M sponsorship and the Trans-Am all but disappeared. IMSA's Camel GT series continued strong growth while USAC's Championship trail was in such disarray that the first rumblings of what was to be the birth of CART were heard. Tracy Bird was out as SCCA's Executive Director, replaced by Cameron Argetsinger, the man behind Watkins Glen and the rebirth of American road racing. On top of all this, the Israeli-Arab war of 1973 led to the Arab oil embargo and the gasoline shortage of 1974. Into all of this turmoil Road America embarked on its 20th season.

The June Sprints had a nine race schedule, four on Saturday June 15th and the remainder the next day. While over the years *Tufte weather*, warm and sunny, has been taken for granted, this year nature did not cooperate. It rained for a good portion of Saturday and Sunday was just plain wet and miserable. Although a record 518 cars entered the Sprints, a not inconsiderable number decided to put their cars on the trailers early due to the wet and slick conditions. Further, the dreary skies held down attendance.

Harvey Templeton, having won FV the year before at the age of 63, decided to do it again. He took his Shadowfax into the lead on the 11th of 12 laps and took the checker. In the big production event, Gene Bothello's Corvette won overall while a herd of Datsun Z cars battled for CP. Logan Blackburn, Dan Parkinson and Bob Sharp had a great tussle with Blackburn prevailing.

A huge field of 71 Formula Fords battled for 12 laps, 48 miles. Vince Muzzin led the first six laps, only to have the engine in his Lola T-340 expire. Steve Lathrop, in a Zink, took over, but had to recover quickly from a spin to save the win over Dale Wilhite's Crossle.

On Sunday, Bob Sharp made up for his CP disappointment by winning BS in a Datsun 710. He passed fast qualifier Dave Frellsen early in the 12 lapper, but was deprived the overall win when Tim Lind, in a DP Jensen-Healey, passed on lap 10.

The last two races were the big formula event and the sports racer go. Jerry Hansen won both, surprising nobody in the process. In the 48 mile formula race, Hansen was driving the ex-Haas/Hall Lola T-330 that Brian

The Leader Card Indianapolis team comes to F-5000. Mike Mosely and A.J. Watson ponder their Lola T-332, perhaps wondering how to make it turn right, as well as left.

Redman had used to such good effect in the 1973 pro ranks. Even though Tuck Thomas was in this year's Lola T-332 he had all he could do to keep the wing of Hansen's red Lola in sight. The FB winner was Mike Hall in a Brabham BT-40, while Bob Schmidt won FC in a Brabham BT-21 and Ed Wachs brought his Lola T-320 home first in FSV.

For the 80 mile sports racing event, the wet surface meant that the power advantage of the big ASR cars would be negated. Therefore, it was no surprise when Hansen's 2.0 BSR Lola T-292 scored an easy win. Jack Hinkle, the only real threat to Hansen, packed up early, not willing at age 63 to unleash 700hp in the rain. Only a couple ASRs actually ran and Dick DeAtley in a Special took the class and second overall, although a long distance behind Hansen. Lee Hall drove his last race, taking third in a BSR Lola T-294, while Jim Trueman was fourth overall, first in CSR, in a Bobsy SR-6.

The mid-July Trans-Am/F-5000 weekend enjoyed far better weather. The Trans-Am race was on Saturday, run over 200 miles. The Trans-Am Series itself was at its all-time low. Its rules and eligibility requirements were almost a copy of those of the IMSA Camel GT series, but the Camel GT offered larger purses, a bigger schedule and more publicity, due no doubt to the marketing punch of Camel. As a result, just about everybody ran in IMSA, and the Trans-Am was a sorry also ran. It was so bad that the RA round was the third – *and last* – race of the season!

The Porsche 911 Carrera RSR was the car so far this year, in both IMSA and Trans-Am. Al Holbert had won at Lime Rock, while Peter Gregg had taken Watkins Glen. Both were at RA, along with threats Hurley Haywood, Ludwig Heimrath and Bob Hagestad. Against these RSRs the top competition would come from the Corvette of John Greenwood and the Camaro of Warren Agor. The rest of the 37 car field could be characterized as club racers out trying to make a couple bucks.

Greenwood took the pole, followed by Holbert and Gregg. Greenwood took his Corvette into an immediate lead as the 200 miler began, but

Holbert was in immediate trouble. He was tapped from behind and did a pirouette into the guard rail. Bodywork thoroughly smashed, he resumed, shedding pieces as he went. Carl Shaffer moved his Camaro into second, followed by Agor as the power of the V-8s told. After 10 laps, Shaffer began fading, and the Porsches of Haywood, Gregg and Heimrath chased Greenwood and Agor. As the thirsty Chevys began pitting for fuel, Agor took the lead, Greenwood's engine sounding sick. Strategy became evident; the big cars would have to pit twice, while the Porsches, if driven a bit circumspectly, could go the distance on one tankful. Agor had his foot in it, trying to build up enough of a lead in order to pit without losing a place.

After Haywood made a stop for a flat tire and Holbert pitted for bodywork repair, it became a two car race. Agor was out ahead and charging, while Gregg circulated behind him doing the math calculations. With 11 laps to go, Agor made his second stop, taking on oil in addition to fuel. When he came back out, Gregg was 20 seconds ahead. Now the chase began. Agor started lopping tenths, then whole seconds from Gregg's lead, who was moving, going as fast as he dared. Into the last lap they went, Agor now right behind Gregg. Into the last corner Agor was poised to make his move, to power by on the straight to the S/F line. But, the best laid plans.... Gregg cannily slipped past two lapped cars going into the turn and Agor had to wait until the exit to get past. That was it. Gregg held off Agor by less than a second to get the win, and with it, the 1974 Trans-Am championship. Agor was second, Holbert recovered to finish third, followed by the Carreras of Haywood, Heimrath, Harry Bytzek and Hagestad.

The Formula 5000 series was in considerably better health, even if L&M had left. The SCCA and USAC had combined to co-sanction the series this year. The idea was that the USAC Indianapolis cars would be eligible for F-5000, while the formula cars could run in USAC championship events. The SCCA was looking to broaden the appeal of its series, while USAC was trying to revitalize its series, which was in trouble. In any case, while the co-sanction did help and lasted three seasons, the crossover of cars was

The wrong way to test aerodynamic pressures. The engine in Sam Posey's Talon blows showing the air flow around the rear wing.

slim. Only at the Phoenix season-ender did any F-5000 cars run USAC, without success, and RA was one of the few F-5000 races where USAC cars appeared.

Dick Simon brought his '73 Eagle-turbo Ford this weekend and was joined by Tom Sneva in Grant King's Kingfish-turbo Drake, a blatant Eagle copy and John Martin, a former sedan racer, in a McLaren M16B-turbo Drake. They were not competitive, Simon even packing up and going home early. Sneva was out on the first lap, while Martin persevered for nine laps before retiring.

The Leader Card Team, three time Indy 500 winners, tried a different tactic. They bought a new Lola T-332 for Mike Mosley to drive. Good idea, but head wrench A.J. Watson was not at home trying to set a car up for a road course, and Mosley could never be accused of being a road racer. Mosley lasted nine laps before retiring.

Besides the three USAC cars, 31 F-5000s were present. Haas/Hall had Brian Redman in its Lola T-332, while Carl Hogan had pared down to one car, entering a T-332 for David Hobbs. Vel's-Parnelli Jones Racing had entered the series this year, with a Viceroy sponsored car for none other than Mario Andretti. The team, a partnership between Vel Militech and Parnelli Jones, had been very successful in USAC racing, with two Indy 500s and three USAC championships to its credit. Dan Gurney had reentered the fray, building F-5000 Eagles for the first time since 1968. Dan had two very sharp looking Eagles present for Brett Lunger and Elliott Forbes-Robinson. The always threatening Eppie Wietzes had a new Lola T-332, as did Evan Noyes and Tuck Thomas. A new nameplate was present as Jack McCormack, previously with the Champ-Carr team, had entered two Talon MR-1s. The Talon was originally a joint venture between McCormack and Graham McRae's shop in England, and the car was originally penned as the McRae GM-2. However, there had been a falling out between the two, and the cars were finished in California by McCormack as Talons. Sam Posey and Jon Woodner were to drive. McRae, meanwhile, hooked up with Chuck

Jones, who had been the entrant of Skip Hudson's cars for several years in the 1960s and was driving Jones' Lola T-332. Add in the usual mix of older Lolas, Marches and the like, and we were ready for the first heat.

The format was similar to 1973. There would be two 48 mile qualifying heats, each for one-half of the field. The top 20, plus four promoter's options, would run the 100 mile feature. Andretti had been the fastest qualifier, followed by Redman, Wietzes, Lunger and McRae. In heat one, Andretti had an easy time, leading all the way to win with Wietzes, Hobbs and Woodner following. In the second heat, Redman was the winner, but he had a harder time than Andretti. Lunger was making the Eagle fly and pushed Redman hard in the early going, who eventually eased away and won by a little over three seconds from Lunger, who had given the Eagle its best outing yet. McRae finished third, while Forbes-Robinson took fourth in the second AAR Eagle, coming up from last place after mechanical difficulties had stopped him from posting any qualifying time.

In the 100 mile feature, Andretti took the initial lead, but Wietzes and Redman were right behind. Mario had his mirrors full of the two Lolas as they swapped second behind him. Lunger led McRae, Hobbs, Woodner and the rest a distance behind. At half distance, Andretti still led, but Wietzes had dropped off the pace a bit and was now third behind Redman. Lunger dropped out of fourth with a flat tire, giving the place to McRae, who shortly thereafter had the same fate befall him.

As the laps wound down, Redman increased the pressure on Andretti. The last couple laps the engine in Mario's Lola began to miss, the fuel almost gone. Andretti stayed on it, though; he would either win or not finish. Redman closed right up, sticking the nose of his Steed Lola alongside. However, Andretti kept his foot in it and in the drag race to the finish took the win just a squeak ahead of Redman. Then, to Redman's chagrin, Andretti's car coasted to a halt, the fuel tank dry as the proverbial bone. Wietzes took third, with Hobbs fourth, Thomas fifth and Woodner sixth. It was a very good race.

The Shadow DN-4s of Jackie Oliver and George Follmer dominated in the abbreviated 1974 season, though both broke at RA, leaving the win to Scooter Patrick in a three year old McLaren M20.

Andretti and Redman fought through the rest of the year. They each won three of the seven races, Hobbs taking the other. Redman won the championship by just a few points over Andretti. The best USAC result was at Riverside, where Bobby Unser won a qualifying heat in Gurney's Indy Eagle. That would be the high point of the USAC challenge.

The Can-Am weekend also enjoyed good weather. A non-championship pro Formula Atlantic (nee FB) race took up Saturday, while a VW Gold Cup Super Vee race was the preliminary to the Can-Am on Sunday.

The Traylor Racing Lola T-360s driven by Tom Klausler and Bill O'Connor were tough to beat in '74. In the 80 mile race Klausler took the lead and cruised to an easy victory. O'Connor led the Doug Shierson Racing Chevrons of Chip Mead and James King, plus Mike Hall's Brabham in a fight for second. O'Connor eventually dropped out with fuel feed problems, then King went to the wayside with a smoking engine. Hall finally bested Mead, taking second behind Klausler.

In the FSV event, Harry Ingle started the 60 mile race from the pole and kept his Zink in front for most of the race. Despite an oil leak, he led a tight group consisting of Bob Lazier, Lola; Fred Phillips, Elden; Richard Melville, Royale; and Freddy Kottulinsky, Lola. Eventually, the leak worsened, and Ingle had to stop at the pits, ending a fine drive. Melville had passed Phillips and now led, with Kottulinsky next, followed by Lazier and the Royale of Peter Moodie. Into the last lap they went, with Melville still ahead. Phillips made his move going into the last turn and outbraked Melville, leading him up the hill to the flag to take an exciting win. Melville was second with Kottulinsky third after Lazier and Moodie collided in turn 12 with Lazier suffering a broken leg putting him out of not only the FSV race but also the following Can-Am.

Due to the world-wide gasoline situation, most motor racing events were cut by 10%. The Can-Am was no different, the 200 total miles being reduced to 180. This was broken up into a 68 mile qualifying sprint, followed by the 112 mile Can-Am. The field itself was quite poor, as pre-season changes by the SCCA had the effect of knocking all the Porsches out. SCCA had imposed a fuel mileage rule, a standard that turbocharged cars could not meet. The intent was to open up competition and bring in new competitors, but the result was just the opposite. All the turbo teams left, the Porsches were gone, nobody was building new cars for sale, and the only new cars built for this year were two works Shadow DN-4s.

The Shadow DN-4 was a fine car, one that would have been able to hold its own in almost any company. The black cars were all new, powered by huge 494ci aluminum Chevys and covered by sensuous body work that seemed to be shrink-wrapped around the mechanicals. Jackie Oliver, who had won all four of the year's Can-Ams to date, and George Follmer were the drivers.

The rest of the small fields were made up of privateers in old cars. All in all, a rather sorry development. Herb Caplan's U.S. Racing had two McLarens, the ex-Roy Woods M20 for Scooter Patrick and an M8F for John Cordts. Brumos Porsche was running its Porsche 917-10 Spyder without turbochargers for Hurley Haywood. Nothing else was newer than three years old, save Gary Wilson's special called the *Sting*. Elliott Forbes-Robinson substituted for Lazier in the Oftedahl McLaren M8E. Only 23 cars were on hand.

The two Shadows qualified on the front row, Follmer first. In the Sprint, Oliver and Follmer loafed their way to an easy 1-2, with Cordts, Haywood, John Gunn in a Lola T-260 and Lothar Motchenbacher's McLaren M8F following. The final had a sudden change almost as the green fluttered. Oliver led, but Follmer was out with a broken drive shaft. Patrick was easily slicing through the thin field and took over second after a mere handful of laps. Cordts ran in third, leading Gunn and Haywood who were disputing fourth. Motschenbacher dropped out with water pump failure, and then Haywood went off course. It appeared to be a procession to the finish but on lap 23 of 28, the engine in Oliver's Shadow let go completely without warning. Patrick was now in the lead and held it to the end, leading Cordts home for a Caplan 1-2 finish. The '71 vintage Lola T-260s of Gunn and Bob Nagel were third and fourth, with Wilson fifth. Although he did not finish, Oliver was the 1974 Can-Am champion.

The fans did not know it at the time, but they were watching the last Can-Am. At a promoters' meeting a few days later, Riverside canceled its event, and the season was over. SCCA presented its plans for further engine restrictions in 1975, limiting engines to five liters. The promoters did not buy it. The Can-Am was done. What killed it? Surely a variety of reasons, but one fact, besides the obvious incessant rule meddling, stands out and will be repeated over time: when the big factories come to play, they drive the smaller guys away. Then, when they tire of the game or have their advertising priorities change, they go away.

1975

With the demise of Can-Am, Shadow entered F-5000. Here the two DN-6 cars go through tech. inspection.

The off-season of 1974-75 was one of great turmoil in the SCCA. The Can-Am was dead, and the Trans-Am was on life support. Meanwhile, IMSA continued to gain in strength and its Camel GT series was in demand. Indeed, several tracks, long thought to be SCCA strongholds, switched from Trans-Am and/or Can-Am weekends to IMSA Camel GT events. Volkswagen took its FSV Gold Cup largely to IMSA, with most of the races now being run in support of Camel GTs. SCCA reacted by making a major change in Trans-Am chassis eligibility which had the effect of temporarily stabilizing the series and increasing the number of events from three to seven. However, a number of these were at second and third level tracks, and its visibility was largely eclipsed by the Camel GT. As far as the Can-Am was concerned, no agreement was reached between SCCA and the promoters, and the series was formally discontinued. SCCA was unable to offer anything in its place, thus moving these now open dates into the IMSA column at many tracks.

At RA, Clif Tufte remained loyal to the SCCA. The June Sprints remained, of course. The event was the club's largest and most prestigious National event. The July weekend also remained unchanged, with a revised Trans-Am on Saturday and Formula 5000 on Sunday. For what had been the Can-Am date, Tufte reached into his bag of promotional magic and pulled out what was probably the oddest, yet most interesting, event, the *252 Handicap*.

The June Sprints ran four races on Saturday, five on Sunday. Two events were for 48 miles while the rest were all 60 miles in length, including the sports racing feature. A far cry from the 140 to 160 mile features of the '60s. Five hundred fifteen cars registered, with some fields of colossal proportions; Formula Vee had 59 starters and Formula Ford gridded 73! The weather was, in a word, *hot*. In fact, it was a sweltering weekend, just the kind that encouraged laying on a blanket in the shade, munching on a brat and consuming some of Milwaukee's finest.

The FV event was a start-to-finish howler, with the leaders running nose-to-tail the entire distance, swapping the lead almost constantly. John Hogdal, Mike Frangkiser, Terry Satchell and Warren Mockler, all in Lynx Vees, gave a great show. They drafted away from the pack, and on the last lap swapped the lead all the way around the four miles. In the last turn, Satchell led, but Hogdal drafted him up the hill and nipped him at the line. Mockler took third with Frangkiser fourth. It was a heck of a race.

The Formula Ford event that immediately followed was almost as frantic. The twin Zinks of Dave Wietzenhof and Tim Evans passed early leader Tim Stiles on lap two and took off, with Steve Lathrop's Zink trying hard to keep up. By lap seven Wietzenhof and Evans were scrapping by themselves when what might be said to be the inevitable happened. They came together, and Evans spun back to 11th place. Rather than give up, Evans drove like a demon, charging back up through the field and retaking second

The brilliant but regrettably short career of B.J. Swanson who came out of nowhere to electrify the 1975 F-5000 series. His RA effort resulted in a fourth place finish. He would be killed at the next race.

place in only three laps! Wietzenhof won by nine seconds but Evans came home second to great applause. Gary Hackbarth took third after starting tenth.

The final race on Saturday was for large production, and it was all Jerry Hansen. His Corvette led those of Tim Startup and Dan Schott home for a Chevy 1-2-3. Logan Blackburn brought his overachieving Datsun 260-Z in fourth overall, first in CP.

On Sunday Hansen put his Corvette on the trailer and took two Lolas off. It would once again be a productive day for him. In the large Formula race, 46 cars started in four classes. But Hansen was the class of the field. Driving his Lola T-330, he simply disappeared at the flag and won going away. Tuck Thomas ran second in a Lola T-332, while Chuck Dietrich took third overall, first in FB in a Brabham BT-40. Jim Miller was the FC winner, while Harry McDonald took FSV in a Royale.

The large sports racer event also was a Hansen benefit. After driving a class BSR two liter car for the past two years, Jerry decided he liked the big bangers better, so he bought his old Lola T-220 back from Dan Kampo. Now in its sixth season of racing, the car was still very capable. He romped to a one minute, forty second win over the McLaren M8FP of Orly Thornsjo with Jack Hinkle third in his familiar Lola T-165. Dick Jordan was fourth in a McLaren M8E, while Jim Trueman took fifth overall, first in CSR in a Bobsy SR-6. The BSR win went to the Lola T-212 of Bud Jackson.

In the fall, at the SCCA's annual National Championship Runoffs, Hansen would win FA and ASR, bringing his tally of titles up to 14. Mike Hall won BSR while Jim Trueman would take CSR. In FB a young driver named Bobby Rahal was the winner. We would hear more from him.

The July Trans-Am and F-5000 weekend again was blessed with good weather. The SCCA's fix for the sick Trans-Am was to stop trying to compete with IMSA. After two years of running to the same specs and getting blown out of the water in so doing, SCCA abandoned that formula completely. For 1975 the Trans-Am was run for strictly production cars as delineated in the rules for A, B and C Production and A Sedan in National racing. While on one hand it reduced the Trans-Am to the level of running club racers for dollars, on the other hand it bought some time and pumped a little life into what was a dying series.

Having said that, 32 cars showed, of which 28 started. Elkhart Lake was the sixth of seven events, and John Greenwood was the points leader,

having won three. However, he would not extend his margin this weekend, as he had a tiff with SCCA officials and withdrew on Saturday morning. This removed whatever competition Jerry Hansen may have had, and he owned the rest of the weekend. Hansen duly took the pole and then led every lap in the race, cruising to a dominant win. Tim Startup was second, also in a Corvette, while the Datsun 280-Zs of Bob Sharp and Walt Maas took the next two places. Indeed the only real interest for the fans was the giant killer act of the two Datsuns, which were running far higher in a field of Corvettes than they should: a case of very skilled drivers coupled with excellent preparation overcoming a horsepower deficit.

Hansen would also win the next Trans-Am, at Brainerd International Raceway. This track, formerly known as Donnybrooke, had recently been bought by Hansen and rescued from the jaws of bankruptcy. Hansen now was promoting as well as racing. Greenwood duly won the 1975 T-A title, with Babe Headley second and Hansen third even though he only drove in two events.

The SCCA/USAC co-sanctioned Formula 5000 event drew 31 entries, with a strong top half of the field. The 1975 Lola was the T-400. However, after the first couple events it became obvious that the previous year's T-332 was better. Hence, the teams that could afford to do so immediately went back to their T-332s. The Haas/Hall Team, of course, did so, with Brian Redman up once again in their T-332. Vel's-Parnelli Jones Racing expanded to two cars this year, T-332s for Mario Andretti and Al Unser. David Hobbs was in the Hogan Racing T-332, while Elliott Forbes-Robinson was driving one for Francisco Mir, and Graham McRae was in Eddie Lewis' example. Patrick Racing traded an Indy Eagle to Leader Card for their T-332 and had Gordon Johncock at the wheel. Among the other T-332s present, the Bay Racing car for B.J. Swanson stood out. Swanson had come out of nowhere this year and leapt into the big time. Driving for a small team he had qualified well and run up front each race, taking a fine third at the previous round at Watkins Glen. He was definitely the coming man.

Having the Can-Am rug yanked out from underneath them, Shadow responded by building a F-5000 car, the DN-6. Jackie Oliver would drive. McCormack Racing had Aussie Warwick Brown in its Talon, while Jon Woodner drove a similar Talon for Interscope Racing. Ted Field, the patron of Interscope, also had a Lola T-400 on hand for ex-drag racer Danny Ongais. Eppie Wietzes had a T-400 also, but his had extensive modifications

The weather-plagued Handicap 252 race weekend. Saturday morning was lost to fog. Here the Heppenstall FSV team waits in the gloom and dampness hoping for better weather.

in an attempt to make it handle as well as the T-332s. Dan Gurney returned with one Eagle for Vern Schuppan. While the '74 Eagle F-5000 was a handsome car, this '75 was, frankly, ugly. Very bare bones, it had an exposed engine sitting behind minimal front bodywork. Also, it must be said, it wasn't very fast. Throw in three Marches and a number of privateer Lolas, and that was the field.

The format again was two qualifying heats of 60 miles each and a 100 mile final. This year Clif Tufte chose to waive the 24 car limit and would allow all 29 to start. In qualifying for the heats, Mario Andretti was fastest, with a clocking of 2:02.077. Brian Redman came next, at 2:02.338. A very fine third fastest was Swanson at 2:03.476.

In the first heat, Andretti won easily. He led the entire 15 laps, initially over Swanson. However, Swanson's brakes began to go away, and he drifted back into the field. Wietzes, Brown and Hobbs chased Andretti, but it was in vain.

The second heat saw Redman trail Oliver's Shadow for the first five laps until he moved past. Just when it appeared that Redman would stretch his lead to the finish, Oliver came by in first with no sign of Redman. A rear hub carrier had broken, and Redman's amazing streak of 36 straight races without a dnf was over. Oliver carried on to win the heat, with Forbes-Robinson second after Unser pitted with a broken rocker arm. John Gunn was third in a Lola T-332 with Woodner finishing fourth.

The 100 mile feature had a lot of passing, but none up front. Andretti took off when the green fluttered and was gone. Twenty-five laps later he came home, winning by half a lap. But behind Andretti there was plenty of action. Oliver ran second, followed by Wietzes, Brown, Hobbs, Forbes-Robinson, Woodner, Swanson and Ongais. Redman followed, slashing his way through the field from a back of the pack start. By lap five Redman was in fourth, and the next lap saw him pass Wietzes for third. Unfortunately for Redman, his charge stalled here, as he lost second gear and his tires were going off. At the 15 lap mark, Redman had to call at the pits when a tire deflated, adding to his misery. This put Wietzes back in third, but behind him B.J. Swanson was on the move. He took Woodner, Forbes-Robinson, Hobbs and Brown in turn and was putting the heat on Wietzes. He caught Wietzes on the last lap, but catching and passing are two different things. They blasted across the line nose to tail, with Wietzes just holding off

Swanson. This was the third straight year and the fourth in the last five, in which Wietzes had finished third. Meanwhile, Brown dropped back with an engine that went off-song, and Hobbs lost a lap with a flat tire. Forbes-Robinson ended up taking fifth place, with Al Unser coming home sixth.

Andretti's win tightened the points chase, as he and Redman now each had two wins. In the remaining five races, Andretti and Redman each won two more, with Unser winning one. Redman took his second consecutive championship, just outpointing Andretti. Most sadly, the season was tinged with tragedy, as at the Mid Ohio round B.J. Swanson crashed badly, and three days later he died of head injuries. A bright young talent, on the cusp of greatness, was snuffed out. What might have been.

At the end of August, on what had been the Can-Am weekend, Clif Tufte staged a most unusual event, the Road America 252 Handicap. There was one support race, a round of the VW Gold Cup. Bad weather plagued the weekend, with rain, sometimes torrential, all three days. When it wasn't raining it was very foggy and damp; not at all conducive to comfortable spectating!

The Super Vee race was scheduled for 15 laps, 60 miles. As the cars were gridded on Saturday afternoon, the skies darkened. Although not raining at the time, the forecast was not promising. Tom Bagley was on the pole in a Zink, with *Fast Eddie* Miller alongside in a Carl Haas entered Lola T-324. Miller led at the start, with Bagley, Herm Johnson, Bill Alsup, Bob Lazier and Fred Phillips giving chase. It was a tight battle, and Bagley was all over Miller. The expected rain arrived on lap six, and the slick-shod cars began sliding all over the place. Bagley and Alsup spun in tandem, and a couple corners later Miller went off. This put Herm Johnson in the lead in his Lola T-324, with Howdy Holmes, also in a T-324 and a fast recovering Miller following. By lap eight, the rain had turned into a squall, with rain coming down in torrents and the track fast becoming awash. Speeds dropped to an almost pedestrian pace, with huge rooster tails obscuring vision. Miller managed to row a bit faster than the rest and regained the lead. He did it just in time, as the red and checkered flags were waved on lap nine. The race was scored as complete after eight laps, 32 miles, with Eddie Miller getting the win over Holmes, Lazier, Bagley and Johnson.

Miller went on to win five of the season's 11 events, taking the championship by a narrow margin over Bagley, who won three times. Howdy

The 252 Handicap belonged to Vern Schuppan in the Mirage M-7. He took an easy win in the 3.0 liter Group 6 endurance racer.

Holmes came in third.

The Handicap race was a weird and wonderful thing. The idea was to take cars from widely varying classes and put them all in the same race. With starting times varied depending upon the probable speed of the car, the theory was that they would all arrive at the finish at the same time. Of course, this works much easier on paper than in reality. John Timanus, SCCA's technical and rules guru, spent many a long day working on the handicapping formula for various cars. He came up with a plan of car classification based upon projected lap times that came fairly close to the mark, with but a few glaring exceptions.

The race had four basic groups. The first group, which would be the scratch group, would start the race. This was essentially for the current breed of Trans-Am car. The second group would be fed into the race 5 minutes 42 seconds after the start. Cars in this grouping were under two liter sports racers and FIA Groups 2 & 4 (race prepped sedans and GTs). The third group would depart 11:10 after the start and was made up of sports racers with engines under five liters pushrod and three liters overhead cam. The last group was for Can-Am cars. They would start 19:38 late. Or as one driver remarked, "enough time for us to have a bratwurst and two hands of cribbage."

The entry was not as good as hoped, but a race that was not part of any championship lost a good amount of its attraction to teams that were points chasing. Twenty-nine cars actually made the show, headed by seven Can-Am cars ranging from three to seven years old. Herb Caplan's McLaren M20 for Milt Minter and M8F for John Cordts led this category. The other five, quite frankly, were all 'tired' and posed no serious threat. Three liter racing cars were represented by the Porsche 908s of Dennis Aase and Gerhard Hirsch and the Mirage M7 of Harley Cluxton, driven by Vern Schuppan. The Lola T-294s of Mike Hall, Bud Crout and Doug Schulz topped the two liter entry. BMW brought its two 3.5 CSLs that had been running the Camel GT for Brian Redman and Sam Posey. John Greenwood had his new "Super Corvette" running with the FIA Group 4 cars, as were the Porsche RSRs of Ludwig Heimrath and Walt Maas. Twelve Corvettes and Camaros completed the field.

The first group boomed off on schedule before 23,000 fans. The Corvettes of Bill Morrison and Babe Headley disputed first for a while, until Morrison lost oil pressure. Headley then led comfortably. The second group entered, and Mike Hall immediately became the fastest on the track, reeling in the leaders at 10 to 15 seconds a lap, even though he was a little over two laps behind. The BMWs were in this set also, but they were not as fast as Hall's Lola.

Almost five laps after the start the third grouped joined the fray. Schuppan immediately showed the speed of the Mirage as he started catching Hall who was catching Headley. Finally, the last group fed into the race some eight laps back, and Minter took up the chase. Cordts was a quick retiree with a broken crankshaft, while Greenwood had parked his car with overheating. The track itself was a sea of activity, as there was constant passing occurring with cars of widely varying speeds passing and being passed everywhere. It was entertaining, and many a fan was seen consulting stopwatches and scratching on paper, tracking who was where and how long it might take Minter, Hall, Redman and Schuppan to catch Headley. Yes, it was entertaining!

Mike Hall had made up his two-plus lap deficit, and at the 100 mile mark rushed past Headley to take over the lead. He hardly had time to enjoy the view from the top, however, as the Hart engine in his Lola was beginning to act up, and he had to call at the pits. He later rejoined the race, but by this time was too far behind. This gave the lead to Redman in the BMW, who had followed Hall through the Corvettes. Minter had been gaining ground prodigiously, but then had a rocker arm break. The 11 minute pit stop ended his chances also.

As the race neared the half way mark, Redman led and Schuppan was now second and gaining. The inevitable was put off briefly when Schuppan made a pit stop, but not for long. On lap 40, just as Schuppan was closing in for the kill, Redman went off course with broken suspension, ending his day. Schuppan was now in front and lapping far faster than anyone else on the course. The 63 laps ended with yet another downpour. Another squall line thundered through as the race had only a couple laps to go. Speeds again dropped drastically as the track quickly became awash. A very damp flag was waved, Schuppan winning by over two laps from Dennis Aase's Porsche 908/2 Spyder. Heimrath was third in a Porsche RSR, while Headley came home fourth. Hall struggled back to take fifth from Hirsch's Porsche 908/2 while Minter finished seventh. Schuppan averaged 101.465 mph for the 252 miles.

It was a worthy experiment and an interesting race, but not quite what Tufte and the SCCA had in mind. They would tinker with the formula and try again the next year.

1976

The FB race at the 1976 June Sprints. James King, Jerry Hansen and Tom Outcault enter turn 3. King would prevail taking the win.

After 20 full seasons of racing, the track was due for a repaving. The entire four miles were given a fresh coat of asphalt during the off season, and the new surface was expected to contribute to faster track times. Clif Tufte scheduled three weekends again, the June Sprints and the Trans-Am/F-5000 weekends as before. For the third weekend, he gave a lot of thought to running a handicap as in '75, but the less than hoped for turnout of cars gave him pause. The date was held open for a few months. Then, as summer started, it became apparent that the F-5000 series was in some trouble, as some cancellations and defections to IMSA's Camel GT reduced the number of confirmed dates to six. Tufte, always an SCCA backer, added a second F-5000 race to the '76 schedule, with the Handicap being an offshoot of it.

The SCCA caught a break when Porsche had a difference of opinion with IMSA over their 934 Turbo car. IMSA would not allow it, while Porsche wanted very much to race it in the U.S. As a result, SCCA restructured the Trans-Am again, giving it its fourth format in 10 years, in order to accommodate the Porsches and the support and visibility that Stuttgart brought to the program. In addition, SCCA created another pro series, this again at the request of Volkswagen. In order to showcase its new Scirocco model, a single make series, sponsored by Bilstein shock absorbers, was to run as support on several pro weekends.

The June Sprints ran eight races, ranging from 12 to 20 laps in length.

Five hundred twenty cars entered, another astounding turnout. Saturday's Formula Vee race was as much a howler as the previous year's had been. Fifty cars started, and David Harris won in a Lynx. In the 48 miles between those two happenings the lead was traded far too many times to count. Long snaking lines of drafting Vees circulated the course, the order changing constantly as cars would slingshot past each other. Denny Ura, J.J. Carlin, Jerry Peterson, Mike Frangkiser, Jerry Knapp, John Haydon and Jim Hall (not the Chaparral Hall!) all had the lead at one time or another. It came down to the last turn, Peterson leading going in and Harris coming out. In a mad dash for the checker, four cars wide, Harris won by an eyelash.

The larger Formula race had a different look. On the non-pro, club level, the FA cars were practically extinct. Virtually anyone who had a top F-5000 car was using it in the pro series, not at the National level. Indeed, Tuck Thomas with his Lola T-332 was the only decent FA car here. Even Jerry Hansen had forsaken the class, as he was driving a FB Lola T-460 this year. In the race, Thomas broke early and James King held off Hansen for the win in his March 76B. The FA winner, Dean Vetrock, was 16th overall in a six season old Lola T-192.

The Formula Ford race had 60 starters with Dave Wietzenhof leading the first lap even though he had started seventh. Bob Paladino fought with Wietzenhof, finally passing him in his Lola T-340. Tony Kester joined in the

Brian Redman exiting turn 14 while lapping the older Lola of Bert Kuehne. Redman won the points-counting 80 mile F-5000 race in August 1976.

fun, his Dulon FF right on Wietzenhof's tail. Dave however, felt that first was his rightful place, and he soon repassed Paladino for the lead. Kester followed Wietzenhof's Zink past Paladino and finished second as Wietzenhof won FF for the second straight year.

The 80 mile feature for A and B SR, A-C Prod, & AS started over 50 cars, most of which were powered by big American V-8s. Jerry Hansen was back with his now seven season old Lola T-220 and had several old Can-Am cars to challenge him. The biggest threat, though, came from Randolph Townsend who brought a Porsche 917-10 Spyder all the way from Reno to challenge Hansen. Townsend gave Hansen a bit of a tussle, even leading the third lap, but Hansen soon reestablished himself in first and pulled away to win. Townsend finished second, ahead of the McLaren M6B of Leonard Janke, the McLaren M8F of Charles Nearburg and the class BSR winning Chevron B31 of Wayne Nelson.

In July the restructured Trans-Am came to RA. The 1975 formula of production cars continued, but now designated as Category I. FIA Group 3 and 4 cars were now eligible, and they were running in Category II. Created on Porsche's behest for the 934, the category was home to many, and they did take most of the year's marbles. However, the category also drew a goodly number of 'silhouette' cars, very potent, highly modified/developed versions of the Camaro and Chevrolet Monza, plus several of the rocket ship-like Greenwood Corvettes. In addition, the Porsche Carrera RSRs were again eligible.

Two Porsche 934s showed at RA. Vasek Polak entered a car for George Follmer while Al Holbert was in his own. A couple big engined C-II Camaros were on hand, for Carl Shaffer and Greg Pickett. Ludwig Heimrath headed the Porsche RSR contingent, while Jocko Maggiacomo led the C-I points category coming into RA, his ex-Penske Javelin seemingly rejuvenated. This was the fifth of eight Trans-Ams this year, and the wins so far had been spread. Follmer and Hurley Haywood had each taken one race in Polak's 934s, while Monte Shelton had pulled a surprise at his home track of Portland in an RSR. The Glen Six Hours was taken by Peter Gregg and Haywood in a BMW 3.5 CSL.

Follmer took the pole in qualifying and was expected to win the race. At the start he pulled into an immediate lead, followed by Holbert. Within a

few laps, though, Carl Shaffer, using all of the horses the 454ci Chevy in his Camaro would give him, started knocking on the door. Shaffer challenged Follmer and eventually passed him for first. Greg Pickett, in a similar Camaro, now pulled onto Follmer's tail and challenged for second. He couldn't quite get to grips with Follmer, however, and had to settle for third. The 100 mile sprint ran out with Shaffer taking his first Trans-Am win with Follmer second, followed by Pickett, Holbert and Heimrath. Don Hager was sixth overall, first in Category I, in a Corvette.

Shaffer won the next Trans-Am, at Brainerd, while Heimrath took Mosport and Follmer copped the season-ender at Trois Rivieres. Follmer won his second Trans-Am championship, with Maggiacomo taking the Category I crown. The Trans-Am had been revitalized and would continue for three more seasons in this form.

The Formula 5000 race drew 24 entries, rather small, but the sharp end of the field was loaded. Haas/Hall had Redman in a Lola T-332. Vel's-Parnelli Jones Racing had its T-332 for Al Unser, while Interscope Racing had a similar car for Danny Ongais. Two very potent teams came from Europe to compete. Racing Team VDS, which had dominated F-5000 racing on the Continent for the past few years, had two 1976 model Lola T-430s for Teddy Pilette and Peter Gethin. Teddy Yip's Theodore Racing had a Lola T-332 for Alan Jones and a March 76A for Bruce Allison. Dan Gurney had given up on the recalcitrant F-5000 Eagle and was debuting a Lola T-332 for Vern Schuppan. Shadow had a DN-6B for Jackie Oliver. The big news here was that the Shadow was powered by a Dodge V-8, breaking the Chevy mold that all the other cars had used for years. Hogan Racing brought a Lola T-332 for Brett Lunger. Other T-332s were for Warwick Brown, Doug Schulz, Randy Lewis, Skitter McKitterick, John Gunn, Bob Nagel, Tuck Thomas, John Briggs and Richard Shirey.

This was the fourth of seven races on the slim 1976 schedule. Alan Jones was the points leader, having won at Mosport in the Lola and at Watkins Glen in the March. The win in the March was the first for anything but a Lola since 1973! The season opener had gone to Redman. In qualifying Unser was fastest, taking the pole for the first heat at 2:01.644. Oliver was second in the Shadow, while Redman was third. Theodore Racing had been very active, but mostly off track. Horst Kroll had crunched his old Lola

71

T-300 big time and had purchased the Theodore Lola for his further use. Then Jones discovered a broken rear cross member on the March and declined to use it further, even when repaired. Teddy Yip thereupon whipped out his checkbook and rented the Lola T-332 entered by Automotive Developments for Richard Shirey. The Theodore crew immediately fell upon it, modifying it for Jones' taste. Yip then put Allison in the March, only to see him take it heavily into the scenery and out of action for the foreseeable future.

This year the two heats were 48 miles each, with the final being 100 miles. The first heat matched Unser against Redman and was greeted with great anticipation. Unser blasted into the lead with Redman right behind him. That is the way it stayed for the entire 12 laps. Nose to tail, hard racing. Unser nipped Redman for the win, with Brown third followed by Pilette and Don Breidenbach in John Cannon's March 75A.

The second heat saw Ongais make a fine start, taking the lead through turn one's right hander. Oliver went wide, jumping over the curbing and deflating a tire. The subsequent stop dropped Jackie well off the pace. Ongais drove a fine race, winning from Schuppan, Jones, Lunger and Lewis.

As the final started, Ongais duplicated his excellent getaway, but at turn three overdid it, sliding off course and letting Unser, Schuppan and Redman by. Unser was trying very hard to pull out a bit of a lead, but he soon did the same as Ongais, sliding off course. Consequently, as the stream of booming cars came up the hill for the end of the first lap, Vern Schuppan had the powder blue Jorgensen Lola in the lead, followed by Redman, Unser, Brown, Jones, Oliver, Pilette, Ongais and Gethin.

Schuppan held onto the lead for three laps until Redman dove inside going into one to take the point. Schuppan held on to second until lap 10 when Unser managed to get by, and then he had Ongais threatening. Unfortunately for the Hawaiian, the Interscope Lola slowed with an electrical fault, eventually calling at the pits. Redman was not extending his lead over Unser, though. In fact, both Redman and Unser were in trouble. Redman had engine trouble, a valve spring having broken. Unser was also slowing, having buzzed his engine when he missed a shift. This was all to Oliver's advantage, and on lap 17 he passed Unser for second and two laps later took Redman for the lead, who retired to the pits shortly thereafter.

Oliver now had the lead and was not to surrender it. Unser, while hobbled by an engine that had lost its edge, still held on to second over Schuppan. Warwick Brown threw away a chance to get Schuppan when he spun, but managed to hang onto fourth because fifth place Jones was also spinning; three times in fact. They were lucky not to lose any places because of ill fortune striking their pursuers. Pilette was slowed with a broken brake disc, Gethin blew the engine, and Lunger had his suspension break.

Consequently, Oliver came home the winner, scoring an impressive first win for Shadow and for Dodge. In fact, Dodge was the first non-Chevrolet engine to win in F-5000 since George Follmer's Ford powered Lotus in 1970! Al Unser held on to second place, while Schuppan came in third, followed by Brown, Jones and Pilette in sixth. A fine race indeed.

A month and a half later, the cast reassembled in the rolling Kettle Moraine country. This year the RA Handicap was to be for F-5000 cars. Clif Tufte again showed his penchant for unique promotion by the program. Since a handicap event could not legitimately be run for championship points, two F-5000 races would be held. On Saturday, the F-5000 cars would run an 80 mile sprint – Tufte dubbed it the *RA Speedster* – for points. No heats, the field gridded on the basis of qualifying times on Friday. Then, the numbers would be crunched. Based upon qualifying times and lap times in the *Speedster* as well as July's race, the F-5000 cars would be launched in groups for Sunday's 100 mile handicap event. Nine groups

would be formed, with times ranging from scratch for the slowest up to a 3:30 deficit for the fastest. In addition, two support races would be held Sunday, a VW Gold Cup Super Vee round and a sprint for A and B sports racers, another doomed attempt to revive the Can-Am spirit.

Much the same field was present as six weeks earlier. There were a few changes, in addition to a somewhat larger field attracted by the two chances to win some money. Vel's-Parnelli Jones Racing and Interscope Racing had merged, now running the cars for Al Unser and Danny Ongais out of the same shop. Alan Jones was absent, F-1 commitments in Europe preventing his attendance. This was unfortunate, as Jones was the points leader coming into the race. Derek Bell took his place in the Theodore Racing entry, which was a brand new, never raced Lola T-332. Bay Racing had pulled out, temporarily leaving Warwick Brown without a ride. However, Racing Team VDS had three cars available, so it picked Brown up to drive a Lola T-430 alongside that of Teddy Pilette, while Peter Gethin would be in the team's Chevron B37. The Shadow team was late getting to the track, not arriving until Saturday morning. Jackie Oliver was second in the points chase, and the late arrival, coupled with the fact that they brought only last year's DN-6, hindered Oliver's chances and put them in a catch-up mode all weekend.

A warm and pleasant Saturday started with final qualifying for the *Speedster*. Redman, not unexpectedly, took the pole with a time of 2:01.573. What was a surprise was Teddy Pilette in second with the VDS T-430. Oliver, Ongais, Unser and Brown filled out the first three rows.

Redman and Pilette took off like scalded cats, Redman leading but the tail of Pilette's Lola wagging furiously in the corners as he tried to get past. Ongais, Oliver and Unser followed in close company. Bell was already out, a stone having pierced his radiator on the first lap. On lap five of twenty Ongais managed to get past Pilette and set off in pursuit of Redman, slowly chipping away at the five second lead. Redman responded with greater speed, and the gap began to expand after contracting slightly. On lap eight Unser muscled his way past Pilette into third, and Oliver saw his championship hopes fade to almost nothing as the Shadow rolled to a silent halt, a short in the electrics.

Unser moved up to Ongais, and the two new teammates dueled furiously. The pace of their battle began to eat into Redman's lead. Redman was dealing with a chunking tire, and prudence was telling him to pit for a replacement. However, as there were only a few laps to go, Redman crossed everything he could and stayed out, going just fast enough to stay ahead of Ongais and Unser. Finally, a brief 42 minutes 59 seconds after the start, Redman came across the line to win, propelling him into the points lead. Ongais and Unser followed in second and third. Gethin came home fourth in the VDS Chevron, while Pilette had faded to fifth as his early race pace had blistered a tire, necessitating a pit stop. Brown, Schuppan, and Lunger all had dropped out, each while poised to place well

Sunday also was a pleasant day. It began with a 60 mile VW Gold Cup FSV race, which was won by Tom Bagley in a Zink over Bob Lazier's Lola. Mike Yoder and Herm Johnson followed, also in Lolas. Bagley would go on to win the '76 season championship. The 60 mile A and B sports racing event was, frankly, an embarrassment. A very small field of under two liter cars and a few old and very tired, weakly driven Can-Am cars vainly chased Mike Hall, who easily won in a Lola T-294.

The math had been done, and the stage was set for the unique F-5000 Handicap. 12 cars would leave on a rolling start with a pace car. Then, at varying intervals, the rest of the field would be fed in from the pit lane. Some of the nine groups had but one or two members, but that is what the projected lap times dictated. All save Al Unser would participate. Unser had made his distaste for the handicap process well known, and he steadfastly

Warwick Brown (third in line) takes the VDS Lola T-430 past the Lolas of John Benton, Richard Shirey and Evan Noyes.

refused to run. Nonetheless, in mid afternoon the first 12 cars were off, with Doug Schulz leading the first couple laps in his ex-Johncock Lola T-332. In the second group, which started 10 seconds after the first, were the Lolas of Richard Shirey, Bob Nagel and Arlon Koops. Pre-race speculation centered around Shirey. A Formula Ford champion, Shirey had shown good speed in his first year in the faster cars. The pundits were right. It took Shirey just a handful of laps to make up the deficit, and he took the ADF Lola – the same car Alan Jones had driven in July – into the lead.

Meanwhile, John Briggs had joined 30 seconds behind, Evan Noyes 1:30 behind, a threesome at 1:50, Derek Bell at 2:10, Schuppan, Lunger, Brown and Gethin at 2:30, Oliver, Ongais and Pilette at 3:10 and all by himself, Redman at 3:30. Granted the format was contrived, it was entertaining as the faster cars moved swiftly through the field, trying to make up the deficit to Shirey. Two cars in particular were on the move. Schuppan had outdistanced the rest in his group and was moving up smartly. Redman was fastest of all, but a seven mile deficit would be hard to overcome.

As the race progressed, Shirey continued to lead, while Noyes had moved from 1:30 down into second. John Briggs, who had started one minute ahead of Noyes, was in third, while Derek Bell, the first of the *really* fast guys, was running fourth, having made up most of his two minute plus handicap. Skeeter McKitterick was in fifth and Schuppan was sixth and closing.

On lap 16 of 25, Schuppan moved past both McKitterick and Bell to take fourth. On lap 19 he caught and passed Briggs for third, and on lap 22 he nailed Noyes for second. Now only Shirey was ahead of him, and the gap was closing. In Schuppan's wake were several cars that had moved up through the field with him. Brown was just a few seconds behind Vern, having started in the same group and having kept him in sight on their mutual charge. Bell, after having been passed by Schuppan, was engaged in a scrap with Brown while Gethin was not too far behind them. As the race entered its last eight miles it appeared that the whole thing might come together with a multi-car dash for the flag!

Entering the last lap Shirey still led, but his mirrors were full. Schuppan fell upon him and quickly passed, followed by Brown and Bell. He went from the lead to fourth inside of a mile. Vern Schuppan brought Dan Gurney's AAR Lola home for the win, the first for Gurney's team in F-5000 in three years. Further, Schuppan had won both RA Handicap races. Obviously, the Aussie was not handicapped enough!

Warwick Brown was 13 seconds behind in the VDS Lola, while Derek Bell came home third in the Theodore Lola after Noyes had spun out of the place on the last go-around. Shirey held on to fourth, just ahead of Peter Gethin in the VDS Chevron. Sixth went to Brian Redman, but that was scant reward for an excellent drive. Redman simply flew around the four miles, setting a new race lap record at 2:01.251. He made up three minutes of his handicap, six miles worth. He finished the 100 miles in the lowest time of all (counting just on track time, not time spent in the pits waiting to start) and would have been right up there if he hadn't had a spin that cost him time. Redman spun? Yes, but it really wasn't a mistake on his part. His seat had broken away from the mounting bolts and the first time thereafter that he stomped on the brakes it was a real adventure!

So ended the F-5000 Handicap, a most interesting weekend. Unser won the next and last race of the series at Riverside, while Redman took his third straight Formula 5000 crown. USAC pulled out of its co-sanction after three years, apparently deciding that a 5.0 liter stock block formula was not going to work in their Indy car series. A few weeks later a big shoe fell, as the SCCA could not get enough promoters to schedule a F-5000 race in order to keep the series viable. As a result, Formula 5000 died. It was a pity, because it was a fine series, with fast, interesting cars driven by top drivers, but the marketplace decides. A few weeks later the announcement was made that the Can-Am would return in 1977. True, it would not be the unlimited Can-Am of memory, but it would carry the name, a name that the promoters felt had a mystique about it. Their thinking was that the Can-Am name would bring the multitudes back even though the product was not the same.

1977

With the turmoil surrounding the SCCA's pro racing program, Clif Tufte had to be a bit imaginative in setting the 1977 schedule. Tufte never lacked imagination, and he devised a three weekend schedule that showed his flair for unusual promotion. The June Sprints would remain as before, but they were advanced to the very start of June. The July weekend would be headlined by the *new* Can-Am, with Super Vee in support. To crank up Saturday's gate the Can-Am cars would run in a short preliminary race to set the grid. For the late summer date, he moved the Trans-Am into its own weekend for the first time. Not being entirely sure if a Trans-Am, at least as constituted in 1977, could carry a weekend, Tufte ran the *Trans-Am Twin 80s*. This was two Trans-Am races, each for 80 miles, one on Saturday and the other Sunday. In addition, a professional Formula race would run in support.

Relations between SCCA and IMSA were testy, with IMSA now allowing Porsche Turbos in their Camel GT series. This meant that with very little variation the Trans-Am Category II rules and those of the Camel GT were virtually identical. This led to arguments, threats and counter threats over schedule conflicts and entries. In reality, this did neither series any good but IMSA had the upper hand with Camel sponsorship, higher visibility races and more dates. It would take the SCCA three more years of playing second fiddle before establishing a separate identity for the Trans-Am.

Another area of contention revolved around the VW Super Vee series. SCCA regained control of the series from IMSA, which had run most of the rounds the previous two years. However, USAC had established a rival series. Also supported by Volkswagen, the USAC *Mini-Indy* series was run on oval tracks in support of the USAC Champ car series. The idea was to have FSV serve as a training ground for future Indy drivers. USAC at this time was just becoming vaguely aware that the short dirt ovals were no longer the road to Indy.

SCCA was to undergo another change of command, as late in the year Cameron Argetsinger returned to his New York law practice and Tom Duvall took over as Executive Director. One big plus in SCCA's column, however, was the gaining of sponsorship for the new Can-Am series. First National City Travelers' Checks was getting into racing in a big way, sponsoring the Can-Am and USAC's Championship Trail plus one or two cars in virtually all major series. In three years they would be gone, as has been seen before and since with such splurges of sponsorship, but while they were present, their money was appreciated! At any rate, they put some of their money into the Can-Am, which officially was called the *SCCA Citicorp Can-Am Challenge*. In addition, they would sponsor the Haas/Hall entry for Brian

The wild and weird Schkees were driven by Tom Klauser and Doug Schulz. The Lola-based McKee built cars were unlike any others that ran in the Can-Am.

Redman.

The June Sprints, June 4-5 this year, again saw huge fields contest several races. Fifty Formula Vees ran 60 miles Saturday before a crowd of approximately 20,000. Jerry Knapp in a Caldwell had a fight with John Hogdal's Lynx early in the race until Hogdal spun. That gave Knapp about a three second lead, big in FV terms. Martin Potashnik and Tom Stephani closed the gap in the late going, actually catching Knapp in the last turn. They came up the hill virtually three abreast, with Knapp nipping Potashnik by less than a car length.

The bigger Formula cars also ran 60 miles, with Dan Johnson leading all the way in a Chevron B24 FA car. Johnson had the only decent FA car in what was now a moribund class due to the axing of F-5000. However, the FB and FC contingent made up for it, as they made up a strong 52 car field. Tom Outcault's new March 77B finished second overall, first in FB. He led Jerry Hansen across the line, Hansen in a new Lola T-560 FB. Bill Anspach easily won FC in a Chevron B34.

Seventy-six Formula Ford cars filled a good portion of the track on a pace lap that seemed to go on forever. Dave Wietzenhof made it three Sprints wins in a row as he took the flag in his Zink. Gary Hackbarth, in a Lola T-440, gave him a fight, even getting alongside on more than one occasion, before settling for second.

The 80 mile feature for A and B SR, A-C Prod and AS also had a big field, 56 cars, but it was heavy on the production ranks. At the amateur, club level, the bigger sports racing cars, as well as the FA cars, were becoming increasingly rare. With increasing pro opportunities, drivers who would have bought a big sports racer in the past and run it in SCCA

Before there were motorhomes, Chris Amon and Gilles Villeneuve relax at the 1977 Can-Am. Villeneuve would place third in the Wolf WD-1 in his only Road America appearance.

Nationals were now buying something to run for bucks, either in SCCA Pro or IMSA.

At any rate, the race shaped up as a three way battle between Jerry Hansen in his now eight season old Lola T-220, Jack Hinkle in his equally aged Lola T-165 and Randolph Townsend in a Porsche 917-10 Spyder. Townsend and Hinkle led the first few laps until Townsend parked with drivetrain failure. Hansen had been loafing back in third, and he now moved up to challenge Hinkle. They traded first place for a few laps before Hinkle went off course and smashed the back of his Lola. Hansen now cruised to the win, his fourth in a row at the Sprints. Mort Platt was second overall, first in BSR, in a Chevron B36, while Bill Morrison brought his Corvette home third, with first in AP. This fall, at the Road Atlanta SCCA Runoffs, Townsend would finish, but he would still be second to Jerry Hansen, who won another ASR National crown.

The Citicorp Can-Am came to RA in July. The formula was radically different from the first, anything goes, Can-Am. The promoters' intent was to bring back the magic of the Can-Am. Hence, they wanted fendered sports racers. Since nobody was building any, and since so many entrants had redundant F-5000 cars in the garage, the rules were structured to allow F-5000 cars to run, but with envelope bodies covering the wheels. Engine displacement would be limited to 5.0 liters pushrod, 3.0 liters overhead cam; turbocharging was not allowed. In an attempt to boost the numbers, a two liter division was created.

Initially, a number of old Can-Am cars were run with the big aluminum 7.0 liter plus engines replaced by the smaller 5.0 units. In reality, this didn't work, as the smaller engines didn't push the cars built strong to handle the big powerplants around with any great speed. Further, the old two seaters were heavier than the formula car based units. The way to go was to drape a F-5000 car with new bodywork. Of course, with the attendant structural changes necessary to mount a body, a domino effect ensued. The cars were now a bit heavier, so brakes, suspension, etc., had to be strengthened. As anyone who has been involved in racing can attest, nothing is cheap, and the more that is done, the more that has to be done, and the more that it will cost. Most cars converted were based on the Lola T-332, which had been the outstanding car of the F-5000 era. The most common conversion was to a kit developed by Jim Hall and his crew at the Chaparral workshops. Quite a number of these kits were sold through Carl Haas. In addition, Lola built a run of new cars to this specification. These were known as the T-333CS, the CS standing for *Chaparral Sports*. A num-

ber of Lolas also were converted by prolific car designer Bob Riley. The bodies on the Riley version were quite different from the T-333CS design. McKee also built some conversions, producing wild-looking, coupe-like cars badged as the McKee Mk. XX, but called *Schkees* in deference to Doug Schulz, who was bank rolling the project as well as contributing his ex-Johncock T-332 to the project as the first car.

Saturday led off the racing with the FSV Gold Cup race. This was Bob Lazier's year, and he won this round on his way to the championship. Eau Claire's Herm Johnson was second, while Fred Phillips took third in a Zink. Both Lazier and Johnson drove Lolas.

The Haas/Hall effort had suffered a severe setback at the first race of the year when Brian Redman had a very bad crash. He suffered a broken neck, among other breaks and bruises, and was out for the year. Haas/Hall also missed the second race while regrouping and had returned to the series at Watkins Glen, the race prior to this. French F-1 driver Patrick Tambay was now behind the wheel. He took the Citicorp Lola T-333CS to victory at the Glen, but got it wrong in Friday's practice at RA, crashing the car rather comprehensively against the turn 13 bridge. The team loaded the car into the trailer and drove 150 miles to their Chicago shop. After 36 hours of repairs, it was back at RA Sunday morning, although with no time it would have to start at the back of the grid.

The Lola was the popular weapon and there were many on the grounds in addition to the Haas/Hall car. VDS had Peter Gethin in theirs, while Hogan Racing's entry was driven by Randy Lewis. John Briggs was using Tropicana Hotel sponsorship for a two car team for himself and Don Breidenbach, who had won the Laguna Seca round. Herb Caplan's U.S. Racing entered George Follmer, while Bill Freeman's entry was driven by Elliott Forbes-Robinson. Other Lolas of note present were for Chip Mead, Bob Nagel, John Gunn, Evan Noyes and Horst Kroll.

Walter Wolf, a Canadian running a F-1 team quite successfully with Jody Scheckter driving, had commissioned the Italian Dallara firm to build a car for this series. The result, the Wolf Dallara WD-1, was driven by Gilles Villeneuve, the '76 and '77 Formula Atlantic champion who had just made his F-1 debut the week prior in a McLaren at Silverstone. Two Schkees were to be driven by Doug Schulz and Tom Klausler, who was the winner in the season opener at Ste. Jovite. Graham McRae was in his own McRae GM-3, a car unique for its transparent upper bodywork, which allowed the spectators to see Graham at work. Bob Brown in a March and Mike Hall and Bobby Rahal in Lolas led the two liter category.

Saturday's 10 lap, 40 mile sprint was to set the grid for the feature on Sunday. Forbes-Robinson did not start due to gearbox problems, while Tambay's car was still in Chicago. However, 26 cars did start, and Peter Gethin led all the way to win in the VDS Lola. Villeneuve, Klausler, Noyes, Briggs, Nagel and Lewis followed, with Brown taking the two liter portion.

Sunday was very wet. A steady rain drenched all on Sunday morning and held the crowd down to an estimated 23,000. After Bill Deters won a 15 lap race for VW Sciroccos, the Can-Am cars were gridded. The rain let up for the race, but it was run under a gloomy overcast. Gethin took the lead at the start of the 38 lap, 152 mile contest, with Klausler and Villeneuve giving close chase. Spearing through the field from the back were Tambay and Forbes-Robinson, joined by Follmer, whose car had not arrived at the track until Sunday morning. Tambay's charge would be blunted by an off-course maneuver which tore off part of the front bodywork. Then he tripped over Lewis and tore off the other half. Follmer's car, without the benefit of any preparation, soon retired.

Klausler stalked Gethin and took the strange-looking semi-coupe past on lap five. The engine in Gethin's Lola was not pulling full revs; apparently a valve spring had broken. Villeneuve closed on Gethin, followed by Forbes-Robinson, Breidenbach, Briggs, Tambay and Lewis. After the first of two mandatory pit stops, the order remained much the same. However it all came to tears for Klausler on lap 24. While still holding the lead, he came up to lap Mort Platt's Chevron U-2, which was three laps down. They both went for the same section of road, and when the dust cleared, both were out.

Gethin now led, able to coax enough speed out of his ailing car to stay ahead of Forbes-Robinson and Villeneuve. Then the engine in Forbes-Robinson's car quit, and Gethin had a cushion. Villeneuve's challenge was blunted with gearbox woes, and Briggs was able to pass Gilles on the last lap to take second behind the winning Gethin. Tambay endured all manner of difficulty to finish fourth, while Lewis snagged fifth on the last lap in the Hogan Lola. Gethin had averaged 105.263 mph; the speeds of these *converted* cars were slower than the F-5000 times of the previous year. Bob Brown came in eighth place overall in his March 77S to win the two liter cup by one place over Mike Hall.

The Haas/Hall Team did nothing wrong the rest of the season as Tambay won all five remaining races to easily take the championship. Gethin finished second and Forbes-Robinson third. Brown won the year's under two liter title.

The unique Trans-Am Twin 80s occupied Labor Day weekend. The hot car, of course, was the Porsche 934, of which three were present, for Peter Gregg, Ludwig Heimrath and Monte Shelton. Three IMSA-spec *silhouette* Chevy Monzas were for Greg Pickett, Tuck Thomas and Roy Woods. John Greenwood was represented by two Corvettes, each outlandish, one even more so. Buzz Fyrhie had a Greenwood *Super Corvette* in Category II, while Greenwood had Jerry Hansen driving his latest. This was a tube frame, big engined version with side radiators set in NACA ducts in the doors. Topped off with a big wing, it was the center of attention. Carl Shaffer had further modified the Camaro with which he won two Trans-Ams the year before. In Category I the two Oftedahl Camaros of Dick Kantrud and Tom Bagley made ready to dice with a herd of Corvettes and the Group 44 Jaguar XJ-S V-12 driven by Bob Tullius.

The two 934s of Heimrath and Gregg led away, with Hansen running third. Heimrath was able to stretch a lead over Gregg, who, as it turned out, was running slightly lesser boost in an attempt to make the car last. Later, a spin would further dampen his chances. Hansen kept the heat on the two 934s until lap 11 of 20. Stefan Edlis, in a C-I Porsche 911 wandered into the much faster Hansen's path and the resulting crash put both out. Heimrath ran home the winner, with Gregg second, Thomas third, Shelton fourth, Pickett fifth and Fyrhie sixth.

A much better contest took place in Category I. Nick Engel's 454ci Corvette led the first eight laps until its engine gave out. John Huber took over in a Corvette, with Bagley right behind. Tullius was in trouble early with brake problems that eventually caused his retirement. On lap 14 Bagley got around Huber and the two led a tight group consisting of the Porsche 911s of Tom Spalding and John Bauer and the Corvette of Don Hager. Huber began experiencing some brake trouble of his own, and a slide off course was all Bagley needed to gain a cushion. Bagley took the class and seventh overall, leading Huber, Bauer, Spalding, Hager and Babe Headley.

On Sunday the various woes had been fixed, and a full field was ready to go once again. But before the second Trans-Am, there were two pro for-

A large field charges through Hurry Downs on the first lap of the Trans-Am Twin 80 race. Porsche 934s dominated: Ludwig Heimrath won the first event and Peter Gregg took the second.

mula races, both free standing and not part of any series. A huge field of Formula Fords ran for 60 miles with Bill Henderson holding off the attacks of Brian Goodwin and Tom Davey, all in Crossles, to win. Bertil Roos, Tim Evans and David Loring also mixed in, but the day belonged to Henderson. A 60 mile race for Formulas A, B, C and SV saw a half dozen FA cars entered, but only the Lola T-330 of Jerry Hansen and the Chevron B24 of Dan Johnson had any speed. Hansen played with Johnson for a good portion of the race before pulling away to win.

The grid for the Trans-Am was based upon the finish of Saturday's race. This meant that Hansen, Shaffer and Tullius, among others, would have to start at the back of the 42 car field. The race began as a replay of the day before. Heimrath took off, with Gregg chasing. Thomas, Pickett and Fyrhie followed. Hansen, meanwhile, was making rapid progress. He gained 20 places on the first lap alone, eight more on lap two, and by lap five he was in fifth place. He passed Pickett on the ninth lap, but by then the leading threesome were quite a ways up the road. Shaffer ended a bad weekend on lap three when the engine gave way while he was following Hansen from the back.

Finally, on lap 15 of 20, Gregg's patience paid off. Just about the time that he was despairing of reliability being a factor, the turbo in Heimrath's Porsche let go, and Gregg was in front. He was able to hold this to the finish, taking the win and extending his championship lead over Heimrath. Thomas came in second, while Hansen had the Super Corvette in third. The Monzas of Pickett and Woods followed.

In Category I Bagley and Huber had continued their duel. On lap 15 Huber passed Bagley, but the problem was in their mirrors. Tullius had come all the way from last to third. Tullius passed Bagley and on lap 17 nabbed Huber for first. Tullius came home sixth overall and first in Category I after a truly superb drive.

Gregg went on to win the Trans-Am title. Or so he thought. Well after the season was over, the FIA overturned his win at Mosport, giving the race win and the title to Heimrath. It seems that Heimrath protested the bumper brackets on Gregg's Porsche as being outside the regulations. That protest was denied at the track, upheld by the Canadian motorsports body CASC, overturned by the SCCA, and then upheld by the FIA. It was all a bit of unpleasantry disliked by all but Heimrath. In Category I, on the other hand, Tullius won the title on the track.

1978

Jerry Hansen in turn six on his way to another win in the 1978 June Sprints driving a Lola T-333CS.

For 1978 a few changes were in order for SCCA racing. First of all, a new series came into being, or should we say was resurrected. The Formula B series which ran from 1967 through 1972 only to die from lack of sanctioning body interest was revived. In Canada the formula had been flourishing, under the name Formula Atlantic, with sponsorship first from Player's, then Labatts. Now the SCCA took a renewed interest, and the series expanded from Canada into the States. It was a co-sanction agreement, with CASC running the Canadian rounds and the SCCA doing the same down here.

The Formula Super Vee scene was burgeoning. For 1978 both the SCCA series, now sponsored by Bosch, and the USAC Mini Indy series had ten dates each. Further, reflecting what Volkswagen was building, the 1800cc water cooled sohc four was introduced. These more powerful engines would quickly run the old air cooled units out to pasture. Volkswagen also changed the car in its one make Bilstein Cup spec series from Sciroccos to Rabbits.

In club racing, the new British class of Sports 2000 appeared. These were two seat sports racing cars powered by 2.0 sohc Ford fours. No wings were allowed. For 1978 however the cars would run in BSR. In 1980 they would get a class of their own. Also, the showroom stock category was now configured into classes SSA, SSB and SSC, based upon performance.

The schedule for RA was similar to 1977. The June Sprints led things off, while the July Can-Am weekend was supported by a round of the new Labatts Formula Atlantic Championship. The September Trans-Am was just one race this year, but at a greater distance than both the '77 races combined and in a split format.

The first weekend in June again saw an enormous field contest the eight races of the June Sprints. 552 cars were entered which made for some very full fields. For example, 54 Formula Vees ran for 60 miles, while 72 Formula Fords finished up Saturday with a 48 mile race. The Vees did their usual multi-car drafting, pass the lead back and forth act with nine cars in the lead group, constantly shuffling positions. Oftentimes three abreast in the corners and four abreast on the straights, the Vees put on a great show. When all was said and done, Jerry Knapp repeated his previous year's win, just edging out Martin Potashnik.

The Formula Ford event was equally as exciting. Dave Weitzenhof led more often than not, but Tony Kester, Gary Hackbarth, Bob Richardson and Carl Anderson all had a turn. It all came down to the run up the hill from corner 14 on the last lap. Weitzenhoff, Richardson and Kester came to the line three abreast for a photo finish. It was Richardson followed by Weitzenhof and Kester, all three cars covered by a tenth of a second!

Sunday Archie Onwiler won the small bore event in a DSR Chimera and D.J. Fazekas took the Showroom Stock event, as he was doing everywhere in those days. Then the big sports racers and production cars came out for 72 miles. Jerry Hansen had finally retired his '70 Lola T-220 and replaced it with the ex-Tambay Can-Am winning Lola T-333CS. He was up against Jack Hinkle, who was still driving his 1970 Lola T-165 powered by a big 7.0 liter plus Chevy. The race saw the two trade first several times; the nimbleness of Hansen's newer Lola offset by the much greater power of Hinkle's. Finally, Hansen was able to draw away and scored yet another Sprints feature win. Mort Platt took BSR in a Chevron, while the Corvettes of Don Hager and Bob Kerns took AP and BP. Logan Blackburn again was the CP winner and Dick Kantrud snared the AS flag.

The big formula cars ran for 72 miles also, and there were as few FA cars on hand as there had been ASR cars the race before. In reality, Dan Johnson had the only fast FA present, a five year old Chevron B24. There was a strong FB contingent, though, led by Kevin Cogan's Ralt. Jerry Hansen, having met with limited success in two years of running Lola FBs, had a new March 78B. Bill Anspach, Rick Koehler, Tom Outcault and Kenny Briggs also were March mounted. Johnson's car would not start, and he was pushed off his pole position. The field was well on its pace lap before the Chevron fired, and Johnson set off in pursuit. The field took the green before Johnson caught up, and the chase was on. Cogan led, followed by Outcault, Hansen, Anspach and Koehler. Johnson was knocking cars off left and right and was in second by lap eight. The next lap he was in first and pulling away. Unfortunately, that is where the racing ended, as the skies suddenly opened and drenched the track. The slick-shod cars were uncontrollable, and the race was prematurely checkered at 10 laps. Johnson had won, with Cogan second, first in FB, followed by Outcault, Koehler and Hansen. Jim Trueman took FC in his March 773.

The July Can-Am weekend had but two actual races. The Formula Atlantic 100 mile go and the 120 mile Can-Am were both held Sunday afternoon. Saturday's only *races* were two short sprints, 7 laps for Atlantics, 10 laps for Can-Am. Unlike 1977, the sprints did not set grid positions based upon finishing position. Instead, if a driver turned a faster lap in the sprint than he had turned in actual qualifying, the sprint lap time would prevail. As a result, the sprints were rather lackluster affairs, with few contestants actually racing. For the record, the winners were Bobby Rahal in Atlantic and Alan Jones in Can-Am.

The Labatts Formula Atlantic Championship race attracted a very competitive field. The expansion of the Canadian series into the U.S. had attracted a lot of interest and the field was full of young drivers on their way up. Bobby Rahal was the fastest qualifier, taking the Pierre Phillips/Red Roof Inns Ralt RT-1 around the four miles at 2:13.836. The title chase was essentially a two man show. The *Flying Finn*, Keke Rosberg, was driving a Chevron B45 for Fred Opert between his F-1 commitments and he had a narrow points lead over Howdy Holmes, who was driving a March 78B for Doug Shierson. However, in the 100 mile race, Bill Brack gave Holmes the toughest time. Brack, in his own March 78B, dueled with Holmes for most of the 25 lap distance, with Rosberg holding off Rahal for third. As the race wound down, Holmes pulled out a few car lengths per lap and won by three seconds over Brack. However, Rosberg's Chevron blew its engine on the last lap, falling out of third place. Rahal took the spot, followed by Danny Sullivan in a March 78B and the March 77B of Tom Gloy. Holmes took command of the points situation and was the first champion of the combined series.

In this second year of the *Son of Can-Am* the cars were even more F-5000 based. Gone were all but one or two of the old two-seater Can-Am cars, uncompetitive with the smaller engines. Development was afoot on the Lola T-332 base that most used. Some teams had modified the cars to such a degree that they were giving them new names. For example, Herb Caplan's U.S. Racing had replaced the outriggers on its Lola with monocoque extensions, modified the suspension and clothed it all in a new envelope body. The result was a car they called the Prophet. George Follmer would continue as Caplan's driver, and he had triumphed earlier at Ste. Jovite. Paul Newman was now an entrant in racing, in addition to his dri-

ving and teamed with Bill Freeman to form Newman/Freeman Racing. They had modified a Lola very similarly to what had been done to Caplan's and the result was called the Spyder NF-10. Elliot Forbes-Robinson was in the cockpit; he had taken the Spyder to a win at Charlotte earlier in the year.

Carl Haas was on his own once again as Jim Hall had formed his own Indy car team and was off winning the Indy 500 with Al Unser. Nonetheless, Haas was still winning. The driver this year was Alan Jones, and the Aussie had won two of the five races leading up to Elkhart. The car, of course, was the latest Lola T-333CS. Another strong Lola T-333CS was the Racing Team VDS entry for Warwick Brown, the winner at Watkins Glen two weeks previously. Al Holbert had transferred over from the Camel GT series, where he had won the championship the two previous years and was driving a new Lola T-333CS for Hogan Racing. Shadow was back with a two car entry for Jean-Pierre Jarier and Randolph Townsend. The Shadow DN-10 was essentially last year's DN-8 F-1 chassis with a 5.0 liter Dodge V-8 shoved in the back and covered with a black envelope body. The added weight thoroughly upset the cars' handling and the team never put in the test time necessary to correct the problem. Jarier and Townsend had long, unhappy seasons.

Jones whipped into turn one ahead of the pack and acted as if he intended to stay there. Brown initially followed in second, until Follmer moved past him on lap five and started to close the gap on Jones. The first round of fuel stops shuffled the order, which then read Jones, Holbert, Brown, Jerry Hansen (Lola T-333CS), Forbes-Robinson, Vern Schuppan (Elfin MR8A), Follmer and John Morton (Lola T-333CS). By half distance both Shadows were out and they were soon joined by Hansen, who dropped out of fourth with two flat tires, and Mike Hall, who also had a flat tire while holding an entire lap lead in the under two liter class.

In the second half of the race positions tended to remain static, affected mainly by pit stop shuffling and dnfs. Alan Jones brought the Haas/First National City Travelers Checks Lola to the checker in first followed by Warwick Brown and Al Holbert. George Follmer fought through handling troubles to take fourth in the Prophet, while Morton took fifth and Schuppan placed sixth. Forbes-Robinson had faded late in the race to seventh in the Budweiser Spyder. David Johnson benefited most from Mike Hall's failure to finish as he won the U-2 category in a Lola T-290. Jones turned the day's fast lap at 2:05.791, still four and one-half seconds slower than the fastest pure F-5000 time.

Jones won two more races this year, for a total of five, as he took the Citicorp Can-Am Championship. Forbes-Robinson and Holbert each took one of the remaining races. Brown was second in points with Forbes-Robinson third and Holbert fourth. Peter Smith in a Chevron was the season U-2 point leader.

On Labor Day weekend Tufte did just about everything differently. First of all, practice was Saturday, qualifying Sunday and the Trans-Am was on Monday, Labor Day. Further, the Trans-Am format was, well, different. The race was run at a distance of 300 kilometers, 188 miles. But it was run in two stages. The first was for 88 miles, at which time the race would be stopped and all cars would have, in essence, a universal 'pit stop'. During this break, the Bosch VW Super Vee race would be run. Following that, the second segment of the Trans-Am would occur. This was not run in heats; rather, the second segment would start where the first ended. Further, the separation between cars at the end of segment one would be carried forward to segment two. This confusing arrangement was a topic of great conversation among the T-A teams all weekend!

The Porsche 935, a faster, group 5 version of the 934, was eligible for both the Trans-Am and the IMSA Camel GT. However, IMSA was allowing twin turbo versions of the 935, while SCCA restricted the Porsche to a single turbo. Hence, most 935s were seen running in the Camel GT series.

Two World Champions to be: Alan Jones and Keke Rosberg confer in the paddock during the '78 Can-Am weekend. Jones would win the Can-Am in the Lola of Carl Haas, while Rosberg had problems in the F-Atlantic race.

Nonetheless, three 935s were at RA, in the hands of Monte Shelton, Ludwig Heimrath and Hal Shaw. Jerry Hansen had bought the Greenwood Super Corvette he drove in the Twin 80s the year before and had promptly sold it to Greg Pickett, acquiring Pickett's Monza in the deal. Pickett had modified the car somewhat, as it no longer carried the side radiators and had won two Trans-Ams so far. Hansen had used the Monza only once, but had won the Brainerd Trans-Am with it. Other Monzas present were driven by Tuck Thomas and Tom Frank. A most interesting entry was the Herb Adams *Silverbird*. An extremely trick Pontiac Firebird, it was still being debugged after a late start to the year. Jerry Thompson would drive.

In Category I the trophy was already in the mail. Bob Tullius had four straight wins coming into RA and the title was in his pocket for the second straight year. His immaculately prepared Group 44 Jaguar XJ-S was simply too much for the hordes of Corvettes that were up against it.

On Labor Day, a slam-bang Bilstein Cup VW Rabbit race that was taken by Bill Deters led off matters. Bill Alsup was the big news of the year in FSV. He was running both series and was leading both points standings. In fact, he won a USAC race at Ontario, California, on Saturday of this weekend. His crew then towed the car for 36 hours, getting to Elkhart Lake in time for Monday's race, even though he would have to start his Argo JM-6 from the back of the field. Herm Johnson had won the previous SCCA round at Brainerd and had his Lola T-620 on the pole.

The Super Vee race, which was held between Trans-Am segments, started with Johnson simply outclassing those around him. He was unstoppable and motored into the distance. Alsup, though, was on a charge from the back. He was up to 10th by lap five of 15. By lap eight, Alsup was fifth. Things were more difficult from this point on, though, as Johnson, Denny Moothart in a Riley, Stuart Moore in a Lola and Steve Lathrop in a Citation Zink were quite a ways ahead. Alsup never slacked off, though, and caught Lathrop just before the finish. Johnson won, followed by Moothart, Moore and Alsup. The points Alsup gained for fourth were enough to clinch the 1978 SCCA FSV title. A few weeks later he would add the USAC crown.

In the Trans-Am, Monte Shelton had two wins in his 935 and was leading the points coming into RA, the eighth race of the ten race season. Greg Pickett was second but close. This situation put Shelton in high panic as

race time approached, since he crashed his 935 in the morning warmup, rendering it unfit for further duty this weekend. Jerry Hansen, who had qualified his Monza fourth, came to the rescue and lent his car to Shelton for the race. A thankful Shelton would have to start from the back of the pack due to the driver change. Pickett and Heimrath were on the front row of the grid, while the Thomas and Hansen Monzas had been the next fastest.

On lap one, Pickett and Heimrath traded the lead three times. Lap two saw Pickett in front and gaining a bit. On the third lap he increased his lead further, and on lap four he held a large margin over Tuck Thomas. Heimrath slowly chugged up the pit lane and into the paddock, the engine having let him down. Thompson was following Thomas, with Hal Shaw next. Shelton was moving through the large field very rapidly, but it all ended after just a few laps as the Monza's engine expired, along with Shelton's points lead.

Segment one ended with Pickett an easy 26 seconds ahead of Thomas, with Thompson and Shaw following. Only Thomas and Thompson were on the same lap as Pickett. In Category I, Tullius caught the leading Corvette of Nick Engels on lap 12 and led the category at the break.

After a couple hours the second segment began. Pickett took off like the hounds of hell were after him. Thomas got bogged behind a backmarker who was ahead of him on the road and was a virtually insurmountable 22 seconds behind Pickett after only one lap. Pickett had it in hand; only mechanical failure could intervene on his cruise to victory circle. Nothing happened, and Pickett took a very easy win 51 seconds ahead of Thomas. Thompson was third, Shaw fourth and Bob Tullius took fifth overall, first in Category I, ahead of the Corvette of Babe Headley.

By winning, Pickett vaulted into the points lead. He would win the next race and finish second in the finale to take the championship. He had four overall wins. In Category I, it was all Tullius. In fact, the Jaguar driver won the last seven races! It was no contest.

So ended 1978. Internationally, Mario Andretti won six Formula 1 Grand Prix races in the ground effects Lotus 79, becoming the second American to be World Champion. The next year would bring major changes to the track, and developments elsewhere would change the face of racing.

1979

Bobby Rahal, back from Europe, passes Jacky Ickx going into turn five in the 1979 Can-Am.

After 1978, Clif Tufte retired. The man whose vision created Road America, whose engineering skills built it, whose business savvy made it prosper and whose promotional abilities made it *the* premier American race track, had decided to take it easy. To replace Tufte as president, which of course could not really be done, the board of directors chose Lee Hall. A retired Chicago banker, Hall had been on the board for many years, and a track vice president for several. Before his retirement from the cockpit in 1974, Hall had been an active race driver, mainly in under two liter equipment. In fact, in 1964 Hall had been the SCCA's Class EM National Champion driving an Elva Porsche. In addition to being president of the track, Hall also became the general manager.

While building upon the legacy of Tufte, Hall decided to do some things differently and to expand the activities at RA. Over the next few years new sanctioning bodies would stage race weekends at RA and the number of spectator events would increase. In his first year Hall made a major change; IMSA would visit the track for the first time. While Tufte had been a staunch supporter of SCCA through thick or thin, Hall realized that it was time to expand the schedule. IMSA was growing at a fast clip for one thing, and tracks had to expand beyond one sanctioning body in order to avail themselves of the markets that were there and were growing; perhaps even to survive.

Hence, RA would still have three weekends in 1979, but they would have a different look. The June Sprints would remain as before. The July

weekend would be a major weekend; all five SCCA professional series would run. The Can-Am would anchor the weekend on Sunday, supported by Formula Atlantic. The Trans-Am would be Saturday, with Super Vee and Rabbits. This was a weekend that the dyed in the wool fan could not possibly miss! The September weekend, which had been Trans-Am the last two years, was now an IMSA weekend. For the headline event Hall revived the concept of the Road America 500. The Winston GT (R.J. Reynolds had changed the name from Camel for '79) cars would run for 500 miles. Further, the race would be sponsored for the first time as the Pabst Brewing Co. affixed its name to the race. Saturday would feature IMSA's support series of small sedans in a 500 kilometer go.

All this was wrapped up in much celebration of the track's 25th Anniversary. The fact that all the hoopla was one year premature apparently made no difference to Hall and the track's publicity department.

Politics was, of course, the staple of the off season. This winter more than the usual bickering and fighting had occurred as a group of USAC Indy car owners, led by Roger Penske and Pat Patrick, broke away and formed their own Indy car series under the CART label. This stood for Championship Auto Racing Teams, and within two years they had taken over all Indy car racing except for the Indy 500, and racing would be forever changed. Indy car racing, which was dying under USAC, would initially be saved under CART, and then would embark on a growth curve that would see it challenging Formula 1 for the world's premier form of motor racing in the '90s. For the first year, in order to have the proper sanctions

80

The 500 was revived as an IMSA GT race. Dick Barbour's team of Porsche 935s played a feature role during the weekend.

and insurance, the CART series would be sanctioned by SCCA.

The first weekend in June again saw the season kick off with the June Sprints. There would be three less classes this year, though. The SCCA had a system for eliminating poorly supported classes, and Formula A, A Production and B Sports Racing had fallen below the 2.5 average cars per race threshold and were eliminated. This put all sports racers over 1300cc in ASR, as were any Formula A cars still running at the National level. The FA cars could run *sans* fenders this year, but by 1980 they had to have envelope bodies. Further, ASR now had a top displacement limit of 5.0 liters. The big seven-plus liter aluminum Chevys were history. The big block Corvettes at the club level were a thing of the past also. The designation *FA* remained, but it now stood for Formula Atlantic and replaced what had been Formula B.

The SCCA, in an attempt to promote club racing, had established the Bonus National concept. A National in each of the club's six geographic divisions would be accorded Bonus National status, which brought some promotion assistance from SCCA as well as the awarding of more points per position than in a standard national. While welcome, the assistance was not really needed at RA, for the June Sprints had always been the top draw in all of SCCA's amateur racing.

Saturday's 14 lap, 56 mile Formula Vee race finally saw the ultimate in close Vee racing – a dead heat! Six cars: John Hogdal, Dave Smith, Scott Rubenzer, Tom Stephani, Dave Harris and Martin Potschnik; all had a chance. They were separated by mere inches the entire last lap, passing and repassing, going down the straights three and four abreast. Hogdal had led into the first turn on the last round and came out of the turn in sixth! It was that kind of lap. Stephani led into the last turn, but then Smith, then Hogdal, then Rubenzer and then Harris all pulled alongside going up the hill. It was five wide, with Harris actually driving, flat out, on the grass! They flew under the flagger's bridge this way, the only change being that Harris tucked back in behind Smith as he was getting a bit uncomfortable driving off road. A roar, a blur, who won? After considerable discussion the decision was a dead heat. Hogdal and Smith both won, both having crossed the line at the same instant. Stephani was third, by just the length of a nose cone, with Rubenzer fourth, another blink back. It had never been closer.

The Formula A and C event was a case of "local boy makes good." Carl Liebich, a school teacher from nearby Plymouth, led the entire 72 miles in a Lola T-560. Second place seemed to be a curse, as Bruce Clark,

Tom Grunnah, Bill Anspach and Ed Midgley all held it at one time or another, and all spun it away. Midgley, luckily for him, had the smallest spin and was able to salvage the position. Mike Plotz took FC in a March water cooled Super Vee.

The BP, CP, AS 72 mile race should have been Logan Blackburn's. Driving a CP Datsun 280Z, Blackburn took the lead at the start and eased away to a comfortable margin. In years past, such a car should not have been leading this race. However, the absence of AP plus the driving skills of Blackburn gave us the surprising sight of a Datsun leading Corvettes. Blackburn held onto the lead until lap nine, when a flat tire took him out of the running, quashing what would have been a storybook win. The lead then went to Stefan Edlis in a Porsche 911. Having started the race 31st, Edlis was a story also. But, like Blackburn, it came to naught. On the last lap Bill Morrison made a move on Edlis in his Corvette. There was contact, and both were out. Vernon Brown led only part of one lap, but it was the one that counted as he drove his Corvette to victory. Jerry Dunbar, who was making his 24th consecutive June Sprints start, was second overall, first in A Sedan, in a Camaro.

The Sports Racing feature, also for 72 miles, was won by Jerry Hansen, his sixth consecutive June Sprints feature win and ninth since 1968. Again driving his orange Lola T-333CS he qualified 8.3 seconds faster than the second man! Perhaps knowing that the race would tend to be a bit dull if he drove at that pace for the whole 72 miles, Hansen pitted on the second lap for a change of goggles. Whether necessary or not (and Hansen later kept a straight face when he insisted that he really had to change goggles), it put him in sixth place, half a lap behind new leader Jim Sechser, McRae GM-1. Giving the fans a show, Hansen knifed through the field, taking the lead from Sechser three laps before the finish. Sechser was second with Larry Johnson third in a Lola T-333. Fourth went to Jack Hinkle. For the first time in over a decade, Hinkle was not able to give Hansen a challenge. His old Can-Am Lola T-165 now had to have a 5.0 liter engine, and it could not propel the tired old car at anything near the speeds the 7.6 liter engine could. The 67 year old Hinkle would finally retire this car at the end of this year, after 10 years together. The next year he would be back in a Sports 2000 Lola, but it would not be the same.

On to the big one. The July 20-22 weekend featured all five of SCCA's pro series. Truly, a racing smorgasbord for the enthusiast. After Gary Benson won the 48 mile Rabbit race, the VW/Bosch Super Vees ran for 60

Dave White spins his BMW at turn five causing those behind to take evasive action.

miles. Herm Johnson made it two in a row at RA, winning in his Ralt RT-1. Johnson was on the pole, but lost the lead at the start to Geoff Brabham. However, Brabham only led the first lap as he lost his engine on lap two. Johnson took over at that point and led until lap seven, when he handed the point to 19 year old Tom Stewart when he went off course. Stewart, in a Bill Scott Racing Ralt, led Johnson, Peter Moodie who was in an Argo, Bob Lazier driving Bertil Sollenskog's March and Dave McMillan's Ralt. All was not well with Stewart's car, though, as the throttle was sticking. Johnson passed on lap 13 of 15 and won, leading Stewart, McMillan, Moodie, Mike Chandler and Lazier to the finish. Even though he won no points this weekend, Geoff Brabham was the season champion in Super Vee, winning five of the eight races.

Saturday's lead race was the Trans-Am. Four Porsche 935s were entered and were heavy favorites for the win. Bayside Racing had two, for Peter Gregg and Bruce Levin. John Paul and Ludwig Heimrath had single entries. Gregg was in the process of winning his sixth IMSA Camel GT championship and his driving in this Trans-Am on an *off* weekend annoyed some of the T-A regulars. But on the other hand, Gregg was a two-time Trans-Am Champion (three by his count; see 1977 dispute) and had his SCCA credentials. The only competition to the 935s was offered by two Chevy Monzas. Tuck Thomas had his usual car, while Gary Wellik was in the ex-Jerry Hansen car. However, on race morning Mexican Daniel Muniz rented the car when his Category I Camaro quit for the weekend. John Paul was the points leader coming into RA, having won three of the first four Trans-Ams this season. In Category I the last two year's champion Bob Tullius was not present. His Group 44 outfit had retired the Jaguar XJ-S and was working on a new Triumph TR8, but they weren't ready for this weekend. Hence, the fight would be among a large number of Corvettes and Camaros.

Paul was the fastest qualifier, but Heimrath took the early lead, followed by Paul, Thomas, Gregg and Mo Carter's Camaro. By lap 11 of 25 Heimrath still led, but Gregg was moving up. After several unsuccessful attempts, Gregg finally got past Thomas to take third. The next lap Gregg managed to outbreak Paul and moved into second place. Paul dropped a few places with a trip down the escape road. Just when it looked as if Heimrath was going to win flag to flag, he pitted with a flat tire, losing the lead to Gregg and second to Thomas. Two laps from the end the rear end in Tuck's Monza broke, and Heimrath was back in second. Gregg took the win, to the chagrin of some, with Heimrath second. Muniz was third in his borrowed Monza, while the Porsche 935s of Paul and Levin were fourth

and fifth. Although Paul was fourth today, he did win the year's Trans-Am Championship winning six of the nine races. Probably just because he was so popular here, Gregg also ran the season finale at Laguna Seca and won that also!

In Category I, the Corvettes of Bill Adam, Dick Danielson and Frank Joyce fought over first. By mid-race Danielson was out with a flat tire while Adam retired a lap later with a broken gearbox. Joyce led, but was in trouble with an ill-handling car. Gene Bothello picked up his pace and took over from Joyce on lap 14. Bothello then led to the end, winning over the Corvettes of Paul Canary and Gary Carlen. Bothello was the year's Category I champ, winning four races. Tullius ran three with the TR8 and won them all for second in the standings.

Sunday's Formula Atlantic race, run for 100 miles, was a first time win for Bob Earl. Driving the NTS Ralt RT-1, Earl took advantage of misfortune that struck pole sitter Kevin Cogan's Ralt, a spin dropping him way back on the first lap. Then, Jeff Wood, who had held the lead from that point, had the engine stop in his March 79B on lap nine. This put Earl in front, but he had to contend with a strong challenge from points leader Tom Gloy. He was able to withstand the pressure from Gloy's Ralt to take the win, with Gloy second. Cogan had recovered to third, but went out in a collision with Howdy Holmes' Shierson March while disputing the position. Cliff Hansen wound up with the spot in his March 79B, while Rick Koehler was next, in the Ecurie Excalibur March 79B. Sprints winner Carl Liebich was next in his Lola T-560. Gloy would go on to win the series title.

This set the stage for the 160 mile Citicorp Can-Am feature. The battle this year was between the Carl Haas Lola T-333CS, driven by Belgian Jacky Ickx and the Newman-Freeman Spyders, a three car entry for Keke Rosberg, Elliott Forbes-Robinson and Randolph Townsend. RA was the sixth round of the year, and Rosberg, with two wins, was leading the standings. Ickx, also with two wins, was second. The Prophet of Herb Caplan was now being driven by Bobby Rahal, while Brit Geoff Lees was in the Racing Team VDS Lola, now clothed in a Riley body and carrying large underbody wings. Hogan Racing had the first car purpose-built for the new Can-Am regulations, as opposed to being an offshoot of a F-5000 car. The Hogan HR-1 designed by Lee Dykstra had a tube frame for simplicity and a body incorporating modest ground effects. Al Holbert was behind the wheel. The rest of the field was a variety of Lolas and under two liter cars.

The front row of the grid was all Budweiser Spyder. Rosberg was fastest at 2:01.760, showing that after three years of development, the times were back in the F-5000 range. Forbes-Robinson was next to him, while

The BMW 320i Turbo of David Hobbs belches flame as it goes up the hill to turn six. The team of Hobbs and Derek Bell won the first IMSA race at Road America.

Ickx and Lees were on row two, and Holbert and Rahal on the third row. The Spyders rocketed away at the start, establishing themselves 1-2 and lengthening the gap to third place Ickx, followed by Lees, Rahal and Holbert. By lap 12 Rahal had moved up to third and was looking to challenge the Spyders when the clutch on the Prophet failed, putting him out. Ickx regained third, which became second on lap 16 when Forbes-Robinson spun out of the race. On lap 20 Rosberg also was out, a valve spring breaking in the engine. Ickx now found himself in the lead, followed by Lees, Holbert, the Lolas of Bob Brown and John Morton, and the Elfin of Vern Schuppan. Ickx held the lead the rest of the distance, relinquishing it only briefly during pit stops. He brought the Haas/Citicorp Lola home first at a 112.950 mph pace, with Geoff Lees second and Al Holbert third. Brown had faded, and Morton, Schuppan and John Gunn in a Lola filled out the top six. In U-2 Tim Evans withstood a stern challenge from Mike Hall to win the category. He was to be the season champ, as was Ickx overall. Ickx was to win five of the ten races, with Alan Jones winning a sixth in Ickx's car while he was off playing at Le Mans. With this championship, Carl Haas had now won six major SCCA titles in a row.

Labor Day weekend was the inaugural IMSA show, headlined by the Pabst 500 for the Camel GT Championship. Saturday was qualifying and the Champion Spark Plug Challenge 500, a 500 kilometer (312 mile) race for IMSA's small sedan series. The win went to Hurley Haywood and Rob McFarlin in a Mazda RX-3 after they withstood challenges from the Starita/Sharp Datsun B210, Roger Mandeville and Jim Downing in Mazdas and the AMC Spirits of Irv and Scott Hoerr, Amos Johnson and Dennis Shaw. The winners' plight was made easier when the two Team Highball AMCs of Johnson and Shaw both went out within seconds and within sight of each other; Johnson after hitting the guardrail and Shaw with an engine fire.

The Pabst 500 featured seven Porsche 935s. Dick Barbour Racing entered three for Brian Redman/Barbour, Bob Akin/Rob McFarlin and Bob Garretson/Skeeter McKitterick/Buzz Marcus. Bayside had Peter Gregg/Hurley Haywood/Bruce Levin in theirs, while Ludwig Heimrath had Brett Lunger co-driving his. The Interscope 935 was for Milt Minter/Ted Field and Charles Mendez had his to be co-driven by Paul Miller. Their top competition would come from the BMW effort. McLaren Cars was running the works effort, a 2.0 liter 320i Turbo driven by David Hobbs and Derek Bell. Jim Busby had a new BMW M-1 coupe, co-driven by Dennis Aase. There were a number of other cars present, Monzas, Greenwood Corvettes and the like, but realistically the winner would be one of the above. In GTO, the usual Corvettes, Camaros and Porsche 911 Turbos were being chal-

lenged by Group 44, which was making its IMSA debut with Bob Tullius/Brian Fuerstenau in the Triumph TR8. GTU featured a horde of Mazda RX-7s against the class leading Datsun 280-ZX of Don Devendorf/Tony Adamowicz.

Peter Gregg was on the pole, at 2:15.675, with Brian Redman alongside. Six of the first seven cars were 935s, the odd car being the Hobbs/Bell BMW. Gregg duly led at the start, until Heimrath passed on the fifth lap. Hobbs was in third, ahead of Redman. Gregg dropped to ninth after a pit stop to fix a loose wheel. However he quickly reeled in those ahead of him and passed Hobbs for second on lap 22. When Heimrath pitted and turned the car over to Lunger, Gregg regained the lead. Hobbs and Redman disputed second for a number of laps until Hobbs had to stop prematurely, as the BMW was suffering from fuel pick up problems.

As the race reached one-third distance, two top contenders dropped out of the running. The Heimrath/Lunger car broke its front suspension, while the Bayside 935, Haywood up, lost two laps when the engine quit as it approached the pits. This put Barbour in the lead, in for Redman, with Bell and Minter following. However, Barbour was no match for Bell, and soon the little BMW took over the lead. Shortly thereafter, Barbour took the red 935 into the pits for a long stop to fix an ignition problem.

When Bell finished his stint and turned the car back over to Hobbs, the die was pretty much cast. The only other cars on the lead lap were the Field/Minter and Mendez/Miller 935s. Fourth place Busby/Aase were a lap down, McKitterick was next, now in the Barbour/Redman car, only to lose a wheel shortly thereafter, then the McFarlin/Akin machine. Despite the fuel pickup problem, which caused the BMW to pit eight times, twice what was planned, the superb driving of David Hobbs and Derek Bell brought the BMW home first, a splendid overall win. Miller/Mendez passed Field/Minter very late in the race for second, while Busby/Aase were fourth and Akin/McFarlin fifth.

Sixth overall and first in GTO was the Tullius/Fuerstenau Triumph TR-8. They had a strong run, leading virtually all the way. Second and third were the Porsche 911 Carreras of Garcia/Herman and DeNarvaez/Naon. In GTU, Bob Bergstrom and Rick Knoop won in a Mazda RX-7. The Devendorf/Adamowicz Datsun led most of the race, but lost the lead on the 81st lap with a lengthy pit stop to try to rectify differential and clutch troubles.

So ended a fine season. RA had been a fairly tranquil setting while political storms swirled about the racing scene: CART vs. USAC, internal clashes within the SCCA, the Trans-Am looking for its identity vs. IMSA.

1980

After much research, Road America added a fourth spectator weekend. In June, the track would run AMA-sanctioned motorcycle races. The event was a big success and continues to this day as a profitable weekend for the track. The first event was greeted with near panic in the surrounding area. Apparently a portion of the local populace had seen Marlon Brando in *The Wild One* too many times and they spent the week of the race boarding their windows and locking up their daughters. It must have almost disappointed the doomsayers when the crowd turned out to be quite average and well mannered. Since the focus of this book is automobile road racing, the motorcycle events will not be covered except as to major developments that affect the track.

There was a second SCCA National at RA as the Milwaukee Region ran a non-spectator event in August. The lure of RA meant that the field would be larger than the average non-spectator National, but at the same time it was not the Sprints, which would remain secure as SCCA's top National.

SCCA continued to be in turmoil. The Board ousted Tom Duvall as Executive Director and replaced him with Buddy Perkins. Perkins hardly had time to warm his chair when he, too, was out, replaced by Jim Melvin, former president of CART. These internal power struggles made the staging of a professional racing series all the more difficult. The Trans-Am rules changed once again, its fifth iteration since 1966. Thankfully, these rules would not be modified in the ensuing years. For the first time – and probably the last – SCCA had all its pro series sponsored. Citicorp was in the last year of sponsoring the Can-Am, while CRC Chemicals came on board to sponsor the Trans-Am. Mamiya cameras had their name on the Formula Atlantics, while Bosch sponsored Super Vee and Bilstein did the same for the Rabbits.

CART and USAC had reached a temporary accord, and the first half of the year saw Indy car racing run under USAC sanction as the *Championship Racing League*. Unfortunately, as soon as the Indianapolis Motor Speedway had run its event and the Pocono 500, which it promoted this year, they pulled out along with USAC, having achieved what was their apparent short range objective of having the CART teams at their race. With the dissolution of the CRL, CART went its own way and proceeded to build

Lap 1 Can-Am scene in Thunder Valley; Stephen South in Paul Newman's Lola T-530 leads Al Holbert in the CAC-1 and Mario Andretti in the Haas Lola T-530.

Indy car racing to heights previously unattained.

IMSA suffered the loss of R.J. Reynolds sponsorship, and their premier series now was just the *IMSA GT*. The sanctioning body and the individual tracks came up with additional dollars in order to have a points fund. Fortunately for IMSA, the loss of sponsorship was temporary, and Camel came back in 1981.

The start of June again saw the June Sprints kick off the racing season. Four races each on Saturday and Sunday was the bill, with Saturday having the better weather, sunny and hot after an early morning thunderstorm. The Formula Vee race was the usual howler. Scott Rubenzer, John Kalagian, John Mills, Fred Clark and Dave Smith swapped places for the entire 60 miles. They pulled away from the rest of the 58 car field and it came down to Clark and Smith going to the line side by side. Clark brought his Zink in first, just a tick of the stopwatch ahead of Smith's Caldwell.

The last race on Saturday was Formula Ford, and an incredible 79 cars took the green. Or tried to take it, as the pace lap had to be red flagged when three overanxious drivers got together and blocked the track at the S/F line. Once underway, though, Gary Hackbarth and Craig Taylor ran the 48 miles as if glued together, with Hackbarth winning in a Lola T-

540 with the Tiga of Taylor in his shadow.

Sunday was cool and overcast, although it did stay dry. Chuck Dietrich won the Formula Atlantic race in his Lola T-460 after early leaders Chip Mead and James King dnf'd. In the sports racing feature, the changing times were evident. Only three old, tired ASR machines were on hand, while 24 new Sports 2000 cars ran. Jeff Miller from nearby Plymouth was the overall winner in his CSR Lola T-496, powered by a 6 cylinder two stroke Kohler engine. Fred Schilplin was second, also in a Lola T-496, while Bill O'Connor was third overall, first in S2000.

The last race of the weekend was for large production and GT cars. SCCA was starting a transition from production and sedan classes to GT classification. Hence, a new category, GT, was instituted. Four classes were in this category, GT1 through GT4. The sedan category was merged into GT, and the large production classes would follow shortly. After last year's disappointment, Logan Blackburn was again a threat for the overall win. Driving his usual CP Datsun 280Z, Blackburn drove furiously, leading most of the way on a track that should favor the big Detroit V-8s. Craig Leifeit took the lead in his Corvette on lap 16 of 18, having come through the field from 44th place. Alas, on the very next lap he tangled with a backmarker and was out. Blackburn came home to claim a giant-killing win.

Mid-July was the return of the SCCA super weekend, with five pro series running in two days. Weather was so-so, with light rain falling on and off.

Saturday's first race was the Mamiya Formula Atlantic 100 miler. Jacques Villeneuve (brother of Gilles and uncle to the Jacques racing CART and F-1 in the 1990s) was on the pole in his Shierson March 80A, but he fluffed the start, and Price Cobb took the lead. Cobb, driving a March 80A, led Villeneuve, Bob Earl, Jeff Wood, Dan Marvin and Rogelio Rodriguez. Earl took Villeneuve on lap four and six laps later passed Cobb into first. With Villeneuve and Wood embroiled in a battle for second, Earl was able to keep his Ralt RT-1 in first for the balance of the race. Villeneuve got past Cobb only to fall off the track on lap 12, giving Price the spot for the duration. Wood spun off in his Ralt, allowing the similar car of Rodriguez to finish fourth. The win was sweet indeed for Earl, who was so broke he had to sleep in the trailer the entire trip coming to Elkhart Lake. Though he finished only third in this race, Villeneuve went on to take the season championship.

The CRC Chemicals Trans-Am was running under new rules this year. Category II was gone, along with the Porsche 935s, et al. The rules now were essentially for production cars, not racers like the 935. However, unlike the very production Category I of the previous few years, the rules now were skewed towards 'silhouette' racers, with tube frames allowed. To put it another way, the Trans-Am was now for road racing sedans with rules and car construction similar to NASCAR. This first year not too many people were fully aware of the tube frame provision, and those cars would not really come on line until the following year.

One car built to the new rules was present and ready, though. Greg Pickett had a new Corvette which he promptly put on the pole. As the 100 miles started, Pickett jumped ahead and started pulling away from the 44 car field. Things appeared to be going all his way when he blew a tire on the seventh lap. The flapping rubber tore the rear bodywork off the car and Pickett was out. Jerry Hansen now took over first in his Corvette and looked to be as dominant as Pickett. Hansen was building up a lead when his motor let go, putting him out. Then Andy Porterfield took up the point, leading handily until he too suffered a puncture. Scratch three fast Corvettes. This put Monte Shelton in first, and that was a bit of a surprise, as Shelton was driving a Porsche 911, which was supposedly slower than the Chevys that were chasing. Shelton nonetheless kept the lead the rest of

the way. Mark Pielsticker was second in a Monza, with Roy Woods closing fast in a Camaro. Woods had come all the way from last place on lap three to the exhaust pipe of Pielsticker. Had the race been a lap longer, Woods would have been second, but it wasn't and he finished third. John Bauer took fourth, also in a Porsche 911. Surprisingly, the little heralded Bauer strung together a season long record of finishes that resulted in his winning the Trans-Am Championship.

Sunday morning, following a Bilstein Rabbit race won by Gary Benson over Randy Zimmer and Peter Schwartzott, the 60 mile Bosch Super Vee race was run. Peter Kuhn won his first pro Super Vee race in a Ralt RT-5, but he did have a bit of luck. On the very first lap front runners Pete Halsmer, Dave McMillan and Josele Garza all spun off, giving Kuhn a very welcome five second lead. He held it for the entire race, with the March 80Vs of Bob Lazier and Mike Chandler following. Excitement was provided by the charge from the tail of the field by Garza and McMillan, the points leader coming in. They managed to bring their Ralts home in fourth and fifth. Kuhn, now that he had discovered how to win, did just that in four of the next five races and made up a huge points deficit to take the Championship.

This cleared the decks for the Citicorp Can-Am, run this year to a distance of 160 miles. In this, the fourth year of the *new* Can-Am, there finally were a number of new, purpose-built cars on hand. Lola had gone into production with the T-530, a car utilizing the new ground effect technology, complete with spring-loaded sliding skirts designed to keep the faster, lower pressure air under the car, thus increasing downforce. The Haas car was again driven by Patrick Tambay, and he had won all four of the Can-Ams run so far. However, for RA Tambay was ill and could not run the Magicolor-sponsored car. To replace him, Haas engaged none other than Mario Andretti. Paul Newman had taken over the Newman-Freeman team completely, and it was now just *Newman Racing*. He had two new Lola T-530s for Elliott Forbes-Robinson and Englishman Stephen South. Racing Team VDS had Geoff Brabham in their T-530. Al Holbert was driving a new car built in his own shops, the Holbert CAC-1. It too was a full ground effects machine, complete with sliding skirts. Garvin Brown Racing had a rather unwieldy beast called the Intrepid GB-1 for Danny Sullivan, while Bobby Rahal was back in Herb Caplan's Prophet. A variety of older Lola F5000-based cars and U-2 machines made up the 29 car entry.

In practice Brabham was clearly the fastest, but a triple roll in the Carousel wrecked the car and relegated him to the backup, which wasn't quite as swift. The pole went to Stephen South, who took Newman's Budweiser T-530 around the four miles at 2:03.359, 116.732 mph. Holbert had his CRC Chemicals-sponsored car alongside, with Andretti and Forbes-Robinson on row two. Under two liters was led by Gary Gove, who was a very fine tenth overall in Pete Lovely's Formula 2 Ralt RT-2-based car.

South took the early lead and held it for the first nine of 40 laps until he had a fast spin at turn five. The resultant pit stop to fix body damage dropped him well back. Holbert had been dogging South since the start and now took over first. Andretti and Forbes-Robinson were chasing in second and third, with Brabham and Rahal trailing. Sullivan was out early and South was moving up fast from well down in the field. On the 19th lap Andretti had the throttle spring break and buzzed the motor of the Haas Lola big time, retiring to the pits with thoroughly bent valves. Brabham closed on Forbes-Robinson and took second when Forbes-Robinson had a slow pit stop due to a slipping clutch. Holbert ran out the distance, a very happy winner in a car bearing his name. The Brabham and Forbes-Robinson Lolas followed, with Rahal fourth. South recovered nicely to take fifth spot, with Colombian Ricardo Londono sixth, also in a Lola T-530. Gove won the under two liter class, after Bertil Roos had to make a long stop to change tires.

Tambay was back at the next race, picking up where he left off. In all, the Frenchman won six of the ten races, easily taking the title for the second time. For Haas, it was the seventh straight major title!

The IMSA weekend featured three races this year, with a Kelly Girl Challenge event joining the Champion Spark Plug Challenge in support of the Pabst 500. The new *American Challenge* series, sponsored by Kelly Girl, was for American sedans and was a playground for Gene Felton. He had won all six events preceding RA, and this round would not be different. Driving a Chevrolet Nova, Felton led the entire 60 miles to make it seven straight. Vern Smith was second early, but Tommy Riggins and Amos Johnson caught him as the race progressed to take second and third. Felton went on to take the last two events, making him a rather unbelievable nine-for-nine on the season.

The Champion Spark Plug Challenge was run for 120 miles this year instead of 312. The winner was the same, however, as Rob McFarlin came out on top. Driving a Datsun 200SX, McFarlin took his fifth win of the year enroute to the title. Irv Hoerr gave him a stiff fight, however, and the finish was one of the closest on record. Hoerr was driving an AMC Spirit, which had more grunt than McFarlin's Nissan. Hoerr dogged McFarlin the entire distance and made his final move in turn 14 on the last lap. He braked impossibly late, scooted ahead of McFarlin going into the turn, only to have McFarlin scrabble by coming out. Then they drag raced to the line, with McFarlin literally winning by a nose. Had the S/F line been just 100 yard further down the track Hoerr would have won as he pulled ahead just after going under the flag. The Mazda RX-3s of Jim Downing, Joe Varde and Roger Mandeville followed, but they were well back of the front twosome.

Sunday was wet. It rained heavily early in the day and on and off during the 500. However, this did not detract from a fine event. As was the case in IMSA at this time, Porsche 935s were the dominant car. Nine were at RA headed by the two car Dick Barbour entry for John Fitzpatrick/Barbour and Bobby Rahal/Bob Garretson. The Bayside car was for Hurley Haywood/Bruce Levin, Interscope for Milt Minter/Ted Field, Akin Racing for Bob Akin/Brian Redman/Paul Miller and Momo for Gianpiero Moretti/Jim Busby. Owner-drivers included Ludwig Heimrath, John Paul and Preston Henn. Most of these 935s were the Kremer-modified versions now dubbed 935K3. Datsun made an effort to counter the Porsche might with a prototype 280-ZX built in Bob Sharp's shop. Of space frame construction, the car featured radiators mounted in the rear fenders and was powered by a twin turbo 4.5 liter V-8. Drivers were Sam Posey and Paul Newman. This being the car's first time out, it was to be constantly afflicted with new car woes.

Fitzpatrick was leading the IMSA points, having won the previous six races. He duly set the fastest qualifying time at 2:09.700, but it was Brian Redman who was the early leader. On lap 11 Fitzpatrick moved into first, a position he was to enjoy most of the day. Redman began dropping back, his car plagued by niggling little problems. By this time Heimrath was already

John Paul Jr. leads the Interscope 935 of Milt Minter at turn 7. The Paul 935 would take an easy win with John Paul Jr. doing the lion's share of driving.

out and Moretti was seriously delayed by a broken drive belt. Haywood was running second in the Bayside car until he had to pit with damage to the front spoiler. Fitzpatrick continued to increase his lead, and at half distance it was three laps over the 935 of John Paul. At this time Fitzpatrick pitted and handed over to Barbour, while Paul did the same, John Paul Jr. taking the wheel. Over the next 100 miles Paul Jr. not only made up the three laps, but was half a lap ahead! This was enough for Barbour, and he came in to give the car back to Fitzpatrick. The Englishman set out after the younger Paul, but the 20 year old built up a big enough lead that he was able to pit and turn the car over to the elder Paul before Fitzpatrick could retake the lead. Fitzpatrick carved away at the deficit, bringing it down to six seconds. But, just when the prospect of a great finish was shaping up, Fitzpatrick had to make a late race stop for fuel. That was it, and the John Paul/John Paul Jr. Porsche 935 won the Pabst 500 by a shade over two minutes from the Fitzpatrick/Barbour Porsche. The 935s of Rahal/Garretson, Henn/Dale Whittington and Redman/Miller/Akin filled out the top five.

Seventh overall was the first GTO car, the Group 44 Triumph TR8 of Bob Tullius and Bill Adam. The only car to threaten the TR8 as it ran to its second straight 500 win was the Bob Bergstrom/Dennis Aase Porsche 911 which finished second in class. The GTU win went to the Electromotive Datsun 280-ZX of Tony Adamowicz and Don Devendorf, which simply ate the field alive enroute to an eighth overall finish. As expected, the Datsun turbo had dropped out with teething problems. Minter had the Interscope 935 well placed for a high finish when the engine blew at the 400 mile mark.

John Fitzpatrick won eight IMSA GT races in all this season as he easily won the championship. Luiz Mendez was the GTO king, winning four times in a Porsche 911. Bob Tullius was second, also with four wins, despite not driving the full season. In GTU the title went to Walt Bohren who notched six class wins in his Mazda RX-7.

1981

The end of the Formula Vee race at the June Sprints with Joe Claudy barely edging out Scott Rubenzer. FV consistently provided close racing and photo finishes.

Over the winter of 1980-81, Clif Tufte, the man who literally made Road America and served as its president and general manager for the track's first 23 years, died peacefully. The track is his legacy and it is safe to say that his influence went well beyond Elkhart Lake. As a respected member of the SCCA's promoters' council, Tufte had great influence not only on the promotion of racing at other tracks but also on the overall conduct of road racing in the U.S. Not only would Road America not have existed without him, but the U.S. racing scene would also look quite different; and not as good.

Road America continued into 1981 with the same lineup as in the past two years. The Can-Am had a new series sponsor, Budweiser, while the Formula Atlantic series had lost Mamiya. The Atlantic series had now been renamed the North American Formula Atlantic Championship, recognizing the fact that there were rounds in the U.S., Canada and Mexico. The Indy car war had been decided in CART's favor, with USAC down to just two events and all the rest belonging to CART. Meanwhile, Watkins Glen had lost the U.S. Grand Prix, to Las Vegas of all places, and the track was in its last year before bankruptcy closed it for a time. Running a motor racing facility is not easy, but RA continued to enjoy good fan support.

At the club/National level, class BP disappeared, integrated into GT-1. This meant that all three of the big production classes of the '60s and '70s, AP, BP and AS, were now all together in one class. Further, Formula Super Vee was gone on the club level, the air cooled cars now in FC while the water cooled cars were in FA.

IMSA not only regained Camel sponsorship, but also introduced a new type of racer that would raise the Camel GT to great heights in the next several years. This was the Grand Touring Prototype, or GTP. These were all-out race cars, two seater coupes powered by a variety of engines from Detroit V-8s to Porsche turbo sixes and Cosworth F-1 engines. It was the start of a new era.

In 1980 all three auto racing weekends were wet to some degree or other. As Saturday dawned on the '81 June Sprints, it appeared that the trend would continue, as it was rainy and foggy. Practice was hindered, but the fog lifted by noon, and the day's four races got underway. David Brown took the small car go in his MG Midget, but the drive of the day went to John Stoesser who started 60th but finished fourth. Following that, 57 Formula Vees fought for 60 miles. Curtis Farley, Scott Rubenzer and Joe Claudy swapped the lead numerous times before it came down to a slip-streaming-drag race out of the last turn. Claudy pulled his Citation Zink out of Rubenzer's draft as they neared the line and pulled ahead to win by a nose. Farley was third.

This set the stage for the Formula Ford race, which gridded 71 cars. The 48 mile race saw a near duplicate of the FV go as the three Fords of Kim Campbell, Craig Taylor, and Brian Goodwin did the pass-and-swap act. Again, it came to the last few feet, and Taylor and Goodwin crossed the line in a near dead heat, Taylor prevailing by just .06 of a second!

The VW Gold Cup FSV race was tight. Bob Earl and Al Unser Jr. both in Galles Ralts lead the March of Arie Luyendyk.

After 15,000 turned out on Saturday, 25,000 came on Sunday, despite the fact that the morning was drenched by thunderstorms. But they passed, and the sun shone in the afternoon. The Formula race was a dice between Stuart Moore in Bertil Sollenskog's Ralt RT-5 FSV and James King in a March 79B. Moore led virtually the entire distance, but King was always in his mirrors, trying to provoke him into a mistake. It never came, and Moore won with King second, followed by Tom Outcault's March 80A in third. Mike Plotz won FC in a March 79V.

The sports racing feature showed the trend in racing at the club level. Gone were all the big ASR cars of the past. Fully 28 starters were from the new Sports 2000 class. While interesting in their own right, they are hardly a replacement for the big bangers of the past. Further emphasizing the decline of the sports racer was the distance of the race – 60 miles. In June Sprints past it was common to have the sports racers run 140 to 160 miles, but times change. As it was, Jeff Miller led 59.75 of the 60 miles; all but the crucial last quarter mile. Miller's Lola T-496-Kohler CSR car rolled to a stop in turn 14 on the last lap, the engine dead; a replay of the same heart-breaking finish that happened to Roy Kumnick in 1964. This time Steve Glassey was the recipient of the victim's largesse, and he swept past in his Tiga SC81 Sports 2000 car to take the overall win.

The final event of the weekend was 64 miles for GT-1. Jerry Dunbar, running in his 26th consecutive June Sprints, finally got the big win that had been eluding him. Dunbar had his Camaro in a race-long fight with the Corvette of Rick Dittman, the lead being swapped several times. Finally, Dunbar managed to trap Dittman behind some lapped cars, giving him the breathing room he needed. Dunbar took the checker, with Dittman trailing by just a couple seconds.

The Can-Am weekend again ran all five SCCA pro series. Finally the weather gave all a break, as most of the weekend was sunny and warm. Saturday's first race was 60 miles for the Bosch Super Vees. Pete Halsmer was on-form all weekend, being the fastest in practice, fastest in qualifying and leading the race from start to finish. It was a perfect weekend for Halsmer and the Arciero Ralt RT-5. While his name was on top of the sheets all weekend, it was not quite that easy. In the race he was constantly shadowed by the Galles Racing pair of Ralt RT-5s driven by Bob Earl and a young 19 year old Al Unser Jr. Earl ran a close second to Halsmer while Unser Jr. and Arie Luyendyk swapped third. On lap 13 of 15 the handling

on Earl's Ralt went off, and he had to slacken his pace, dropping to fourth. The race went to Halsmer, with Unser Jr. in second and Luyendyk third in a March. Young Unser would go on to take the FSV championship, the first of many in his brilliant career.

The 100 mile CRC Chemicals Trans-Am was headed by last year's winner, Monte Shelton. This year Shelton was in a Porsche 930 Turbo and was considerably faster than in 1980. He took the pole with Greg Pickett's trick Corvette next to him. Filling out the first five were Doc Bundy in the Holbert Racing Porsche 924 Turbo, John Bauer's Porsche 911 and the Jaguar XJ-S of Bob Tullius, the Group 44 entry now built around a tube frame.

As the race started Shelton showed that qualifying was not a fluke. He bolted into the lead, followed by Pickett, Tullius, Eppie Wietzes in a Corvette, Bundy and Bauer. Probable threat Jerry Hansen was already out, his Corvette breaking an oil line on the first lap. He was soon joined by Pickett, who stopped with electrical problems. The same problem hit Tullius, who had to stop for lengthy repairs. This put Wietzes into second and Bauer third, after Bundy broke a hub carrier. Shelton serenely whooshed his Turbo around the 25 laps, taking a fairly easy win. Wietzes and Bauer followed. Half the 49 car starting field was still running at the finish. Wietzes continued to enjoy his return to racing after having sat on the sidelines since F-5000 folded and went on to win the '81 Trans-Am title.

Sunday led off with a 52 mile Bilstein Cup Rabbit race. Bill Deters led the first 11 laps, but Peter Schwartzott got past on lap 12. The last two laps saw the two pass the baton back and forth, but Schwartzott prevailed by a whisker as the two cars slipstreamed to the line.

The 100 mile North American Formula Atlantic Championship race began with Jacques Villeneuve on the pole. Driving a Doug Shierson Racing March 81A, Villeneuve was well on the way to his second consecutive Atlantic title, matching the two Canadian crowns collected by his brother Gilles in 1976-77. Villeneuve led from the start, stretching it by a second a lap. Ten laps into the 25 lap race he led Norm Hunter, Dan Marvin, Rogelio Rodriguez, Tom Grunnah and Whitney Ganz. Soon Hunter began dropping back with gearbox troubles and then Marvin blew a head gasket. This put Rodriguez in second and Ganz third, Whitney having caught Hunter and Grunnah when they both spun. With 17 laps completed, Villeneuve pulled into the pits and retired, a sure win gone with a failed wheel bearing. This put Rodriguez into the lead, looking for his first win. Alas, his engine began

Under dark skies Monte Shelton dominates the 1981 Trans-Am in his turbocharged Porsche 930.

to overheat, and he slowed, allowing Ganz, Grunnah, Tim Coconis and Chris Kneifel to pass. Ganz then led the final few laps, taking his first win. Grunnah, Coconis and Kneifel followed, then a downcast Rodriguez.

The Budweiser Can-Am had three Lola T-530s this year, facing a challenge from the new March 817 Can-Am cars and a new Holbert. Carl Haas had Jeff Wood in his car with Landmark Petroleum sponsorship. Geoff Brabham was in the VDS T-530, while Garvin Brown had replaced the horrid Intrepid with a T-530 for Danny Sullivan. Paul Newman had switched from Lolas to March and had two 817s for Al Unser and Teo Fabi. Al Holbert's CAC-2 was a slightly more compact version of his 1980 car. The top runners were completed by Irishman David Kennedy in Herb Caplan's Prophet, now clothed in a Frissbee body. The Frissbee was yet another Lola F-5000-based car, and one was present for Rocky Moran. The rest of the small 20 car field was made up of old Lola-based cars and under two liter equipment.

In practice Teo Fabi, who had won two of the first three races coming into RA, went off at the kink and demolished his March in the trees. After some dithering it was decided that even though he was the points leader it was probably best that he sit out the rest of the weekend. Hence, Unser drove the only Newman Budweiser March in the race. Fabi had been fastest qualifier, at 2:01.290, and with his absence Sullivan moved into the top spot. Wood was alongside in the first row, and behind them were Brabham, Unser, Holbert and Moran.

Sullivan outdragged Wood at the start of the 160 miles and started stretching out a lead. Wood, Brabham and Holbert followed, Unser being slowed by brake problems. In the under two liter category, Jim Trueman was leading easily in the same Ralt RT-2 that Gary Gove had driven the year previous. Brabham made an early pit stop in an attempt to get out of a battling group that was allowing Sullivan to escape. He now ran fifth behind Sullivan, Wood, Holbert and Unser. With a clear track in front of him, Brabham was moving and set a new race lap record at 2:00.268, finally breaking Brian Redman's mark which had stood since 1976. This was aided, no doubt, by the sliding skirts that greatly increased downforce. As the pits readied for the first round of regularly scheduled pit stops Sullivan rolled to a stop on the course. His pit crew had miscalculated, and the fuel tank in the Brown Lola was bone dry. Brabham was now in the lead and his fast laps on a clear track made the difference as he was able to make his

second stop without losing the lead, still ahead of the rest, all of whom yet had to make their second stops.

As the laps ran out, the main battle was for second, where Holbert and Wood were rubbing paint. With two laps left the inevitable happened. Wood got a bit too aggressive and punted Holbert off the track, not only taking second, but allowing Unser to pass for third. That is how the race ended with Brabham taking a finely judged win followed by Wood, Unser and a decidedly unamused Holbert. Jim Trueman came in fifth overall, first in under two liters. After the race the stewards fined Wood and docked him the second place points, but otherwise allowed the finishing order to stand.

Brabham went on to win the Can-Am Championship. He had two wins on the year, as opposed to Teo Fabi's four and Al Holbert's three, but he was far more consistent than either the Italian or the Pennsylvanian. Trueman easily won the under two liter hardware.

Unlike 1980, the IMSA weekend was run in splendid weather on the weekend of August 22-23. The first race of the weekend was the Kelly American Challenge, contested for 60 miles. This year IMSA had opened up the class to American pony cars, and as a result the field was largely populated by Camaros. Vern Smith was on a roll, having won the four previous races coming into Elkhart. Robert Overby led Smith at the start, with Gene Felton having spun to the rear of the 16 car field. Tommy Riggins took his Camaro past Craig Carter's for third on lap three, while Felton was back up to seventh place. Halfway through, Overby spun away first, but recovered in time to keep second. He then closed on Smith, with Riggins following. Then on lap 12 of 15 Overby and Smith came together, not once, but three times, with Smith spinning off into the guardrail. Riggins had to slow to a crawl to avoid the melee, and Felton was past into second. On the final lap, Overby suffered a flat, spinning him out, and Felton completed his last to first run by taking the checkered flag. Riggins, Overby and Carter followed.

The 120 mile Champion Spark Plug Challenge was a walkaway for the Mazda rotaries. Three RX-3s took the top three spots, with Jim Downing leading Roger Mandeville and Joe Varde at the finish. Mandeville led for three laps in the middle, but the day belonged to Downing. The Archer brothers, Tommy and Bobby, tried hard in their Renault Le Cars, but the little front wheel drive French cars just could not keep up with the Japanese sedans. Tommy Archer took fourth, a fair distance behind third place Varde. Downing won the last four races of the season to take the title.

The Cooke-Woods Lola T-600 initiated the GTP class in IMSA and Brian Redman took the Camel GT championship in this car. Here the car is driven through turn 7 by Sam Posey in his last race.

The Pabst 500 saw three of the new GTP cars on hand to challenge the usual horde of Porsche 935s. Lola had built a mean-looking Chevy powered coupe, the T-600. Brian Redman was the points leader, having won five races this season, four in the Cooke-Woods T-600. Chris Cord had just taken delivery of his T-600, and RA would be its first race. Sam Posey was Redman's co-driver, while Jim Adams would drive with Cord. The third GTP was entered by BMW for David Hobbs and Vern Schuppan. The car was a March, and this 81G was the prototype for a long line of March GTPs in the next several years. The car was powered by a 2.0 liter turbocharged four.

Ten Porsche 935s were on hand, led by the Pauls' car, now tube framed as opposed to the standard platform frame. Momo Corse had two present, a long-tail ex-factory car for Bobby Rahal and Gianpiero Moretti and the 1980 Joest-bodied car for Derek Bell and Mauricio de Narvaez. John Fitzpatrick had won two races so far this year in his, and he was partnered by Jim Busby. Andial, a noted Porsche tuner from California, entered a much-modified ex-factory long tail for Rolf Stommelen and Harald Grohs. Add in Bob Garretson's, the Interscope car, Edgar Doeren's from Germany and a couple Latin American entries, and it was a stout field.

The BMW M-1s were now in GTO and were the car to have in that field. The Dave Cowart/Kenper Miller Red Lobster car was the easy points leader. Their only threat came from the turbocharged Datsun 280ZX of Don Devendorf and Tony Adamowicz. In GTU, the Mazda RX-7s were being challenged by Toyota, which entered a factory backed two car effort through Toyota Racing Developments of California. The team was managed by its lead driver, George Follmer.

Stommelen took the lead at the start, with Paul Jr. right behind. Then came Fitzpatrick, Redman, Moretti, Ted Field starting the Interscope Porsche and Hobbs. The March-BMW did not hang around long, though, as the gearbox was slowly breaking up. The car was retired before the 100 mile mark. The Pauls' strategy was to have young John drive the first and last two hours, with John Sr. taking just the middle stint. Further, they would pit out of sequence with the rest in an attempt to get clearer road. Hence, Paul Jr. was in early, moving Redman up to second. Their strategy appeared to be valid a while later when both Stommelen and Redman pitted. Paul Jr. moved into the lead and appeared to be in charge. Grohs, Posey, Bill Whittington, Rahal and Busby followed. The Cord Lola was experiencing some new car blues, as the fuel pump would not pick up the last

10 gallons in the tank. As a result, they were forced into making extra pit stops.

The Paul Porsche continued to lead after Junior gave way to Senior. But it was apparent that Junior was the faster driver, as the Stommelen/Grohs team ate into their lead. After a brief rest Junior was back in the car and the situation stabilized. Unfortunately for them, though, a turbo failed, and they lost four laps replacing it. Their try for two in a row was finished. Soon thereafter, their race was also finished when the engine failed.

This put Stommelen/Grohs into the lead, with the Lolas of Redman/Posey and Cord/Adams next, the latter four laps down after the extra fuel stops. Both the Moretti/Rahal and Field/Whittington 935s were slowed by fuel injection difficulties while the 935s of Bell/DeNarvaez, Akin/McKittrick and Doeren/Sullivan had dropped out. The last 100 miles ran out without incident, and Rolf Stommelen and Harald Grohs brought the Andial Porsche 935 to the finish line in first place, 4 hours 44 minutes after starting, a speed of 105.415 mph. Second and third were the Lola T-600s of Redman/Posey and Cord/Adams. Four Porsche 935s took fourth through seventh in the order Garretson/Gloy, Moretti/Rahal, Fitzpatrick/Busby and Field/Whittington. Second place virtually clinched the '81 Camel GT crown for Redman, and he emphatically handled that technicality by winning the next race.

In GTO the Devendorf/Adamowicz Datsun led the first part of the race until a broken exhaust header put them out. The BMW M-1 of Cowart/Miller took over, seeking to win its tenth of the year. However, they lost their engine and the similar BMW M-1 of Dennis Aase, Chuck Kendall and Pete Smith took the class. Cowart did go on to win two more races, a total of 11, to easily win GTO.

The GTU challenge from Toyota ended fairly early. The Lee Mueller/Walt Bohren Kent Racing Mazda RX-7 had an easy run to the win, but Follmer ran second until the differential failed at the 100 mile mark. The second Toyota was already well off the pace, and even the transfer of Follmer to that car could not fill the gap. Bohren/Mueller finished eighth overall, two laps up on second in class Logan Blackburn/Dave Frellsen in a Datsun. Mueller was the year's champ.

So ended 1981 in the Kettle Moraine. 1982 would bring more change to the track with the addition of a new event, a major new event.

1982

Paul Newman put the Newman-Sharp 280-ZX on the pole and led the first half of the GT feature. Here he has a pre-race discussion with Jerry Hansen.

1982 saw the addition of not one, but two new weekends at Road America. One of the burgeoning trends in racing was vintage car racing—the running of old race cars, obsolete by the day's standards, but worthy of admiration, both at rest and on the track. In July Road America ran its first spectator weekend for vintage cars. Masterminded and promoted by Joe Marchetti, proprietor of the Como Inn and International Autos in Chicago, the weekend would be known as the Chicago Historic Races. From a small start, with a meager turnout by RA standards, the weekend has grown to the point where it became the second largest spectator turnout of the year.

The other new weekend was the big one. In September the PPG Indy Car World Series came to RA. CART now ran all Indy car racing except the Indy 500 and was expanding its series into new arenas. One of the areas of growth was road racing, and in the 1982-84 period classic road courses such as RA, Mid Ohio, Laguna Seca and Portland would become CART venues. CART was *the* area of growth in racing, and already the Truesports team had established a CART team with Bobby Rahal as driver. Following the 1982 season Carl Haas, Paul Newman, Racing Team VDS and Galles Racing would all follow from the Can-Am into CART. The September CART weekend was the first of an annual visit by the Indy cars to RA, and the event quickly grew into the biggest weekend of the season.

At the track one of the first changes noted was the absence of the wooden roof along pit lane. Over the winter a windstorm had carried a

portion of it away. Rather than repair what was getting in everyone's way, the rest was torn down.

Before the new events, though, there was the June Sprints. Again, fine weather greeted a very large field with very close racing. After Dieter Griesinger bested 58 other cars in the small production event, 45 Formula Vees staged their usual close fight. This time it was Scott Rubenzer's turn after being close for a couple years. After a very close slipstream battle with John Hogdal and David Bennett, among many others, Rubenzer led them to the line, his Caldwell D-13 nipping Hogdal by a nose. John O'Steen took the medium production race in a Porsche 924, and then it was the Formula Ford race. A large field of 64 FFs ran for 48 miles, but this year did not have the usual bare knuckle brawl to the finish. Danny Edwards, better known on the PGA golf tour than as a race driver, simply dominated the race in his Lola T-640. In a surprisingly easy race, Edwards took a comfortable win over Kim Campbell's Van Diemen and Curtis Farley's Zink.

Sunday, Larry Rehagen led things off with a showroom stock win in a Ford Mustang. James Opperman and Carl Liebich put on a fine show battling for first in the FA & FC race, passing the lead between them. At the finish Liebich was just ahead of Opperman, both drivers in March 79Bs. Tom Outcault was third in a March 80A, while Peter Heckman took FC in an Argo JM4.

The 60 mile sports racing event was notable for the return of Jerry Hansen. After having missed the past two Sprints due to a conflict with an

The 1982 Can-Am race was taken by Al Holbert in the VDS 001.

IMSA race at his own Brainerd track, Hansen was back in the same Lola T-333CS with which he had captured the past five ASR National Championships. By this time Hansen's total National Championship count was up to 23, with a few more to come before he retired in 1986. In this race it went much as expected. Driving the only ASR car in the race that was remotely competitive, Hansen simply walked away with the win. Jeff Miller finished second overall, first in CSR, in his Lola-Kohler, while third and fourth went to the two top Sports 2000s, Larry Campbell in a Lola T-592 and Steve Glassey in a Tiga SC80.

The final race of the weekend was 72 miles for GT1 and CP. The attraction here was the entry of Paul Newman in a Datsun 280ZX Turbo. Newman was in fine form and qualified on the pole. In the race he moved out smartly, led the opening laps, only to be felled by turbo failure. The movement noticed in the spectator areas at this time was all the females packing up and leaving... What they missed was none other than Jerry Hansen, now in a Camaro, moving into first and holding it to the finish for his second win of the day. Rick Dittman and Buzz Fyhrie followed in Corvettes, with Morris Clement winning CP in a Datsun 280ZX.

In early July the Chicago Historic Races held their initial event. There is a marked difference between vintage events and modern racing. While racing today has become very much a business proposition, vintage racing is in many ways a throwback to the early days of road racing. Matters are far less commercial, camaraderie is far more apparent and an atmosphere of *pour le sport* prevails. These are enthusiasts who appreciate fine cars and who feel that these veteran machines should not be museum pieces , admired statically, but rather should be dynamic objects to be seen in the proper setting – at speed. In deference to the age and value of the machines, most vintage races are of relatively short duration. Classes are determined largely by car age, engine displacement and original intent, as well as performance. Drivers run the gamut from flat-out racers bent on winning to *gentleman drivers* airing out a thoroughbred. Overall, the sanctioning bodies (of which there are many) tend to put the emphasis on the spirit of friendly competition and mutual enjoyment of classic cars, rather than a *win at all costs* philosophy. It is a time and place to simply enjoy cars, at rest and at speed. In view of that, this book will not go into in-depth race descriptions of vintage events, but rather will give an overview and touch on some of the more significant cars present.

Never before or since has Road America seen so many Ferraris. In

these days before the boom in speculation on vintage car values sent prices skyrocketing, people brought their cars out to show, to play and to race. There were over 70 Ferraris in the paddock, including several GTOs, a 625 F-1, a rare '61 Dino 206 racer, many SWB Berlinettas, and on and on. One of the world's two Aston Martin DBR-2s was present. There were Listers, Porsches, the occasional Maserati, Lotuses, Elvas, Ford GT-40s and various specials. It was a treat for the eyes of even the most jaded car enthusiast.

On the track a noteworthy car was Charlie Gibson's 1959 Costin Lister-Corvette. Painted in proper Lister works colors of British Racing Green with a yellow stripe, it brought back memories of what racing was like in the '50s. Gibson led the pre-1960 event. The run for later sports racers was taken by Steve Cohen, who was driving a one-off Porsche 907 Spyder. While the Chicago Historic Races were not necessarily a box office success this first year, it was indisputably an artistic success.

The last weekend in July all the SCCA's pro series congregated at RA. Saturday held round five of the Bosch/VW Super Vee Championship. Ed Pimm, driving a Red Roof Inns Ralt RT-5 for Jim Trueman, qualified on the pole and was the race's initial pacesetter. His cause was aided on the first lap when Mike Rosen made a vastly overenthusiastic passing attempt on Michael Andretti, taking both off. Andretti, who had won the first two rounds of the season, regained the track, but in twelfth place. Pimm was steadily increasing his lead, trailed by Davy Jones and Peter Moodie. The 18 year old Jones had just become eligible for U.S. racing, having driven previously in Canada. Moodie was in an Anson SA3C, a new English chassis that was making its U.S. debut. The car was entered by engine builder Bertil Sollenskog, who had previously run a Ralt. Unfortunately for Pimm, his romp at the front ended with a failing gearbox. His pace slowed, and Moodie, Jones and a recovering Andretti passed, relegating Ed to fourth. Moodie took the win, a sparkling first time out triumph for the Anson. Andretti's third put him back into first in points, a position he was to hold the rest of the season, notching six wins enroute to the title.

Saturday's feature was 100 miles for the CRC Chemicals Trans-Am. The Mecham Racing Team Pontiac Trans-Ams of Elliott Forbes-Robinson and Steve Saleen were the cars to beat this year. Forbes-Robinson had won three straight races coming into RA and had a comfortable points lead. The day belonged to Jerry Hansen, though, as the Minneapolis driver continued his mastery of the four miles. Hansen qualified his big-block Corvette on the pole at 2:21.001 and proceeded to lead every lap as he romped to an

Jaguar returned to the prototype arena for the first time since 1960. The XJR-5, which debuted at RA, was built by Group 44. Here Bob Tullius is lapped by the winning Porsche 935 of David Hobbs.

easy win. Forbes-Robinson's day ended early as he missed a shift and bent the valves on lap five. His teammate Saleen went out spectacularly, completely destroying his Pontiac in a series of flips and rolls, fortunately without serious injury. Behind Hansen, Tom Gloy ran second in a Mustang, then Milt Minter's Trans-Am, Carl Shaffer in an Oftedahl Pontiac Trans-Am and Loren St. Lawrence in the most interesting racer, a Mercedes-Benz 450SL. In the last few laps the positions behind Hansen shuffled as Minter blew his engine and St. Lawrence spun off course. Thus, Shaffer came to the line in second place behind the winning Hansen, with the Corvettes of Phil Currin and Rick Stark third and fourth, Doc Bundy fifth in the Holbert Porsche 924 Turbo and St. Lawrence recovering for sixth. Hansen only ran three Trans-Ams in 1982, but won two of them. Forbes-Robinson, on the other hand, won five all told and the season championship.

Sunday morning the brothers Hacker won a 52 mile Rabbit/Bilstein Cup race with Karl first and Paul second. Gary Benson was the only non-Hacker to lead, but he had to relinquish the point when his gearbox broke.

The 100 mile North American Formula Atlantic Championship event had a 25 car field. Pole sitter Tim Coconis had to start his Ralt RT-4 from pit lane after his car failed a pre-race skirt check. Dave McMillan took advantage of this to lead the first two laps in his Ralt, but then John Briggs moved to the front. McMillan later lost a lap changing a flat, putting him well down. The Lane Sports Ralt duo of Norm Hunter and Josele Garza now chased Briggs, with the Shierson March 82A of Allan Berg nipping at Garza's heels. The race ran out that way, with Briggs making a fine return after having broken his leg just five weeks before (he fell off his motorcycle!). He averaged 109.307 mph in his Ralt RT-4. Hunter, Garza and Berg followed. The season itself was harder fought than this race, and McMillan emerged as the champion with one win.

The Budweiser/7-11 Can-Am race also had 25 entries of which 14 were *traditional* American V-8 powered cars. Al Unser Jr. had won two of the three events run so far and was the points leader. He was driving a Frissbee for Galles Racing. For RA Galles debuted a new car, a Frissbee variant (which itself was a Lola variant!) built in his Albuquerque shops. Utilizing a new monocoque tub and suspension, the car was dubbed the Galles Frissbee GR-3. Racing Team VDS had built its own car, the VDS 001. Somewhat similar to the Lola T-530 in layout, the VDS was designed by Tony Cicale. Al Holbert was the driver and had won the previous round of the series. In order to boost the shrinking Can-Am grids, the SCCA had

opened the series to FIA Group C endurance racers. The RA round was the first to see such an entry, a Lola T-610. The somewhat ugly coupe was powered by a 3.9 liter Cosworth DFL V-8. It was entered by Cooke Racing for Jim Adams. Can-Am specification cars powered by 3.0 ohc engines were also eligible, and Colin Bennett Racing of England entered a F-1 March 811 for Val Musetti. The 3.0 F-1 car was cloaked in a March 817 body and sounded glorious. Paul Newman was running one car this year, a March 827 for Danny Sullivan. A rules change had eliminated sliding skirts. They had been costly, work intensive and prone to breakage, so they really were not missed. However, the distinctive scraping sound the cars made as they passed was now gone too. Realistically, in the Can-Am this year, barring an upset, the battle was strictly among Unser Jr., Holbert and Sullivan.

Al Unser Jr. ran a tremendous qualifying lap, taking the pole at 1:59.695. Significantly, this was the first sub-two minute lap since Mark Donohue's turbo Porsche record run in 1973! Holbert was second fastest, also under two minutes, while Sullivan and John Morton's Frissbee were in row two. The fastest U-2 car was Bertil Roos in a *Marguey*, a March F-2 based machine.

At the start Unser bolted from the pole, led lap one and was stretching his lead on the second lap when a halfshaft suddenly snapped. The fastest car was out, practically before the crowd of 20,000+ got settled. Holbert took the lead with Sullivan closely following. Morton, Randy Lewis in the ex-Holbert CAC-1 and Roos followed. The Group C Lola of Adams was already out, but truthfully was never more than a curiosity. Musetti lasted only until lap eight when he, too, dropped out. Up front Holbert led most of the race, giving the lead to Sullivan only during the pit stop shuffle. Holbert won his second straight race fairly easily, with Sullivan second and Bertil Roos taking a fine third overall, first in the under two liter class. John Kalagian was fourth in a Frissbee, followed by the two Holberts of Lewis and Frank Joyce.

Unser Jr. and Holbert disputed the Can-Am title all season, both winning four of the nine races. Sullivan was the other winner. The 20 year old Unser won his second SCCA Championship in two years, having also been the 1981 Super Vee king.

The weekend of August 21-22 was the annual IMSA Pabst 500. As usual, the Kelly American Challenge and the Champion Spark Plug Challenge were the support events on Saturday. First, though, there was a free-standing pro race for Sports 2000 cars. Sixty miles in length, it was

The big show comes to Road America. Rick Mears, Bobby Rahal, Mario Andretti and Al Unser scream through turn 7 in the early laps of the '82 CART 200.

won by Bob Lobenberg in a March 82S, beating Bill O'Connor's Lola T-592 by three seconds. Tommy Riggins took the 60 mile Kelly race in a Camaro, leading most of the way. His drive to victory was made easier when closest competitor Craig Carter was black flagged for passing the pace car. (In Carter's defense, it was a different car than had paced the race.) Carter was able to recover from last to finish second behind Riggins. Gene Felton was third, also in a Camaro. Nonetheless, Carter won six races this year to win the championship.

The Champion Spark Plug small sedans again ran for 120 miles. The race was a two car duel, between Jim Downing in a Mazda RX-3 and Richard Gordon in a Volvo 142E. They each took turns leading before Downing established a margin which he expanded to the finish. Top threats Tommy and Bobby Archer both experienced bad luck on lap two in their Renault Le Cars. Tommy stalled with electrical failure, and Bobby had to pit to change a flat. Bobby charged back, but the margin was too great, finally settling for fifth. Chuck Ulinski, who finished fourth in a Mazda RX-3, was the season champion.

The Pabst 500 had a fine field which included seven GTPs doing battle with seven Porsche 935 variants. Attracting most interest was the debut of the Jaguar XJR-5. Built by Group 44 and entered for Bob Tullius/Bill Adam/Brian Fuerstenau, this was the first non-XKE based Jaguar purpose-built racer since the E2A of 1960. Three Lola T-600s were here, the Chris Cord/Jim Adams car and two from Ted Field's Interscope Team. That was reduced by one when Danny Ongais hit the barrier in the kink during practice. Two March 82Gs were entered, the Red Lobster car with a 3.5 liter BMW six for David Cowart/Kenper Miller and a Chevy V-8 version for Marty Hinze/Randy Lanier. From Europe came the Grid S-1, a 3.9 liter Cosworth V-8 coupe for Emilio de Villota/Fred Stiff and a Rondeau M382 with a Chevy V-8 for Bill Koll/Skeeter McKittrick. John Paul Sr. entered three 935s; a monocoque chassis car built in his shops for himself and Hurley Haywood, the tube framed car for John Paul Jr. and Mauricio de Narvaez and a *regular* one for M.L. Speer/Terry Wolters. Bob Akin's 935 also had a monocoque frame for himself and Derek Bell. By this time the various owners of 935s were taking it upon themselves to modify/rebuild their cars in order to stay competitive with the new breed of prototypes. The latest 935, though, was the K4 version from the Kremers in Germany, owned and run by John Fitzpatrick and co-driven by David Hobbs.

In GTO the class leader was the Electromotive Datsun 280ZX Turbo for Don Devendorf and Tony Adamowicz. Their chief opposition would come from the pair of Oftedahl Camaros. In GTU the Toyota factory effort had been shifted to Kent Racing, which was running two Celica coupes. The usual swarm of Mazda RX-7s would provide opposition.

It would be nice to report that the race was a knock-down, drag-out affair between the 935s and the prototypes, but in truth the team of Fitzpatrick and Hobbs had things under control. They led the race almost all the way, turning over the lead only during pit stops. In the early going they were closely pursued by Ted Field in the Interscope Lola, but Fitzpatrick was able to hang onto first. Even when Ongais got behind the wheel he could not catch the white and blue 935K4, Hobbs holding him off. In the first part of the race, Fitzpatrick led Field, then came Paul Jr., Cord, Bell, de Villota, Tullius, McKittrick and the others. Attrition set in, as usual, and one by one the challengers fell by the wayside. Ongais went out after spinning on another car's oil and damaging the front of the Lola. The Cord Lola had a fuel pickup problem – exactly the same as last year – and had to pit twice as often to refuel. Bill Koll crashed the Rondeau big time when the suspension failed. The Akin/Bell Porsche lost an engine. John Paul Jr.'s Porsche made it to the finish in second place, but de Narvaez was far slower than Paul behind the wheel. The Jaguar had a very satisfactory debut run, slowed only by minor new car troubles and it finished third. Cord/Adams were fourth and the two Marches finished fifth and sixth, Miller passing Lanier for fifth five laps from the end. A trio of 935s followed, all several laps down.

The Devendorf/Adamowicz should have won in GTO, but a long stop to repair a broken gearbox cost them a sure victory. Bob Raub and Chris Gleason were the beneficiaries, bringing their Oftedahl Pontiac to the line tenth overall, first in class. In GTU the Kent Toyotas were dominant. For much of the race Lee Mueller and Kathy Rude led, followed by the team car of Rick Knoop/Ron Grable. Unfortunately, gearbox and throttle linkage problems, respectively, dropped them from the running. The Jim Downing and Roger Mandeville Mazdas then were felled by engine failures, and Logan Blackburn's Datsun suffered from long pit stops. All this allowed the Joe Varde/Jeff Kline Mazda to take the win.

For the season, John Paul Jr. had the Camel GT championship in his pocket, winning nine races, both in Porsche 935s and a Lola T-600. Don Devendorf and Jim Downing took the GTO and GTU crowns.

The season then ended in early fall, with the CART Indy cars in town

The burgeoning vintage car movement saw a spectator weekend of historic cars added to the program in 1982. Of course, some of the most popular of these cars are red.

on September 19. The sole support race was a 60 mile affair for Sports 2000 cars. Steve Glassey was the winner in a Tiga SC82 with Charlie Rush second, also in a Tiga and Bill O'Connor third in a Lola T-592. The two free standing Sports 2000 races here, plus a similar event at Mid-Ohio, would gel into a pro series next year.

As any Wisconsinite can tell you, anytime after Labor Day is getting "iffy" in terms of weather. Sure, there are some very good days, but there are just as many that are not so good. But, when offered a CART PPG Indy Car World Series event, one takes it. The weather this weekend was marginal; it was cool and overcast, but at least the rain held off until the race was almost over. Somewhere in the neighborhood of 40,000 fans turned out for the weekend, the largest gate of the year. All the usual runners were present, and the prospect for a fine race was present.

In qualifying, somewhat surprisingly, only two drivers got below the two minute mark. Rick Mears took the pole in the Penske PC-10 at 1:57.710; still not as fast as Donohue's 1973 mark! Bobby Rahal was alongside Mears on the front row, his Truesports/Red Roof Inns March 82C clocking 1:58.983. Al Unser Sr. was next in the Longhorn LR-3, followed by Mario Andretti and Gordon Johncock, Patrick Racing STP Wildcat Mk. VIII-Bs; Howdy Holmes, Shierson/Domino's Pizza March 82C; Tom Sneva, Cotter/True Value March 82C; and in eighth, making his Indy car debut a startling one, John Paul Jr., in the Wysard March 82C. Given little notice in the fifth row was Mexican Hector Rebaque in the Forsythe/Indeck March 82C. In all there were 25 cars in the field.

In practice and qualifying it became apparent that pit stops would be crucial. Indy cars at this time, and up to 1997, were limited to a minimum of 1.8 mile per gallon of ethanol. This being the first time on RA's four mile course, fuel consumption was critical. It became apparent that the pit stop windows would be very narrow and to miss would be fatal to any chance at winning because here there would be no coasting into the pits.

Mears jumped into the lead at the start, but on lap two both Rahal and Andretti moved past. By lap three, Paul Jr. was also past, running third in this Indy car debut! Rebaque, Mears and Unser followed. John Paul's time up front was sadly limited, as he drove his smoking March into the pits and retirement on lap 12. Meanwhile, Rahal and Andretti were having a great time, passing and repassing each other for first.

The first round of pit stops came early, as most teams called their cars in a lap or two sooner than expected, fearful of high fuel consumption and wanting to see how much was actually used so they could do their math for the rest of the race. Andretti re-established himself in first with Rebaque, Rahal, Unser, Mears, Holmes and Geoff Brabham in the second Cotter March trailing. Kevin Cogan was out with engine failure in his Penske, and the same fate befell the Kraco March of Vern Schuppan. Johncock had retired with a broken gearbox. As the second round of pit stops approached, Andretti seemed to have things under control. But suddenly the gearbox broke, and Andretti rolled to a halt halfway up the hill at turn five. He had hardly stepped from his silent Wildcat when Brabham pulled up alongside, out with the exact same malady.

Following the second round of stops, Rahal now was in control, followed by Unser and Rebaque. Rain had been threatening all day, and now it began. A sprinkle at first, it soon developed into a steady shower as the race neared conclusion. Cars began coming into the pits to change to rain tires, taking advantage of the situation to add whatever fuel they had left. Unser, Rebaque and fourth place Josele Garza all stopped for wets, but Rahal stayed out, gambling that the race would be red flagged. He was wrong. His March coughed and died on the back straight, the tank bone dry. By the time he was towed into the pits, he had lost a lap. This put Unser in the lead and looking very good to score his first Indy car win since 1979. The senior Unser took the white flag and started his last lap, a good margin to second place Rebaque. Heartbreakingly, the white Longhorn coughed, sputtered and died at turn five – out of fuel! A surprised Hector Rebaque motored past, leading only two miles of the 200, but nonetheless, he took the checkered flag, winning his first ever major race. Unser was scored second, Rahal was third and Josele Garza was fourth in his own Penske PC-9B. Taking fifth place following a troubled run with fuel injection bothers, was Rick Mears. However, the points he collected for fifth were enough to clinch the PPG Cup for him, his third title in four years. Remarkably, Rebaque never drove in another Indy car race!

So ended 1982. It was a fine year for the track with two new weekends which would grow to be the two biggest weekends of the track's season. In 1983 CART would give the track a summer date, vastly increasing the chances for good weather and a bigger gate. The only negative was the Can-Am series, for which the new year's prospects were not good, all the top teams switching to CART.

1983

The SCCA expanded the rules in the Can-Am to admit Group C cars in an attempt to save the faltering series. The only such car to win was John Fitzpatrick's Porsche 956 at the RA round in 1983.

While the schedule for 1983 contained the same five automotive racing weekends as the year previous, there was considerable change. Principally, the Can-Am was going into its death throes, virtually all the top runners having gone to either CART or IMSA. Despite Budweiser sponsorship and promotion, the entry lists were small, and the names were virtually nonexistent. RA still had this year to go on its contract, but the weekend was just a two day affair, the first time in decades that the track was not open for at least practice on Friday of a race weekend. The Trans-Am and Super Vee races were moved to the CART weekend, which now was in midsummer, much to everyone's delight.

Sponsorship at the track had also changed. After four years Pabst was no longer the title sponsor of the 500. Arch rival Budweiser replaced Pabst, and their presence was noted everywhere, as the silos at stations two and thirteen now were giant Bud cans. In addition, Bud was the featured beer at the concession stands. To further cement the new relationship, Budweiser brought its famous Clydesdales to the track in June and the Bud beer wagon did a two mile lap of the *short course* on both Saturday and Sunday. The CART Indy car race, unsponsored in 1982, now had Provimi Veal as the title sponsor.

The SCCA now had Budweiser sponsoring both the Can-Am and the Trans-Am series. The Formula Atlantics, on the other hand, did not have a sponsor, but were ostensibly part of an international series called *Formula*

Mondiale. While the U.S. and Canadian promoters tried, they received no support from either national or international sanctioning bodies. The Atlantics struggled through the year in fits and starts, and at the end of 1983 were gone. The Sports 2000 cars did have a pro series, though. The Pro-Motion Agency of Chicago, headed by Vicki O'Connor, put together a four race series, all at Road America. Dubbed the *Road America Cup*, it would prove a hit with entrants and fans alike.

IMSA ran two single make series, much like the SCCA's VW Rabbits. They were both for Renaults, one for Le Cars and the other for the new Alliance, being built in conjunction with American Motors. Facom Tools sponsored the Le Car series. However, their big gun was, of course, the Camel GT. The GTP concept had taken off, and Camel GTs now were everything the post-1976 Can-Am tried to be, but wasn't. It was a big success and draw.

June 18 & 19 brought the June Sprints to the track. Four races each on Saturday and Sunday gave the crowds plenty of action. Saturday's FV race was the usual howler, with Scott Rubenzer, John Hogdal and Jerry Knapp again giving us the musical chair routine for first. For the second straight year Rubenzer timed his out of the last turn slingshot perfectly and won over Hogdal and Knapp. The Formula Ford race saw Curtis Farley lead more often than not as he took his Citation Zink to the win.

Sunday's four races all had a common element: Jerry Hansen. Jerry was attempting something never done before, four national wins in a single

Turn 12 can be tricky, as this slightly off-line Indy car shows....

day. He brought four cars to the track and was on the pole for all four events! First of all, he easily won the Showroom Stock race in his Datsun 280ZX Turbo. But his historic attempt was thwarted in the GT 1 and 2 race. His Pontiac Trans-Am broke an axle in the warmup and the last minute renting of Doug Rippie's Corvette turned sour when the engine overheated on the first lap. Rick Dittman took the win in a Corvette. Race three was for sports racers. This was an easy win for Hansen. Having sold his Lola T-333CS, Hansen replaced it with a VDS 001. The rest of the field was vastly overmatched. Though he would deny it, Hansen gave the fans a 'show' by idling around behind Ebby Lunken's March-BMW for over half the race. As the race neared its conclusion, he put his foot the rest of the way down and blew the field away. Finally, the Formulas A and C event went to Hansen in a Ralt RT-4. The race was behind him with Paul Barnhart's Anson just nipping Nick Wrzesinski's March for second. While Hansen did not get his four wins, three ain't bad!

July 10-11 was the Chicago Historic Races. The first race in the Road America Cup for Sports 2000 cars took place as part of this weekend. Twenty-seven S-2s ran, with Bill O'Connor taking the pole and the race. Steve Glassy chased O'Connor for the entire 60 miles, but his Tiga SC83 just could not quite catch O'Connor's Lola T-594. Syd Demovsky and Andy Blank contested third, until Blank lost out on an outbraking contest at turn five and shot down the escape road. Blank got his March going again, but had lost a lap. Demovsky finished third, only to be disqualified for rough driving.

The important part of the weekend, of course, was the historic cars. Again, the paddock was full of rare and wonderful cars. There were no less than five Ferrari GTOs present, a D Jaguar, a couple Listers, Ford GT-40s, a Cheetah, two Ferrari 250 Testa Rossas, an Alfa Romeo 8C-2300, a Cobra Daytona Coupe, more Ferraris, a Maserati 200S, and on and on. The feature race was called the *Ford vs. Ferrari Challenge*. This race, like the preceding all-Ferrari race, was taken by Peter Sachs in the 1961 Le Mans winner, a Ferrari 250 TR-61. Charlie Gibson took the later years race in a McLaren M6B, while Steve Cohen again took his Porsche 907 Spyder to a win. But again, the pleasure was just walking around and seeing these works of art.

One week later was the Can-Am weekend. The Rabbits and Formula Atlantics would run on Saturday, with Sports 2000 and Can-Am on Sunday.

The Rabbit/Bilstein Cup 52 miler was again taken by a Hacker, this time Paul. Brother Karl wrapped his Rabbit into a ball on the first lap. Peter Schwartzott led most of the race but Paul Hacker outbraked him going into Canada Corner on the last lap to take the win.

The Formula Atlantic race was a three way battle among the Ralt RT-4s of Mike Rosen, Roberto Moreno and Michael Andretti. Moreno and Andretti were on the front row, and both waited for the other to brake first into turn one. They waited too long, and both went off course. Moreno got right back on, but Andretti dropped to last, over two miles behind, before he could restart. That gave the lead to Mike Rosen, with a healthy cushion over John Briggs. But a full course caution for a brief rain shower not only allowed Moreno to close, but Andretti to catch the pack. Briggs soon dropped out, Moreno was around Dan Marvin, and shortly after the restart, past Rosen for the lead. Andretti moved up to fourth behind Marvin, which became third when Marvin broke a suspension piece. He soon was past Rosen, but the 100 mile ran out without his being able to catch Moreno. Moreno and Andretti would battle all year, with Andretti taking the championship.

Sunday morning the pro Sports 2000 cars ran for 60 miles. Bill O'Connor again won, but he had a much harder time than a week before. O'Connor passed pole sitter Steve Glassey on lap three, only to skate off course on lap five, Glassey and Larry Campbell getting by. Campbell quickly returned the favor, sliding off and giving second back to O'Connor. But Glassey was up the road and gone, and it looked like he would take his Tiga to the win. Then, with only a little more than a lap to go, Glassey went off at turn 12 and dropped to sixth. O'Connor was past, and he took his Lola T-594 to the win. Campbell was second in a Lola T-590, while Andy Blank took third in a March 83S.

The Can-Am race really had only three cars in it. Although there were 22 entered, the vast majority were old, tired, or both. Canadian Tire had bought the Galles cars from last year and had Jacques Villeneuve driving. In practice he thoroughly trashed the Galles GR-3 when he took it into the trees at the kink, just as Brabham did in '80 and Fabi in '81. He reverted to the older Frissbee for the race. Scot Jim Crawford was in an Ensign N180 Formula 1 car converted to Can-Am specs. He had won the previous race. The third car in with a shout was entered by John Fitzpatrick. Last year the sole Group C option entry, the Lola T-610, had been a bust. Nobody else tried this option until this weekend, when Fitzpatrick brought his Group C Porsche 956 to the race. The rules called for air restrictors on the turbos and a limited fuel allotment, both designed to harness the turbo power. The rest of the field were under two liter cars and backmarkers. Herb Adam's entry merely caused a lot of head scratching. The unnamed special was built in his shops, and it was a catamaran! The driver, Walt Bohren, sat between the wheels on the left side of the car, while the Chevy V-8 engine was similarly situated on the right. Between the two 'booms' was a huge airfoil. A lot of thinking went into it, but on the track it was a brick.

Villeneuve led the 160 miles early, Fitzpatrick running second and Michael Roe already out as he damaged the nose on his Walker Racing VDS trying to overtake the Porsche. Villeneuve was pulling away until he felt a vibration and pitted to investigate. Fitzpatrick led until his first fuel stop, handing the lead to Crawford. Villeneuve closed in on Crawford and passed into first, but then felt another vibration and pitted to have a wheel changed. He came out only to discover that they had changed the wrong wheel, and he had to go back in the next lap to do it again. Crawford retook the lead, which he then stretched out to over 40 seconds over Fitzpatrick. It was not to last, however, as on lap 34 his Cosworth V-8 burned a valve. Fitzpatrick now was in the lead, but very worried about his fuel. He leaned down the mixture and dropped the revs in an attempt to make the finish. He could only watch in frustration as Villeneuve roared by on lap 38 of 40. After only one lap in the lead, the engine in Villeneuve's Frissbee began coughing; out of fuel! Villeneuve crept into the pits as Fitzpatrick rolled by on an economy run. Is this called *racing?* Fitzpatrick drove around the last four mile lap quite slowly, while Villeneuve, now with a few gallons of fuel, blasted out of the pits in pursuit. Not enough time though; Fitzpatrick came home the winner, just 12 seconds ahead of the charging Villeneuve. Charles Monk was third in a Frissbee, while Bertil Roos again took the U-2 portion, fourth overall in a Chevron-Hart.

This Can-Am was the last at Road America. Not only was the field substandard, but less than 10,000 fans came, the smallest turnout on a Sunday since the '56 NASCAR race. Fitzpatrick's win in a Group C Porsche did not save the Can-Am. It was a one-off and was not repeated. Villeneuve went on to win the series title. 1984 would see SCCA downgrade what was left of the series by farming out its administration to Don Walker in Dallas. Though Walker ran 10 races, they were mostly all at second level tracks and attracted little in the way of entries or interest. Walker bailed out at the end of '84 and the series struggled for two more rather pathetic years, carried on only by a few of its own entrants, until it was mercifully laid to rest at the end of 1986.

Such was not the case two weeks later, though. The PPG Indy Car World Series returned to RA, supported by the Budweiser Trans-Am, the Bosch Super Vees and the pro Sports 2000s. The move from September to July was everything RA's General Manager, Lee Hall and the track hoped it would be; the weather was wet on Friday, but perfect the rest of the weekend and the crowds came in droves, a most successful weekend.

Round three of the Road America Cup for Sports 2000 cars had the same man on the top step of the podium as rounds one and two – Bill O'Connor. Bill put the Como Inn Lola T-594 on the pole, ahead of Andy Blank's March, Larry Campbell's Lola and 29 other starters. O'Connor led Campbell early, but Blank moved into second and closed the gap. On lap 13 of 15 the gap closed to zero and Blank collided with O'Connor. O'Connor kept going, but Blank dropped back, his bodywork damaged. Blank salvaged second, with Steve Glassey third.

The Bosch Super Vees ran for 60 miles and Price Cobb led all 60. Cobb, out of a ride after several years in Atlantics, had dropped down to FSV and was driving a Ralt RT-5 for Witt Racing. He was doing well too, as

he had won two of the four races coming into Elkhart. His closest competitor was Ed Pimm, who was driving an Anson for Truesports. As Cobb led away, Pimm, Mike Rosen and Roger Penske Jr. diced for second. Arie Luyendyk joined the fray, and briefly got his Anson up to third before the engine gave way. At two-thirds distance Pimm had closed on Cobb and just when it seemed that it might get very interesting the Anson rolled to a halt with ignition failure. Cobb took the checker, with Rosen and Penske following. Pimm may have failed here, but he won the next four races in a row to put the title safely in his pocket.

In this year's Budweiser Trans-Am the hot team was DeAtley Racing. After having run the St. Lawrence Mercedes in 1982, DeAtley came back with two superbly turned out Camaros, Budweiser sponsorship and David Hobbs and Willy T. Ribbs at the wheel. Hobbs and Ribbs each had won twice so far and were 1-2 in the points. Last year's champion, Elliott Forbes-Robinson was their closest competition. Driving the Huffaker Racing STP Pontiac Trans-Am, Forbes-Robinson had won once. Tom Gloy had not won yet, but was knocking on the door with his Mercury Capri.

Qualifying for the 100 mile race saw Hobbs and Ribbs one-two, followed by Forbes-Robinson and Gloy. In the race Hobbs jumped into an immediate lead and led the rest of the way, 54 cars chasing him. In turn five, Gloy and Paul Miller came together, the Capri and Porsche 924 Turbo both shedding fiberglass like confetti. On the second lap Ribbs lost his engine and dropped out. All this gave Hobbs a several second lead, and he was followed by Paul Newman in the Bob Sharp Datsun 280ZX Turbo, Forbes-Robinson, Darin Brassfield in a Corvette and the dueling pair of Ludwig Heimrath in a Porsche 930 Turbo and Jerry Hansen in a Pontiac Trans-Am. At half distance Brassfield was out when a brake disc broke and caused the tire to explode. Darin went off course in a big way but luckily escaped injury. As the race neared conclusion, Hobbs led Newman, Forbes-Robinson, a recovered Miller and Gloy. Then the turbo failed on Newman's Datsun, and the fuel pump quit on Miller's Porsche, allowing Forbes-Robinson, Gloy, Heimrath and Hansen to follow Hobbs home. The year also belonged to the Englishman, as Hobbs won the Trans-Am Championship.

The Provimi Veal 200 fielded 26 cars. Several new teams were in the series this year, essentially the heart of what had been the Can-Am. Paul Newman folded his Can-Am team and Budweiser sponsorship in with Carl Haas, producing Newman-Haas Racing. Mario Andretti was the driver, and he was in the only Lola in the series, a new T-700. Racing Team VDS sold their Can-Am cars to Jerry Hansen and Don Walker and bought a pair of last year's Penskes. John Paul Jr. would drive, and he had already notched his maiden victory, having sensationally taken the Michigan 500 two weeks prior. Galles Racing, after disposing of its Can-Am equipment to Canadian Tire, was running Al Unser Jr. in an Eagle. Al Unser Sr. led the points chase with one win and four seconds in the five previous events. The senior Unser was in a Penske PC-11, as was his teammate Rick Mears. Patrick Racing had suffered through a tough year so far, both of its drivers, Gordon Johncock and Johnny Rutherford, out with broken legs. Interscope Racing came to the rescue, loaning Patrick Danny Ongais and a pair of March 83Cs. Ongais would drive the March while Patrick's other driver, Chip Ganassi, was in a Wildcat Mk. IX. Forsythe Racing had the sensation of the year, Teo Fabi, in its Skoal Bandit March, while Cotter Racing was running a pair of Theodores for Tom Sneva and Kevin Cogan. The local Provimi Racing Team had a pair of Marches for Derek Daly and Tony Bettenhausen. Also of interest was the entry of South African lady driver Desire Wilson in the Wysard March.

In qualifying Mario Andretti captured the first ever pole for the Newman-Haas Team and the Lola T-700. His time of 1:58.898 meant that Mark Donohue's 10 year old record was safe for another year. Teo Fabi was

While the sun shone at the RA 500, Al Holbert in a March 83G is pursued by Klaus Ludwig's Mustang GTP through turn 7.

alongside, while row two was Bobby Rahal in the Truesports/Red Roof Inns March and John Paul Jr. Then came Derek Daly and Chris Kneifel in a Primus Longhorn LR-3, the Unsers son and father and Pete Halsmer's Arciero Penske and Howdy Holmes' Shierson/Domino's Pizza March. There is an art to road racing, as was evidenced by the fact that the three slowest qualifiers, Mike Mosley, Pancho Carter and Dick Simon, dyed in the wool oval trackers all, were at least a second shy of the man immediately ahead of them, Drake Olson, who was making his one and only lifetime Indy car start in a two year old Penske.

As the race started, Rahal took the lead, followed by Fabi, Paul, Andretti, Unser Jr., Daly, Halsmer and Unser Sr. Dead last was Josele Garza in the Machinists Union Penske PC-10 who had to start from pit lane when a duff ignition switch prevented his car from firing on time. Rahal and Paul stopped for fuel during an early yellow, which put Fabi first with Andretti chasing. Andretti got around Fabi on lap 20, whereupon Fabi spun out, losing four laps and all hope. At the same time Paul, who was running a fine third, spun and lost the best part of one whole lap getting restarted.

After the first round of pit stops were complete, Rahal led comfortably from Andretti, followed by the junior and senior Unsers, Halsmer, Mears, Daly, Garza (up from last!) and Holmes. This order ran fairly static until Mears and Holmes tangled, bringing out another yellow which saw all pit for the final time. After the restart, Unser Jr. was leading, then Andretti, Unser Sr., Rahal and Garza. The 20 year old Mexican was really flying, and he took Rahal, Unser Sr. and Andretti to move into second behind Junior's Eagle. On lap 40 of 50, Garza outbraked Unser Jr. and took the lead, completing a run from last to first! It was tight behind him, as Unser Jr. dropped to fourth and then Rahal passed Andretti for second. Rahal began eroding Garza's lead and then on lap 44 Garza gave it to him when he spun. However, in an agonizing replay of last year, Rahal's March started stuttering and coasted to a halt, out of fuel. Only three laps remained, and Andretti sailed past the stalled March, home free to score the first win for Newman-Haas. Unser Jr. came in second, followed by his father. Tom Sneva drove very well, staying out of trouble and was rewarded with fourth place. John Paul Jr. recovered only part of the distance lost in his earlier spin and

had to settle for fifth. In a race of high attrition, only 10 cars were running at the finish.

The race was a success at the box office also, as over 50,000 fans were present on Sunday, the largest RA crowd in years. Al Unser had a successful year, winning the PPG Cup, his first Indy car title since 1970. Teo Fabi was the rookie of the year, winning four races and finishing only two points shy of Unser.

The Budweiser 500 weekend was three weeks later in mid August, and it was apparent that the Indy car weekend had taken all the good weather. The weekend was overcast with on-and-off rain, including a deluge on Sunday. However, the whole IMSA show was in town, and a goodly crowd of 25,000+ turned out to see it. Four preliminary races would be on Saturday, with the 500 occupying Sunday.

The fourth and final round of the Road America Cup for Sports 2000 cars was won by Bill O'Connor. Making it a clean sweep of the four races, O'Connor took his Lola T-594 past Steve Glassey's Tiga on lap three and never looked back. Andy Blank gave Glassey a fight for second before he had to slow when his March overheated. Glassey took second while Blank persevered for third.

Twenty-eight Renault Le Cars ran for 32 miles for the Renault/Facom Cup. Willy Lewis was the winner, holding off Kurt Roehrig at the flag with a controversial blocking maneuver. Al Salerno and Kurt Kelly followed. The Kelly American Challenge cars ran for 60 miles, with Craig Carter taking the win and the season championship. Carter led all the way in his Camaro, winning for the fifth time this season. Tommy Riggins was second in a Chevrolet Monte Carlo, barely holding off Robert Overby's Buick Regal.

The Champion Spark Plug Challenge had an eligibility change this year which shed the series of the fast but long out of production Mazda RX-3s. New this year was the Proformance class, front wheel drive cars, which gave the series a whole new look. Rear wheel drive cars were still eligible, but they were essentially handicapped out of contention. Joe Varde mastered the new formula best, as he clinched the season title with his sixth win. Dave Frellsen led the first portion of the 60 miler in a Nissan Sentra, followed by Varde's Dodge, the brothers Archer in Renault Alliances and

As the skies darken, the turbo of the winning Ford Mustang GTP glows cherry red. Klaus Ludwig and Tim Coconis gave a storybook debut to the unique front-engined racer.

Dave Jolly in a Mazda GLC. On lap 10 of 15 Varde got around Frellsen and carried on to victory. Frellsen was second, followed by Tommy and Bobby Archer.

The big news in the Bud 500 was the debut of Ford's new Mustang GTP. A very much up-to-the-minute racer, it was a carbon fiber tubbed coupe powered by a 2.3 liter turbocharged dohc four. However the most startling thing about it was that it was front engined, completely contrary to current race car design! Ford wanted to carry some identity to the road cars, so it dictated a front engine. The German Zakspeed outfit, which ran Fords in European sedan racing, was engineering and running the effort. Two cars were entered, driven by Klaus Ludwig/Tim Coconis and Bobby Rahal/Geoff Brabham. Holbert Racing entered its CRC Chemicals March 83G, powered by a Porsche turbo six, for Al Holbert and Jim Trueman. This team had dominated the season, Holbert having already clinched the Camel GT championship. A second March 83G, this one Chevy powered, was the Red Lobster car for David Cowart and Kenper Miller. Three Lola T-600s were entered. Conte Racing's car was driven by Bob Lobenberg/John Morton and John Kalagian had the ex-John Paul Jr. car for himself and John Mills. Both these Lolas were Chevy powered while the Bayside T-600, for Jim Adams and Bruce Levin, was powered by a Porsche turbo six. Three Porsche 935s were present, their numbers down drastically from previous years as the GTPs took over. Preston Henn had purchased the Andial car and his co-driver this weekend was John Paul Jr. Bob Akin had his monocoque L-1 variant for himself and John O'Steen.

Amazing all who watched, as well as all who were in the know, the Ford Mustang GTPs were fast right out of the box. Holbert was on the pole, but Ludwig was right alongside, with the second car starting fifth. After the first lap shake-out, Holbert led Ludwig, but they exchanged places on lap six to give the Ford the lead in its first race. Brabham pitted the second car, though, to check a fluid leak. Lap after lap the Ludwig Ford led, it must be said to the surprise of most. As the race came up on 100 miles the order was Ludwig, Holbert, Morton, Miller, Kalagian and Paul, the latter slowed by severe brake imbalance. As the cars started pitting around the 125 mile mark, Miller parked the Red Lobster March with a broken gearbox, and the Holbert March made a lengthy stop with a severe misfire. Coconis took the Ludwig Ford back into the fray with a comfortable lead over Lobenberg, now in for Morton. An off course excursion damaged the Lola's nose, costing the Conte car considerable time. The Paul/Henn 935 was also out with a broken turbo wastegate.

As the race passed half distance, Ludwig/Coconis led, Kalagian/Mills were second, Rahal/Brabham third and fourth was the leading GTO runner, the Adamowicz/Devendorf Datsun 280ZX Turbo. Yes, attrition was high. In GTU the Mazda RX-7s of John Maffucci/Jim Downing and Amos Johnson/Roger Mandeville were easily leading the rest of the category and were moving up the overall leader board, as well. The second Ford was delayed by two mishaps. First, the fire extinguisher went off in the cockpit, nearly gassing Rahal. He managed to pit, the car was aired out, and Brabham took over. The next pit stop saw a fuel overflow ignite, causing a brief but alarming flash fire. That put them behind the GTO leading Datsun.

The lead Ford was beginning to slow, troubled by an intermittent misfire. The Kalagian/Mills Lola was closing in, ready to pounce. Unfortunately, on lap 107, just when they got within visual distance, the clutch failed and they were out.

Drama increased dramatically, as not only was the lead Ford slowing, but the all-day overcast had now developed into a steady rain that was growing in intensity. The clouds finally fully opened, and the rain became a deluge. The two Fords popped and banged around the course, water dousing the electrics. Devendorf was now faster than Coconis, although three laps behind. Could he make it up by lap 125? The answer was no. The rain was now coming down so hard that the track was awash in places, and it was just too dangerous to continue. The checkered flag came out at 115 laps, 460 miles, and the race was over. Incredibly, in their first race the Ford Mustang GTPs had finished first and third, the Ludwig/Coconis car winning with Brabham/Rahal third. Second overall, first in GTO, was the Adamowicz and Devendorf Datsun. Paul Canary and Eppie Wietzes were fourth, second in GTO, in a Pontiac Trans-Am, while Roger Mandeville and Amos Johnson were next, winning GTU, in a Mazda RX-7.

It was a soggy finish to the 1983 season. Winter would pass and soon the sun would be shining on 1984.

1984

A large throng watches from the outside of turn five as Paul Newman leads eventual winner Richard Spenard in the '84 Trans-Am.

The turmoil surrounding SCCA's pro racing series was reflected in the 1984 lineup. The June Sprints stayed, of course, but the Can-Am weekend disappeared, the track deciding not to promote such a race this year. Since the Formula Atlantic series was allowed to die, that, too, was off the card. Hence, after the Sprints July held the Chicago Historic Races, while the CART weekend was now the first weekend in August. Besides the CART Provimi Veal 200, the Trans-Am and Super Vee series would run. Three weeks later the IMSA boys would be in town for the Budweiser 500 Camel GT. Lee Hall wanted to hold a fifth car weekend and held the date of September 16 open. However, as the spring moved into summer it became apparent that there was no event available at that time around which a weekend could be built so the date was deleted from the schedule.

What had in 1983 been the Road America Cup had now segued into the Budweiser Pro Sports 2000 Series. Three races would be at RA, with two at Mid-Ohio. In future years this would grow to as many as ten races spread across the country.

The SCCA had a new boss, Nick Craw taking over as president from Jim Melvin. Craw, a race driver himself and past head of the Peace Corps, was SCCA's seventh head since 1969. Fortunately, he brought stability to the post and as of 1997 was still at the controls. Membership, which had been static if not in decline, more than doubled during Craw's tenure. Melvin, meantime, became a principal at Pinnacle Marketing. When Carl Haas

became promoter of the Milwaukee Mile, Melvin became the track's general manager.

While early June weather was unsettled, the middle of the month was dry, which was just fine because it was time for the June Sprints. Eight fine races filled the two days with some things being the same as in past years (Jerry Hansen wins) and some different (FF and FV not being photo finishes). Hansen put RA win number 29 after his name in the Showroom Stock race. Driving a Nissan 300ZX Turbo, Hansen easily led 43 other muffled cars around for 48 miles. In the sports racing feature, he did much the same thing for 60 miles, this time driving his VDS 001 Can-Am car. Only two other A sports racers were in the 42 car field, and they were *old.* Dick DeJarld was second in a Schkee. Thirty Sports 2000 cars tried to fill the gap, and Larry Campbell emerged victorious, eking out a win over rookie sensation Scott Overbey.

The Formula Vee race was taken by Dave Smith, no surprise, but his margin of victory, 7.9 seconds over Chris Shultz, was. Unlike the past several years, Smith was able to take the race by the scruff of the neck and make it his. Following Shultz, perennial battlers John Hogdal, Scott Rubenzer and Jerry Knapp were running close, with Knapp's son Steve mixed in with them. They finished Hogdal, Rubenzer, Steve Knapp and Jerry Knapp, third through sixth. The Formula Ford race saw John Dekker win by 8.2 seconds; again a relatively huge margin. Curtis Farley and Ulf Berggren followed. The big formula race was taken by Bill O'Connor in a Ralt RT-4, leading the like

Pit activity during practice for the CART 200; Tom Sneva departs as major engine work goes on in the Cotter pits.

cars of James Opperman, Eric Lang and Michael Angus. Chris Strong topped FC in a Shannon.

GT1 and GT2 also ran for 60 miles. Class CP had now disappeared, incorporated into GT2. Rick Dittman took another Sprints win in his Corvette; Don Sak and Doug Rippie followed, also in Corvettes. Jerry Hansen was in the race, but had ignition troubles with his Pontiac Trans-Am and finished 10th. Gerry Mason took GT2 in a Datsun.

At the end of this season A Sports Racing fell afoul of the SCCA's 2.5 average rule and disappeared. This was the end of what arguably was SCCA National racing's most glorious class: the class that had seen Ferraris and Maseratis, D Jaguars and Listers, Scarabs and Chaparrals, 917 Porsches, McLarens and Lolas. Why did this come about? Evolution and expansion. Race cars evolved with formula cars gaining in popularity. Twenty plus years ago there was just SCCA National racing, fourteen classes in all, seven production and seven *modified*. That was the only show in town. Now there were a dozen pro series including IMSA in addition to new categories such as formula cars, showroom stock and so forth. Simply put, there were many more places for a racer to put his money. With expansion came dilution. New series came, old series left.

July gave us the Chicago Historic Races. Again there was much to see. Over 300 historic and vintage cars were in the paddock, a visual feast. Not as many Ferraris, perhaps, as before, but there were some remarkable examples present. Take for instance the 1954 Le Mans winning 375 Plus, or one of three straight six 121LMs ever made, or Bob Sutherland's 375MM coupe, three GTOs and more. Three Porsche 917 coupes were on the track, as was Sutherland's other entry, a 1971 Tyrrell 002 F-1 car. Joel Finn took the formula race in a 1959 Cooper T-51 F-1. The event for rear engined sports racers was taken by George Follmer in the ex-Revson, ex-Hansen Lola T-220, now back in its L&M livery from 1970. Spending a summer weekend looking at all this automotive history and beauty has to be one of the great pleasures in life.

On the same card as the Historics was a round of the Budweiser Pro Sports 2000 Series. The year's first round at Mid-Ohio had been taken by Bill O'Connor, making it five straight for the Chicagoan. However, his streak was to be broken this weekend. Steve Glassey took the pole in his Tiga

SC84, but Scott Overbey jumped him at the start, leading the first five laps in his Lola T-596. Glassey caught him, though, and they spent the next few laps disputing the lead. Glassey was able to move ahead, while Overbey was challenged by Steve Ave in a Lola for third. Glassey finished the 15 laps in the lead, breaking O'Connor's string, while Overbey, Ave and Mike Yoder followed, trailed by O'Connor in fifth. Fifty cars had started the race.

Over 70,000 fans came two weeks later to the Trans-Am/CART weekend, with some 50,000+ on hand Sunday. After showers on Saturday, the weather was sweltering, with temperatures in the mid 90s. Once again, Elkhart Lake drew 'em in!

The Budweiser Pro Sports 2000 cars led off with round three. Fifty-three cars made the show, a fine turnout. Steve Ave had the pole in a Lola T-596, but the first lap was led by Larry Campbell. Ave led lap two, while Scott Overbey was in front the third time around. He held it for the next several tours, while Campbell filled his mirrors. Bill O'Connor moved up to third, helped by Steve Glassey and Ave going off in tandem while they fought over the spot. On the 11th lap O'Connor spun off, while Overbey went wide, giving Campbell the break he needed. Campbell was through into the lead with Overbey second and Ray Stover third in a Royale. That's the way they finished, with O'Connor keeping the points lead by recovering for fifth.

The Bosch/VW Super Vee race was a three car dice. Chip Robinson was on the pole, driving a Bill Scott entry, while his closest pursuers were Arie Luyendyk and Ludwig Heimrath Jr. Robinson led Heimrath and Luyendyk in the early laps. Luyendyk was able to pass Heimrath when young Ludwig fell off course while he was shadowing Robinson. That gave Robinson a bit of a cushion to Luyendyk, and he held it for the rest of the 60 miles despite Luyendyk's fast lap. Heimrath recovered to finish third trailed by John Briggs, Jeff McPherson and Ted Prappas. The top nine finishers were all driving Ralt RT-5s. Luyendyk and Robinson fought to the finish for the season crown, with Luyendyk prevailing.

The Budweiser Trans-Am ran for 100 miles just before the Indy car race. This year five major teams fought for the season title. DeAtley Racing, which won the title the year before, had switched to Corvettes for 1984. David Hobbs and Darin Brassfield were the drivers, although Richard Spenard would drive the Hobbs car at RA due to Hobbs having a prior commitment. Bob Sharp had two cars, a Nissan 300ZX Turbo for Paul Newman and a Datsun 280ZX Turbo for Jim Fitzgerald. Huffaker Engineering had installed Bob Lobenberg and Jim Miller in its Pontiac Trans-Ams while there were two Ford teams. Roush Racing had entered the Trans-Am and was running two Mercury Capris for Greg Pickett and Willy T. Ribbs. Tom Gloy had his own team, with a Mercury Capri for himself. Coming into RA the wins had been spread, with Pickett and Ribbs each with two, while Brassfield, Lobenberg and Gloy had one each.

Lobenberg started his STP Son-of-a-Gun Pontiac from the pole and looked unbeatable. He was on form all weekend, fastest in practice as well as qualifying. Lobenberg led Newman, Gloy, Spenard, Pickett and Ribbs for the first few laps. Pickett then began to move and shortly was up to third. Newman's Nissan had great speed, the fastest on the straights, but he was discovering that the brakes did not measure up. His Nissan began a slow descent on the leader board as his braking distances became greater and greater. Ribbs was out with a broken water pump, and Spenard was up to fourth. The order Lobenberg, Pickett, Gloy, Spenard, Newman held static through the middle portion of the race, with Jim Miller moving up. With but a few laps to go, things began to change. Spenard caught Gloy, and the two began to swap third. Then suddenly Pickett slowed, his engine sounding horrible. Spenard made the pass of Gloy for what was now second, and Gloy's tires were shot, preventing retaliation. Then, just two laps to go, and Lobenberg was out! Unbelievably, his car ran out of fuel! Spenard shot past, winning the race. Gloy was second, maintaining his points lead, with Miller and Newman following. Lobenberg never recovered from this heartbreak, not winning the rest of the season. Gloy, with a victory in the season's final race, took the Trans-Am crown.

The Provimi Veal 200 qualifying finally saw it happen: the breaking of Mark Donohue's eleven year old lap record. Mario Andretti lapped the four miles in 1:55.187 to smash Donohue's record by two seconds.

Andretti was in the midst of a marvelous season, a season in which he won six times and locked up the PPG Indy Car World Series championship. Andretti was driving a Budweiser-sponsored Lola T-800 for the Newman/Haas Team and was on top form all year. March had virtually taken over the Indy car market, and 25 of the 31 entries were Marches. Besides Andretti's, the only other Lola present was the Doug Shierson/Domino's Pizza car of Danny Sullivan, who was fourth on the grid. A surprising second on the grid was Roberto Guerrero in his first year in Indy car racing. Guerrero was in the Cotter/Master Mechanic March 84C. Third in qualifying was Bobby Rahal in the Truesports/7-Eleven March. Row three was Rick Mears, Pennzoil/Penske March 84C and Geoff Brabham, Kraco March 84C. The fourth row held Al Unser Sr., Miller High Life/Penske March 84C and Tom Sneva, Texaco/Mayer Motor Racing March 84C. Making his Indy car debut was Arie Luyendyk, who qualified 18th in the Provimi March 84C.

Andretti led away from the green and his cause was aided early when Guerrero spun at turn five, sowing fear and confusion through the rest of the field. Andretti held a large early lead over Rahal, Sullivan, Mears, Guerrero, Sneva, John Paul Jr. in the STP/Patrick March, Michael Andretti in a Kraco March, Unser and Josele Garza's, Machinists Union March 84C. Guerrero clawed his way back up to second and began closing on Andretti when he did it again, spinning at turn five. This time he stalled and lost two laps. During the shuffle for the first round of pit stops Andretti lost the lead to Sullivan, who then began to slowly extend his lead as Andretti lay back in second, nursing his brakes for the final third of the race.

Sullivan led through the middle portion of the race, but lost the lead to Andretti as both made their second and final pit stops. Sullivan pursued Andretti, closing the gap bit by bit, but suddenly a fuel line worked loose

and the Lola was on fire. Sullivan abruptly stopped the car and frantically bailed out, unhurt but his race was run. This put Rahal back into second, but Andretti was well up the road and, barring the unforeseen, the race was over. Nothing happened, and Mario Andretti came home a fairly easy winner, averaging a record 116.347 mph. Rahal was second, over a minute behind, followed by the Penske entries of Unser and Mears. Brabham took fifth, just holding off John Paul Jr. who took a splendid sixth in a one-off appearance for Patrick, handicapped by bent suspension sustained in the first lap melee. Luyendyk finished eighth, behind Garza, after a fine inaugural run.

Andretti went on to win the PPG Cup, his fourth Indy car title. Tom Sneva was second in points, scoring three wins along the way. It was a good *rookie* Indy car season for Teddy Mayer's team, Mayer having sold his interest in McLaren at the end of 1983. However, this would be Mayer's only season in Indy cars as a team owner, as the next year he accepted Carl Haas' offer to form an F-1 team, Team Haas USA, using their own Force chassis.

At the end of August the IMSA circus came to town for the Budweiser 500 weekend. This year the weather was fine, and there was an excellent turnout of both entries and spectators. Four preliminary races ran Saturday, with the Bud 500 on Sunday.

Round four of the Budweiser Pro Sports 2000 Series kicked off Saturday. After knocking on the door the previous two rounds, it finally was Scott Overbey's day. Overbey, driving the CSK Sports Lola T-596, was second on the grid to Steve Glassey's Tiga. He took the lead over the 50 car field as they rolled into turn one for the start of the 60 miles. He led until lap five when he briefly went off course, dropping to third behind Larry Campbell and Ray Stover. A lap later both he and Glassey were past Stover, and then Overbey took Campbell for the lead on lap nine. Behind, Stover passed Campbell for second, spun and was collected by Campbell. Glassey thus took second behind the winning Overbey, with Steve Ave third in a Lola. Overbey went on to win the season finale at Mid-Ohio to take the 1984 championship.

The Renault/Facom Cup, for showroom stock Renault Encores, fell to Charlie Downes. He led most of the 32 miles, spinning down to fourth once, but regaining the lead in less than two laps. Al Salerno finished second and John Fuchs third.

The Champion Spark Plug Challenge, once contested over long distances, ran for 60 miles this year. The work that the Archer brothers had performed on Renaults over the past couple years was coming to fruition this year, and their French cars were the ones to beat. In this race Bobby won in a Renault Encore while Tommy was second in a Renault Alliance. They moved up front on lap four of 15 when Joe Varde, who had led the first three laps in a Dodge Daytona, pulled off with a blown head gasket. Dennis Shaw was third in a Mazda GLC, while Cat Kizer took fourth in her Renault Alliance. Brother Tommy Archer went on to take the title.

The Kelly American Challenge also ran for 60 miles and was a three way fight between the Camaro of Craig Carter, the Buick Regal of Tommy Riggins and the Oldsmobile Cutlass of Gene Felton. Riggins led at the start from Carter and Felton. Felton's Olds took Carter on lap two and Riggins for the lead on lap four. Riggins retaliated on lap seven, and with some pushing and shoving, retook the lead. Carter also got by and started to close on Riggins. However, his Camaro shortly pulled off, through for the day. Riggins came home the winner, with Felton second and Bruce Nesbitt third in a Camaro. Riggins also went on to take the season championship.

This set the stage for the Budweiser 500. To say that the field was stellar is an understatement. There were 27 prototypes on hand! New were the Porsche 962s. The menacing coupes were an IMSA version of the all-con-

The advent of big rigs made paddock space a premium. What used to comfortably hold a weekend's worth of cars and support vehicles was stretched to the bursting point by 1984.

quering 956 cars that had conquered the World Championship of Makes three years in a row. Three were on hand; the Holbert Racing Lowenbrau car for Al Holbert/Derek Bell; the Bayside Racing entry for David Hobbs/Bruce Levin and Bob Akin's red Coca-Cola car for himself/John O'Steen. Group 44 had two Jaguar XJR-5s for Bob Tullius/Doc Bundy and Brian Redman/Hurley Haywood. There were no less than nine March GTPs present, headed by the two car entry of Blue Thunder Racing for the brothers Whittington and Randy Lanier. The Kreepy Krauly (a swimming pool cleaner) 83G was driven by South Africans Sarel Van der Merwe and Ian Scheckter. It was powered by a Porsche six. Conte Racing had an 84G for John Paul Jr. and John Morton, while Conte's Lola T-600 was in the hands of Mike Brockman/Rob McIntyre. John Kalagian had sold his Lola to Corvette driver Bard Boand and replaced it with a March 84G. Last year's winning car, the Ford Mustang GTP, was back, but as a single entry. This was a 7-Eleven sponsored machine for Bobby Rahal/Klaus Ludwig. Add in the rest of the GTPs, the GTOs and GTUs, and 60 cars were ready to take the green.

Holbert lead away from his pole position, and as the race unfolded was followed by Redman, Bill Whittington, Van der Merwe and Rahal. On lap 15 Whittington moved inside Redman, but instead of gaining second, acquired a broken nose piece and pitted for repairs. Redman took the lead when Holbert made a stop was in turn passed by Scheckter, now in for Van der Merwe. Bell, Haywood, Ludwig and Paul Jr. followed. But Scheckter couldn't stand prosperity, for he soon spun his way down to third. As an exclamation point, he promptly did it a second time, but was collected by the Bundy Jaguar. Both had to pit for repairs. Don Whittington pitted and retired the second Blue Thunder March with a shot clutch. Lanier, who was running for the title and hedging his bets by being entered in both cars, was now down to just the Bill Whittington March.

By half distance Holbert/Bell lead, but the Rahal/Ludwig Ford was but a few ticks behind. Two miles further back came the Paul/Morton March, the Hobbs/Levin Porsche and the B. Whittington/Lanier March. Then it all went wrong for the Ford; the turbo wastegate failed and it was out. The Lowenbrau Porsche now had a handy lead over the Paul Jr./Morton March, the Bayside Porsche of Hobbs/Levin, the Kreepy Krauly March and the sur-

viving Blue Thunder March. Despite going through three nose pieces, the Blue Thunder car was flying, and Whittington and Lanier managed to move it up into third.

As the race wound down, Holbert and Bell were firmly in command. However, just five laps from the end the Conte March lost its engine, and Paul Jr. and Morton dropped out of second. No sooner had this happened than the Blue Thunder March, now second, pitted with a punctured radiator. The crew managed to repair it with the loss of only one place, to the Bayside Porsche.

The race ended with Al Holbert and Derek Bell scoring a convincing win. David Hobbs and Bruce Levin were second for a Porsche 962 one-two. Despite all their troubles, Bill Whittington and Randy Lanier took third in the March 84G, while the March 83G of Van der Merwe and Scheckter was fourth. The surviving Jaguar of Haywood and Redman took fifth with the Akin/O'Steen Porsche 962 sixth. Bard Boand and Rick Anderson took seventh in Boand's Lola T-600, while the Paul Jr./Morton March was classified eighth.

In GTO there was a lot of attrition, but the Chet Vincentz/John Mullen Porsche 934 came through for the win. Dan Schott and Jim Fay were second in a Pontiac Firebird, while Gene Felton and Billy Hagan took third in the Stratagraph Camaro. They had stopped on the first lap with a broken transmission, and the Stratagraph crew replaced the whole unit in 30 minutes. The Roger Mandeville/Amos Johnson Mazda RX-7 finished fifth after spending a lot of time in the pits with a clogged fuel system. Nonetheless, Mandeville took the series title.

In GTU, Dan Gurney's All American Racers had received the Toyota contract for running the works team. They had one Celica on hand for Chris Cord and Jim Adams. They led the first 200 miles with great ease. Unfortunately, that was all it ran, and the class win went to the Mazda RX-7 of Jack Dunham/Jeff Kline. Again, there was a lot of attrition. The Kelly Marsh/Don Marsh/Ron Pawley Mazda took second, two laps behind. Jack Baldwin, who was to win the GTU championship, finished fifth.

Another fine year was in the books. But for 1985 there would be big changes at Road America, both in the schedule and the physical plant.

1985

The Formula Vee race continues to this day to be the most closely fought class at the June Sprints. Here fourteen Vees snarl up the hill out of turn 14.

The most noticeable change at RA was the new tower. The track recognized that the pagoda, charming as it may be, was terribly outdated, so they replaced it. Actually, the pagoda still stood, but it was no longer used. A new, state of the art two-story structure was built across the track from the pagoda. This permanent building housed race control and the media room in addition to nine suites that were available for rent for VIP entertainment. After years of laboring in the decrepit pagoda this was practically a dream. The only thing wrong with the new tower was that it was on the wrong side of the track. While it gave a good view of pit action for those who would not be leaving the building, its location was very inconvenient for the press and officials who had to make many trips to the paddock. This now involved hiking all the way down to the bridge at the top of the hill, then crossing the track and hiking all the way back up the course to the pits and paddock. A bridge or tunnel was now badly needed, but it would be several years before it could be funded.

The second change was the addition of a fifth spectator weekend for cars. After a false start the year before a September date was added to the Sprints, Historics, CART and IMSA weekends. Both the SCCA and IMSA had created professional showroom stock series this year and Lee Hall chose the IMSA version as the centerpiece of the September date. This would take

the form of an eight hour showroom stock endurance race.

The silos were repainted again this year, as Miller Brewing Company took over from Budweiser as the *track beer*. The chosen brand was Lowenbrau, and their two shades of blue appeared, with the IMSA feature becoming the Lowenbrau 500.

More than just showroom stock was new this year. SCCA had created a new class of race car, a class wherein all cars were to be identical, absolutely alike. These *specification* racers were powered by four cylinder Renault engines, transversely mounted at the rear and were known as Sports Renaults. The idea was, of course, that with identical cars the driver would make the difference. Besides being a class at the National level, a pro series, sponsored by Lucas, was initiated. A second new National class was Formula 440. Essentially this was a class for cars that were little more than go-carts powered by 440cc two-stroke motorcycle engines. The Trans-Am had a different sponsor, as Budweiser left and was replaced by Bendix Brakes. Budweiser had also dropped its support of Sports 2000. The SCCA's showroom stock series was sponsored by *Playboy Magazine* and known as the Playboy United States Endurance Championship. The Formula Atlantic cars were beginning a comeback, though not orchestrated out of Denver. Vicki O'Connor and her Pro-Motion Agency started a midwest-based series for Atlantics similar to what she was doing with Sports 2000s. The East Coast Atlantic Racing series (ECAR) was essentially self-funded out of entry fees and various small deals. It scheduled five events this year, although none were at RA.

IMSA's version of showroom stock racing had picked up sponsorship from Firestone tires. The series would be known as the Firestone Firehawk Endurance Championship, with all cars naturally running on Firestone Firehawk brand tires. IMSA also made a change in the Camel GT with the creation of the Camel Lights class. Essentially this was for GT Prototypes under three liters unsupercharged, though there were variations based upon weight, etc.

The 30th edition of the June Sprints came on the sunny summer weekend of June 22-23. Again, over 400 cars were on hand, viewed by a crowd of over 25,000. The first appearance by the new Sports Renault cars saw 13 of the little *spec racers* on the track, with Mike Berryhill taking the first win. In the same race, which had a total of 56 cars running, Tim Wiest started dead last in his HP Sprite, yet came through the pack for a splendid class win.

Michael Leathers notched the first F440 win in race two, which also had the Formula Vees. In that portion it was a very similar story to the past several years. Scott Rubenzer, John Hogdal and Jerry Knapp fought it out for the win. This year, however, the Knapp doing the challenging was Jerry's son Steve. It came down to the final corner, as usual, with Steve Knapp leading onto the main straight with Rubenzer tucked into his slipstream. At the right moment Rubenzer pulled out of the draft and shot by Knapp for the win.

The GT1 and 2 race was taken by Jerry Hansen, once again. This year Hansen had a Ford Mustang, and he loped to an easy win, made easier when Rick Dittman's Corvette dropped out. Bobby Fehan's Mustang was second for a Ford 1-2. Hansen's luck was not as good in the Showroom Stock event, as his new Corvette suffered transmission troubles which gave the win to Bob McConnell's Corvette. For the second year in a row Gerry Mason won GT2 in a Datsun 280Z.

The big formula event was a 1-2-3 for the Ralt RT-4s of Mike Angus, Jim Opperman and Dan Carmichael. Doug Vermeer took FC in an Anson. The Formula Ford race was won by Dave Weitzenhoff who led the 54 car field in his Citation. English F-3 star Calvin Fish was second in a Van Diemen, while last year's winner, John Dekker, came in third in a Swift.

The sports racing feature was dominated by Sports 2000 cars after Jeff Miller's 6 cyl Lola-Kohler dropped out of the lead. Tom Knapp took the win in the CSK Sports Lola after a late race pass of Scott Overbey's similar car. Steve Glassey also managed to get past Overbey, who had led the class most of the race, to take second in his Tiga.

Mid-July gave us the third annual Chicago Historic Races. Among the hundreds of interesting cars present two of the most interesting were Scarabs. Don Orosco had recently purchased the first Scarab built from Cheryl Reventlow. It had been converted to street use by Lance Reventlow, and after his passing in an air crash his widow had lent it to the Cunningham Museum for display. Orosco converted it back to race trim, as it appeared in 1958. The second Scarab present was the second built and was the ex-Nickey, Leader Card, Meister Brau car. Augie Pabst had bought it a couple years earlier from the Peter Hand Brewery. The brewery had the car stored for almost 20 years, since they last ran it in 1963. Pabst completely restored it and chose to do so in the Meister Brauser livery in which he had won so many races. Unfortunately, Orosco's car did not run due to mechanical difficulties. Pabst's car did, but was subject to *new-old car* blues.

Peter Sachs again had two interesting Ferraris present, the 1961 Le Mans winning 250 TR-61 and one of the three 1964 GTO-LMs. An even rarer Ferrari was the *Breadvan* owned by Joe Marchetti. The Breadvan was built on a 250 SWB chassis by Scuderia Serenissima in the early '60s and was an attempt at streamlining. The result was what looked very much like a Ferrari station wagon, but without windows aft of the doors, hence the nickname *Breadvan*. Don Walker brought some interesting Ferraris, including one of only three 1956 4.9 liter 410-S cars, the only one known in this hemisphere.

In on track action, Sachs won the pre-'63 race in the TR. The race for formula cars was taken by Joel Finn in a '59 Cooper T-51 F-1. The post-'63 race was taken by George Follmer, driving the same Lola T-220 with which he won the previous year.

The CART weekend led off August. The Pro Sports 2000 series had expanded to ten races, of which three would be at RA; this weekend was round five. Scott Overbey led away and appeared to be well on his way to a win when his Lola T-598 died on lap 12 of 15. This let Tom Knapp (cousin of Jerry and Steve) through to win. Knapp had qualified eighth, but had moved up to be in position when things went his way. Calvin Fish recovered from an early spin that had put him midway down the 47 car field to take second in a Tiga SC85. Scott Goodyear, also in a Lola T-598, was third.

The 60 mile Bosch/VW Super Vee race was led start to finish by Davy Jones. He had spent the previous two years in Europe, racing with limited success in Formula 3. Jones was now back home, trying to reestablish his career on this side of the Atlantic. He was driving a Ralt RT-5 for Garvin Brown and was in the championship chase. His stiffest competition came from the similar cars of Jeff Andretti, the brothers Steve and Cary Bren and Ken Johnson. In this race Jones led much as he pleased, but the battle for second raged the entire distance. Jeff Andretti had the greater straight line speed but Cary Bren had the edge in cornering. Hence their duel went back and forth, coming down to the last lap. Andretti made his final move entering turn one on the last lap, only to find his way blocked by the lapped car of Steve Bren (!). That gave Cary Bren the margin he needed to hold onto second. Jeff McPherson was fourth and Ken Johnson, who would win the season title in the Provimi Ralt, took fifth.

The Bendix Brakes Trans-Am was a factory battle. Roush Racing entered three Motorcraft-backed Mercury Capris for Wally Dallenbach Jr., Willy T. Ribbs and Chris Kneifel. In addition, Tom Gloy ran two more Mercurys for himself and Jim Miller. Their strongest competition would come from the Sharp Racing Nissans of Paul Newman and Jim Fitzgerald. A dark horse was the Buick Somerset of Elliott Forbes-Robinson. Coming into RA Ribbs had won four Trans-Ams, Dallenbach two and Forbes-Robinson one; however, RA looked as if it might be Nissan's turn. In qualifying, Paul Newman took the pole in the Nissan 300ZX Turbo, over a second faster than Ribbs. Teammate Fitzgerald was third.

The race started with the Nissans using their turbo power to jump ahead. Ribbs followed closely, but the rest of the 36 car field was soon left behind. Ribbs caught up to Fitzgerald and passed, only to have Fitzgerald take it back the next time around. This went on for a few laps before Ribbs finally was able to make it stick. Meanwhile, Newman was stretching his lead and looked every inch the winner. Alas, it was not to be. On lap 11 Newman came into the pits, trailing fluids. The valve train had broken and his splendid ride was over. Ribbs now was in first and holding a several second lead over Fitzgerald. This lasted until lap 18 when Fitzgerald's Nissan broke a camshaft. Gloy, Kneifel and Forbes-Robinson, who had been in a close scrap all race long, now were disputing second place. Kneifel set Gloy up for a last lap pass, but a waving yellow prevented it. The 100 mile race ended with a Mercury Capri 1-2-3 with Ribbs first and Kneifel third in the Motorcraft Roush cars, with Gloy in second in his 7-Eleven copy.

Alan Jones made his only CART appearance at the 1985 Provimi Veal 200. The 1980 World Champion drove the Newman-Haas Lola T-900 in place of the injured Mario Andretti.

Forbes-Robinson took fourth, with Dallenbach fifth in the third Roush Mercury.

Roush Racing had a stellar year, winning twelve of the 15 Trans-Ams. Although Dallenbach had five wins to Ribbs' seven, Dallenbach took the title on points. Forbes-Robinson scored twice, and the last win went to Paul Miller in a Porsche 924.

The Provimi Veal 200 began with Danny Sullivan on the pole. Sullivan, driving the Miller High Life Penske March 85C, lapped in 1:52.029 to smash the lap record. Beside him on row one was Bobby Rahal in the Truesports/Budweiser March 85C. Row two held a surprise as third fastest qualifier was Roberto Moreno, driving in only his second ever Indy car race. Moreno was in the Galles March 85C. Equally surprising was the other half of row two, Jacques Villeneuve. After winning the '83 Can-Am title, Canadian Tire moved to CART, taking Villeneuve along. Roberto Guerrero had the Cotter/Master Mechanic March on row three, as was Arie Luyendyk in the Provimi Lola T-900. Absent from the field was Mario Andretti, who was missing his first race ever due to an injury. Andretti had broken his shoulder two weeks earlier at Pocono. Sitting in for him was 1980 World Champion Alan Jones. He qualified 12th in the Newman-Haas/Beatrice Lola T-900, getting used to a new type of racing. Of interest were the two Eagles. Dan Gurney had secured Skoal Bandit sponsorship and was making his most concerted Indy car effort in years. Tom Sneva and Ed Pimm were driving the AAR Eagle 85GC cars. Unfortunately, the Cosworth powered machines were not terribly competitive, qualifying 19th and 21st.

The race began under threatening skies, but nonetheless 50,000 fans were on hand. Sullivan was on form this weekend, immediately took the point and was already three seconds ahead after two laps. Moreno was second, then came Guerrero, Michael Andretti in the Kraco March, Luyendyk, Al Unser Jr. in the Shierson/Domino's Lola and Rahal. Sullivan's lead over Moreno stabilized, then it began coming down. As the first round of pit

stops approached, Moreno was right on Sullivan's rear wing. Getting a better run out of turn 14, Moreno pulled out and passed Sullivan for the lead. The next lap he was almost two seconds ahead. As the cars made their first stops, it all went wrong for Moreno. His air jacks would not work, and he lost considerable time. Unser Jr. made the best stop of all and took the lead with Sullivan second. They were followed by Andretti, Villeneuve – who also had made a lightning pit stop – Rahal, Luyendyk, Moreno, Raul Boesel in the Simon/Break Free March, Jones and Guerrero.

Unser Jr. steadily increased his lead, aided by Sullivan losing several laps with a broken throttle linkage. Light rain now began to fall, and the complexion of the race was changing. Drivers and crew agonized over whether or not it was wet enough to go to rain tires. For Moreno, the answer was obvious, as he slid off the slick track and stalled, losing all hope for victory. The second round of pit stops saw many opt for the grooved rubber, but those who stayed on slicks were back in a lap or two later as the skies opened up and the rain pelted down. While this was happening, Josele Garza went off at the kink and comprehensively reduced his Machinists Union March to scrap as he flipped three times, fortunately without injury. Hardly had the safety crews attended to this when the leader was off. Al Unser Jr., seemingly headed for an easy win, crashed into the guard rail in Thunder Valley, splitting the Lola in half and breaking his ankle.

When all the added stops for rain tires were over, who should be in the lead but Villeneuve! His first lap out of the pits saw him spin at turn five, but amazingly he not only restarted, but kept the lead. Second place Michael Andretti was hampered by the loss of second gear and could not launch a full-fledged assault on Villeneuve, who ran out the 50 laps, taking a most surprising win, almost as much of a stunner as Rebaque's win three years earlier, also done in the rain. Andretti came in 10 seconds later to take second, while Alan Jones showed considerable wet weather prowess to move up to third ahead of Rahal. In fifth was Emerson Fittipaldi, also mov-

The Kelly Challenge Series often caught bad weather at RA. Here a portion of the field splashes into turn 8, just hoping to stay on the track.

ing up several places in the closing laps. Fittipaldi's Patrick Racing/7-Eleven March passed Luyendyk and Al Unser Sr.'s Penske March on the last lap for the position.

A most surprising finish; as with Rebaque, it would be Villeneuve's only Indy car win. As for Jones, this would be his only Indy car race ever. Al Unser Sr., who began the season only as a sub for the injured Rick Mears, went on to win the PPG Cup by a narrow two points over his son.

Three weeks later the IMSA show was in town, accompanied by two SCCA support series. The Sports 2000 race went to Tom Knapp once again, his fifth straight. Steve Ave led the first six laps, Knapp never far behind, until he spun the lead away. Knapp led the rest of the way in his Lola T-598 with Bill O'Connor second and Calvin Fish third in the 46 car field.

The Lucas Sports Renault 40 mile race was taken by Gene Harrington. He took the lead for good on lap seven when the skies opened, drenching the track. His three closest pursuers all spun off, allowing Harrington to splash home first ahead of Dorsey Schroeder and Ben Burrell.

The Champion Spark Plug race was a battle between Kal Showket and Tommy Archer. Showket led the first six of 15 laps in his Dodge Daytona before Archer took over in a Chevrolet Cavalier. Showket remained in contact and repassed Archer on lap 10, leading the balance of the 60 miles. Joe Varde's Dodge was third. In fourth was Dennis Shaw, who would be the season champion in his Mazda GLC.

The Kelly American Challenge race had a new twist this year. Instead of the 60 mile sprint as in past years, the race would be run for 300 kilometers, 47 laps, 188 miles. The race was long enough to have two rain showers, thoroughly muddling the picture with much tire swapping. Tommy Riggins was the pole man in a Buick Somerset, but he was passed on the third lap by Irv Hoerr, who led the next 28 in his Camaro. Running in third was Patty Moise, who found that her Buick liked the wet track. She held this position for over half the race until her engine blew. Hoerr had been in and out of the pits and was cruising when his engine suddenly quit, a victim

of ignition problems. This put Riggins back in the lead and he held it the balance of the race. Clay Young was second and Jerry Thompson third. Riggins would win his second straight Kelly title as the year progressed.

The Lowenbrau 500 had an excellent field of 55 cars, of which 24 were prototypes. Attracting great interest was the debut of the Corvette GTP. The car, in reality a Lola T-710 powered by a turbo V-6, was entered by Hendrick Motorsports and driven by David Hobbs and Sarel Van der Merwe. Nissan also entered a Lola-built prototype with a turbo V-6. Entered by Electromotive Engineering, the California-Cooler sponsored Lola T-810 was driven by regulars Don Devendorf and Tony Adamowicz. Ford had given up on the front engine GTP and was back with a *proper* rear engine racer, the Probe. Klaus Ludwig and Doc Bundy would drive the 7-Eleven sponsored turbo four Probe. Porsche 962s were out in force, with six entered. The Holbert Lowenbrau car was for Al Holbert and Derek Bell, with the Bayside car under the control of Bob Wollek and Bruce Levin. Bob Akin was back in his red Coca-Cola car, with Jim Mullen co-driving. Jim Busby entered two 962s, sponsored by and shod with BF Goodrich tires. Jochen Mass/Busby and Pete Halsmer/John Morton would drive. The final 962 was Rob Dyson's Budweiser car driven by Bobby Rahal and Drake Olson. Group 44 ran two Jaguar XJR-5s for Brian Redman/Hurley Haywood and Bob Tullius/Chip Robinson. Add to that five Marches, led by the two turbo Buick V-6 cars of Conte Racing for John Paul Jr./Bill Adam and Whitney Ganz/Bob Lobenberg and it was a strong field indeed.

In qualifying the pole went to Klaus Ludwig in the Ford Probe. He turned the first sub-two minute lap for prototypes, at 1:59.881. Rahal was alongside in the Budweiser 962, while Whitney Ganz was third in one of Conte's March 85G-turbo Buicks. The 962s of Wollek, Holbert, Halsmer and Mass followed.

Race day dawned overcast, with rain forecast. Ludwig dragged away from the line, but his lead only lasted one lap before he was overtaken by Wollek. After the early lap shakeout, Wollek continued to lead, followed by

One of the best ever sports car drivers, five time Le Mans winner, Derek Bell had many fine drives at Road America.

Mass, Holbert, Ludwig, Olson, Robinson, Halsmer, Devendorf, Ganz, Paul Jr. and Redman. Attrition began to set in as Ludwig retired the Probe with overheating, Devendorf crashed, Halsmer was delayed when he lost a wheel, Ganz was out with failed ignition, and Paul Jr. had a cylinder head crack. After the first round of pit stops Tullius took the lead in the Jaguar, but was out just two laps later with a broken axle. The race now became all Porsche at the front as Wollek retook the lead, followed by Olson, Bell and Mass. The Redman/Haywood Jaguar was moving up and began to claw at the heels of the Porsches. The Akin 962 went out spectacularly, going over the guard rail at turn six and wound up suspended in the trees several feet off the ground. Fortunately, Jim Mullen was uninjured.

The mid-race pit stop shuffle ended with Holbert leading followed by Rahal and Redman. The Lola-Corvette joined the others on the sidelines when the engine expired at 70 laps. Holbert began experiencing valve train difficulties, eventually retiring the Lowenbrau 962 at 96 laps. By this time the expected rain had arrived, starting slowly but soon developing into a goodly shower. Rahal was in the lead, but Haywood was following closely in the Jaguar with the Wollek/Leven and BF Goodrich 962s chasing. Sadly, only 10 laps from the finish a water hose came off the Jag V-12 and its goose was cooked along with the engine. Rahal/Olson now stroked it to the finish, a lap ahead of second place Wollek/Leven and four up on the third place 962 of Mass/Busby. The second BFG car of Halsmer/Morton was next, followed by two March 85G-Porsches of John Kalagian/Steve Shelton and Al Leon/Randy Lanier.

Al Holbert may not have finished this race, but he had a superb season, winning nine races and his fourth Camel GT championship. His other three were in 1976, 1977 and 1983.

In Camel Lights, the Argo JM-16s of Kelly Marsh/Don Marsh/Ron Pawley and Jim Downing/John Maffucci stayed in contact the entire 500 miles. Indeed, on lap 124 of 125 they went around the entire lap side-by-side! Marsh worked traffic a little better and won the class. Both cars were powered by Mazda rotary engines. Downing went on to win the first Camel Lights crown.

The GTO race within a race was all Ford. Darin Brassfield was fast qualifier and led the first six laps in the Brooks Racing/7-Eleven Ford Thunderbird before the engine blew. Shortly thereafter, the Roush Racing Motorcraft Ford Mustang of 19 year old John Jones and Lyn St. James took over and led the rest of the way. The Porsche 934 of Chet Vincentz and Kees Nierop finished second while the second Roush Mustang of Scott Pruett and Olympic decathlon winner Bruce Jenner finished third after losing seven laps changing a water pump. It was indeed a fantastic year for Roush, for besides dominating the Trans-Am the team won nine GTO events with young Jones becoming the Champion.

The AAR Toyota Celica of Chris Cord led the first 80 laps of the GTU portion. The Huffaker Pontiac Fieros of Terry Visger and rock musician John Oates provided an early challenge until Visger went out and Oates crashed. Then the Malibu GP Mazda RX-7 of Jack Baldwin and Jeff Kline moved into second and kept the Toyota in sight for hours. They finally took the lead following a pit stop shuffle, but the matter was not decided until the Cord/Dennis Aase Celica went for a long trip off course in the rain. Baldwin not only won the race, but went on to take his second straight GTU title.

In mid-September the IMSA Firestone Firehawk series came to RA. Saturday's only race was a round of the Pro Sports 2000 series, and it was won by Scott Overbey. This surprisingly was the first win of the year for the 1984 Champion. His Ove Olsson Lola T-598 led all the way, winning over the Lolas of Scott Goodyear, Bill O'Connor and John Fergus. Tom Knapp finished ninth, but accumulated enough points to clinch the championship.

The eight hour Firehawk enduro finished with Porsche 944s first and second. Jon Milledge and Walt Maas were in the winning car, completing 160 laps, 640 miles, in the one-third of a day run. Jack Lewis, Shawn Hendricks and Pepe Pombo were second. The only real threat to them was the Nissan 300ZX Turbo of Tom Kendall, Ron Grable and Max Jones, which led for a good portion but eventually ran out of brakes. Forty-four cars started the race. The race itself did not prove to be the spectator draw anticipated, as the hillsides were noticeably bare.

1986

Early in the 500 Geoff Brabham leads in the Lola-based Nissan GTP followed by Sarel Van der Merwe in the Lola-Corvette GTP and David Hobbs in the March-BMW.

The number of car weekends increased to six this season as the Trans-Am was split off from the CART weekend into one of its own, supported by several SCCA support series. In addition, a round of the Pro Sports 2000 series was scheduled for the Sunday of the early June AMA Motorcycle weekend. Unfortunately the track found itself on the short end of the stick when it came to the CART schedule. The track's summer date, which it had enjoyed for three years, was given to a new street race in Toronto, and RA wound up with a late September date. Lee Hall was not pleased, as the weather in eastern Wisconsin is notoriously unsettled at that time and his fears were well founded, as we shall see.

The much-rumored CART *B Series* came into being with the launch of the American Racing Series. To be run as a support event at most CART weekends, it was a *spec car* series, with everything being the same except for the driver and color of the car. The cars were all March 86A chassis, powered by 4.2 liter Buick V-6 engines. A round was scheduled for RA.

SCCA had changed sponsors for its Showroom Stock Series, Escort radar detectors replaced Playboy. If nothing else, it would mean a change in the appearance of the trophy queens.

IMSA also had a new series, masterminded by Skip Barber. The Barber-Saab Pro Series was a unique concept. It not only was a *spec car* series, with all the cars being tube frame Mondiale chassis powered by turbo Saab fours, but all cars were owned by the series. The drivers rented the cars by the weekend, with the rental including all at track service in addition to the car. It quickly grew to be a fine training series.

On June 8 the Sports 2000 cars ran round one of their 1986 series. R.K. Smith, making his first RA appearance, led all the way to victory. Smith was driving a Swift DB-2, a west coast built S-2000, and it was the first win by a Swift in this series. Curtis Farley was second, also in a Swift, while Steve Knapp took third in a Carl Haas-supported Lola T-86/90. Grids continued big, as 39 cars started the race. The experiment to have this during the motorcycle weekend turned out to be a one-off. The idea was to interest fans of bikes and fans of cars in each others' sport, but apparently made few converts.

Two weeks later the June Sprints started its fourth decade. The Formula Ford race did not go to Dave Weitzenhoff this year; he only managed to finish second. Kirk Stevens won in a Swift over Weitzenhoff's Citation. In the Formula Vee race, however, Scott Rubenzer kept the status quo as he notched another Sprints win. He led the usual snarling pack in his Citation, narrowly beating the Predators of Mike Stiffler and Dave Smith. Mike Leathers won his second straight F-440 class in the same race.

The GT race marked the last appearance by Jerry Hansen at RA. The 27-time National Champion retired at the end of the year and moved to Florida. His last run was not to be a success, though, as his Ford Mustang broke a coil after Hansen had easily led the first seven laps. This opened

Al Unser Jr. gives son "Mini Al" a spin on his mini bike through the paddock during the CART 200 weekend.

the door to Rick Dittman who passed Don Sak's Corvette on the last lap to win in his Pontiac Firebird.

The sports racing event did see a win for Dave Weitzenhoff. While he lost the FF race, he won this race overall and in Sports 2000 in a Shrike. The Lolas of Tom Jagemann and Steve Knapp finished second and third. The Beasleys, father Al and son Al Jr. had a good run. Young Beasley dominated CSR, winning the class in a LeGrand-AMW, while Dad Beasley was second in DSR in a Decker-AMW, losing the class lead on the last lap to Bob Atkinson's Lola-Kohler.

The Formula feature went to James King in a Ralt RT-4, leading most of the way. Tom Grunnah was second in a similar Ralt, while Cliff Ebben took third in an *ancient* March 81A. In the same race the Ralts of Robert Stocker, Mike Plotz and Hiro Nishioka finished in that order in FC.

One face missing on the track was Jerry Dunbar, who had started every June Sprints for 30 consecutive years! Dunbar had lost his Camaro in a crash and had no car for the weekend. Fortunately, he acquired another and resumed his participation, including the 40th Anniversary Sprints in 1996!

The Chicago Historic Races again tantalized the senses. Highlighting the cars on hand this year was Joel Finn's Mercedes-Benz W-163, the 3.0 liter supercharged V-12 1939 GP car. Sadly, Finn was unable to get the finicky engine fired, thus depriving all of what would have certainly been an aural treat. An old F-1 car that did run, though, was a 1957 Maserati 250-F, and it was impressive. A fine crop of front-engine sports racers were present, led by Augie Pabst's Scarab. Nick Soprano had the one-off 5.7 liter Maserati 450-S which had raced in the fifties in the hands of Masten Gregory, Carroll Shelby and Jim Hall, among others. Peter Livanos, part owner of Aston Martin, brought one of two DBR-2s as well as a couple DB-4 coupes and a DB3-S. The race for these cars was taken by Peter Sachs, again in the '61 Le Mans winning Ferrari 250 TR-61, by a car length over Pabst. Joel Finn again took the all formula car event in his Cooper T-51 F-1. Bill Wonder was the winner of the later sports racer event in a McLaren M8F. Among the many cars on display were three Ford Mk. IVs, including the 1967 Le Mans winner on loan from the Henry Ford museum.

After that delightful weekend it was back to modern racing as the Bendix Brakes Trans-Am headlined the final weekend in July. A 52 mile VW Cup race, now being contested by Golfs rather than Rabbits, saw the win go to Al Salerno even though he was third across the line. Unfortunately, the first two VWs of Mark Behm and his father Les were disqualified after the race for illegal engines. The 52 mile Lucas Sports Renault Challenge was taken by Ray Kong, who led only the last mile. Kong had shadowed Scott Lagasse from the start, and it paid off in Canada Corner when Lagasse spun out.

Formula Atlantic returned to RA with the running of round four of the E-Z Wider ECAR Challenge. Scott Goodyear was on form all weekend and took the pole and led every lap of the 60 mile race. Behind him things were more dicey, and Ted Prappas prevailed over a scrapping group including Calvin Fish, Tom Grunnah, Bill O'Connor, Steve Shelton and Mike Greenfield to take second. Greenfield finished third, with Shelton fourth and James Opperman fifth. All were in Ralt RT-4s. Goodyear would continue to run well and won the season championship.

Also on the program was a round of the Bosch/VW Super Vee Series. The 60 mile race began with Steve Bren leading away from the pole, followed by Tom Knapp, Didier Theys, David Kudrave and Gary Rubio. Theys got by both Bren and Knapp for the lead before the end of the first lap and he proceeded to lead the first 11 of 15 laps. While virtually all the cars in the 60 mile race were Ralt RT-5s, Theys was in a Martini MK50. He had won the previous SV round at Watkins Glen, becoming the first non-Ralt winner since early 1983. Different car or not, Theys was defending his lead from the strong assault of Steve Bren, an assault that was physical at times as the two cars banged wheels and swapped paint. On lap 12 the inevitable happened and both were off course in a cloud of dust. This allowed third place Knapp through to a lead that he would hold to the finish, winning his first Bosch Super Vee race. Second was Steve Bren's brother Cary while David Kudrave finished third.

The Bendix Brakes Trans-Am in 1986 saw the re-emergence of Chevrolet. Chevy was practically invisible in the previous year, but was backing the Protofab Team this year which had won five of the first six

111

The 1986 CART 200 was postponed two weeks due to weather and it was little better on the second attempt. Here Bobby Rahal leads the pack into turn 5.

races. Protofab was running three Camaros, V-8 cars for Wally Dallenbach Jr. and Jim Miller and a lighter weight V-6 car for Greg Pickett. Dallenbach had three wins and Pickett had two. The Roush Racing Ford effort was concentrating on the 2.5 liter four cylinder turbocharged German Ford-built Merkurs this year, believing that turbo power was the way to go. Roush also was a three car team with Merkur XR4Ti turbos for Pete Halsmer and Mike Miller while hedging their bets somewhat with a V-8 Mercury Capri for Chris Kneifel. Competition to these two juggernaut teams was mainly limited to Elliot Forbes-Robinson in a Buick Somerset and the Bob Sharp Racing Nissan 300ZX Turbos of Paul Newman and Jim Fitzgerald.

Although Dallenbach was on the pole it mattered little because, in the best tradition of Clif Tufte, Lee Hall scheduled a 60 mile non-points race on Saturday that set grid positions for Sunday's 100 mile points race. A purse of $23,000 ensured that there would be racing, and Pete Halsmer won, taking the lead from Dallenbach, who missed a shift on lap four of 15. Miller was third, followed by Kneifel and Forbes-Robinson.

Sunday's Bendix Brakes Trans-Am was led away from the green by Halsmer, followed by Dallenbach and Miller. However, Miller's Camaro was out early, elevating Kneifel to third. Pickett lost the engine in his Camaro on lap six, and the Protofab effort was down to just one car. Dallenbach was all over Halsmer's Merkur, but could not pass. Once the turbo was at full blat, even the Chevy V-8 was left behind. Dallenbach got alongside Halsmer a couple times in the closing laps, but could not complete the pass. Halsmer came in first, scoring the first win for the Merkur. Kneifel finished third followed by Fitzgerald and Mike Miller. Paul Newman, who ran so well here in 1985, had a tough time as his Nissan went out on lap 22 with a broken wheel. He had been running as high as fifth. Newman would rebound though by winning the next Trans-Am at Lime Rock. The Merkurs went on to win the last three races, but it was too late by then; Wally Dallenbach Jr. took his second straight Trans-Am crown.

The Lowenbrau 500 weekend came August 24-25. The weekend's first race was round five of the pro Sports 2000 series. Engine builder Curtis Farley put his Swift DB-2 on the pole and led the opening lap only to be passed on lap two by the Swift of Scott Harrington, whose lead was equally brief. On the next lap Dave Weitzenhoff tried to overtake him, but instead they collided and both spun off. Farley observed all this from third and found himself back in first, which he held to the finish. Steve Knapp took

his Lola past the Swift of John Fergus on lap seven of 15 to take second. Fourth behind Fergus was Weitzenhoff in his Shrike, having made an excellent recovery. R.K. Smith and Steve Ave followed.

The first Barber-Saab race at RA went to Bruce Feldman who took the lead after mechanical difficulties knocked out front row starters Willy Lewis and Brian Till. Eric Kielts finished second with Van Roberts third. This dnf notwithstanding, Willy Lewis was the first Barber Saab series champion.

Kal Showket won his second straight RA Champion Spark Plug Challenge 60 mile race. Showket led all the way in a Dodge Daytona. The Chevrolet Cavaliers of the brothers Archer provided the strongest competition but Tommy Archer spun out of the race on lap seven while running second. Doug Peterson's Acura Integra took second from Bobby Archer, but Showket was too far ahead for any more progress. Peterson did take the year's title, though.

The final race on Saturday was the 300 Kilometer Kelly American Challenge. Irv Hoerr was the man to beat this year as he had won seven of the eight rounds leading to RA. However Dick Danielson took the pole in a Buick Somerset with Hoerr's Oldsmobile Toronado second. Danielson used the pole to take the lead with Hoerr running second while Patty Moise was third in her Buick Somerset. Danielson led for over half the 47 lap distance, until his pit stop on lap 28. It was excruciatingly long, and both Hoerr and Moise were in and out while he sat there. Hoerr now led by over a minute over Moise, and he led her to the finish, clinching the season title in the process. Moise was second, Danielson third, while Robin McCall took fourth in her Oldsmobile Calais.

The factories were out in force in the Camel GT this season. The top end of the field was very strong indeed. BMW had joined the fray and was running two March 86G cars powered by 2.1 liter BMW turbo fours. Drivers were David Hobbs/John Watson and John Andretti/Davy Jones. Ford was back with two Probes for Klaus Ludwig/Tom Gloy and Bobby Rahal/Pete Halsmer; both were turbo fours. Chevrolet had Sarel Van der Merwe/Doc Bundy in its Lola T-710 Corvette GTP, while Nissan's Lola T-810 derivative was in the hands of Geoff Brabham/Elliott Forbes-Robinson. Group 44's Jaguars were updated XJR-7 models, and the drivers were Brian Redman/Hurley Haywood and Bob Tullius/Chip Robinson. Of course there were Porsche 962s, seven to be exact, headed by the Holbert, Dyson and Bayside teams. With Derek Bell otherwise occupied this weekend, Al Unser

Last lap, up under the bridge and to the checker. Fittipaldi fends off the attack by Michael Andretti to win by three car lengths.

Jr. was co-driving with Al Holbert in the Lowenbrau car.

The Lowenbrau 500 began with a bang, as Davy Jones lost his March-BMW in the kink on lap two while trying to overtake the leading Lola-Nissan of Brabham. He ricocheted off the guard rails on both sides of the track, thoroughly trashing the car. Van der Merwe was the only other car taken out in the melee, although Gloy in the Probe and Paulo Barilla and Price Cobb in 962s all pitted to repair damage. Brabham led, followed by Watson. On lap 10 Watson took Brabham for first and opened it up by a second a lap as they passed the 100 mile mark. Cobb brought the Dyson 962 back into the pits for more repairs, having collided with the spinning BFG 962 of John Morton. Cobb's day was not going well.

Hobbs was in for Watson and continued to lead. The two Jaguars were threats, running in the top five. They were getting better fuel mileage and aimed for one less stop than the turbo cars. The Brabham/Forbes-Robinson Nissan and the Holbert/Unser Jr. 962 filled out the top five. Forbes-Robinson dropped out of this group when the smoking Nissan V-6 expired. At half distance Watson had replaced Hobbs and had a minute lead over Unser Jr. with the third and fourth place Jaguars a lap behind. However on lap 71 of 125 the BMW engine quit, and the March was parked at turn five. This sudden development put the Lowenbrau 962 of Holbert/Unser Jr. in the lead, with the Haywood/Redman Jaguar less than a minute behind and with one less pit stop to make. On paper, the Jag could do it. In reality, it didn't, because a half shaft snapped on lap 92, dropping the pair out of second in the closing stages for the second year in a row. Further adding to Group 44's woes, the second Jaguar had its engine go a few laps earlier while running third.

Holbert and Unser Jr. cruised to the finish, taking the win over five laps ahead of the second place Porsche 962 of Rob Dyson and Price Cobb. Despite two crashes, they had hung on as attrition weeded out most of the opposition. Indeed, the third place GTP was the Akin/Nierop Porsche 962 which finished sixth overall behind two GTO cars and a Camel Light. Fourth in GTP was the Darin Brassfield/John Morton 962 which was 11th overall.

Holbert was enjoying a good year, winning six races and his fifth Camel GT championship.

In the Camel Lights category, the Alba AR6 powered by a 3.0 Ferrari V-8 and driven by Ruggero Melgrati, Martino Finotto and Carlo Facetti was first in class, fifth overall. They led to the first pit stop when David Loring took over in his Denali. Loring built up a lead of over a lap until he handed the wheel over to Pierre Honneger. Unfortunately, Honneger was nowhere near as fast as Loring, and he quickly lost the lead. By the time Loring was back in the car, the Denali was third. The Alba won, with the Chip Ganassi/David Sears Spice CL86 second. Jim Downing finished fourth enroute to his second straight Camel Light title.

In GTO it was Roush vs. AAR. Toyota had moved up from GTU this year, with turbo engined Toyota Celicas. Gurney entered two, for Chris Cord/Juan Fangio II and Dennis Aase/Rocky Moran. Roush entered one Mustang for Scott Pruett and Bruce Jenner. The Toyotas led most of the way with the Mustang occasionally grabbing second. Late in the race the Cord/Fangio Celica broke its shift linkage, dropping out of the lead. Moran/Aase then led, but when Pruett replaced Jenner the Mustang carved into it. Moran picked up the pace and finished 12 seconds ahead of Pruett, third and fourth overall. It was the first GTO win for Toyota. Pruett did win seven times to take the year's title.

The GTU class was initially led by Roger Mandeville in a Mazda RX-7. A long pit stop gave the lead to Tom Kendall, also in an RX-7. Kendall's co-driver Irv Hoerr took over at half distance, but his unfamiliarity with the car allowed Mandeville to catch him. Mandeville went on to win, co-driving with Danny Smith, with Kendall/Hoerr second. Kendall held a healthy lead in points, though and won the class championship at year end.

The second weekend in September was headlined by the IMSA Firestone Firehawk Showroom Stock series. The race was shortened to six hours, down from eight. It would run on Sunday, with a Pro Sports 2000 race on Saturday. Sunny but cool weather held forth for the 60 mile race. Mike McFarland had bought Curtis Farley's Swift and suddenly was going

113

faster than he ever had in the past. McFarland took the lead from his position outside the front row and held it for all 15 laps. Pole sitter Steve Knapp ran second until his gearbox broke, taking third and fourth place Colin Trueman and John Fergus out with him when they could not avoid the abruptly slowing Lola. Meanwhile, Dave Weitzenhoff and Scott Harrington collided for the second race in a row while disputing second, spinning both out. Steve Ave finally took second behind McFarland, with Kevin Whitesides third.

The Six Hour enduro went to the Porsche 944 of Tom Bagley and Jim Goughary. They covered 121 laps, 484 miles in the six hours. The similar Porsche of Pepe Pombo/Shawn Hendricks/Jack Lewis was second. It was a long drawn out affair that had the very sparse crowd dozing. The crowd was so small, in fact, that PA announcer Ed Conway half jokingly inviting them all to come to victory circle to meet the winners. This was the second and last IMSA SS weekend at RA.

The CART weekend, held in late September, was cursed with miserable weather. To say it never stopped raining would only be a slight exaggeration. It was *wet!* Cold, miserable, gloomy, muddy, it was all of that. Almost all Friday was fogged out. Lee Hall's displeasure with CART president John Frasco's pushing of the RA date to late September was well founded.

The Bosch VW Super Vee race ran for 60 very wet miles. Mike Groff was on the pole, but his Ralt was off at turn five, dropping to 11th. David Kudrave then took his Ralt RT-5 into the lead, but before the lap was out he too had slid off the slick track, handing first to Tom Knapp. Cars slid off left and right, but Knapp kept his Ralt on the road and led all 15 laps for his second straight RA FSV win. Didier Theys put on the drive of the day after starting in the last row following a practice crash. He sliced through the field in his Martini MK50, taking second place behind Knapp. This was a drive befitting a champion, which Theys would be in FSV this year. Cary Bren was third with brother Steve fourth, both in Ralts, while Kudrave recovered for fifth.

A slim field of 11 cars started the 76 mile American Racing Series event. Mike Groff took the win, passing pole sitter Juan Fangio II on the run into the first turn. Fangio was soon out with bad electrics while Fabrizio Barbazza, who was to be the series' inaugural champion, had to pit to tighten a loose wheel. All this allowed Groff to spurt away to an easy win. Jeff Andretti came in second after starting last with no time following a practice crash. Tommy Byrne was third with Ross Cheever fourth. Eight cars were running at the end, which is quite slim for a four mile track. There would be no ARS race at RA in 1987.

After a very wet Friday and Saturday, an equally wet Sunday's first race was for Pro Sports 2000. Rain has always been a great equalizer, and this race again proved it. Unheralded Barry Sitnick took the win, gaining the top spot when Steve Knapp's Lola fell out of first after leading nine of 14 laps when the electrics in his Lola drowned. Sitnick was there to take over and led the balance of the 56 miles in his Swift with the similar cars of Scott Harrington, Colin Trueman and Mike McFarland following. Knapp won only one race this season, but he finished consistently and took the title his cousin Tom had won the year before.

Twenty-five Indy cars were on hand for the CART Race for Life 200. Penske Racing was working on the new Chevrolet-Ilmor V-8 engine, and although it had not yet won, it showed great promise. One would be in the tail of the Pennzoil March 86C for Rick Mears. Friday's practice and qualifying was rained and fogged out, so Saturday had everything riding on one session. Bobby Rahal made the most of it, taking the pole in the Truesports/Budweiser March 86C at 1:55.829. This was considerably slower than Danny Sullivan's record from the year before, but the conditions were not conducive to record setting. Sullivan was second on the grid in

the Penske/Miller High Life March while row two was Roberto Moreno in the Galles Racing Lola T-86/00 and Kevin Cogan in the Patrick Racing/7-Eleven March. The second Patrick/Marlboro March of Emerson Fittipaldi was next, followed by the Andrettis, father Mario in the Newman/Haas Lola T-86/00 and Michael in the Kraco March 86C. Rounding out the top ten were Mears, Al Unser Jr. in the Shierson/Domino's Pizza Lola T-86/00 and last year's winner, Jacques Villeneuve, driving the Hemelgarn/Living Well Spas March 86C. The only other non-Cosworth powered car besides Mears and Dale Coyne's stock block Chevy was down in 13th place. Geoff Brabham's Galles/Valvoline Lola T-86/00 was powered by a Judd V-8 based upon a Honda F-3000 block.

Sunday was wet, but it was not raining as the cars gridded. As the pace lap commenced, rain began falling, increasing in intensity by the minute. Rahal took the lead just as the heavens really opened up, the rain simply pouring. Rahal was leading and only going 40 mph in so doing! Behind him nobody could see, and cars began sliding off course and colliding. While these cars can race in the rain, this was simply too much. Visibility was nil, giant puddles were forming, and it simply was not safe. The race was red flagged after two laps.

The rains persisted to fall heavily for the next two hours. By the time they began to abate, what light existed was failing. The race was postponed for two weeks.

On October 4 the cast reassembled to pick up the race at lap three. Unfortunately, the fall weather this year was the worst in years and it had rained every day in the intervening two weeks. Race day was sodden, with a steady rain coming down. After a morning warm-up, the cars were gridded for a noon restart.

After two laps under yellow, the cars were unleashed into the mist and gloom. Rahal took the point, but Michael Andretti moved past on lap eight. Sullivan was also on the move and he took second on the tenth go-around. They were followed by Rahal, Moreno, Mario Andretti, Mears, Brabham and Fittipaldi. Incredibly, the rain was picking up in intensity, and cars were slithering off course everywhere.

After the first pit stop shuffle, Sullivan assumed the lead over Michael Andretti and had extended it to 15 seconds. There were big spreads between the cars as the rain made visibility difficult. Mario Andretti was in third, then came Rahal, Mears, Moreno, Robert Guerrero in the Cotter/True Value March, Fittipaldi and Villeneuve. On lap 32 the rain had become a downpour, and Tom Sneva, in the Curb/Skoal March, although two laps down, went off course in turn five and came back on directly in Sullivan's path, who had no choice but to spin to avoid a collision. He lost the best part of a lap getting restarted.

The second round of pit stops rearranged the order. Some very astute pit strategy saw Moreno take the lead, followed by Fittipaldi, Villeneuve, Mears, Michael Andretti, Rahal, Mario, Guerrero and Sullivan. Villeneuve moved past Fittipaldi and started reeling in Moreno. On lap 44 of 50 Jacques was right behind when Moreno spun in turn 12 with Villeneuve having to spin in avoidance. Both were eliminated from the chase.

This put Fittipaldi in first with Michael Andretti closing. As the laps ran out, Andretti closed dramatically, but Fittipaldi was able to hang on to win by less than a second. Mears came in third, followed by Guerrero, Rahal and Sullivan. The points were important to Rahal, as he was in a close battle with Michael Andretti for the PPG Cup. Rahal held on and won the prestigious championship, winning six times enroute.

Lee Hall was right. The track should not have a major race this late in the year. Although some 30,000 fans braved the inclement weather, the gate could have been larger. There would be some lengthy negotiations over the matter of the date before next season.

1987

The Spec Racers (nee Sports Renaults) quickly became a popular entry level class. Several shops ran teams of rental cars for drivers not wanting to commit to car ownership.

Lee Hall's protestations were heard, and RA received a CART date at the end of August. The Trans-Am would share this weekend as the Saturday feature, the separate Trans-Am weekend of 1986 not being repeated. In addition, the September IMSA Firestone Firehawk weekend also was eliminated, with the Firehawk race being shortened and scheduled on the IMSA Camel GT weekend. Further, there would be no car event at the motorcycle weekend and no ARS event. This meant that there would be four car weekends for 1987, the Sprints, Historics, IMSA and CART weekends.

SCCA had created a new series for compact pickup trucks. They would run in showroom stock configuration and would be known as the SCCA Racetruck Challenge. RA chose not to schedule one. SCCA would sanction the American Racing Series for CART for a second year. The ECAR Series picked up HFC as the series sponsor, while Lucas left as the Sports Renault sponsor.

IMSA had also suffered the loss of sponsorship. Kelly Services ceased its support of the American Challenge Series, while Champion Spark Plugs did likewise for the small sedans. Both series would continue, but without title sponsors.

Following a meeting of the Board of Directors of RA, Lee Hall resigned as president and general manager of the track. There followed a brief period when the track effectively had nobody at the helm. Former driver and successful Milwaukee car dealer Bill Wuesthoff, who was a member of the board, took the presidency on an interim basis. SCCA HQ lent RA Jim Haynes who was its Vice President of Special Projects to the track as general manager. Before going to SCCA Haynes was the general manager of Lime Rock Park. Haynes would do double duty with SCCA and as general manager of RA until he made the move permanent. Later he would also assume the presidency of the track.

Wisconsin Governor Tommy Thompson instituted the Governor's Cup Award, designated to be given to a deserving individual to highlight amateur athletic and recreational resources unique to Wisconsin. The Road America Governor's Cup was to be given to a top amateur racer who exemplified sportsmanship, effort and achievement. This award would be given annually at the June Sprints to a person selected by the Governor's office and the RA officers. The initial recepient was Dr. Hiro Nishioka, a Green Bay neurosurgeon who had driven a variety of formula cars at RA for years.

The June Sprints entry was down from previous years, with 350 cars registered. Again, the proliferation of pro series tended to dilute the talent pool. Nonetheless, 53 cars ran in Sports Renault, 46 in Formula Vee, 45 in Formula Ford and 25 in Sports 2000.

The Formula Ford race was won once again by Dave Weitzenhoff, who had made it quite a habit. His Citation led most of the race, beating the fellow Citation of Brian Williams fairly handily. The Sports Renault race appeared to belong to Lynn Trapp, but after leading eight of the 12 laps his engine quit. Dudley Fleck spun out and Mike Alexander was in first. He kept it to the finish, with Pat Berryhill second and Robbie Buhl in third. Michael Gray took the Formula Vee race in his Lynx, benefiting from a battle for second that allowed him to draw away. Emory Pavol won that, with William Styczynski and Joe Claudy following.

The Formula Atlantic race was decided on the last lap when James King and Eric Lang collided. King had led since the start in his Ralt RT-4, but Lang was always there to pester. Lang made his move at turn five, there was contact, and after the dirt cloud settled, Lang got moving first to take the win. The sports racing event was taken by Al Beasley Jr. in a LeGrand-AMW. Jeff

The Historic weekend continued to grow in stature. At the 1987 event Aston Martin brought several cars from England and had the legendary Stirling Moss drive its DBR-2.

Miller had led most of the race in a Lola-Kohler, only to have the ignition box overheat, putting him out. Beasley had started last in the large field, but had moved into second when Miller failed, thus taking the overall win as well as CSR. In DSR his father, Al Beasley Sr. also won, having an easy drive to the checker in his Decker-AMW.

July 17-19 was for the Chicago Historic Races, this year dubbed the Chicago Sun-Times International Challenge. The main event would be the Aston Martin International Challenge, open to pre-1965 cars eligible for international racing at that time. Peter Livanos brought a big Aston Martin contingent from England to compete in this race. Livanos had no less than Stirling Moss to drive his DBR-2, plus noted English drivers Ray Mallock and Mike Salmon driving DB-4s. He also brought a DB-2 and a DB3-S. A goodly assortment of cars ranging from Augie Pabst's Scarab through Listers, Jaguars and Ferraris to Triumphs and MGs ran against the Astons, but to no avail. Mallock won in a DB-4 with Moss second in the DBR-2.

Among the hundreds of wonderful cars on display was an Eagle F-1. This particular chassis, #103, had won the 1967 Brands Hatch non-points Race of Champions in the hands of Dan Gurney. Unfortunately, it was not run, and all were deprived of hearing the sounds of its Gurney-Westlake V-12. Another F-1 car was the Shadow DN-3. The world's one and only Brabham BT-17 was here. This was a car built by Brabham for the Can-Am but never developed. The post-1964 sports car event was taken by a name from the past, Don Devine, driving a McLaren M20. Add in the usual blend of Ferraris, Lotuses, Porsches and scores of others and once again it was a memorable weekend.

In mid-August the IMSA show came to town again. Unfortunately, they were greeted by bad weather. Most of Friday's practice was useless, fog and rain blighting the day. Saturday was occasional rain, while Sunday was awful. Saturday's first race was for Pro Sports 2000. Due to a very crowded weekend, the race was run for 12 laps rather than its customary 15. For ten of those laps Steve Ave appeared to have it in the bag. Pole sitter Ave had his Lola T-87/90 ahead of Steve Knapp's like example, but Knapp's brakes were going. On lap 11 Knapp, now out of brakes, rammed Ave, putting him out. Knapp led the last two laps to win over the Swifts of Greg Wenkman and Kevin Whitesides.

The Firestone Firehawk race was contested over three and one-half hours. The winning Nissan 300ZX Turbo of Shawn and Scott Hendricks covered 264 miles in that time. They took the lead for good on lap 44 of the 66 covered. The John Petrick/Scott Lagasse Camaro finished second.

On Sunday morning the American Challenge cars ran for 12 laps, 48 miles. This was quite a change from the 300 kilometer distances of the previous two years. Dick Danielson scored a fine victory, one for which he had to fight the entire distance. He led the first lap in his Buick Somerset but was passed by Irv Hoerr's Oldsmobile Toronado on lap two. Danielson made a fine move at turn five on the fifth lap to reclaim first, Jerry Thompson also passing Hoerr at the same time when Hoerr went wide on the exit. Thompson then got ahead of Danielson, leading laps 10 and 11, and the two went around the last lap virtually side by side with Danielson outdragging Thompson up the hill to the line, winning by half a car length. It was a fine race. Hoerr, despite finishing out of the points after getting mired in a gravel trap, did go on to nip Danielson for the season title.

As the IMSA International Sedans came to the grid for their 48 mile race it began to rain. Not hard at first, but it was rain that would continue most of the day. Amos Johnson and Parker Johnstone fought it out for the entire 12 laps with Johnson taking the win in a Mazda 626 by less than a car length. They swapped the lead many times, including twice on the last lap. The second place points were enough for Johnstone to clinch the season championship.

The Camel GT field had a bit of a different look about it. Only 10 prototypes were running, although there were 16 cars in Camel Lights. Seven of the 10 GTPs were Porsche 962s; two from Holbert, plus the Dyson, Akin and Bayside entries as before. John Hotchkiss had replaced his March with a 962 and had Jim Adams co-driving. From Switzerland came the Walter Brun team, with a 962 for Oscar Larrauri. Co-driving the Dyson 962 this weekend was Scotsman John Chrichton-Stuart, the Earl of Dumfries, better known by his *nom de corse* Johnny Dumfries. The two Lola-based cars of Nissan and Chevrolet were present and were fastest in qualifying as their V-6 turbo motors were putting the power down better than before. However, reliability was still suspect. Elliott Forbes-Robinson was on the pole in the Nissan Lola with Sarel Van der Merwe alongside in the Corvette Lola.

As the noon start time for the Lowenbrau 500 approached, the rain became heavier. As the cars were gridded it was raining so hard that a start was impossible. Eventually the rain stopped, and the race got underway 1:40 late. Pole sitter Forbes-Robinson shot out ahead, with Van der Merwe following. In a few laps the field of 53 cars had created a dry line, and the pit stops to change to slicks began. After this shuffle, Forbes-Robinson had about a half minute lead on Larrauri followed by Van der Merwe, Al Holbert and Derek Bell in the twin Holbert Lowenbrau 962s, Price Cobb in the Dyson

The start for the '87 500 was delayed and the checker flew early. Chip Robinson pits the third place Porsche 962 to hand over to Al Holbert.

962 and Hurley Haywood in the Bayside example.

The first round of regular pit stops came shortly after 100 miles and John Morton, in for Forbes-Robinson, resumed in the lead. Holbert had moved up and was now in second ahead of Doc Bundy in the Corvette Lola. Positions had stabilized to a degree when the rain returned. By the 200 mile mark it was raining so hard that visibility was nil and the track was awash in some places. The leading Nissan stalled on course with water in the electrics, and the third place Corvette was out after running through a puddle so deep that the engine was flooded. Out came the red flag.

Eventually the rains let up and the race was restarted after an hour and a half's delay. Chip Robinson, in for Holbert, led the pack away on lap 60. Of course the rain started almost simultaneously. Dumfries was quickly showing that he was an excellent *mudder* as he was moving the Dyson Porsche up rapidly. He was quickly past Robinson and started pulling away. Larrauri also showed wet weather prowess, taking second from Robinson. By this time it was already well past five o'clock and getting quite dark. The word was passed that the race would end at six, as the light was fast fading in the rain and gloom. This announcement was not disputed by anyone as all just wished to get somewhere dry and warm. A crowd of 20,000 fans had come through the gates this morning, but by this time far fewer than that were still on the grounds.

At 6:00 PM the checker came out and Johnny Dumfries took the win. The Earl and Price Cobb had covered 82 laps, 328 miles in the on-and-off 3:21:26 of actual racing. Following their 962 were five more 962s. Larrauri was second in a solo drive, Holbert and Robinson third, Bell fourth also driving solo, Vern Schuppan and James Weaver fifth in the Bob Akin 962 and the Hotchkiss/Adams car sixth. This year Chip Robinson won the Camel GT title in the Holbert Porsche as Holbert was phasing himself out of the cockpit to spend more time as the head of Porsche Motorsports North America and its Indy car project.

In Camel Lights the Spice of Charles Morgan and Jim Rothbarth prevailed, taking the class lead in the final half hour of running when the leading Spice of Jeff Kline and Don Bell made an ill-timed pit stop. Once again David Loring led a good portion of the race in his Denali, but the rain eliminated his chances as the car refused to refire after a pit stop. Taking third was the Jim Downing/John Maffucci Argo JM-19, the points helping Downing to his third straight Camel Lights title.

The Morrison-Protofab Team scored a 1-2 finish in GTO. The winning Camaro was driven by Chris Kneifel and Paul Dallenbach, while the second place Corvette was in the hands of Greg Pickett and Tommy Riggins. The AAR

Toyota Celica Turbo of Rocky Moran and Wally Dallenbach Jr. was third. The other AAR Toyota of Chris Cord/Juan Fangio II went out in a big crash on the front straight, fortunately without injury. The Roush Ford Mustangs of Scott Pruett/Tom Gloy, Bruce Jenner/Bobby Akin Jr. and Gloy/Lyn St. James all dropped out of the race. Though Cord crashed, he would be the '87 GTO champion.

Tom Kendall was the GTU story. He drove solo to the win, challenged only by Amos Johnson in the Team Highball Mazda RX-7. Kendall would win his second straight GTU crown.

Two weeks later on the last weekend in August the CART and Trans-Am series came to town. The weather, unbelievably, was periodic rain! Fortunately Saturday and Sunday afternoons were dry, with rain Sunday morning just clearing in time for the CART race.

The first race on Saturday was the Bendix Brakes Trans-Am. Roush Racing was dominating the season with its Turbo Merkurs and Scott Pruett had a strangle hold on the championship. He and Pete Halsmer would drive Merkurs at RA with Deborah Gregg in the Roush Mercury Capri. GM again was not giving any Trans-Am team factory support, so the GM challenge was limited to privateers. The Merkurs of Pruett and Halsmer were on the front row with Paul Gentilozzi in the Rocketsports Olds next. Pruett led the first lap, but dropped back suddenly as his Merkur overheated. Also out at the start was Paul Newman, who blew the Nissan 300ZX Turbo's engine as he shifted into second gear.

With Pruett's departure Les Lindley took the point in his independent Camaro. Driving superbly, Lindley kept Halsmer at bay until lap 22 of 25. Going into turn five, Lindley went wide to avoid some oil while Halsmer didn't, going for the apex instead. Halsmer's gamble paid off as he emerged from the corner ahead of Lindley. Try as he might, Lindley could not catch Halsmer, who came home the winner of the 100 mile event. Behind Lindley there was a race-long scrap for third. Gentilozzi, Irv Hoerr in a Olds Toronado, Gregg, Dick Danielson in a Buick Somerset and Jerry Thompson in a Chevy Beretta fought long and hard. Deborah Gregg came out on top, finishing third, which was the highest finish for a woman in Trans-Am history to that point.

Saturday's final race was 13 laps, 52 miles for the HFC Atlantic Challenge. It didn't get underway until almost six o'clock as two false starts — and agonizingly slow regridding and general bumbling — caused a delay of over one hour. By this time most of the fans had left, and they missed watching Ted Prappas lead all 13 laps in a Ralt RT-4. Steve Shelton ran second for the entire distance in his Swift DB-4 but a slipping clutch did not allow him

The non-spectator Fall Vintage Festival follows a theme each year. In 1987 it was Bugatti and over 20 of the fabled French cars were on hand.

to challenge Prappas. He did manage to stay ahead of Calvin Fish who finished third in Bill O'Connor's HFC-sponsored Ralt and added to his point lead that would see him collect the championship at year end.

Sunday's three support races were all flag-to-flag runs. In the Pro Sports 2000 event, Steve Knapp took the win in the Carl Haas Lola T-87/90. Richard Bahmer was on the pole in a Swift DB-2, but Knapp nailed him at the start. Bahmer finished second in the 48 mile race, while Kevin Whitesides was third in another Swift. Knapp would win his second S-2000 championship in a row when he made a pass for the lead in the last turn on the last lap of the season's final race!

The Barber Saab Pro Series spec cars ran for 44 miles with Jeremy Dale leading all the way. Ken Murillo, who would win the title, ran second for the entire 11 laps, but third place was a scramble ultimately decided in favor of Bruce Feldman.

David Kudrave scored his first win in the Valvoline/Bosch VW Super Vee race. He started on row two, but took the lead with a bold move into the first turn. He led all 15 laps in his Ralt RT-5. Ken Johnson took an equally untroubled second place, but the battle for third lasted almost the entire distance. Dennis Vitolo, Scott Atchison and Robbie Groff passed the position around constantly, finishing in that order behind the lead two. Atchison was to be the series champ this year and would go on to run portions of two Indy car seasons with the Machinists Union team.

The Living Well/Provimi Veal 200 got off to a wet start as most of Friday's practice and qualifying was rendered useless by rain. Saturday was better, times dropped and the grid was set. Mario Andretti was in control and he grabbed the pole with a time of 1:52.287 in the Newman/Haas Lola T-87/00 now powered by an Ilmor/Chevrolet turbo V-8. This was just 0.2 off the lap record set by Danny Sullivan in 1985. Roberto Guerrero was alongside Andretti on the front row in the Granatelli/True Value March 87C with a time 1.4 seconds slower than Mario. Row two comprised Michael Andretti in the Kraco/STP March 87C and Bobby Rahal in the Truesports/Budweiser March 87C, which was appropriate because the two were very close atop the point standings. The third row consisted of Sullivan in the Penske/Miller March 87C and Geoff Brabham's Galles/Valvoline March 87C, powered by the Judd Honda engine. The balance of the top ten held Rick Mears driving the Penske/Pennzoil March 87C, Al Unser Jr. in the Shierson/Domino's Pizza March 87C and the two Patrick/Marlboro March 87Cs of Emerson Fittipaldi and Kevin Cogan.

As the pace car began rolling a light rain was falling. Fortunately, this soon blew over and after a few laps the sun broke through, warming a

crowd of over 60,000. Mario Andretti had this weekend under control, and the race was no different. He took the lead at the start and held it all the way. He did not surrender the point even during pit stops. There was a race, but it was not for first place.

At the 10 lap mark the race had shaken out to Mario leading, followed by Sullivan, Brabham, Rahal, Fittipaldi, Cogan, Mears, Michael Andretti, Arie Luyendyk in the Hemelgarn/Living Well-Provimi March 87C, Fabrizio Barbazza in the Arciero March 87C and Unser Jr. Brabham, Rahal and Fittipaldi got past Sullivan, with Rahal and Fittipaldi having an especially close dice. They soon passed Brabham as he was wrestling with a duff clutch.

After the first round of pit stops Mario led Sullivan, Fittipaldi, Mears, Michael Andretti and Brabham. Rahal was out with ignition problems, while Sullivan lost a gearbox oil filter plug, losing a lap. Then Mears had his gearbox jam, and he dropped well back. All this left Mario leading Fittipaldi, Michael, Brabham, Guerrero, Cogan and Unser Jr. On lap 30 disaster struck the Patrick team as both Cogan and Fittipaldi coasted to silent halts, Cogan with a blown engine and Fittipaldi with a dry fuel tank. On lap 31 Michael Andretti's engine quit, and he also was out.

All this attrition was affecting everyone except Mario Andretti, who was serenely cruising around the four miles. Brabham was now second, even without a clutch, followed by Unser Jr., Luyendyk and Guerrero. Sullivan and John Andretti, in his first Indy car race, got past a stumbling Guerrero and that is how the race finished. Mario won a crushing victory, with Brabham second, then Unser Jr., Luyendyk, Sullivan and John Andretti's Curb/Skoal March 87C. Andretti averaged 120.155 mph in his victory run. This also was the first win at RA for the Chevrolet-Ilmor V-8 race engine.

Mario's win tightened the points chase, but in the end Rahal prevailed to take his second straight PPG Cup. Fabrizio Barbazza won the Jim Trueman Award, given to the year's top rookie in honor of the late head of Truesports, Mid Ohio and the Red Roof Inn motel chain.

In early October the Vintage Sports Car Driving Association (VSCDA) ran the second of what would become an annual event, the Fall Vintage Festival. While this was a non-spectator event, it drew a great variety of vintage and historic cars. This year, the Festival featured Bugatti, and over 20 were not only on hand, but on the track in a special all-Bugatti race. Famed Bugatti *pilote* and New York restaurateur René Dreyfus was the Grand Marshal. Dreyfus, winner of the 1930 Grand Prix of Monaco in a Bugatti, though in his 80s, cut a dapper figure as he greeted people in the paddock. In addition, he did a lap of the track in a Bugatti; a truly memorable weekend.

1988

The famous Pagoda, expanded several times since 1955, overlooks the start of the sports racing event at the 1988 June Sprints. Its end came in late 1989 when the new paddock was constructed.

The silos were painted again as Miller Brewery's marketing strategy switched to the High Life brand. Further, the Lowenbrau 500 became the Miller High Life 500. The base schedule for 1988 remained similar to '87 with the Sprints, Historics, IMSA and CART/Trans-Am weekends. In August a round of the Escort Endurance Challenge was staged at RA, but interestingly, it was a non-spectator event! Escort wanted to have a round of the series at RA, as did SCCA and the participants, but the track was loathe to have a free standing spectator weekend for this type of race, following the gate receipt disasters of the two IMSA Firehawk weekends. Of the two pro weekends, the IMSA weekend, of course, was out, while the CART/Trans-Am weekend was already running to a tight schedule and any type of race more than an hour in length was out of the question. The result was a three hour Escort Endurance race on the Saturday of a Chicago Region non-spectator SCCA regional. It is believed that this is the only time that there ever has been a non-spectator pro race in the history of either SCCA or IMSA, but such is the draw of RA.

There were a lot of name changes as sponsors came and went. Bendix Brakes departed from the Trans-Am, replaced by Escort radar detectors, which also continued to back the SCCA's showroom stock series, now called the Escort Endurance Championship. Coors added its name to the Racetruck Challenge, as did Valvoline to the Super Vees, while Wolverine Boots and Shoes sponsored the Pro Sports 2000s. In response to the urging of General Motors, as well as the complaints of some competitors, Corvettes were split out of the Escort Endurance series and given a series of their own, the Corvette Challenge. HFC added its sponsorship to the American Racing

Series, while continuing its support of the Formula Atlantic ECAR series.

The June Sprints also had sponsorship this year as Nissan put its name on the event as part of an overall program in which they also supplied the course vehicles. In addition, Country Time Lemonade put up a purse for the GT-1, 2, 3 race and titled it the *Country Time Old Fashioned Shoot-Out.* Before that was run the fans were treated to another Dave Weitzenhoff win, but this year Weitzenhoff took the FC race instead of his usual FF romp. Driving a new FC Citation, Weitzenhoff did receive some luck as leaders Steve Knapp and Steve Ice were taken out in an altercation with a wandering FA car. After that, Weitzenhoff led the last 12 of 14 laps. Eric Tremayne won Formula Vee this year in yet another close race.

The sports racing event was taken by Jeff Miller, whose record in the Sprints showed that after three straight wins in the early '80s he broke every year since and always while in the class lead. Fortunately, his Lola T-540-Kohler held together this time and he got the elusive checker. Al Beasley Sr. was the DSR winner, while Jay Hill took Sports 2000. James Opperman won the formula feature on the last lap as leaders Jim Brouk and Cliff Ebben collided. This happened only two corners from the finish and a very surprised Opperman did not realize he was first until he reached the impound paddock after the race.

The Country Time Old Fashioned Shoot-Out saw Rick Dittman lead all 60 miles in his Pontiac Firebird. Jerry Dunbar, also in a Firebird, challenged, but Dittman had his measure. Ray Irwin was third in a Camaro. In the GT2 portion, David Finch fought with Rick Mancuso before easing away to the win. Finch was in his usual yellow Porsche 944 while Mancuso was driving a red (of course) Ferrari 308GTB.

The Historic weekend saw two Scarabs go head to head for the first time since the early 1960s. Heading into turn five, Augie Pabst leads Don Orosco by a nose.

IMSA favored RA with a mid-July date for the Miller High Life 500 Camel GT. Unfortunately, at RA IMSA seemed to mean rain, and despite this summer being of near drought proportions, it was very wet on Friday and Saturday. Sunday, mercifully, was dry and warm.

Saturday's only race was a six hour Firestone Firehawk race. Despite the fact that a good portion was run in the rain the winning Camaro of Leighton Reese and Brad Hoyt covered 117 laps, 468 miles. Reese and Hoyt actually were second on the road, but the first car across the line after six hours, the Pontiac Firebird of Mark Hutchins and Tim Evans, was disqualified in impound for illegal body modifications.

Sunday morning led off with a 60 mile HFC Formula Atlantic race. Colin Trueman was on pole in the Truesports/Red Roof Inns Swift DB-4 but it was Robbie Buhl in a Ralt RT-4 who led the first two laps. On lap three Buhl began dropping back and Trueman, Steve Shelton and Jocko Cunningham, all in Swifts, passed him. Shelton closed on Trueman, and the twosome engaged in a tense duel for the balance of the 15 laps. On lap 11 Shelton passed Trueman when he dropped two wheels off course, opening the door. Two laps later Shelton returned the favor, running wide through turn 12, and Trueman repassed. This held to the finish, with Trueman squeaking out a half second win. Cunningham was third, followed by the H-Promotions team Ralts of Buhl and Scott Harrington. A late season rush saw Shelton take the season championship.

The Barber Saab 60 mile race was all Rob Wilson. He grabbed the lead, after a little contact, in the first turn from pole sitter Bruce Feldman and led the entire distance. Jay Cochran, Ken Knott and Jeremy Dale led the balance of the 21 starters to the finish. Feldman, who would be the season champ, finished sixth.

The third Sunday prelim was a 60 mile International Sedan race. Parker Johnstone notched the fourth of six wins this season enroute to his title. He took the lead in his Acura from pole sitter Amos Johnson on lap two and never looked back. Johnson finished second in a Mazda 323 while Johnstone's teammate, Doug Peterson, was third in another Acura.

In the Camel GT the Nissan had come of age. After using a Lola T-810 based car for the past three seasons, Nissan Performance Technology had built its own car, the Nissan GTP-88. The car had worked so well coming into RA that Geoff Brabham already had a strangle hold on the Camel GT title, having won five straight races. His co-driver would be John Morton. The Corvette GTP was still using a Lola chassis, but this year it was a new T-

88/10. Further, Hendrick Motorsports had ditched the 3.0 turbo V-6 in favor of a good old 5.7 liter Chevy V-8. Sarel Van der Merwe and Elliott Forbes-Robinson were up. Jaguar had switched its factory team from Group 44 to Tom Walkinshaw Racing. TWR had two new XJR-9s present with the formidable driver lineup of John Nielson/Martin Brundle and Jan Lammers/Davy Jones. As usual, a slew of Porsche 962s were present, headed by the Holbert Racing entry of Derek Bell/Chip Robinson. Add prototypes from Spice, Fabcar, March and others and it was a big field.

While this race was the Miller High Life 500, it was in kilometers, not miles. Hence the race would run for 78 laps, 312 miles. This year IMSA was using a confusing qualifying procedure, which saw the fastest six after regular qualifying go into a separate session with single car qualifying. Only problem was that it was raining hard when this occurred, so even though Geoff Brabham was quickest in the Nissan at 1:58.352, the pole went to Oscar Larrauri in the Brun Porsche 962 at 2:19.487.

Larrauri led lap one, but slid wide in the Carousel on lap two and Brundle was past in the Castrol TWR Jaguar. The Brit then began to pull away, and as the race settled down led Larrauri (until the timing belt broke), Lammers, Brabham, Price Cobb in the Dyson Porsche 962, Robinson, Van der Merwe and Bernard Jourdain in the Porsche 962 of John Kalagian. The Momo March 86G-turbo Buick was already out, the engine blowing after only seven laps. Lammers and Brabham came together while disputing third, both sliding off and losing several places.

The first round of pit stops saw Brundle surrender the lead as the Jaguar suffered fuel pick up problems. This would plague the car the rest of the day, and it would not again challenge for the lead that it held for almost a third of the race. Derek Bell now was leading, having taken over from Robinson, with James Weaver second in the Dyson Porsche he inherited from Cobb. Morton was third after Brabham had pushed the Nissan up the chart after his early spin. At two thirds distance a full course yellow to clean up the mess created when Dominic Dobson crashed his Camel Light saw the Electromotive Nissan crew time their second pit stop superbly, and Brabham found himself with the lead. This held through the final routine pit stop, and the Brabham/Morton Nissan won easily, the sixth straight for Brabham. Bell/Robinson were second, followed by the Cobb/Weaver Porsche. The two TWR Jaguars were plagued with minor glitches and finished fourth-fifth in the order Brundle/Nielsen and Lammers/Jones. The John Hotchkis/Jim Adams Porsche 962 finished sixth for the second straight year. Brabham went on to win his first Camel GT championship, winning nine races in all, including eight in a row.

Terry Visger and Dan Marvin won Camel Lights after the leading Spice of Dominic Dobson crashed heavily in the kink. Dobson was cruising in the lead when he moved over for a Jaguar that was approaching rapidly. He moved a bit too far as the Jag blasted past, dropped two wheels off, lost it and trashed the machine against the guardrail. John Grooms then took over the lead in an Argo JM-16, but late in the race had the suspension break. Marvin was left with the lead and he brought the Huffaker Spice CL88 to the win over the similar Spice of Bill Koll and Skeeter McKittrick. Tom Hessert finished fifth in a borrowed Tiga after the car he was sharing with David Loring broke early. The points he earned were crucial, as he narrowly beat out three time class champion Jim Downing for the '88 title.

GTO was a four car battle between the two AAR Toyota Celicas of Willy T. Ribbs and Dennis Aase and the two Roush Merkurs of Scott Pruett and Pete Halsmer. Ribbs led the first portion of the race followed by Pruett. After a full course yellow had bunched the field, Ribbs and Pruett came together, dropping themselves back. Aase now assumed the lead, holding it to the finish. Halsmer was second, but could not challenge because of failing boost pressure. Ribbs wound up third, with Pruett fourth. Pruett, however, did go on to win his second GTO crown in three years. For Aase the win was particularly sweet, for in a serious testing accident the year before he had smashed his legs so badly that doctors feared he would never walk again. This, his first win since, confounded them.

The GTU prize went to the Fulltime Racing Team Dodge Daytonas of Dorsey Schroeder and Kal Showket. They finished one-two, the first win for Dodge in GTU. Third was Amos Johnson in the Team Highball Mazda RX-7. Having started 58th due to a heavy practice crash, Johnson had to pit in the opening laps to repair some more crash damage. Johnson drove superbly from the very end of the field; third was not a good enough reward for a magnificent drive. Tom Kendall held on to finish fourth, his C&C Chevrolet Beretta running on only five cylinders and subsequently went on to win his third straight GTU title.

Two weeks later the Chicago Historic Races ran in fine weather. Don Orosco attracted the throngs in the paddock with the three cars he brought; a Scarab, Maserati Tipo 61 and Porsche RS-60. Augie Pabst had his Scarab here also, and the two put on a great show. The two Scarabs went around the track in tandem, first one leading, then the other. They thundered down the straights and did power slides through the corners. It was awesome and had the fans jumping up and down. They finished their seven lap race side by side; who won? It really didn't matter – everybody won!

The featured event this weekend was a 45 minute *enduro* for cars that were eligible to contest the world sports car championship in the '60s and '70s. Bib Stillwell, of Australia, was the winner in a Mirage M7. There were three other Mirages in the race as well as Ferraris; 275-LMs, 312PB, GTOs, 250 GTs and 512-M – a lot of V-12 music!

The last weekend in August saw the three hour SCCA Escort Endurance race. It ran on Saturday of the Chicago Region, SCCA, regional race weekend and was a non-spectator event. A good portion of the three hours were run in the rain. The winning Camaro of Don Knowles, John Heinricy and Stu Hayner covered 56 laps, 224 miles. They averaged 73.64 mph beating the second place Camaro of Sean and Scott Hendricks by six seconds. In third came the Saleen Mustang of Steve Saleen and Desire Wilson.

It must also be mentioned that in the accompanying regional, actor Tom Cruise appeared, winning GT4 in the Newman-Sharp Racing Nissan. Apparently word had leaked out, and there were some fans hanging on the outside track fence watching. Further, it seems that there were an extraordinary number of teenage girls, who normally never accompany their fathers to the race track, who did so this weekend.

The weekend after Labor Day witnessed the CART and Trans-Am show. After having an August date in 1987, the track was again saddled with a date in September. At this time there was a debate between various parties in CART over even having a race at Road America. Certain CART board members thought the track was too long, was too remote, did not have convenient hotels and so forth. Fortunately, the pro-RA members of CART, led by Carl Haas who was recently elected to the track board, were able to retain dates for the track, although not at a favorable time of the year. This struggle was to continue on and off for several years until the coming of Andrew Craig as CART president in 1994. Craig displayed a far more catholic view of racing than either his predecessors or some CART board members. He and Jim Haynes ultimately came to an agreement that would ensure CART participation at RA for the balance of the century.

Having said that, this year's September date featured an outbreak of sunny and warm weather! After three previous CART weekends plagued by bad weather, this was indeed a most pleasant change, even if it was in September.

The SCCA Escort Trans-Am was the first race on Saturday, running for 100 miles. The Audi factory entered the series this year with two cars tended by Group 44. Hans Stuck and Hurley Haywood drove the four wheel drive, five cylinder turbo cars. They were the ticket that year and had won seven of ten races coming in to RA with Haywood well on his way to the '88 championship. As a response, Roush was running four cars this weekend. Ron Fellows, Lyn St. James and Deborah Gregg were in Merkur XR4Ti four cylinder turbos, while Scott Pruett was brought in from the IMSA GTO series to *guest drive* a special Merkur XR8 powered by a 5.7 liter Ford V-8. This took advantage of a rules loophole that specified that in order to be eligible, the car/engine combination had to be available to the public. Ford, it turns out, sold a V-8 Merkur in South Africa, making it eligible for the Trans-Am.

Pruett dutifully took the pole with Irv Hoerr alongside in the factory-aided Oldsmobile Supreme. Darin Brassfield was third in the Pacific Summit Corvette before Stuck in the first of the Audis. Pruett jumped into the lead immediately and was able to watch the fight for second in his mirrors. Stuck was just ahead of Brassfield, Hoerr, Willy T. Ribbs in Les Lindley's Camaro, Fellows, Mike Ciasulli in the second Hoerr Oldsmobile Supreme and Paul Newman in the Newman-Sharp Nissan 300ZX Turbo. Soon Stuck was edging away in second, so with the first two places static the battle became one for third. Hoerr dropped out with a punctured oil cooler while Brassfield had a distributor fail. Haywood moved up from a bad start and started mixing it up with Ciasulli and Fellows. As the race neared conclusion, Pruett cruised in first while Stuck started closing the gap. Before it could get tense, though, Stuck had to back off as his brakes were going away. Consequently, Pruett won with Stuck second, followed by Ribbs, Haywood, Fellows and Ciasulli.

The final Saturday race was for the Corvette Challenge. Thirty of the fiberglass flyers ran for 88 miles with Andy Pilgrim taking the lead from Mark Dismore on lap five and going on to win. Stu Hayner came up from tenth to take second, while Peter Cunningham finished third.

Sunday morning started with a 60 mile Wolverine Shoes and Boots Sports 2000 race. Interestingly enough, Road America which gave birth to the series and had run up to four events a year had only one this season. The series had matured and now was running across the country. At any rate, this year's event was a fine race, with many lead changes. Tom Jagemann led the early laps from the pole in his Lola T-88/90. Jim Miller moved his Swift DB-2 up steadily from seventh, stalking and passing Jagemann for first on lap 12. Most unfortunately, Miller then spun in turn

A.J. Foyt ran Road America several times during the twilight of his career never running with the leaders. Nonetheless, his Copenhagen-liveried March was a fan favorite.

six and the closely following Jagemann hit him, putting both out. Pat Hill took over the top rung in a Swift with Jay Hill (no relation) following in a Lola T-87/90. Jay Hill made the pass for first in turn five but Pat Hill took it back in turn six. Not discouraged, Jay again passed, this time in turn 12 and made it stick, taking his first pro win. Third finishing John Fergus would go on to claim the title.

The 60 mile Valvoline/Bosch VW Super Vee race was all Robbie Groff. He led the entire distance in his Ralt RT-5, besting the similar cars of Mark Smith, Ken Murillo, Bernard Jourdain, E.J. Lenzi and Paul Radisich. There was much pushing and shoving behind Groff with the attendant shuffling of positions. For Groff it was his second FSV win, the first coming at Milwaukee in June. The local air must agree with him. Murillo was in the Provimi Ralt which was the car of champions during this period. Murillo took the '88 championship, following in the footsteps of Arie Luyendyk in '84 and Ken Johnson in '85 who also won the title driving for this team.

The HFC American Racing Series race was for 15 identical March 86A cars running 76 miles. Englishman Calvin Fish started from the pole and led the first seven laps followed by Juan Fangio II, Tommy Byrne and Jon Beekhuis. Paul Tracy was already out after two laps, his March handling atrociously. However that was not the case up front as Fangio closed on Fish. Just when Fangio was sizing him up, Fish pulled off track with a dead engine. Beekhuis, who was to win this year's title, closed on Fangio, who responded by dropping his lap times and holding first to the end. Beekhuis was second, followed by Ted Prappas, Gary Rubio and Mike Groff.

After five years of title sponsorship in some form or other, Provimi had cut back its race involvement, and this year's CART race was the Briggs & Stratton 200. In qualifying Danny Sullivan again was fastest, taking pole with a time of 1:51.567, breaking his 1985 track record. After several years of using customer Marches, Penske was back with his own cars. The PC-17 was good, as evidenced not only by Sullivan's pole time, but by the fact that Sullivan would be this year's PPG Cup winner. Further underlining the Penske's pace was Rick Mears, who had the Pennzoil PC-17 next to Sullivan's Miller High Life PC-17 on the front row. Al Unser Jr. was next in the Galles/Valvoline March 88C. This was the only March that had any type of speed this year, as the Lola chassis was the preferable customer car. Indeed, several March teams switched to Lolas during the season. One of these was Patrick Racing, which switched from March to a year-old Lola T-87/00 for Emerson Fittipaldi, whose Marlboro car was fourth on the grid. These first four were all Ilmor-Chevrolet powered. Sitting fifth was Bobby

Rahal in one of the only two Judd powered cars running. Rahal was in a Truesports/Budweiser Lola T-88/00. Mario Andretti was alongside Rahal in the Newman-Haas/Amoco/K-Mart Lola T-88/00. Row four held the first Cosworth powered cars, the Machinists Union/Schaeffer March 88C of Kevin Cogan and Michael Andretti in the Kraco Lola T-87/00. Filling out the top ten were Didier Theys in the Dick Simon/Uniden Lola T-88/00 and Derek Daly driving the Raynor Lola. Of interest in the field was the Porsche entry. Porsche entered CART with its own car at the end of '87, but to develop an engine and chassis simultaneously is almost impossible. Consequently, Porsche put its turbo V-8 in a March 88C chassis. The car was run by Holbert Racing under the name Porsche Motorsports North America, was sponsored by Quaker State and driven by Teo Fabi. So far this season it had struggled, and here Fabi was 13th on the grid.

As expected, Sullivan took the lead at the start, Fittipaldi shadowing him closely. These two slowly broke free from the pack, comprising Unser Jr., Mario Andretti, Mears, Michael Andretti, Rahal, Raul Boesel in the Shierson/Domino's Pizza Lola and Fabi. The first round of pit stops started on lap 16 of 50 which was not a moment too soon for the Penske team. Sullivan barely made it, and Mears ran dry on course. This put Fittipaldi in the lead, with Sullivan second, but keeping a wary eye on his fuel mileage. Mario Andretti was third, then Rahal, Unser Jr., Michael Andretti, Arie Luyendyk in the Simon/Provimi Lola, Daly, Boesel, John Jones in the Arciero/Labatts March and Fabi. Rahal attacked Mario, finally getting past into third on lap 24, bringing Unser Jr. along with him. Mario was hobbled a bit by an engine slightly down on power.

The second round of pit stops were heralded by Sullivan running out of methanol coming out of Thunder Valley. Fortunately he had enough momentum to get up the pit hill where his crew met him and pushed him to the pits. His car was refueled and back on the track quickly, but all hope of victory was gone. Fittipaldi was now first, with Rahal close behind. Rahal was worried about fuel mileage also and could not mount the charge he would have liked. Third place Al Unser Jr. had to give up the spot in the final laps with a third stop for the last of his fuel. The race finished with Emerson Fittipaldi winning and Bobby Rahal less than a second back. Mario Andretti took third while Sullivan managed to salvage fourth. Michael Andretti took fifth, Derek Daly sixth, while Al Unser Jr. had dropped back to seventh, just ahead of Teo Fabi in the Porsche entry. An interesting race, but it could have been better if everyone had enough fuel to run flat out.

1989

Jaguar entrusted its IMSA challenge to Tom Walkinshaw Racing, winning frequently, but never taking the Camel GT crown. Here Chip Robinson's Nissan GTP pulls up on the tail of John Nielsen's Jaguar XJR-9

The program for 1989 was virtually identical to the previous year with four weekends. The SCCA Endurance Series would not run a non-spectator event as in 1988 and as a result was not on the schedule. Dates remained similar, with IMSA in July and CART in September. Prange's Department Stores and Levi Jeans had signed on as title sponsors for the June Sprints, while Texaco Havoline had replaced Briggs & Stratton as the CART sponsor. Miller High Life remained on board for the IMSA weekend.

SCCA had lost Escort as the title sponsor for both the Trans-Am and the showroom stock-based Endurance Series. Wolverine Boots and Shoes had also departed from Pro Sports 2000, but Sisapa Records had replaced them. HFC had left the Formula Atlantic series, concentrating on the ARS, but in a major move Toyota came on board as sponsor. This was part of a long range plan that would see Toyota engines become the standard Atlantic powerplant. Over the years Atlantics had used variations of the Ford Cosworth 1600cc four. Now the much newer Toyota 1600cc four was eligible and after a two year grandfather period would become the required engine.

During the off season, John Bishop retired. He sold the organization to Mike Cone twenty years after founding IMSA and changing the face of U.S. road racing. Mark Raffauf, long-time IMSA employee, took over as the sanctioning body's second ever president.

The Prange/Levi's June Sprints saw over 350 cars play to 20,000 spectators. The weather cooperated and it was a good weekend of fun in the sun. The large formula race was decided by a yellow flag, but not in the usual way. Duane Smith had led the first 13 of 15 laps in his Ralt RT-4, but then Cliff Ebben got past him in an old March 81A. However, when they came upon a local yellow, both backed off. Smith's engine backfired so loudly that Ebben thought the engine had blown. Ebben then motored away from the corner in too leisurely a fashion, and Smith blew by to take the win. In FC, Dave Weitzenhoff did not win; Craig Taylor relegated him to second place.

Fifty-four Sports Renaults ran for 12 laps with Mike Alexander winning after Dudley Fleck and Doug Kimbrough collided while disputing the lead. The drive of the day went to David Tenney, who came all the way from 54th to finish eighth. In the sports racing event, Al Beasley Sr. won CSR in his Dekker-AMW, but only after borrowing an oil pump from a spectator's car to replace the one he blew in practice! Jerry Dunbar was awarded the Governor's Trophy for his service to the sport over the years. It would have been nice if he could have won his race also, but alas, he finished second in GT-1 to the Corvette of Morris Clement.

The Miller High Life 500 Camel GT weekend, again in mid-July, was finally blessed with good weather after having endured storms the past two years. Saturday saw a four hour Firestone Firehawk Endurance race, down from 1988's six hours after many complaints about the crowded schedule. Leighton Reese had a great day finishing both first and third. He co-drove the winning Camaro with Mitch Wright and the third place Camaro with Brad Hoyt. Between these two was the Camaro of Don Knowles and John Heinricy. The winners covered 320 miles in the four hours.

Sunday started with a 60 mile Sisapa Pro Sports 2000 race. Tom Jagemann finally had everything hold together in his Lola T-88/90 and drove to an effortless win, leading all the way. John Fergus, who was to win his second straight series title this year, and Jay Hill swapped second place in their Lolas until Fergus spun, dropping back a few places. Hill wound up

The '89 Trans-Am was a wet race, but that mattered little to Dorsey Schroeder who won the race and the championship in Ford's 25th Anniversary Mustang.

second, with Ken Winters third and a recovering Fergus in fourth.

Robbie Buhl added the RA round to his total as he drove to the Barber Saab pro series title. Today he led all 60 miles for an impressive win. Rob Wilson, Justin Bell, Brian Till and Bernard Santal all disputed second until Santal and Till collided. Wilson finally took the spot with Bell (Derek's son) third, Jim Pace fourth and Ian Ashley fifth.

The IMSA International Sedan series was sponsored by LuK Clutches this season. Dave Jolly started the 60 miles from the pole, but Dennis Shaw put his Mazda MX-6 in first at the start. Jolly steamed ahead on lap two, and his Mazda MX-6 was not headed thereafter. Scott Hoerr finished third after the two Mazdas driving an Oldsmobile Calais. Amos Johnson was fourth in the Team Highball Mazda mate to Shaw, while Parker Johnstone was only fifth today in the Comptech Acura. This was Jolly's fourth straight win enroute to the season title.

The Camel GT season was a fight between factories. Nissan was on a roll and Geoff Brabham had won six of the year's first eight races on his way to a second straight Camel GT championship. He would share his Nissan GTP-88 with Chip Robinson. Jaguar was their closest threat and TWR had two cars entered. One was the V-12 XJR-9 driven by Davy Jones and John Nielsen. The other was a new XJR-10 powered by a 3.0 liter twin turbocharged V-6. This would be driven by Jan Lammers and Price Cobb. After working their way through GTU and GTO, Toyota had moved up to the GTP category. Dan Gurney's AAR team was building its first fendered Eagle, the Mk. I. It would be driven by Willy T. Ribbs and Rocky Moran. AAR was also running a Group C Toyota 88C in order to give a benchmark while they were getting the Eagle into shape. This was for Drake Olson and Juan Fangio II. Both cars were powered by 2.1 liter turbo fours. Four Porsche 962s faced them, led by the two Jim Busby cars in Miller High Life livery for Bob Wollek/John Andretti and Derek Bell/Steve Bren. Two Spice GTPs with big V-8s were also on hand.

Once again the 500 was run in kilometers, not miles, with all classes combined. The TWR/Castrol Jaguars occupied the front row with Jones on pole in the V-12 car. The two Jags and Brabham's Nissan were chased by Olson in the Toyota for the first few laps until Olson fell off the track, losing a couple laps. Brabham got around Jones, but though he constantly harried

Lammers, could not get past the lead Jaguar. This scenario lasted for the first 100 miles until the first round of pit stops and driver changes. Nielsen took over in the lead with Robinson chasing, but the second Jaguar of Cobb was shortly back in the pits for a brake pad change. This elevated the Andretti/Wollek Porsche to third. Robinson chased Nielsen closely and took over first when Nielsen had to pit when a tire went down. Wollek and Cobb were slowly catching the leading Nissan and had it in sight when the second round of stops began. All were in and out in good shape except for the Wollek Porsche, which was held in the pits by IMSA officials for an agonizing two minutes while faulty brake lights were repaired. A decidedly unamused Wollek slammed the door on his way out while a surprised Andretti was hustled back into the Porsche.

The laps ran out with Brabham back in the Nissan, winning his seventh of what would be nine Camel GTs this season. The Jaguars filled the next two spots in the order Lammers/Cobb and Jones/Nielsen. The Andretti/Wollek Porsche was fourth while Olson and Fangio took fifth in the Toyota, finishing one lap back. Costas Los was sixth in a solo run in a Spice, angering many along the way by being involved in no less than three collisions. Three 962s, Moretti/Ricci, Adams/Hotchkis and Bell/Bren followed.

The Camel Lights portion was as placid as the overall race was frantic. Scott Schubot, who was enjoying a dream season on his way to the Camel Lights championship, led effortlessly with little opposition. His Buick V-6 powered Spice SE88 finished 13th overall, one lap ahead of second in class Charles Morgan/Tom Hessert, also in a Spice.

GTO was a factory battleground this year. Nissan had jumped in with a factory effort fielded by Clayton Cunningham Racing. Steve Millen was the driver in a twin turbo 300ZX. Audi, having conquered the Trans-Am in '88, switched its attention to IMSA GTO and was running two turbo Quattros. Hans Stuck/Walter Rohrl and Scott Goodyear/Hurley Haywood were the drivers. The third factory effort was from Roush Racing for Ford. This year they were using Mercury Cougars, two with 2.5 liter turbo fours for Pete Halsmer and Wally Dallenbach Jr. A third V-8 Cougar was run by Roush for Craig Carter, co-driven this day by Andy Petery. Millen took the early lead, followed by Haywood, Halsmer and Stuck. Halsmer only lasted until lap six when his gearbox broke. Then Stuck ran afoul of Costas Los. While lapping the Audi, Los ran right into the Quattro, sending Stuck into the guard rail at a high rate of speed. A furious Stuck dragged the wrecked car back to the pits and retired. Except for pit stop shuffles, Millen held the lead for the entire race to win Nissan's first victory in GTO. His Nissan also was eleventh overall. The Goodyear/Haywood Audi was second with Dallenbach third. Even though he was out early, Halsmer constantly scored points this season along with four wins and took Roush Racing's fourth GTO championship in five years. Stuck finished the season in a rush, winning four of the last five and seven in all, but could not overtake Halsmer's consistency.

The GTU race was a howler, as almost everybody led. Amos Johnson led early in a Mazda MX-6 rotary, but was soon passed by Bob Leitzinger's Nissan 240SX V-6. A few laps later Jeremy Dale and Kal Showket, both in Dodge Daytonas, moved past both to lead. Then Dale broke a steering shaft and Showket led. However he blew a piston on lap 22 and John Hogdal took over in a Mazda RX-7. That held until his pit stop when a frightening pit fire cost him two laps. Leitzinger now was back in front but Johnson was catching him. Finally, 12 laps from the finish, Amos passed Leitzinger to take the lead, which he held to the finish. Leitzinger, who would be the season champ, finished second, followed by the Mazdas of Lance Stewart and Hogdal. This race definitely had a lot of action!

In late July the Chicago Historic Races again brought a fine collection of mouth-watering machinery to the Kettle Moraine. Among the many interesting cars on hand was the Lotus 78 F-1 car driven by Gunnar Nilsson in 1977, the Cooper T-53 driven by Stirling Moss in the 1961 ICF races, Pabst's Scarab, several Can-Am McLarens and Lolas, a McLaren M19 F-1, a Corvette Grand Sport, a Porsche 936, a Porsche 956, a Porsche Abarth Carrera, a Porsche 917, two Cobra Daytona coupes and an Eagle F-1.

Augie Pabst and Bob Akin put on a show in the race for pre-'63 sports racers. Pabst in a Scarab and Akin in a 2.5 Cooper Monaco T-49 dueled the entire distance with Pabst coming out on top. Interestingly enough, Pabst fastest lap of 2:39.911 was faster than he turned in the heat of battle 29 years earlier, when both he and the Scarab were much younger! Finishing fifth in this event was John Mecom in Pabst's Aston Martin DB-4. Yes, the same John Mecom whose racing team was one of the world's best in the mid '60s.

The race for large production cars was also taken by an historic racer, Bob Bondurant, in a Cobra, just like 1964. The race for post-'63 sports racers went to Joel Finn, driving a McLaren M8F this year. Steve Cohen was second, now driving a Lola T-330 instead of his familiar Porsche 907. Dropping out early was yet another great, Brian Redman, who was in a Chevron B-19. Although it seems that the class was just introduced, Formula Ford is old enough that its earliest cars are now running here. Indeed, John Marconi beat a wealth of Formula Juniors to take the formula race in a Lola T-202 FF.

This year's early September date for the CART weekend was not as fortunate as the last. While the weather was sunny and warm on Sunday, Saturday was very wet. CART qualifying was virtually washed out, with Friday's times having to stand. In addition, the Super Vee and Trans-Am races were run in very wet and unpleasant conditions.

The Valvoline/Bosch VW Super Vee 60 mile race was controlled by rain. It was dry as the race started, but rain started as the slick-shod cars were on their first lap. Leader Robbie Groff immediately slid off, dropping to the back. Harald Huysman reveled in the sudden rain, moving from sixth to a lead of 13 seconds as he completed lap two. Unfortunately for Huysman, SCCA stopped the race as a safety measure to allow the fitting of rain tires. Cars were sliding everywhere with no traction in the wet on slicks. This was a break for Groff, as it allowed him to restart within sight

of Huysman. On the restart, Huysman immediately moved ahead again, leading second place Stuart Crow by 20 seconds on the sixth lap. Groff was on the move, though, rapidly gaining positions. On lap seven he passed Crow and set out after Huysman. However the Norwegian sped up some more and stabilized the lead at a dozen seconds, winning the race over Groff. Third was a photo finish as Crow and series points leader Mark Smith came across side by side with Crow ahead by a thick coat of paint. All were driving Ralt RT-5s. Mark Smith won five times this season to take the championship.

Over the winter the SCCA had changed the rules for the Trans-Am in that turbos were no longer allowed. This meant that it now became a battleground for American thumpers; the Trans-Am had heavy factory participation this year. Ford was making a major effort to mark the 25th year of production for the Mustang. Roush Racing was running four Mustangs, for Dorsey Schroeder, Ron Fellows, Lyn St. James and Finn Robert Lappalainen. Chevrolet was represented by the C&C Berettas, having moved over from IMSA GTU and replaced the 3.0 liter V-6s with 4.5 units. Tom Kendall and Max Jones were behind the wheel. Oldsmobile was supporting three teams, all running Supreme bodied cars. Hoerr Racing had Irv Hoerr and Mike Ciasulli, Rocketsports ran Paul Gentilozzi and Newman-Sharp ran Scott Sharp.

The race was very wet and the start saw the 35 car field tip toe around the first four of 100 miles. Tom Kendall led in the Beretta with Schroeder, Fellows, Jones and Gentilozzi following. Schroeder made a move on Kendall at turn five on the third lap, taking the lead. Fellows soon followed, and the Mustangs were 1-2. The rain had stopped, and a dry line was appearing. On lap eight Fellows moved past Schroeder for the lead, and Hoerr had moved up from well down the field to take third from Kendall, who shortly thereafter pitted to change to slicks as did teammate Jones. They then were the fastest cars on course and swiftly began moving back up front having a decided advantage over those on overheating rain tires. At half distance Fellows led Schroeder but Kendall was up to third, with Sharp, Gentilozzi and Lappalainen following.

The rain began again. This time it came down very hard, but for a lap or two Kendall managed to stay with the leaders, displaying masterful car control. Then his engine blew, and he was out. Fellows then spun, dropping to third behind Schroeder and Lappalainen. The order behind Schroeder changed constantly, as the rain affected the drivers to varying degrees. As the soggy checker flew, Dorsey Schroeder brought his Mustang across the line first, his fifth win of the season on his march to the title. Irv Hoerr was second, followed by Fellows, Sharp and Gentilozzi.

Sunday's weather was much better, and a record crowd of approximately 60,000 turned out for the Texaco Havoline 200 and three support races. The 56 mile Corvette Challenge was a flag to flag win for Shawn Hendricks. Bill Cooper, Boris Said III, Scott Lagasse and Stu Hayner filled out the top five in a field of 24 Corvettes. The HFC American Racing Series ran for 76 miles. Ted Prappas was the initial leader, followed by Tommy Byrne, David Kudrave, Steve Shelton, Johnny O'Connell, Gary Rubio and Paul Tracy. Points leader Mike Groff was at the end of the 14 car field, having been punted off course on the first lap by P.J. Jones. Prappas spun the lead away on lap seven of nineteen, and Byrne had a ten second lead over O'Connell. Prappas moved back up from sixth but misjudged an overtaking move on Steve Shelton. The resulting collision took both out. Irishman Byrne went on to win, with O'Connell second, Rubio third, Groff fourth after a fine recovery and Kudrave fifth. The points that Groff picked up were very important, as he barely nipped Byrne for the season title.

The ECAR Toyota Atlantic cars ran for 60 miles. Jacques Villeneuve, making his first RA appearance since crashing in the '86 CART race, took

1989 was the last year for the old pits. Cramped, outmoded and very muddy when it rained, it was overdue for a change.

ROAD AMERICA 1989

the pole in a Swift DB-4. However his lead was short lived as Claude Bourbannais overtook him at turn five on the first lap and led the balance of the race. Villeneuve's engine was a bit off, and though he held onto second place for a good portion of the race, he held up the rest of the field allowing Bourbannais to disappear into the distance. Finally, on lap 10 of 15 Colin Trueman forced his way by Villeneuve, but Bourbannais was too far ahead. Bourbannais ran out the race firmly in front, bringing his Toyota-engined Swift home first. Trueman was second, with Jocko Cunningham third, Villeneuve fourth and James King fifth, all in Swifts. Trueman led Cunningham in points with two races to go, but Cunningham took the season crown.

The Texaco Havoline 200 saw Danny Sullivan on the pole once again. He set a new track record in his Penske/Miller High Life Penske PC-18 at 1:50.367. His Penske teammate, Rick Mears, was again alongside him in the front row in the Pennzoil PC-18. The second row held Michael Andretti, who had joined his father Mario in the Newman-Haas team this year. Michael was in a K-Mart/Havoline Lola T-89/00. Next to Michael was Arie Luyendyk in the Simon/Provimi Lola T-89/00. This was a splendid showing for the Dutchman, as he was driving not only for a team that admittedly was not top line, but also was powered by a Cosworth engine at a time when the Chevrolet-Ilmor engine was the thing to have. Row three was Emerson Fittipaldi in the Patrick/Marlboro Penske PC-18 and Al Unser Jr. in the Galles/Valvoline Lola T-89/00. Mario Andretti was next, then Scott Pruett driving well in the Truesports/Budweiser Lola T-89/00, though he was hindered by having to use a Judd engine.

The 29 car entry was dominated by Lolas, as March had virtually been run out of the customer car business. Their 87C and 88C cars were markedly inferior to the Lola, and customers switched in droves. For 1989 March did not produce a customer car, but rather built cars only on commission. Porsche had March custom build cars for its V-8, and the resulting 89P was a fairly good car. Indeed, Teo Fabi had won the Mid Ohio CART race just the week before in a March 89P, giving Porsche its first Indy car win. Alfa Romeo had entered Indy car racing this year with its V-8. They were being run by the Alex Morales Autosports team and were using a custom built March, the 89CE. While driver Roberto Guerrero was trying hard, the learning curve for Alfa was steep.

The rain that washed out Saturday played a major factor in Sunday's race, as the teams had been unable to run the usual Saturday mileage checks. As a consequence, fuel consumption and guessing on pit stops would determine the outcome of the race. Sullivan took the initial lead with Michael Andretti right behind. Fittipaldi ran third, followed by Unser Jr., Mears, Mario, Luyendyk, Pruett, Fabi, Bobby Rahal in the Kraco Lola and Derek Daly in the Raynor Lola. Sullivan slowly pulled away from Andretti with Fittipaldi following. Rahal and Daly departed with blown engines. The first round of pit stops saw a lead change as Sullivan had to come to a complete stop in the pit lane to avoid another car. This allowed Michael Andretti to get out first and with a healthy 10 second lead to boot. Mears, Unser Jr., Mario, Fabi and Luyendyk followed; Fittipaldi was well back after a very long stop.

The middle portion of the race was fairly static as Michael Andretti led Sullivan with Mears ahead of the rest. However, concerns about fuel were high, and the second round of pit stops began on lap 28 of 50, six or seven laps earlier than normal. This indicated that fears of running dry were high and that three pits stops would be the norm. Michael Andretti kept the lead, which by this time was over half a minute. Sullivan still was second, but Mario was up to third, then Mears, Unser Jr., Fabi and Fittipaldi. Al Jr. was not fifth for long as his engine quit on lap 36. Three laps later Michael was in the pits for his third and last stop. His lead was such that he was able to get the last of his methanol and get back on course five seconds ahead of Sullivan. Danny worked on it and cut it down to less than a second as they completed lap 48. Suddenly, though, Sullivan peeled off into the pits to pick up the final drops of his methanol. He was in and out in a flash, but now 12 seconds behind Andretti. But fate smiled on Sullivan. On the final lap Michael Andretti coasted to a halt at turn 11, completely out of fuel. A crushing loss for the strongly competitive Andretti. Sullivan led the final mile and a half, taking the checkered flag ahead of Teo Fabi in the Quaker State March-Porsche. Fabi? Yes, although fifth heading into the final lap, he advanced three places when Mears pitted for fuel, Michael Andretti dropped out, and incredibly, Mario also stopped with dry tanks! Mears took on the last of his fuel and rejoined to finish third, with Luyendyk fourth, Fittipaldi fifth and Michael and Mario classified sixth and seventh. The luck of the Irish was with Sullivan today. Emerson Fittipaldi, though not a factor for first this day, did win five times this season to take the PPG Cup.

126

1990

The June Sprints GT race was a runaway for NFL great Walter Payton in the Newman-Sharp Oldsmobile.

oad America had a new president as Jim Haynes was elected to the post by the board of directors. He retained the position of general manager. Jonathan P. Laun was elected Chairman of the Board. Bill Wuesthoff, who had been president for three years on an interim basis became vice president, along with Jim Jeffords.

The biggest change since the erection of the new control/press/VIP building took place over the winter. The woods south of the pits and paddock were cleared, and a new pit complex was built. Further, the entire area was paved so that the big rigs would not sink into the mud when it was wet. The old and venerable pagoda was gone. Its last service was to the local fire department as they burned it as a field exercise. In all, this was a major renovation and gave an entirely new look to the front straight area. Of course, change at RA also includes the silos, and in line with Miller's introduction of Genuine Draft the gold of High Life gave way to the black and gold of MGD.

On the sponsorship front, Bugle Boy joined Prange's as sponsor of the June Sprints. Miller took its name off the IMSA race after a run of five years, but Nissan stepped in to sponsor the weekend. Texaco Havoline remained as the title sponsor of the CART event.

Dates were shifted, and the IMSA weekend moved from mid-July to mid-August. The CART date, unfortunately, moved farther back, to the weekend of September 21-23. The memory of the 1986 debacle was still fresh, and the track objected to such a late date, as the chances of inclement weather were great. However, CART's president, John Frasco, had given Vancouver and Denver the Mid Ohio and Road America dates, pushing these two great road courses back into late September. People in Ohio and Wisconsin were not pleased. However, shortly after the year began, the CART board bought out the balance of Frasco's contract, temporarily installing John Camponigro as head. This lasted but a short time until the board hired Bill Stokkan as the new president. The hope was that he would be more receptive to the needs of both RA and Mid Ohio.

Early June brought the Prange's/Bugle Boy June Sprints. Fine weather prevailed but for the second straight year, Dave Weitzenhof did not. He was second again in FC, this time losing to the Reynard of Ken Gerhardt. Weitzenhof was testing new Firestone radials on his Citation, and they went off during the race. Steve Overton won the FA portion in a Swift DB-4 after Carl Liebich dropped out with a flat battery. Second was Jay Hill who stepped into Duane Smith's Ralt RT-4 just before the race when Smith became ill. Despite his unfamiliarity with the car and the fact that this was only his second ever FA race, Hill drove well indeed, finishing a close second to Overton.

Five time World Champion Juan Manuel Fangio was the Grand Marshall of the 1990 Chicago Historic Races. While patiently signing autographs, Fangio displayed his charm and legendary gentlemanly manners.

The Sports Renault 48 mile race was the usual close battle. In fact the foursome of Robert Urich, David Downey, Jeff Beck and Kyle Konzer swapped the lead so many times that a lap chart was useless. In the end they finished that way, but the result would have been different if the race were a mile shorter or longer. Kevin West took the FF race but was closely followed by Bill Weidner and Bruce May. The first 13 cars in the 46 car field were Swifts.

The sports racing event was again won by Al Beasley Sr. who had an easy run in his Decker-AMW. Bob Schneider was a distant second in a Ralt-based special. In Sports 2000 Tom Jagemann enjoyed another win in his Lola, aided greatly by Duke Johnson who spun in front of the pack in the first turn and delayed everyone but Jagemann. Webb Bassick ran second for a good portion of the race, but Jay Hill was closing. After dispensing with Ken Kroeger's Swift DB-5 and Barry Sitnick's Lola T-90/90, Hill caught Bassick's Swift DB-2 late in the race for second.

The final race of the day was the GT feature, and the fans were waiting with great anticipation. Newman-Sharp Racing had entered a GT-1 Oldsmobile Supreme for NFL great, Walter Payton. The future Hall-of-Famer had driven in Sports 2000 for the past two years since retiring from the Chicago Bears. Even in Packerland Payton was respected for his on field prowess and off field demeanor, which had earned him the nickname *Sweetness*. He qualified on the pole over two seconds faster than Rick Dittman. He was snookered on the start, but it took only until turn five for Payton to pass for first. He led effortlessly until a red flag due to Jerry Dunbar's blown engine which thoroughly oiled the track. Walter was not snookered on the restart. He was hard on it up the hill and led the balance of the distance for his first ever race win. The Pontiacs of Chip Boatwright and Ron Rosenmerkel were far behind, while the GT-2 winner again was David Finch in a Porsche 944.

The Chicago Historic Races in mid-July scored a coup by the presence of the great Juan Manuel Fangio as the Grand Marshall. Arguably the greatest race driver ever, the five time World Champion graciously spent an hour and a half each day sitting at a table in the paddock, signing autographs and greeting the spectators. The lines were always long as fans waited to meet the Great Man.

Augie Pabst not only brought his regular Scarab, but was displaying the one-off Scarab Mk. IV. This was the rear engine sports racer built by Reventlow in 1962 and raced briefly by him before he retired. The car was sold to the Mecom Racing Team and it won several major races driven by A.J. Foyt and Walt Hansgen. Pabst acquired it in 1965, raced it twice and then had it converted to street use. It was present in this guise, but Pabst would shortly begin a restoration reverting it to race trim. On the track Pabst and Bob Akin resumed their duel of a year before. This time it was Akin's turn to win, and Bob, driving a Cooper Monaco, just nipped Pabst.

Also on display was the Chevrolet CERV II, a rear engine sports racer built in the early '60s as an engineering exercise. It was never raced, but one wished that it had been. McKee was a featured marque, and five of the 12 sports racers that Bob McKee constructed under his own name were present. The one-off Lang Cooper-Ford was present, as were several Mirages, including a rare BRM V-12 powered coupe. The race for later sports racers again was taken by Joel Finn in a McLaren M8F.

The Nissan Camel GT race had a different format this year. For the past couple years IMSA was urging RA to run the GTO/GTU classes in a separate race from the Camel GT feature. The track objected, reasoning that a field of semi-fragile GTPs and Lights might get a bit thin towards the end of 500 kilometers. This year the impasse came to a head, and IMSA insisted on separate races. Not wishing to lose the 'Road America 500' title, a format was devised which would run the 500 in two 250 kilometer segments. Between these the GTO/GTU cars would run for 300 kilometers. The second part of the 500 would not be a heat per se, but rather would be a continuation of the first segment. The reasoning was that cars that dropped out of the first portion could be repaired and rejoin in the second, thus raising the chances of a goodly number of cars still running at the completion. Because of this format, the supporting events were just a four hour Firestone Firehawk race on Saturday and a Barber Saab race on Sunday morning.

In keeping with what seems to be the *modus operandi* for the IMSA weekend over the past few years, it rained. It rained Friday. It rained

Saturday. It rained Sunday. The Firestone Firehawk race started in the dry but a squall line came through during the four hours, complete with lightning, thunder and darkness. The pace car was dispatched during the height of the storm, when cars were sliding off course at 20 mph, and the race finished under yellow. Nonetheless, the winning Camaro of Joe Varde and Don Wallace covered 76 laps, 304 miles in the time allotted. In second place was the Porsche 944 of Bobby Akin and James Weaver. The Brit Weaver happened to be watching from the pits when spotted by Bob Akin, who talked Weaver into driving the car instead of him. As it turned out, Weaver probably stayed dryer.

The Barber Saab cars ran for 48 miles on Sunday morning. The race started in the rain, but it stopped and a dry line developed during the 12 laps. Rob Wilson led the first three laps until he spun and John Tanner took over first. Not being content with doing it once, Wilson spun again a few laps later, dropping to fifth. Tanner led the rest of the distance to take the win with John Robinson second, followed by Briggs Phillips, Bob Reid and Wilson. For Wilson fifth place was sufficient to clinch the 1990 season championship.

Sunday dawned very, very wet. A heavy storm had gone through the area Saturday night, leaving standing water everywhere. Further it was still raining fairly hard. The rain continued all morning and into the afternoon before it slacked off to a light shower. This caused a major change in schedule. The heavy morning rain and large puddles pushed activities well back with the warmups and Barber Saab race delayed considerably. As the noon hour passed it became apparent that the schedule had to be changed. Hence, the Camel GT was shortened to just one 250 kilometer heat/race while the GTO/GTU event was shortened to one hour. In view of the atrocious weather, there was little complaint.

The GTO battle this year had been among three works teams, each with two cars. Ford had Roush, of course, and they were running Mercury Cougars with 2.5 turbo fours for Dorsey Schroeder and Robby Gordon. Clayton Cunningham Racing ran the works Nissan effort with 300ZX twin turbos for Steve Millen and Jeremy Dale. Mazda had expanded its involvement to GTO in addition to GTU and had Pete Halsmer and Elliott Forbes-Robinson in four rotor RX-7s. For this race Ferrari of France made the most welcome entry of two Ferrari F-40s for Jean-Pierre Jabouille and Michel Ferte.

The Roush Mercurys made the most of dodging the rain drops in qualifying and occupied the front row, Schroeder up over Gordon. But Millen was missing as the grid formed. He had a big crash in the soggy warmup and the CCR crew was still repairing his car. Finally, as the pace lap started, Millen roared out of the paddock to take up his fourth place on the grid. Gordon, the off-roader, made it immediately apparent that he was a fine *mudder* as he moved into first at the start. He proceeded to hold the point for the first seven laps, with Jabouille, Dale, Schroeder, Millen, Ferte and Forbes-Robinson following, Halsmer well back after a spin. On lap eight Jabouille jumped Gordon for the lead in turn five, Gordon falling off the road a turn later trying to retaliate. Dale took up the chase and managed to lead lap 15 but the Ferrari was back in front by turn one. That was the best Dale could do, as his turbo began failing and he dropped back.

Steve Millen had thoroughly acclimated himself to his rebuilt Nissan and steadily decreased the gap to the Ferrari. As the rain slackened into a light shower, Millen closed on Jabouille and moved in for the kill, as the hour neared its end. On lap 22, of what would be a 24 lap race, Millen moved inside Jabouille in the Carousel and passed. The tires on the Ferrari were gone, and Jean-Pierre could not hold the inside line. Millen moved ahead by a second a lap and finished the 96 miles 2.5 seconds ahead of Jabouille. Dale was third, with the Cougars of Gordon and Schroeder fourth

and fifth followed by the Mazdas of Halsmer and Forbes-Robinson. Despite his semi-off day, Schroeder would win the GTO crown to go with his Trans-Am title of the year before.

In GTU David Loring should have won. Driving the second Nissan 240SX V-6 of Bob Leitzinger, Loring led effortlessly, opening up a 30 second lead. Unfortunately, Loring had to pit at the 43 minute mark to change a flat tire. When he rejoined, he was in second, but 40 seconds behind the Mazda MX-6 of Lance Stewart. Loring, now with fresh tires under him, simply flew around the four miles, knocking huge chunks of time off Stewart's lead every lap. With two laps to go the lead was 13 seconds, with one lap, six seconds. Stewart pedaled furiously as Loring filled his mirrors. At the flag the white Mazda led the blue Nissan across the line by just under two seconds. One more lap and Loring might have been first rather than second; but this year Lance Stewart was winning the GTU championship, and he was not to be denied.

The Camel GT this year looked similar to the past two seasons. Geoff Brabham was doing most of the winning, and the Jaguar and Toyota teams were struggling with inconsistency. Brabham was well on his way to his third consecutive Camel GT crown, having won four races leading into RA, while no one else had won more than two. Nissan had built a new car, the NPT-90, and Brabham and Chip Robinson were driving. Jaguar had Davy Jones and John Nielsen in the TWR twin turbo V-6 XJR-10s while Toyota was represented by Juan Fangio II and Rocky Moran in the AAR Eagle Mk. IIs. Fangio had broken the ice for Eagle, winning twice so far this season. There was only one Porsche 962 present this year, James Weaver in Rob Dyson's war-weary car. Jim Busby had replaced his Porsche 962s with a Nissan GTP-88, but at mid season sold the team to Canadian David Seabrooke. John Paul Jr. was in the car at RA. Three Spice-Chevys filled out the 11 car GTP field.

By the time the GTO/GTU race ended, it was mid-afternoon and the rain had stopped for the time being. All made the decision to start on slicks. Brabham had the pole and led the first lap but the Davy Jones Jaguar moved past on lap two, taking Nielsen with him for a Jaguar 1-2. This held for a few laps until Brabham repassed the Dane for second. Weaver ran fourth with Fangio, Robinson, Moran, Jay Cochran and Wayne Taylor following, the latter two in Spices. Paul Jr. was well down, his Nissan suffering from chronic engine and boost problems. The race would be a one pit stop affair and, as the time approached, it began to rain again. However the rain seemed to be confined to the backside of the course, while the front remained dry. Confident that the rain would soon spread, all the front runners came in and changed to rain tires except Brabham, who gambled that it would not get any wetter. Brabham was right. His slick tires, nicely warm by now, kept their grip while the treaded tires were coming up to temperature. He took over first from Jones, gave it back and then retook it for good on lap 32 of 39. Brabham managed to keep the lead even when the rain spread over the entire track in the late stages, driving masterfully on slicks when rain tires definitely were preferable.

Geoff Brabham duly took his fifth win of the year, a superb job when the elements were against him. Jones was second, Fangio II third, Weaver fourth, Paul Jr. fifth and Nielsen sixth. Cochran, Taylor, Robinson and Moran completed the top ten, with the Spice of Jim Adams being the only GTP not to finish.

The Camel Lights portion had a similar scenario. The Uli Bieri-entered, Ferrari V-8 powered Spice driven by Ruggero Melgrati and Martino Finotto was kept on slicks at its mid-race pit stop while the rest changed to wets. Melgrati had little trouble winning by over a minute. Second was the Spice-Buick of Tomas Lopez, who was parlaying a series of consistent high finishes into the '90 Camel Lights title, aided considerably by co-driver Parker Johnstone.

Darin Brassfield leads Tom Kendall up the hill as the skies darken during the rain-shortened Trans-Am. Kendall took the win in this 80 mile race.

The late September CART weekend predictably had bad weather. Saturday was steady rain, the only question being how hard. Sunday was mercifully dry, but very cold. Heavy jackets, hats and even gloves were the garb of the day. How the track wished that CART would realize that anything after Labor Day is very chancy in Wisconsin.

The Valvoline/Bosch VW Super Vees were the first race of the weekend, running 60 miles in damp and cold conditions. The story, as it turned out, centered around Kim Campbell, who had broken his neck in a race crash in 1989. This race would be his first since he suffered his potentially career ending injuries. Campbell very quickly got the rust off, qualifying his Ralt RT-5 second on the grid to three time winner Christopher Smith, who was locked in a close struggle for the points lead with Stuart Crow. The effervescent Crow, who had won twice this year, was third on the grid. Chris Smith led the first four laps with Crow following. Crow had led a couple times so far, but not at the S/F line. On lap five Smith's engine began to misfire, which was all Crow needed. Stuart moved in front with Campbell following him past Smith. Campbell closed the gap and was right on Crow's wing as they entered the last lap. The light mist had developed into a steady rain, and traction was terrible. Nonetheless, Campbell managed to squeak past Crow on the last go-around and won his comeback race in true Cinderella fashion. Crow finished second, regaining the points lead from Smith, who took third. Matters went Crow's way the rest of the year, and he took what turned out to be the final Super Vee championship.

An aside to the race was the presence of Viktor Kosankov, a Russian driver making his first U.S. appearance. Kosankov may have been the first ever driver from the former Soviet Union to run in an SCCA event. He furthered the cause of *glasnost* by qualifying ninth and finishing seventh.

Saturday's second race was the 100 mile SCCA Trans-Am. Factory battles were in full force, with Ford represented by the four car Roush Mustang entry of Ron Fellows, Max Jones, Robert Lappalainen and Lyn St. James. Chevrolet had three C&C Berettas for Tom Kendall, who had already clinched the 1990 championship, Chris Kneifel and R.K. Smith. Oldsmobile supported three teams. Newman-Sharp had Supremes for Scott Sharp, Paul Newman and Walter Payton. Rocketsports also had Supremes for Darin Brassfield and team owner Paul Gentilozzi while Irv Hoerr was in his team's car. Sharp was fastest and was on the pole.

The red, white and blue Oldsmobile of Sharp dutifully leapt into the lead with Hoerr following, who held second until lap 10 when his differential broke. Then the Berettas of Kendall and Kneifel moved up to challenge Sharp, and Kendall spent the next few laps rubbing fenders. Finally on lap 13 Kendall got by, but Sharp would not let him get away, retaking the lead on lap 17. However, the next time around the skies opened, and a deluge came down. Lap times went up dramatically as cars slithered all over the place. Kendall handled it better than others and passed Sharp on the outside of the Carousel. Kendall had anticipated a heavy wall of water on that part of the course and actually backed off, allowing Sharp and Brassfield to hit it first. His plan worked brilliantly, as both spun off, and Kendall was through to lead until the finish. That came quicker than expected as officials ended the race prematurely at 20 laps, 80 miles, due to the horrid conditions. Kendall won, with Brassfield recovering for second. Kneifel was third, Sharp fourth, Fellows fifth in the first Ford and Scott Lagasse sixth in the Morrison Corvette.

Sunday was bright but very cold. Just the kind of weather that would not allow tires to come up to temperature. The first cars to test this would be the March 86As of the American Racing Series. The 1990 ARS season can be summed up in one name: Paul Tracy. The young Canadian had dominated the year, winning eight of the 11 races run so far. The season championship, needless to say, was already firmly in his pocket. At RA today Tracy made it nine out of twelve as he led all but the first lap to win the 76 mile race. Robbie Buhl would finish second with Mark Smith third, Eric Bachelart fourth and Robbie Groff fifth. Bachelart provided the most conversation by having an almighty spin in the kink, escaping without hitting anything! Only 14 cars started the race and the action on the four mile track was pretty thin. As a result, this was the last ARS race at RA.

The Toyota Atlantic Championship also ran a 76 mile race. From the time the ECAR series was born in 1985 through this year there had been two such series: ECAR and its west coast equivalent, WCAR. This RA round would be a *shootout*, a race in which both divisions were to participate with each giving points in their respective categories. This was a prelude to 1991 when both series would be merged into one U.S. wide championship. As such, a full field of 29 Atlantics were present, all powered by Toyota engines as the transition year of 1989 was the last that allowed the Ford Cosworth that had served since the early '70s. Mark Dismore came into the race leading the WCAR points, while Brian Till was the ECAR leader.

The new paved paddock and pit area opened in 1990, just south of where the old Pagoda was located.

However, a *ringer* in the form of Jimmy Vasser mixed matters up. Vasser had driven WCAR on and off, but had only driven once prior this season, having concentrated his efforts on Canadian FF2000. Vasser had talent and duly took the pole.

Brian Till led the first lap, but Vasser was ahead on lap two followed by Till, R.K. Smith and Jovy Marcello. Dismore was knifing through the field after starting at the back due to having lost an engine in qualifying. Also starting at the back was Claude Bourbannais, who missed all of practice and qualifying due to his being in France for a F-3000 race. Bourbannais, in the Comprep Reynard 90H, was even faster than Dismore and had moved into second place when a full course yellow massed the pack. Marcello, for whatever reason, didn't realize the cars were slowing and rammed the rear of Bourbannais' Reynard. The subsequent pit stop to replace the rear wing meant that Bourbannais was doomed to finish 17th, ending his title hopes. Vasser went on to an easy win with Brian Till second, clinching the ECAR title for himself. Jocko Cunningham took third, followed by Smith and Dismore, who was a splendid fifth, giving him the WCAR title.

The 1990 PPG Cup was contested by two men. Coming into RA Al Unser Jr. had won six races in the Galles/Valvoline Lola T-90/00 while Michael Andretti was first four times in the Newman-Haas/K-Mart/Havoline Lola T-90/00. However, Unser had a fairly comfortable points lead as he had been a more consistent finisher.

Although Saturday was wet, fast times had been turned in Friday's qualifying session. For the third year running and fourth out of the last five Danny Sullivan took the pole. He set yet another new track record at 1:49.682 in the Marlboro Penske PC-19. He was the first to turn a lap under 1:50. The only other was his teammate Rick Mears, who was along side him on the front row. Mears turned 1:49.775 in the Pennzoil Penske PC-19. Penske was running three cars this year and his third driver, Emerson Fittipaldi, was fourth quickest in a Marlboro Penske PC-19. Splitting the Penske drivers in third was Mario Andretti in the second Newman-Haas/K-Mart/Havoline Lola T-90/00. The title protagonists, Michael Andretti and Al Unser Jr., occupied row three. Unser's Galles teammate Bobby Rahal headed the next row in the Kraco Lola T-90/00. The first seven cars were powered by the Chevrolet-Ilmor engine with Teo

Fabi the first non-Ilmor in eighth. Fabi was in the Porsche entered and powered Foster's March 90P. The first ten were rounded out with Arie Luyendyk in the Shierson/Domino's Pizza Lola T-90/00 and John Andretti in the second Foster's March 90P-Porsche. In all, 25 cars would start.

The three Penskes led at the start with Sullivan setting the pace. Unser Jr., Michael A., Eddie Cheever in the Ganassi/Target Lola T-90/00, Rahal, Luyendyk, John A. and Fabi followed. Mario was already dropping back fast with a broken turbo connection. Michael made a fine outside pass on Unser in turn five to take fourth, then took Mears for third on lap six. It took Michael six more laps to catch Fittipaldi, but on lap 13 he was through for second place.

At this point the first flurry of pit stops got underway and when they were over Michael Andretti was in the lead, helped immensely by very quick pit work. Sullivan was second, trailed by Unser Jr., Fittipaldi, Mears, Rahal, Luyendyk, Mario, Roberto Guerrero in the Patrick/Miller Genuine Draft Lola T-90/00-Alfa Romeo (first non-Ilmor) and Cheever. It had been a bad day for Porsche, as Fabi was out with broken suspension and John Andretti parked his with overheating.

On lap 26 Foyt had a bad crash in his Copenhagen Lola. He went off course in turn one and hit an earthen bank hard. The race went to full course yellow for several laps, then was red flagged to allow a helicopter to land on the track. Foyt was airlifted out, suffering severe injuries to his legs and feet. He recovered, but it would be a lengthy convalescence.

The race was restarted after a delay of over an hour. It resumed on lap 34, and Sullivan took off into the distance. By lap 38 he had a five second lead and was visibly stretching it every lap. Then, with things seemingly under complete control, the gearbox broke. Sullivan was out and Andretti led, a complete reversal of 1989. Michael had a lead of six seconds over Fittipaldi, and that remained static until the finish. Mears overtook Unser Jr. for third on lap 42 while Mario Andretti finished fifth, the faulty turbo hose having been repaired during the stoppage. Luyendyk and Rahal were next, with Guerrero placing eighth in the Alfa Romeo powered Lola, the first non-Ilmor home.

Al Unser Jr. went on to win the PPG Cup at the next race, his first Indy car title. Michael Andretti had a fine season, but not as good as Unser's. His turn would come next year.

131

1991

Club racing remains the realm of the little guy: no big transporters, no big budgets, not even the clout to get into the paved paddock area.

Over the winter a major gripe was eliminated. Ending six years of constant complaint, a tunnel was built under the track at the start/finish line. No longer would people have to take what seemed like a mile hike to get from the tower to the new pit and paddock area. Smiles were much in evidence.

The 1991 program was much the same as 1990. Prange's/Bugle Boy continued to sponsor the June Sprints, while Nissan did the same for the IMSA weekend and Texaco/Havoline for the CART weekend. Sponsorship expanded greatly at the Sprints, as the individual class races also acquired sponsors. This allowed some prize money to be given out, which of course is the complete opposite of what National racing was in the '50s and early '60s. Times do change.

A change in pro racing was the end of Super Vee. Volkswagen decided to end its support of the class and the series; just like that it was gone. In its 20 year run it produced many a driver who went on to success in higher series. Among its champions were Elliott Forbes-Robinson, Geoff Brabham, Al Unser Jr., Michael Andretti and Arie Luyendyk. The Trans-Am series picked up Liquid Tide as its title sponsor. What had been known as the Escort Endurance Championship was still sponsored by Escort, but was now the Escort World Challenge. The car preparation rules were changed

considerably and were now more in line with FIA GT rules than the strict showroom stock as before. Further, the Corvette Challenge had been folded back into World Challenge. The race distance was also altered from endurance format to short sprints. The Pro Sports 2000 series, which curiously did not play at RA in 1990, even though the track had been its base for years, underwent a big change. Oldsmobile began a three year sponsorship agreement which saw the 2.3 liter Oldsmobile Quad 4 engine become the motive power. Regular Sports 2000 cars were grandfathered for 1991 only. Thereafter all cars in what was now called the Oldsmobile Pro Series would have to be Olds powered.

In IMSA, Exxon had come on board to sponsor the GTO/GTU/ American Challenge series, which would be known as the Exxon Supreme Series. The American Challenge, which had faded away to practically nothing, was rejuvenated as a class in the new Exxon Supreme Series. Entries jumped and numbered more than the GTO class, which was now dominated by factory teams. IMSA also debuted a new series, dubbed the Bridgestone Supercar Series. It was designed to attract exotic GT cars and had car prep rules similar to the SCCA's World Challenge.

On the club level the success of the Sports Renault spec racer had led to the creation of a larger version of the idea. Carroll Shelby developed a single-seater, envelope bodied tube frame car powered by a 3.4 liter pushrod Dodge V-6. The cars would be identical, with modifications not permitted. These Shelby-Dodge spec cars would spawn the inevitable pro series in 1992 but support for this class and concept was always thin, and by the end of 1996 the class faded away. The integration of the large production classes into the GT category was complete, and now GT-1 through GT-5 ran with the production category containing only EP, FP, GP and HP.

The Prange's/Bugle Boy June Sprints again enjoyed good weather. Close racing among the over 400 entries was the norm. For example, Jack Wheeler took the EP race in his Triumph TR4 by the narrowest of margins over Vic Skirmants' Porsche 356, the two side by side under the checker. Jim Render won the FF race by a margin that was just slightly larger. He and Bruce May flashed by the S/F line together, Render's Swift just ahead of May's. However, the Formula Vee race was the closest. At the finish of 48 miles the four cars of Eric Tremayne, Peter Guillan, Bill Wallschlaeger and Jeff Otto swept under the checker in one mad group. Tremayne and Guillan both punched the air in victory, but when Tremayne arrived in victory circle he was dismayed to find Guillan already there. It was that close.

An incredible 81 Sports Renaults (now called *Spec Racers*) ran for 48 miles. Keith Scharf, Robert Mumm, Kyle Konzer and Jeff Beck broke clear of the rest and passed first around. The race came down to the last corner and traffic played a big role. Scharf, Konzer and Mumm all dithered a bit about which way to go, while Beck merely kept his foot down and passed all three to win.

Steve Overton won the formula feature in a Swift DB-4 with Ken Gerhardt taking FC. Dave Weitzenhof had to settle for second once again, his Citation not quite able to get to grips with Gerhardt's Reynard. The sports racing event went to Bob Schneider's Ralt-based special while Tony Ave won the Sports 2000 class in a Lola T-88/90. The new Shelby class had 10 entries and David Tenney came in first.

The Historic Races were the usual visual treat. Attendance at this event was continuing to grow, with the crowds now rivaling the June Sprints. Augie Pabst and Bob Akin went at it again, with Akin winning in his Cooper Monaco over Pabst's Scarab. Joel Finn won another event, this time the formula race in a McLaren M4 Formula Atlantic. As always, there were many interesting cars in the paddock, including a rare Jaguar XK-SS that was a winner in the annual Concours judging.

The late August Nissan Camel GT weekend was dry! This was quite a departure from former years and had people rubbing their eyes and blinking in astonishment. The four hour Firestone Firehawk endurance race on Saturday was taken by Joe Varde and Mark Sandridge in a Porsche 944. They covered 336 miles in the time allotted. The lead changed hands eight times during the race. Second place Al Mitchell and Chris Cook did a fair amount of leading, but when Varde relieved Sandridge at the midway point, it was over. Varde was just too fast.

Sunday morning's 60 mile Olds Pro Race was led all the way by Tony Kester. He got a terrific, yet legal, jump at the start and simply motored away in the Jagemann Stamping sponsored, Olsson Engineering Lola T-89/90. Bob Thomas followed in a Lola with Ken Kroeger third in a Swift. Mike Borkowski made up two places on the final two laps to finish fourth. Class B for regular Sports 2000 cars was taken by Alan Andrea in a Lola T-89/90, ninth overall. Kester ran well all year and took the inaugural Olds Pro title.

The Barber Saab race was also a flag to flag event as Englishman Johnny Robinson led all 40 miles. Bryan Herta, Tony Leivo, Page Jones and Robert Amren followed.

The Exxon Supreme Series ran for 200 kilometers. Three factory teams were battling this year. Ford was represented by Roush Racing, of course, and they had three Mustangs for Dorsey Schroeder, Robby Gordon and Mike Dingman. While Dingman's car was V-8 powered (he also was running in SCCA Nationals in GT-1), the other two had 2.5 liter turbo fours. Nissan had two CCR entered 300ZX twin turbos for Steve Millen and Jeremy Dale. Mazda again ran two four rotor RX-7s, this year for Pete Halsmer and Price Cobb.

Steve Millen routinely did well at RA; this year was no different, as he won his third straight GTO race. While he led all 31 laps, he did not have it as easy as it sounds. The first part of the race saw Schroeder, Dale and Gordon follow him closely, not letting Millen get any room to breathe. Pit work told the tale; Millen had a very fast stop as did Halsmer, while the Fords suffered. Halsmer resumed in second, followed by Gordon and Schroeder. Dale had fallen back with failing oil pressure while Cobb had lost touch with the leaders. Millen dutifully won, with Halsmer second, then Gordon, Schroeder and Cobb. Sixth overall was Tommy Riggins, leader of the AC class. Halsmer had a fine season, going on to win his second GTO championship.

The GTU portion was a Dodge vs. Nissan struggle. Dodge Daytona driver John Fergus took the win on his way to the GTU championship, but it wasn't easy. The Nissan 240SX V-6s of David Loring and Bob Leitzinger pressured him for the first half of the race, trading the lead many times. Fergus began easing ahead, though, as the race entered its middle stage, and his Full Time Racing Dodge pulled out a half second or so every lap. Fergus held on to win, with Loring and Leitzinger next in the Nissans ahead of the second Dodge of Jeff Purner.

The Camel GT series had been a real dog fight this year. Geoff Brabham was heavily challenged this season, the competition such that, even though he was leading the points, he was not scoring wins. His consistency was making the difference, though, as while different folks were spreading the wins, Brabham was always there in second or third. Most unfortunately, Brabham would not be able to defend his lead this weekend. In Thursday's open test he blew a tire passing the pits at full speed and his Nissan NPT-90 became airborne, flipping three times and sending Brabham to the hospital with broken ribs and crushed vertebrae. Mercifully, he would recover to race again at the next and last Camel GT of the year which was two months away.

Nissan was making a major effort, running three NPT-90s. Derek Daly was brought in to drive in Brabham's place, alongside Bob Earl and Chip Robinson. Dan Gurney's AAR team ran the Toyota effort with Juan Fangio II in the latest Eagle Mk. III while Rocky Moran was in last year's Eagle Mk. II. The TWR Jaguar team was using new XJR-16s for Davy Jones and Raul Boesel. The Jaguars were carrying Bud Light livery this year in place of Castrol. Jim Miller, who had run a Chevy engined Spice the last two seasons, had his own Pratt & Miller shops build a new Chevy powered GTP, the Intrepid. South African Wayne Taylor would drive. Somewhat surprisingly, after all these years there still were three Porsche 962s running. The Dyson car had James Weaver up, while Momo Corse ran Derek Bell along with owner Gianpiero Moretti, and the German Joest team had a 962 for the very fast German Bernd Schneider, partnered by the car's owner, John Winter.

This year RA gave up on trying to keep the *Road America 500* name. The race would be run for 300 kilometers, 188 miles. In qualifying Jones took the pole with the remarkable time of 1:51.822. This was top Indy car time just a year ago! Jones took immediate advantage and led the first lap, beating back the challenge of Taylor. Fangio passed Taylor on the second lap and closed on Jones, looking for a way past the Jaguar; however, before he could make a serious attempt, his Eagle rolled to a halt at turn five on lap 12. The throttle cable had snapped. His teammate Moran moved into second and took up the chase, followed closely by Robinson. After a num-

Years of effort finally produced results for Jaguar as Davy Jones scored an easy win in the '91 Camel GT race. His XJR-16 was never seriously challenged.

ber of laps Robinson managed to pass Moran, then the differential on the Eagle failed and Moran was out.

The race now was stabilized, the mid race pit stops came and went, and Jones finished the 47 laps 20 seconds ahead of Robinson. Taylor finished third, while Raul Boesel drove well from last to finish fourth. Bob Earl was fifth and the leading Porsche 962 of Schneider/Winter was sixth. The days of the 962 appeared to be at an end. Despite his crash Brabham remained the points leader just ahead of Jones. At Del Mar two months later he gathered enough points to win his fourth straight Camel GT championship.

The Camel Lights class had Jim Pace take the win, passing on the last lap. The race had belonged to the Comptech Spice-Acura of Dan Marvin, but his car stopped on the last lap with contaminated fuel. Pace moved past in his Kudzu-Buick to take his first Camel Lights win. Marvin's teammate, Parker Johnstone, who had already clinched the Camel Lights title, was leading at 40 laps when his car also fell victim to dirty fuel. It seems the Comptech team had brought its own fuel to the track, not wishing to risk using what they feared might be suspect track fuel. As it turned out, their fuel was bad. Marvin had completed enough laps to still be classified second while Charles Morgan and Ken Knott were third, also in a Kudzu-Buick.

Late September drew a large crowd, upwards of 50,000, for the CART weekend. As could be expected from the late date, the weather was cool and threatened rain. Indeed, the final portion of the Indy car race was run in a light rain, and the Bridgestone Supercar race, which followed the CART event, saw very wet and foggy conditions.

Saturday, though, was sunny, if not too warm. The Escort World Challenge had a one hour timed race. In that time the leaders covered 23 laps, 92 miles. The winner was actor Bobby Carradine who overtook leader Shawn Hendricks on the last lap. They had dueled a good portion of the distance and the margin of victory was only 0.3 seconds. Carradine drove a Lotus Esprit as did Doc Bundy in third and Mike Brockman in fourth, all for the Lotusports Team. Hendricks was in a Corvette.

Saturday's feature was the Liquid Tide Trans-Am 100 miler. Local sponsorship for this event had been procured from Piggly-Wiggly and Banquet Foods, and their name was on the event. Ford was not in the Trans-Am this year, so it was mainly Chevrolet vs. Oldsmobile. Chevy was backing Buz McCall's team of Scott Sharp and Jack Baldwin in Camaros. Oldsmobile had consolidated its backing to the Rocketsports Team. Irv Hoerr had folded his Olds team into Rocketsports and was driving one of

four Supremes entered, along with team owner Paul Gentilozzi, Chris Kneifel and Darin Brassfield. Morrison Racing ran a Corvette for John Heinricy and a Camaro for Stu Hayner, but although they were well turned out, they were not able to successfully challenge the works assisted teams. The top Fords running the T-A this year were independent efforts. Ron Fellows was driving for Wayne Akers while Steve Saleen was in his own Saleen Autosports entry.

Scott Sharp was enjoying a fine season, and all he had to do here was place in the top ten to win the championship. He dutifully took the pole and the lead. However, Darin Brassfield was not letting him get away, and the following 23 laps produced some of the closest sedan racing ever seen at RA. Sharp and Brassfield left the field behind as they dueled relentlessly, constantly shifting the lead and never more than a few car lengths apart. It was riveting. Then, sadly, the front suspension broke on Brassfield's Olds and he went straight into the bridge at turn 13, fortunately without injury. Sharp was home free and cruised to the victory and the championship. Chris Kneifel had broken free of the pack and had been third for a good portion of the race. With his teammate's demise, Kneifel finished second. Irv Hoerr finished third in another Rocketsports Olds, but his story was not so simple. He had to start dead last after a post-qualifying engine change. He drove through the 33 car field brilliantly, finishing third ahead of a string of Camaros driven by Steve Petty, Stu Hayner, Jack Baldwin, Les Lindley and George Robinson.

Sunday morning's Barber Saab race covered 52 miles in the 30 minute time limit. Leo Parente scored his first Barber win, as he held off the challenge of Johnny Robinson. Once Robinson went out with a broken clutch Parente had some breathing room, as second place Bryan Herta had his hands full with Robert Amren. Herta, who had led the first lap, was passed by Amren on lap 11 and the finishing order was Parente, Amren, Herta, Page Jones and Alex Padilla.

This year's PPG Cup race was led by Michael Andretti. The Newman-Haas/K-Mart/Havoline Lola T-91/00 driver had won six races coming into RA and led Bobby Rahal in the points. The race had a new pole sitter this year as Danny Sullivan, who had won it four of the last five years, was struggling with the Patrick Racing/Miller Genuine Draft Lola T-91/00-Alfa Romeo. Penske had pared down to two cars from three, and Sullivan was the odd man out. While Patrick may have been a good ride, clearly the Alfa engine was not on the same level as the Chevy Ilmor. Rahal was the pole sitter, lapping his Galles/Kraco Lola T-91/00 at the new record time of

The Trans-Am race was a hard fought battle between the Camaro of Scott Sharp and the Oldsmobile of Darin Brassfield.

1:47.090. In fact the first ten places were all under the old lap record. Rahal's Galles teammate, Al Unser Jr., was alongside in his Valvoline Lola T-91/00. Michael Andretti was third and in fourth was Scott Pruett, driving the first American built Indy car since 1986, the Truesports 91C. The Budweiser sponsored car was small and compact, but it was severely hindered by using a Judd engine. Nonetheless, Pruett was driving it extremely well. Emerson Fittipaldi was next in the Marlboro Penske PC-20 with Mario Andretti alongside in the second Newman-Haas Lola. Seventh fastest was John Andretti who was driving Jim Hall's Pennzoil Lola. Rounding out the ten record breakers were Rick Mears, Marlboro Penske; Arie Luyendyk, Vince Granatelli Racing Lola T-91/00; and Eddie Cheever, Chip Ganassi/Target Lola T-91/00. The Judd engine in Pruett's Truesports was the only non Ilmor in the first 10.

After a morning warm-up run in a light rain, the grid formed in dry but overcast conditions. Unser Jr. and Michael A. got the jump on Rahal and moved into first and second, with Pruett holding down fourth. By lap 10 the first four had remained static, with Mario, Luyendyk, Mears, Cheever and Fittipaldi following. John Andretti had dropped out of eighth with a broken gearbox. The first round of pit stops produced a bit of a surprise, as Michael Andretti came out first, even though he spent more time in the pits than Unser. The difference was that Michael was apparently turning a faster out lap than Unser, getting up to speed faster on cold tires. Al Jr. was fighting back, however. He was on Andretti's gearbox quickly, and on lap 23 he made the classic inside pass at turn five. Scott Pruett was holding down an excellent third place, with Mario, Rahal, Mears and Luyendyk following. Pruett made an early second pit stop, falling to fifth, but shortly thereafter his fine run ended with a broken gearbox.

The middle portion of the race saw Unser Jr. run in first with Michael Andretti several lengths behind. While not making any cut and thrust moves, Andretti was so close nonetheless that if Unser sneezed, he would be past. The second round of pit stops began with Unser on lap 29. Andretti passed into first, not stopping until lap 32. Those three laps on lighter tanks made a difference, for Michael kept the lead through his stop. Mario ran in third, ahead of Rahal, Luyendyk, Sullivan, Mears, Fittipaldi, Cheever, Mike Groff in the Foyt/Copenhagen Lola T-91/00, Scott Goodyear driving the Tezak/McKenzie Financial Lola T-91-00 and Willy T. Ribbs, who was in the Walker Lola T-90/00. Sadly for Sullivan, the electrical system failed on his

Alfa Romeo engine on lap 35. Sullivan did note with some glee that he was ahead of both Penskes when he retired.

Unser Jr. now repeated the earlier script. He closed on Michael and made the pass for the lead in turn five on lap 37. Al Jr. remained in the lead until lap 41 when he stopped for a third time. Andretti moved in front yet again and stayed out on the track. As the laps approached 50, the big question was whether or not Michael would have to pit a third time, as Unser. It was expected, yet the end of the race was rapidly approaching. Finally, on lap 48 Andretti peeled into pit lane, stopped, received the last few gallons of methanol and roared back on course, ahead of Unser Jr.!

With two laps to go, Al Jr. was right on Andretti's tail. Whether he could pass once again was to be influenced by an outside factor: it began to rain. Lightly at first, but by the last lap the back of the course was experiencing a steady drizzle. Unser Jr. made a move in the Carousel, but the slick surface would not allow it. Unser slid sideways, retaining control, but Andretti was now out of reach. Michael came home the winner, his seventh of the season. Al Unser Jr. was second, Mario Andretti third, then Rahal, Luyendyk, Fittipaldi, Cheever, Groff and the first non-Ilmor, the Judd-powered Goodyear in ninth. Arguably, this was one of the best Indy car races ever at RA. The fight for the lead was continuous, with two exceptionally talented young second generation drivers fighting cleanly. It doesn't get much better. Andretti would win once again, making it eight on the season, as he would win the PPG Cup.

After the CART event, the IMSA Bridgestone Super Car series ran for 30 minutes. By this time the rain was steady and cold, fog hung in the trees, and it was the most dedicated spectators who continued to hang on the fence. The two Brumos Racing Porsche 911 Turbos of Hurley Haywood and Don Knowles led into turn one, where Knowles promptly spun, holding up the rest of the field and allowing Haywood to get a tremendous lead. Indeed, Hurley led by 15 seconds after the first lap! The field could never recover after spotting Haywood such an advantage. Haywood eased off the last two laps but still won by 50 seconds, covering 10 laps, 40 miles, in the 30 minutes. The Lotusports Lotus Esprits that had run the previous day's SCCA World Challenge made the minor changes necessary in order to run this race and their four Lotuses finished second with Bobby Carradine, third with Doc Bundy, fifth with Paul Newman and sixth with Bo Lemler. The interloper in fourth place was Rob Wilson in a Dodge Stealth.

1992

The good news at the track as 1992 dawned was that CART had granted RA a date in August rather than September. With the weather always very risky, the move to a summer month was welcome indeed.

An addition to the track and to the schedule was off road racing. A 1.1 mile dirt course was gouged out of the area outside turn seven down into the Carousel. Viewing would mainly be from the hill on the east side of Hurry Downs. This course was used several times a year for four years, both for off road vehicles and motorcycles. The downside was that it did tear up the land and took a segment of the track out of the picture for spectating. After the 1995 season the experiment would be dropped, and the rutted land allowed to go back to nature.

SCCA continued to enjoy Tide sponsorship for the Trans-Am, but Escort withdrew as sponsor of the World Challenge. Further, the Racetruck series was discontinued, going the way of other support series such as Sports Renault, Super Vee, Corvettes and VW Cup. The Shelby-Dodge spec cars now had a pro series, though, with RA on the schedule. SCCA also revived the Formula Continental name for a pro series for Formula Ford 2000 cars. This would rival a similar series that had been started by USAC.

Carl Haas expanded his operation once again. He became the promoter for the race track at the Wisconsin State Fair grounds in Milwaukee. Haas renamed it the *Milwaukee Mile* and immediately began to improve the track, which was in danger of losing its CART date due to physical rundown and managerial conflicts. Haas brought in the same marketing firm that RA used and the tracks began a loose working relationship. Jim Melvin would be the general manager of the Milwaukee track.

SCCA instituted a pilot program in its Central Division to try to boost attendance, entries and awareness of its National racing program. The Nationals designated as "Showcase" Nationals would get promotional assistance from SCCA National, among other benefits. The June Sprints received a Showcase designation, although with the event's history of entries and attendance, little help would seem to have been needed.

The Prange's/Bugle Boy June Sprints again attracted more than 400 entries and the weekend attendance

Beauty is all around when the Historic weekend is at hand. Here the tall intake stacks and blued exhaust on an aluminum Chevy Can-Am engine.

Famed Can-Am driver Denny Hulme returned to Road America as Grand Marshall at the 1992 Chicago Historic Races and drove an orange McLaren to victory in the Can-Am Thunder race.

topped 20,000. The Formula Vee race was normal; that is, it was a flag to flag shuffle of places as a train of 10 Vees constantly mixed it up for first. David Bennett won in a Lazer, but Peter Guillan, Bob Lybarger, Bill Noble, Dave Smith and Bill Wallschlaeger all were knocking on the door. Bennett passed Wallschlaeger for the win on the last lap on the run up the hill from turn 14.

The large formula race had John Schaller winning overall and FA in a Ralt RT-5, while Dave Weitzenhof was back on top in FC after a couple years of frustration. This year he beat Ken Gerhardt, reversing the results of the previous two races. Jeff Miller's bad luck returned in the sports racing feature, as his Lola-Kohler once again dropped out while leading. David Tenney won overall and in the Shelby class in his Shelby-Dodge. Augie Pabst III, son of the famous Augie Pabst of the '50s and '60s, was second in his Shelby-Dodge. Al Beasley won yet again, taking DSR in his Decker-AMW.

Sixty-eight Spec Racers had at it with Tom Van Camp the winner. He led most of the time but was challenged by Warren Stilwell, Jeff Beck and Denny Marklein who finished in that order behind him. The GT race was taken by the Camaro of Ray Irwin, the owner of Blackhawk Farms, a 1.8 mile club racing track just over the state line from Beloit, WI. No professional courtesy at work here, though. Irwin had to drive a hard race and was in position for the win, when the Camaro of Max Lagod and the Oldsmobile of Mitch Bender retired. In Formula Ford the race was atypical; Tony Kester led the distance in a Reynard, challenged only by Mike Sauce who got alongside a couple times, but could not pass.

The Historic Races had a very special Grand Marshall: Denis Hulme, winner of so many Can-Am races (including two at RA) and the 1967 World Champion. He not only spent a couple hours signing autographs in the paddock, but was here to drive in the weekend's designated feature, a reunion of Can-Am cars.

Among the many interesting cars in the paddock were the three of Don Orosco. He brought his Scarab sports racer, Old Yaller III and a Scarab Formula One car. The one and only Ferrari 612 Can-Am car from 1969 was present, as was a Lotus 19, three Ferrari GTOs, a Jaguar XK-SS and Augie Pabst's Meister Brauser Scarab. The Can-Am portion of the activities brought out over 20 of the cars, Lolas, McLarens, McKees and Shadows, almost all with some type of interesting race history. As usual, wherever you looked in the paddock there were Ferraris, Lotuses, Elvas,

Porsches, Coopers, and on and on.

Fans were deprived of seeing Pabst and Orosco duel in their Scarabs, as Pabst's broke its gearbox on the first lap; however, Bob Akin with his Cooper Monaco and Orosco went at it for the distance of their race, just as Akin and Pabst had done the past few years. This time it was the Scarab's turn, and Orosco won. An all Ferrari race drew a good entry with all manner of red cars running, from Dinos to Mondials, Testa Rossas to a 375MM. Robert Dusek won in the ex-Amon 612.

The feature was the Can-Am reunion and fittingly, it was won by Denis Hulme. He drove Bob Lee's McLaren M20, his car from the 1972 season. Hulme roared around the four miles, enjoying himself immensely, as he led a mixed bag of late '60s and early '70s Can-Am cars. It was a precious moment, made all the more so when Hulme passed away of a heart attack just a couple months later.

The weekend of August 8-9 held the Nissan Camel GT. For the second year in a row weather was fine; maybe the IMSA jinx had been broken! The GTO/GTU/AC cars were again split out in a separate race, running for one hour. The GTP/Camel Lights would run for two hours. Before then, however, there were three support races.

The Oldsmobile Pro Series and the Dodge/Shelby Pro Series both ran on Saturday afternoon. Tony Ave had a seemingly effortless run to win the Olds Pro race, which was for 60 miles. Ave led all 15 laps in the Olsson Engineering Lola T-88/90. Second was a scrap, though, as Steve Knapp, 1986-87 series champion, made a one-off return at the wheel of a Vestal Cars entered Swift DB-5. Knapp swapped second many times with Bob Thomas' Lola BHP-19, with the Vestal Swift of Ken Kroeger lurking just behind. On the last lap Knapp and Kroeger had contact, Knapp spinning back to fourth with Thomas third behind Kroeger.

The Dodge/Shelby Pro Series ran for 13 laps. Scott Harrington and David Tenney were side by side for much of the first two laps before Harrington was able to ease away, leading the balance, winning over the identical Shelby-Dodge spec cars of Tenney, Chris Winkler, Augie Pabst III and Bennett Dorrance. At the end of the season Harrington and Dorrance would be tied in points, but Harrington was the champion on the tie breaker of number of wins.

Sunday morning the Barber Saab series, now sponsored by Zerex, had a 52 mile race. Leo Parente and Robert Amren shared the lead in the early

The Clayton Cunningham Nissans of Steve Millen and Jeremy Dale and the Rocketsports Oldsmobiles of Darin Brassfield and Paul Gentilozzi were the cream of the IMSA GTO class.

going until Amren got just far enough ahead that Parente could not attempt an outbraking maneuver. Amren won by little more than a second over Parente, with Ashton Lewis and Elton Julian following.

The Exxon Supreme Series again had factory teams dominating a small GTO entry. Oldsmobile had entered the fray this year with Rocketsports moving over from the Trans-Am. They were running Darin Brassfield and Paul Gentilozzi in GTO plus Irv Hoerr in AC. Nissan, as usual, was represented by the CCR team with 300ZX twin turbos for Steve Millen and Jeremy Dale. The first two-thirds of the 26 lap, 104 mile go was between Millen and Brassfield. They ran in very close company, occasionally exchanging the lead. Dale was already well behind, a misfire slowing his pace. Gentilozzi, on the other hand, was running in third according to plan. Unlike the others, Gentilozzi had hard compound tires on his Olds, gambling that he would have more grip at the end. Gentilozzi began to move as the race passed the 40 minute mark. First he passed teammate Brassfield, who was in some discomfort from belts that were too tight. Then he closed on Millen, who was struggling not only with tires that were going off, but also with a gearbox in which fourth gear was failing. With much more grip, Gentilozzi made a fairly easy pass on lap 21 and led the balance. Millen was second, Brassfield third and Hoerr fourth, first in AC. A good day for Rocketsports.

In GTU it also was a factory battle. Nissan, through Bob Leitzinger's team, was running three 240SX V-6 cars for Bob and Butch Leitzinger and David Loring. Dodge had two Daytonas run by Full Time Racing for John Fergus and Don Walker. The race went all Butch Leitzinger's way. He got a good jump, with Fergus following and Loring dropping out with a broken axle. Butch used a strong engine to good advantage, running up with some AC cars and using them as a buffer to the pursuing Fergus, Bob L., Bill Auberlen in a Mazda RX-7 and Walker. Butch Leitzinger led to the finish with his father second and Auberlen third. Fergus broke a half shaft near the finish and dropped to fifth.

On the season, Steve Millen would win the GTO championship and David Loring the GTU crown, justifying Nissan's monetary outlay. Irv Hoerr would take AC, adding it to his crowns of 1986-87.

The Camel GT was a factory battle between Toyota and Jaguar. The Eagle Mk. IIIs of Dan Gurney's AAR team had worked out the bugs and were now the fastest. Jaguar, through Tom Walkinshaw Racing, had reacted

to the speed of the Eagle by making an IMSA-spec version of the XJR-14 World Championship of Makes racer. It was a small, compact car powered by a 3.5 liter Ford HB F-1 engine. Eagles had won six races coming into RA, five by Juan Fangio II and one by P.J. Jones. Jaguar's Davy Jones had won twice in the Bud Light XJR-14. Geoff Brabham was having a tough year. He had one win in the Nissan NPT-91C, but the Nissan clearly was showing its age compared to the Eagle and Jag. The fourth factory involved this year was Mazda. They developed two sharp-looking RX-792P racers for Price Cobb and Pete Halsmer. If looks were wins, they would have swept the year. As it was, their first year in GTP was a learning experience. They had several good placings, but no wins.

A moderate crowd of approximately 20,000 showed up for the race. Fangio was on the pole, clocking an astonishing 1:47.913 which was less than 0.9 second slower than Rahal's absolute track record, set in an Indy car! P.J. Jones was alongside while Davy Jones was third. Most unfortunately, Davy Jones had a major crash in the Sunday morning warmup. His Jaguar broke something going into the Carousel, and the XJR-14 went into, up and over the guardrail, coming to a rest upside down. Jones was unhurt but the car was beyond immediate repair. Since TWR did not have a spare at the track, Jaguar was done for the day.

This all but assured a monumentally dull race. Fangio and P.J. Jones led all the way, spending the two hours driving around in formation. They started 1-2 and finished 1-2 without any challenge whatsoever. Brabham was a lonely third with the Mazdas of Cobb and Halsmer finishing fourth and fifth. John Paul Jr. and Gianpiero Moretti finished sixth in the Momo Porsche 962. The only possible threat to the Eagles was the Intrepid MR-1 of Tom Kendall, but it was out after five laps with broken suspension. So crushing was the superiority of the Eagle-Toyotas that they would not lose a race that they entered from mid-1992 through the end of 1993! Fangio would easily win the Camel GT championship both years.

In Camel Lights there was a bit more action. Ruggero Melgrati led the early laps in the Comptech Spice-Acura until losing a cylinder at half distance. Parker Johnstone, in the sister Spice-Acura then led until a cam belt broke. Kudzu-Buicks now took over with the Charles Morgan/Tommy Riggins car winning over the like examples of Jim Downing/Tim McAdam and Fermin Velez/Andy Evans. Johnstone did not have to worry though, as the title was already in his pocket for the second straight year.

The Camel GT series in 1992 was a romp for the Toyota-powered Gurney Eagles of Juan Fangio II and P.J. Jones.

Two weeks later the track was open for business again for the CART/Trans-Am weekend. Warm and generally sunny weather greeted this summer date, an improvement over the September dates of the immediate past. The first race of the weekend was the 100 mile Tide Trans-Am on Saturday afternoon. With the Oldsmobile effort having moved to IMSA, this left Chevrolet vs. Ford. However, a third player entered the picture as Dodge supported the Archer Brothers who entered two Dodge Daytonas for Tommy and Bobby. Tommy had already drawn blood with a win at Detroit. The Chevrolet effort was headed again by Buz McCall's two Camaros for Scott Sharp and Jack Baldwin. They were leading the standings and it appeared that one of them would carry off the crown. The main standard bearer for Ford this year was Tom Gloy Racing. He entered three Mustangs for Ron Fellows, Jerry Clinton and Walter Payton. Roush Racing had a very subdued presence, just running one car for Ford Director Michael Dingman in the occasional Trans-Am and IMSA AC race.

The McCall pair of Baldwin and Sharp were on the front row, with Sharp taking the lead at the start. He would lead the first four laps before Baldwin got around him in turn five on lap five. Behind these two were Greg Pickett, Camaro; Fellows; George Robinson, Camaro; T. Archer; Jim Derhaag, Camaro; Jim Stevens, Mustang; and Dick Danielson, Olds Supreme. On lap seven Pickett made full use of the strongest engine in the field to power past both Baldwin and Sharp to take the lead. His time in front lasted just until lap 14 of 25 when that strong engine cried, "enough!" and coasted to a silent stop on the back straight, elevating Baldwin to the front once again.

Ron Fellows was on the move, though. He was now lapping faster than anyone else and dispatched first Sharp, then on lap 16, Baldwin. Once in first he inched away from Baldwin and Sharp, leaving them to dispute second. Dispute it they did. With the title likely to go to one or the other, they were racing each other, as well as Fellows. This went down to the last lap where Sharp passed Baldwin going into turn 12, only to put two wheels off on the exit and spin, handing the place to Baldwin. Fellows took the win, Baldwin second and Sharp recovering for third. Robinson, Derhaag and Dingman filled out the top six. It was a fine race, one of the most competitive Trans-Ams seen at RA. The season championship did come down to the last race, with Baldwin winning the title.

After the Trans-Am, the World Challenge cars had a one hour timed race, during which Bill Cooper traveled 24 laps, 96 miles. He took the lead in his Corvette on lap 20 after playing a waiting game. The threesome of R.K. Smith, Boris Said III and Kim Baker all had a taste of the lead as they spent the early laps swapping first. Then, one by one, they fell by the wayside. First, the hood on Said's Mustang came undone, necessitating a pit stop. Then Smith's Corvette began smoking, and he dropped back. Next, Baker's Corvette began to misfire. Cooper then was first, followed by the Corvettes of Jim Minneker, Smith, Baker, Mike Maloney and the Camaro of Lou Gigliotti.

Sunday morning was warm and overcast. The 30 minute Zerex Barber Saab race saw Swede Robert Amren win the race, and in so doing, win the season championship. Amren took the lead on lap two from Elton Julian, then withstood a furious assault by Leo Parente to win the 13 lap, 52 mile contest. Parente dropped back after a big spin while trying to pass Amren. Ashton Lewis took second, followed by Julian, Ricardo Dona, Rick Pollock, Craig Hall and fast lady driver, Andrea Kasiewicz.

Then it was time for the Texaco Havoline 200. Many things had changed on the Indy car front since 1991. Ford had tired of Chevrolet getting all the headlines with its Chevy-Ilmor engine and had commissioned Cosworth to build a replacement for the very long in tooth Cosworth DFX. The result was the Ford XB. This first year two teams were using it, Newman-Haas with Mario and Michael Andretti and Chip Ganassi with Eddie Cheever and Robbie Gordon. Both teams used special Lola T-92/00XBs, built exclusively for the new Ford unit. Chevrolet answered with the 'B' version of the Ilmor. Penske Racing was the only team that had its use, and it powered the two Marlboro PC-21s of Emerson Fittipaldi and Paul Tracy. Rick Mears had retired at mid-season, and Tracy had taken his seat full time. Chevrolet also released the 'A' version of the Ilmor to all who wanted it and most of the field had this in the back of their cars. Besides the Ford and the Ilmor B users, the only teams not with the Ilmor A were Dale Coyne and Euromotorsports, who still used the Cosworth, and Arciero, which labored on with the totally uncompetitive Buick V-6.

The points chase was led by Bobby Rahal, who was having great success in his first year as a car owner. He and partner Carl Hogan, who had run a F-5000 team during the years of that series, had purchased Patrick Racing and renamed it Rahal-Hogan Racing. Rahal had run at the front all year, winning three times. He would qualify fourth here, not in the front row, but still at the sharp end of the grid. Pole was taken by Paul Tracy, his first ever Indy car pole. His time was 1:48.210, not quite as fast as Rahal's record of the year before. The lap after Tracy set his fast time he lost it in turn 13 and crashed heavily, wrecking the car but without personal injury. The second Marlboro Penske of Emerson Fittipaldi was alongside Tracy. Third fastest was Michael Andretti, alongside Rahal in row two. Father

Christian Danner pulls his Euromotorsports Lola off into the gravel as the engine lets go during the '92 CART 200.

Mario shared row three with Scott Goodyear, having a fine run in the Walker/Mackenzie Financial Lola T-92/00. Scott Pruett did very well to place the Budweiser Truesports 92C seventh on the grid. Team owner Barbara Trueman had suspended all development on the Truesports in May. As a result, team president Steve Horne and a number of key individuals left and the car dropped back in the field with respect to the other teams. Only Pruett's skill kept the car in a semblance of competitiveness. At the end of the year, Truesports would shut down completely. Eighth and ninth fastest were the Galles pair of Al Unser Jr. and Danny Sullivan, both driving Galmer G92s. Rick Galles had commissioned Galmer Engineering of England to build an Indy car, and the Galmer was the result. Despite being on a steep (and slippery) developmental curve, the Galmer had two wins so far, one for each driver. Rounding out the top ten on the grid, which contained 25 cars, was John Andretti in the Hall-VDS/Pennzoil Lola T-92/00.

Tracy and Fittipaldi led into turn one, with Michael following. Before the lap was out, both Mario and Unser Jr. slipped past Rahal, who was a bit slow getting started. Ross Cheever, who was A.J. Foyt's driver of the week in his Copenhagen Lola, was already out, having nosed into the barriers at turn three. As the race settled down, the two Marlboro Penskes of Tracy and Fittipaldi led, followed by the two Havoline/K-Mart Lolas of the Andrettis, Michael and Mario. Unser Jr., Rahal, Pruett, John Andretti, Goodyear, Sullivan, Gordon, Cheever, Raul Boesel in the Simon/Duracell Lola and Stefan Johansson in the Bettenhausen/Amax Penske PC-20.

On lap six Tracy followed team orders and let team leader Fittipaldi past. Having done a noble deed, he proceeded to blot his copybook thoroughly. He ran off the road at turn three, dropping to 11th. He regained three places before he made a mistake in turn 12, spinning into the gravel and losing four laps. A very promising start had been ruined.

Fittipaldi now was in control, with a comfortable lead. The pit stops went uneventfully, and Michael resumed in second with Rahal, Mario, Unser Jr., Pruett and Goodyear following. Pruett and Goodyear came together when Goodyear attempted to overtake going into turn five, spoiling Pruett's fine run. Mario was experiencing braking troubles and began to fall back, being overtaken by Unser Jr., Goodyear and Gordon.

The second round of pit stops saw Fittipaldi in and out in good order, but Michael botched his, pulling into Rahal's pit! He had to pull out of the pits and do another lap and try again, while Rahal was delayed waiting for

Michael to move. Some of the time lost was regained when a full course yellow flew for Goodyear's crash in the kink. The Canadian became yet another who discovered that the kink could not be taken flat out. The car was destroyed, but Goodyear was unhurt.

When the track went green, eight laps remained, and Fittipaldi had enough in hand to withstand a furious assault by Unser Jr. Rahal trailed in third while Michael Andretti moved up quickly from seventh, where his gaffe had put him. Fittipaldi held on to win, just .775 seconds ahead of Al Unser Jr., with Bobby Rahal another tick behind. Michael had improved to finish fourth, with his father Mario in fifth and cousin John sixth for an Andretti 4-5-6. Sullivan, Boesel, Pruett and Ted Prappas in the P.I.G. Lola T-91/00 filled out the top ten. Brian Till lost a top ten finish on the last lap when his Robco Racing Truesports 91C ran out of fuel.

Rahal would win one more time this season and win his third PPG Championship. Michael Andretti signed with McLaren to drive Formula One in '93 and Carl Haas replaced him with 1992 World Champion Nigel Mansell. Surely one of the greatest coups in CART's history.

After the Indy car race, the Firestone Firehawk cars ran a three hour enduro. This scheduling had a benefit the local police appreciated. The crowd of over 50,000 filtered out all during this race rather than leaving in one massive bunch. Traffic was spread, making the trip home somewhat less taxing than normal. Traffic was also on the track during this time as over 50 cars started the three hour race. Nick Ham, assisted by Rich Moskalik, won in a Porsche 944, but only after Ham passed Joe Varde on the last lap. Ham was fourth starting lap 51 of the eventual 63, then took third from the Bobby Akin Porsche. He then ran down Doug Goad's Pontiac for second on lap 58. Only Varde headed him, and Ham nailed Varde on the last lap for a splendid win.

The Sunday after Labor Day the Oldsmobile Pro Series paid its second '92 visit to RA. However, like the Escort Endurance race in 1988, it was with a non-spectator regional race. A mid-year schedule change had knocked out two Olds Pro races, and in order to fulfill the contract with Oldsmobile, another race had to be run. This race was much the same as the one a month earlier as Tony Ave led from start to finish in the Olsson Engineering Lola. Bob Thomas started 10th but finished second in his Lola with Mike Borkowski third in a Shannon. This was Ave's year, and he duly went on to win the season championship.

1993

Changes from the previous year were relatively few. The schedule remained essentially the same, while sponsors changed for the June Sprints and the IMSA Camel GT race. Younkers came on board to sponsor the Sprints, while the new title sponsor for the Camel GT was Piggly Wiggly. A minor shuffle took place for support series, but the features remained as before.

IMSA was experiencing significant difficulties as its flagship Camel GT series was in big trouble. Nissan, Jaguar and Mazda had all withdrawn their teams, leaving Toyota as the only factory participant. The problem was exacerbated by the fact that over the previous few years the factory teams had forced out most of the independents. Now that the factories were gone, so were the independents. The result was very slim fields and a Toyota walkover. IMSA saw the problem developing and had announced at the start of the year that this would be the last for the GTP cars. A new class, World Sports Car, would take over in 1994. While the technical specifications

Andrea Kasiewicz leads David Finch, David Downey and Tom Jagemann as their Sports 2000s contest the lead at the 1993 June Sprints.

were many, briefly stated a WSC was a two seater, open topped sports racer powered by a production-based engine. No turbocharging would be permitted. It was designed to be cheaper than a GTP, especially in the engine department. During 1993 WSC entries were encouraged, even though they would be competing in the GTP category against the Toyota-backed Eagles. The first year or two most WSCs would be Camel Lights with their tops chopped off. Further complicating IMSA's troubles, Camel disclosed that this would be their last year of sponsorship.

The SCCA also had sponsorship problems, as Tide left after two years sponsorship of the Trans-Am. The result was that SCCA had to move forward without title sponsors for either of its two top series, the Trans-Am and World Challenge. Its Formula Atlantic series, on the other hand, picked up sponsorship from Player's Ltd. and was now known as the Player's Ltd./Toyota Atlantic Series. However, it should be pointed out that this series, as well as the Oldsmobile Pro Series, were both being run and administered by the Pro-Motion Agency and the SCCA's role was limited to mainly being the sanctioning body.

The end of June was the time for the Younkers June Sprints. Some 474 cars, the highest in years, entered the showcase National. Over 20,000 fans turned out in glorious warmth and sunshine to enjoy the action. The Formula Vee crowd provided the usual thrilling race that spectators had

come to expect. Peter Guillan led more often than not, but a snarling group of Jeff Salcedo, Tom Stephani and William Bonow caught him at half distance. These four then traded first until Dave Smith caught them, up from twelfth. On the last lap the usual howling mob headed out of turn 14 to the line with Salcedo nipping Smith by an eyelash. The Formula feature was anticlimactic, as both FA and FC were easy wins. Greg Ray won overall and FA in a Swift DB-4 by 22 seconds, while Dave Weitzenhof added yet another win to his RA total as he took FC.

The sports racing event belonged to Jeff Miller. For a pleasant change, his Lola-Kohler CSR entry held together for the distance and Miller won by an easy 37 second margin over Alan Andrea's Lola-Olds. In Sports 2000 Andrea Kasiewicz was the early leader in her Lola, but first David Downey, then Michael Finch got by and they finished in the order Finch, Downey, Kasiewicz. The Spec Racer event drew an astounding 74 entries! The first few laps saw Warren Stilwell, Jeff Beck, Robert Mumm and Leo Capaldi mixing it up, but Stilwell managed to eke out a couple seconds lead and that was all he needed to carry it to the checker. Frank Emmett won the GT race in a Camaro, while Tom Patton was the GT-2 winner in a very old Sunbeam Tiger. In Formula Ford, Tony Kester almost made it two in a row, but he could not get his Reynard past the Swift of Dennis O'Neal. Tom Van Camp was third in the field of 41 cars.

July 10-11 brought the IMSA show, featuring the Piggly Wiggly Camel GT. The Firestone Firehawk enduro was back on this weekend and ran for three hours on Saturday. Unlike the usual enduro, this race went down to the last lap. Three Pontiac Firebirds, Doug Goad/Larry Schumacher, Don Knowles/John Heinricy and Heinricy/Stu Hayner, had played in the lead most of the 63 laps. With 20 minutes left, Goad made his final pit stop. Heinricy and Hayner ran one-two and looked safe. At the start of the last lap Hayner passed Heinricy for the lead as Heinricy's Firebird began to stutter, the fuel almost gone. Incredibly, Hayner's car then also began sputtering, its fuel gone! Goad, almost a lap back at the start of the final go-around, came out of Thunder Valley and was greeted with the incredible sight of both Pontiacs weaving from side to side, trying to pick up the last dregs in their tanks. Goad passed both as they weaved and banged their way up the hill, going from third to first in the last 200 yards of a three hour race!

The '93 Chicago Historic Races featured Ford. All three Fords which collectively won four Le Mans races were there including the Gulf/Wyer GT-40 which won the 1968 and 1969 races.

In contrast, Riccardo Zona had an easy win in the Zerex Barber Saab race which led off Sunday. He led all 10 laps in the 30 minute race, which only had 16 minutes of green flag running. The USAC Formula Ford 2000 48 mile race was also an easy win as Chris Simmons took the lead from Kevin West on lap two and led for the duration.

The Camel GT reached its low point at RA this year. The track took note of the low grid counts at previous races and stood fast that the GTPs and Lights would run with the GTO/GTU/AC cars in one race. The justifiable fear was that the track could look very bare in the late stages with only the prototypes. IMSA agreed, and a combined class race was scheduled for the somewhat curious length of two and three-quarter hours. However, this produced an immediate downside, for the AAR Eagle team, which had won every race this year and for whom Juan Fangio II would win his second straight Camel GT title, withdrew. They did not wish to run in a combined race with the much slower GTU cars. This left only four GTPs.

The race itself was very mild, to put it kindly. Reinhold Joest entered two Porsche 962s and the Manuel Reuter/John Winter car led the entire 73 laps, 292 miles. One of last year's Nissan NPT-91Cs, now owned by Momo Corse, ran second in the hands of Gianpiero Moretti for the first 100 miles until the engine blew. The second Joest Porsche then took and held second to the finish. John Paul Jr. drove this car solo and was delayed by a broken nosepiece and a flat tire. The fourth GTP, the Intrepid MR-1, was driven by Wayne Taylor and also was out early. Two GTPs finished, and they were one-two.

Two Rocketsports Oldsmobile Supremes were third and fourth, one-two in GTS, formerly known as GTO. Scott Pruett, doing a guest drive, led the class for a good share of the distance until he moved over for team leader Paul Gentilozzi, who was chasing points. They then finished that way, with Tom Kendall third in class, seventh overall, in the Roush Ford Mustang. Kendall was a bit faster than the Oldsmobiles, but his strategy of an extra pit stop in trade for lighter racing weight due to less fuel did not pay off. Kendall would take the season GTS crown, however.

Fifth and sixth overall were the first two Camel Light cars, both Spice-Acuras. Parker Johnstone, winning the class championship for the third straight year, and Dan Marvin drove the winning Comptech car, while Bob Earl and Bob Schader were second in the Brix entry. Charles Morgan took

GTO, formerly known as American Challenge, in his Oldsmobile Supreme. In GTU, Bill Auberlen won in a Mazda RX-7, finishing a lap ahead of the Nissan 240SX V-6 of Bob and Butch Leitzinger. Butch would take the GTU crown, the same that his dad won in 1989.

The fan enthusiasm for this year's Camel GT was reflected in the attendance. Less than 10,000 bothered to come, the lowest ever for a spectator race at RA except for the two Firestone Firehawk races of 1985-86. As a result, RA removed IMSA from its schedule.

The Historic Races ran the weekend of July 24-25. The feature again this year was the Can-Am reunion, and 27 were on hand. Not all raced, of course, but even if they did not go onto the track, they still were worth gawking at in the paddock. The race itself was a contest between George Follmer, in an *over restored* McLaren M8F (the car featured a thicker tub, bigger engine and ground effects tunnels, among other modifications, that went well beyond the original) and the ex-Parsons 1969 Lola T-163 of Craig Bennett. They raced hard the entire 10 lap distance with Bennett taking the win.

The Indy cars returned to RA on the weekend of August 21-22. Texaco Havoline again was the title sponsor for the CART 200 and the other races on the card were the Trans-Am, World Challenge, Zerex Barber Saab and the Dodge/Shelbys.

The SCCA Trans-Am ran its 100 mile event early Saturday afternoon. The factory-assisted Chevrolet team of Buz McCall was the one to beat, as Scott Sharp had already won five races and was poised to take his second T-A title. His teammate was last year's champion, Jack Baldwin. Dodge had expanded its effort to four cars, all entered by the Archer Brothers. The red Daytonas would be driven by Tommy and Bobby Archer, Mitch Wright and Bill Saunders. Tommy Archer had one win so far this season. Ford's main effort came from the shops of Tom Gloy. He had entered four Mustangs for Ron Fellows, Jerry Clinton, Walter Payton and rookie Chris McDougall. Roush was running his main driver Tom Kendall in IMSA this season, but had a 'B' team of Michael Dingman, Jon Gooding and Jim Stevens present.

In qualifying the McCall Camaros of Sharp and Baldwin took the front row. However, the talking point was Payton's big escape. He was following Dick Danielson's Olds down the Moraine Sweep when Danielson missed a gear, slowing abruptly. Payton collided with the Olds, flew up and over him, bounced, went through the guard rail, tearing off the fuel cell which exploded and cart wheeled over the fence into the spectator area, coming to rest upside down. A trail of gasoline ignited the car, and Payton scrambled out, more shaken and bruised than he ever had been after an NFL game. Shortly thereafter, Payton decided that he'd rather be on the other side of the pit wall and retired as a driver, buying into Dale Coyne's Indy car team.

Scott Sharp was on a roll; he grabbed the lead at the flag and led all 25 laps in the Rain-X Camaro to win his third straight and sixth of the year, putting the title well into his pocket. His teammate Jack Baldwin had an early dice with Fellows and then a banging-rubbing battle with Greg Pickett to finish second. Pickett brought his Camaro home in third place with Fellows fourth. Those positions had been reversed until the closing laps when Pickett made a fine overtaking move in turn eight. The Dodges challenged early, but dropped back as the race wore on with Tommy Archer being the best placed in fifth.

The Dodge/Shelby Pro Series was also on Saturday's card and was taken by Kyle Konzer. David Tenney had the pole, but Konzer passed him on the first lap. Tenney fought back and retook the point on lap three, but Konzer repassed him two laps later. Scott Harrington moved past Tenney and challenged Konzer, but could not get past. His water pump failed a couple laps from the end and he faded to sixth. Augie Pabst III moved up from seventh on the grid, battling past Gene Harrington, Richie Hearn and Robert Amren, taking second behind the winning Konzer. Gene Harrington, Tenney and Amren followed ahead of Scott Harrington. Konzer's two wins and four seconds would be enough to take the season championship ahead of Hearn and Pabst.

Sunday morning dawned partly cloudy and warm. A track record crowd of 65,000 spectators streamed through the gates, ready for a great day of action. The Zerex Barber Saab cars ran for 30 minutes in the late morning and put on a great show. Bill Adams led the first of 10 laps but was passed first by Diego Guzman and then by Kenny Brack on lap two. Brack then took Guzman in turn eight to lead the lap, but Guzman repassed going into turn one on the third lap. The next lap they traded the lead twice, while Jerry Nadeau joined the fray, pushing Brack down to third. It stayed this way until the last lap when Brack passed Nadeau going into turn three, then set out after Guzman, who he caught going into five and out dragged him up the hill to six. Brack held onto first for the remaining two miles to score a fine come from behind win. Guzman was second, Nadeau third and Riccardo Dona fourth. Brack's charging style was rewarded at season's end with the series title.

The 1993 CART season was memorable. Nigel Mansell had joined the Newman-Haas team, the first time a reigning World Champion had raced a full Indy car season. He had already won four races and was leading the title chase. His teammate in the Texaco/K-Mart Lola T-93/00s was Mario Andretti, who had one win. The Ford engines were now available to more teams, and the Foyt, Dick Simon and Walker teams were using them in addition to Newman-Haas and Ganassi. Chevrolet Ilmor responded with the 'C' version of their engine, which was being used by Penske, Rahal-Hogan, Bettenhausen, Galles, Hall and Kenny Bernstein teams. Last year's Penskes with the 'B' engine were sold to Arciero and Turley. The balance of the 29 car field used the Chevy Ilmor 'A' with the exception of the woebegone Leader Card team, which used a Buick, and Euromotorsports, which used the last Cosworth running.

Paul Tracy took the pole in the Marlboro Penske PC-22. Just like the previous year, he had a huge crash, this time in the kink. He destroyed the Penske and damaged his ankle. He spent a large portion of his time in the CART medical trailer, getting therapy to ease the pain. He used crutches around the pits, but still was able to drive. Tracy's pole time was 1:47.405, still short of Rahal's 1991 record. The Newman-Haas pair came next, Mansell ahead of Andretti. A fine fourth fastest was Raul Boesel in the Simon/Duracell Lola T-93/00, ahead of Emerson Fittipaldi in the second Marlboro Penske PC-22. Al Unser Jr. filled out row three in the Galles/Valvoline Lola T-93/00. The team had given up on the Galmer after one year, much to the chagrin of Unser, who felt that it could be developed into a consistent race winner. Row four held Scott Goodyear in the Walker/Mackenzie Financial Lola T-93/00 and Robby Gordon in A.J. Foyt's Copenhagen Lola T-93/00. Rounding out the top ten were Mark Smith, the 1989 FSV champion moving up from Indy Lights in the Arciero/Sears Craftsman Penske PC-21 and Bobby Rahal in his Rahal-Hogan/Miller Lola T-93/00.

The race itself was fairly anticlimactic. Paul Tracy duplicated Mario Andretti's 1987 feat of leading every lap from the pole. Tracy simply just checked out and was gone. In second, Nigel Mansell could keep Tracy in sight, but was never close enough to try to overtake him. Mansell also was dominant, spending the entire day in second place. The racing started for third, that place being shuffled numerous times.

Tracy led the first third of the race easily, and going into the first round of pit stops it was Tracy, Mansell, Andretti, Gordon, Arie Luyendyk in the Ganassi/Target Lola, Fittipaldi, Rahal, Eddie Cheever driving the Simon/Menard Lola, Teo Fabi in the Jim Hall/Pennzoil Lola, Unser, Goodyear, Boesel, Smith and Christian Danner, first of the 'A' engine cars. Fittipaldi got nabbed for speeding in the pit lane and dropped back after a stop and go penalty. Shortly thereafter, Unser rolled to a stop with a broken CV joint. Luyendyk had moved up to fourth, but spun it away while lapping a car.

At 30 laps Tracy led Mansell by 16 seconds. Andretti, Gordon and a fast recovering Luyendyk followed, then Rahal, Boesel, Fittipaldi and Cheever. Tracy was now in some pain, as his injured leg was going numb. He slackened his pace slightly, depending upon his gearbox more than the brakes to slow him. Rahal got past Luyendyk, then outbraked Gordon for fourth. Boesel was also on the move, following Rahal up the charts. This pattern lasted through the second round of stops, and as the race moved to conclusion, Andretti's engine broke a valve spring on lap 48, dropping him out of a sure third place. Luyendyk lost positions when he had to pit with a flat tire. The race then finished with Paul Tracy a most dominant winner, his fourth of the season. Mansell was second with Bobby Rahal a fine third. Raul Boesel took an equally fine fourth, followed by Fittipaldi and Cheever, rounding out the top six.

Tracy and Mansell would each win another race, with Nigel adding the 1993 PPG Cup to his World Championship. At RA, the CART president, Bill Stokkan, announced his resignation. He cited personal reasons, but it had been no secret that his management style and ideas of series expansion did not sit well with a goodly portion of the CART membership. A search committee would be formed to find a new leader, and early in 1994 Andrew Craig would take over as head of CART. This move that would be a major plus for CART as it moved into a contentious period in American racing.

The World Challenge race which wound up Sunday's activities was also a flag to flag romp. In this instance Elliott Forbes-Robinson was the beneficiary, leading all 24 laps completed in the one hour timed race. He was driving a Nissan 300ZX Turbo. R.K. Smith was right on Forbes-Robinson's tail for the first 15 laps until his Corvette slowed in order to conserve fuel. Nick Ham in the Kelly-Moss Racing Porsche 911 Turbo was there to pass Smith and take second. John Schneider in the team car to Forbes-Robinson finished fourth, while Lou Gigliotti won class B, fifth overall, in a Camaro. Forbes-Robinson would win five of the eight races this year to be the champion.

1994

Over the winter much happened with the major road racing sanctioning bodies. IMSA was sold to Charles Slater who immediately installed Hal Kelley as president. Dan Greenwood had been IMSA's president in the very difficult period involving the switch from GTP to World Sports Car and had been saddled with the difficult task of having to work with the non-visible owner Michael Cone. Greenwood was immediately snapped up by SCCA and made president of SCCA Pro Racing Inc. IMSA's troubles were not over for it carried a lot of debt. Further, overambitious marketing and television plans would add to the debt. Another sale in September, 1996, apparently rescued IMSA from impending insolvency. Camel did bow out as the title sponsor for IMSA's major series, but Exxon stepped in and gave its name to the new World Sports Car series.

Andrew Craig was hired as the new president of CART. Craig's no-nonsense style and superb diplomatic skills immediately gained him the support of the CART members and the series continued to grow and prosper.

Road America had only three spectator weekends for auto racing in 1994. The IMSA weekend was not replaced on the schedule, leaving the June Sprints, the Historic Races and the CART/Trans-Am weekends. However, each of the three weekends was a good draw and proven to be profitable. The Historic weekend had surpassed the June Sprints in spectator count, an occurrence not thought possible a few years earlier and evidence of the exploding interest in historic or vintage car racing. The CART event again was in September, the 10th and 11th to be exact, due to now familiar CART scheduling concerns. However Andrew Craig promised the track a summer date in 1995, and he delivered when the final schedule showed RA down for an early July date. However, the September date hurt this year, as the crowd was down about 10,000 from the year before. In Wisconsin, one cannot go head to head with the Packers and not expect some runoff.

June 25-26 was the weekend for the Younkers June Sprints. As the last couple years, individual races and some individual classes had sponsorship, with prize money and/or accessories awarded. As usual, the Formula Vee race provided close exciting competition. Bill Wallschlaeger led more often than not in his Lazer, but Eric Tremayne, Bill Noble, Jeff Salcedo, Bob Lybarger, Peter Guillan and Dave Smith hounded him constantly, one mad

Eventual winner, Dorsey Schroeder gets ready for battle in the Trans-Am as the Tom Gloy Team prepares his Ford Mustang.

pack of snarling Vees pounding around lap after lap. As usual, it came down to the drag race out of turn 14 on the final lap. Wallschlaeger led, but Tremayne pulled out of his draft and inched by as they crossed the line. But where did he actually pull ahead? Tremayne pulled up to the starter's bridge, said he won and took the checkered flag for a victory lap. Meanwhile, after a good deal of studying instant photos of the finish, the officials said that Wallschlaeger actually was ahead at the line! They gave him a flag and he too, did a victory lap.

The Spec Racer event started 91 cars, which not only was a record at RA, but surely must have been an all-time record of some sort. The Renault engines were starting a three year phase-out, due to Renault not being in the U.S. market anymore and its parts becoming scarce. Ford four cylinder engines were chosen to replace Renault and for three years there would be two sub-classes of Spec Racer. David Tenney led all the way, a rarity in this equalized class. In the Renault class James Marinangel nipped Lee Fleming for first.

The sports racing feature was won by Jeff Miller for the second straight year. He was accosted constantly by Randy Zimmer in a Royale-Mazda, with the pressure only ending when Zimmer ran out of fuel on the last lap. In Sports 2000 four cars put on a great fight. Webb Bassick led early in his Swift with Robert Sollenskog passing on lap three. The next lap, however, Sollenskog got his Shannon tangled up with a CSR car, spinning back in the field. Alan Andrea moved ahead, but he had his mirrors full of the Lola of Andrea Kasiewicz. She had passed Bassick on lap five and on lap seven made a fine pass in turn five. The next lap Alan Andrea tried to retaliate with the same move, but he spun instead. Kasiewicz led the balance of the race, becoming the first woman to win at RA since Denise McCluggage in 1960.

The Formula Ford race officially had only two lead changes. In actuality, the lead changed hands many times away from the S/F line. Bruce May prevailed for the win in his Swift, but he had Tony Kester, Dennis O'Neal, Keith Brown and Steve Kelly constantly harassing him. O'Neal finally finished second, followed by Brown and Kester.

Max Lagod finally took the win in GT-1 after six years of trying, with Tom Patton again taking GT-2. Then the Formula feature ran, with John Schaller winning in his Ralt RT-5. Tony Ave was his only competition, but Ave had two things against

Tom Kendall, Ron Fellows, Scott Pruett and Jack Baldwin race though turn seven during the '94 Trans-Am race.

him. He spun from second to eighth on lap two, and he was driving the one-off XFR Formula Atlantic based on a 1989 design and decidedly obsolete. Ave recovered nicely and came through to second. In FC Dave Weitzenhof broke, ending his seemingly annual domination. Tony Stefanelli won driving a Piper although it wasn't easy, since he had Bill Weidner filling his mirrors the entire distance.

One month later the Historic Races ran on July 23-24. The feature this year was the Ford GT-40 reunion. Over 500 cars were on display with over 40 GT-40s. Among those on display were the three Mk. IIs that finished 1-2-3 in the 1966 Le Mans 24 Hours, the Mk. IV that won the 1967 Le Mans and the GT-40 that won both 1968 and 1969 Le Mans. Historic indeed. In the all-Ford race Brian Redman was first in a GT-40.

Augie Pabst had completed the restoration on the 1962 rear engine Scarab Mk. IV and his son, Augie III, drove it while Augie was in his usual Meister Brauser Scarab, a good show indeed as the two thundered around the four miles, airing out America's best. A horde of over 20 Can-Am cars ran, with the Bennetts, Craig and Kirk, leading in their Lola T-163s. Fred Cziska in a Shadow Mk. III kept them honest though. Also running was Dave Cowart in the Lola T-70 that John Surtees had used to win the first Can-Am series in 1966.

The 1994 Trans-Am Series saw a step up in factory participation from the previous couple years. Roush Racing was back in force representing Ford with Tom Kendall and Jon Gooding in Mustangs. Gloy had four Mustangs at RA, driven by Dorsey Schroeder, Ron Fellows, Boris Said and Brian Simo. Chevrolet had Buz McCall in its camp, as usual. This year McCall was running Scott Pruett and Jack Baldwin. Greg Pickett had three Camaros for himself, Jamie Galles and R.J. Valentine. Rocketsports had switched from running Oldsmobiles in IMSA to Camaros in the Trans-Am. Paul Gentilozzi was up. The only negative from the year before was that Dodge had pulled out. The Archers switched to Mustangs for themselves and Bill Saunders.

Scott Pruett in the Royal Oak Charcoal Camaro took the pole and from there the lead as the race began. Through the first half dozen of 25 laps Pruett led Kendall, Baldwin, Gentilozzi, Schroeder, T. Archer, Pickett, Fellows and Gooding. On lap eight Schroeder moved past both Gentilozzi and Baldwin to move into third with Archer following him past Gentilozzi.

Pruett could not shake Kendall, who was constantly probing for a way past. This played into Schroeder's hands on lap 14. Kendall tried an outside pass on the run into corner five with Pruett responding by moving slightly off line to the right. Schroeder pounced at the opening and moved inside, passing Kendall. Then, since he was somewhat off line, Pruett accelerated slower than usual up the hill and Schroeder moved past him and into the lead in turn six.

Three laps later Kendall again tried Pruett in turn five, only this time for second. The two cars made contact and Kendall was past. Shortly thereafter Fellows also moved by Pruett, putting Mustangs 1-2-3. A frantic last lap which saw Fellows hood explode off the car on the main straight ended with the checker flying over Schroeder, Kendall, Pruett, Fellows, Picket, Tommy Archer, Gentilozzi and Said. However a post-race inspection found the fuel cell in Kendall's car "not in specification" and he was disqualified, moving everybody behind Schroeder up one notch. Pruett's second place was enough to give him the 1994 Trans-Am Championship, his second, and the fourth in a row for the McCall team.

The one hour World Challenge race was somewhat of a non-event. The two Kelly Moss Porsche 911 Turbos simply had too much speed on RA's long straights. Price Cobb and Mauro Baldi ran 1-2 for the entire 22 laps, 88 miles. Steve Dinan finished third in a BMW 540i, but he was well behind.

The Barber Saab series ran two separate 30 minute races, one Saturday afternoon and the other Sunday morning. The first race saw Jaki Scheckter, 18 year old nephew of 1979 World Champion Jody Scheckter, rocket from fourth on the grid to the lead by turn one. Scheckter led the first nine of 13 laps but his low downforce setup was cooking the tires in the corners and he fell back into the grasp of Mark Hotchkis, who took him in turn one while Scheckter had to fend off the advances of Geoff Boss, Juan Pablo Montoya and Diego Guzman. Hotchkis won, followed by Scheckter, Boss, Montoya and Guzman.

Race two the next morning seemed to be an instant replay. Scheckter again started fourth, again led in turn one, and Hotchkis followed him for the first several laps. Then on lap nine of 12 Hotchkis again passed Scheckter going into turn one. The laps ran out with Hotchkis and Scheckter repeating their one-two finish, with Guzman, Montoya and Boss following.

The CART season was interesting in a number of ways. Most noticeable was the Penske domination. Penske got everything right this season and the three Penske drivers, Al Unser Jr., Emerson Fittipaldi and Paul Tracy, would finish 1-2-3 in the championship, winning 12 races along the way. Reynard had entered the customer car derby and had won twice so far, both times with Michael Andretti, back from the F-1 wars, in the Ganassi/Target car. Mario Andretti had announced his retirement at the end of the year, and his career was being recognized with the *Arrivederci, Mario* tour. Indeed, at RA Wisconsin Governor Thompson was on hand with a proclamation and a gift for Mario.

On the engine front Honda had joined the fray and was powering the Rahal-Hogan Lolas of Bobby Rahal and Mike Groff. The rest of the field was split fairly evenly between the Ford XB engine and the latest "D" version of the Ilmor. Chevrolet had sold its interest in Ilmor Engineering, and the engines were badged as *Ilmor* this year rather than Chevrolet. At the end of the season Mercedes-Benz

After taking the lead in the 1994 CART 200, young Jacques Villeneuve II withstands intense pressure from Paul Tracy and Al Unser Jr. to take the win.

would buy into Ilmor and starting the following year the mills would be badged *Mercedes-Benz*. There still were two "A" versions here, in the possession of the more impecunious teams.

Qualifying saw Paul Tracy take his third straight pole at RA; however, this year he did not crash after doing it! Further, his time of 1:45.416 handily broke Rahal's three year old lap record. Next to him on the front row was a very interesting story. Jacques Villeneuve II, the son of Gilles Villeneuve and the nephew of the Jacques Villeneuve who had won the 1985 race here, had entered Indy car racing. In 1993 young Jacques had won five races in the Player's Ltd./Toyota Atlantic Series. This year he and the team for whom he drove, Forsythe-Green Racing, moved into Indy cars with Reynard 94I-Fords sponsored by Player's Ltd. This was the best qualifying effort of his very young career. Row two held Nigel Mansell in the Newman-Haas/K-Mart/Havoline Lola T-94/00-Ford and Unser Jr. Fifth and sixth on the grid were Robby Gordon in the Walker/Valvoline Lola T-94/00-Ford and young Mexican driver Adrian Fernandez, who was in the Galles/Quaker State/Tecate Reynard 94I-Ilmor. The next row was Mario Andretti, Newman-Haas/K-Mart/Havoline Lola T-94/00-Ford and Mark Smith, Walker/Sears Craftsman Lola T-94/00-Ford. Rounding out the top ten were Emerson Fittipaldi and Raul Boesel, Simon/Duracell Lola T-94/00-Ford. In all 30 cars started the Texaco Havoline 200.

With the flick of the green Tracy took off, hoping to duplicate his flag-to-flag win of the prior year. Villeneuve stayed on his tail, while Mansell dropped back, his car not pulling maximum revs. Before fans had settled back on their blankets Claude Bourbannais and Franck Freon were out, their tired equipment from back-of-the-pack teams having expired. Jimmy Vasser would follow shortly as his Hayhoe Reynard just wouldn't handle. The Andrettis were having an atrocious time, Mario losing many places with a flat and Michael having to pit not once, but twice for two flat tires.

At one-third distance Tracy led, but Villeneuve remained right with him. Unser Jr. ran third, then came Gordon, Mansell, Fernandez, Eddie Cheever in the Foyt/Copenhagen Lola T-94/00-Ford and Smith. Gordon, Cheever and Smith all dropped out in short order just before the pit stops began with engine woes. Villeneuve stalled leaving his pit, and Unser was able to rejoin the race in second. Villeneuve came back out in third, fol-

lowed by Mansell, Mario back up to fifth, Fernandez, Fittipaldi, Teo Fabi in the Jim Hall/Pennzoil Reynard 94I-Ilmor, Dominic Dobson and Scott Sharp in the PacWest Racing Lola T-94/00-Fords and Rahal in his Miller Genuine Draft Lola T-94/00-Honda.

The middle portion of the race produced minor changes, but a full course yellow was called to clean up the mess when Arie Luyendyk crashed his Indy Regency Racing Lola T-94/00-Ilmor in the kink. This occurred within the second fuel stop window, so all stopped under yellow and prepared to run to the finish. The pivotal moment of the race was as the cars came up the hill to take the restart beginning lap 36. Tracy and Unser accelerated away, but Villeneuve got just a bit better jump and went into turn one intent on taking the lead. He moved inside Tracy while Unser moved outside. Tracy and Villeneuve touched wheels but Jacques was on the inside. They went around turn one side by side, then Villeneuve accelerated down to three, ahead of both Tracy and Unser! It was not only the pass of the race, but probably of the year.

The next several laps flew by with the two Marlboro cars all over the tail of Villeneuve's Player's Ltd. car. Tracy made several attempts to overtake, but Villeneuve displayed a maturity beyond his tender age in fending them off. On lap 44 Tracy slowed on the Moraine Sweep and pulled down the escape road at five, his engine gone. Unser now harried Villeneuve, hoping to coax him into a mistake. However, no mistakes were made, and Jacques Villeneuve II swept under the checkered flag, winning his first Indy car race. Unser finished second and in so doing wrapped up his second PPG Cup. Fittipaldi was third with Fabi fourth, having taken that position on lap 48 when Mario Andretti pulled off with engine failure. Fernandez and Boesel filled out the top six. It was a great race, full of excitement and marked the arrival of a great new talent.

After the exciting Indy car race the Dodge/Shelby Pro Series ran for 52 miles. The race was fought between Scott Harrington and Kyle Konzer. Harrington led from the pole with Konzer in close attendance. Both pulled away from the balance of the field, which was led by Augie Pabst III. Konzer passed Harrington for first on lap five, but Harrington took it back on lap eight. That was it, as Harrington, Konzer and Pabst finished in the top three spots.

1995

The big news in racing as 1995 dawned was the split between the Indianapolis Motor Speedway (IMS) and CART. The reasons are many, some known, and probably some unknown. Tony George, president of IMS, desired to not only have more control over Indy car racing but also wanted to reestablish the Indianapolis 500 as the event around which all other Indy car races revolved. CART had grown to such an extent in the past several years that it viewed each race as being a major event and was not willing to give control to George and to subjugate its series to the Indy 500. The result was a split, with George forming his own series, the Indianapolis Racing League (IRL), which would start in 1996. This would run strictly on oval tracks. Further, also starting in 1996, places in the Indy 500 would be guaranteed to the top 25 drivers in IRL points. The predictable result was each series going its own way, CART without the Indy 500 and the IRL and Indy 500 without the top teams and drivers.

This split did serve to help RA, though. Andrew Craig, president of CART, negotiated a series of long term contracts with most CART tracks, including RA. This assured RA of a CART date through the end of the century, far more peace of mind than the track enjoyed with Craig's predecessors.

To replace the IMSA date, vacant in 1994, the track negotiated for a major event. In early August the motorcycle Grand Prix of the United States was scheduled. This would have brought in riders from all over the world and would indisputably have been the top bike race in the U.S. However, it did not happen. The F.I.M., motorcycling's world governing body, demanded that the track construct chicanes in the middle of the three main straights. Needless to say, the track objected strongly to such butchering, and the race was not held. RA scheduled a round of the North American Super Bike Series instead.

Besides the two motorcycle and off road events the track would have three car weekends as in 1994; the June Sprints, the Historics and the CART/Trans-Am. Texaco Havoline would continue as title sponsor of the CART Indy car race, while Cousins Subs came in as the June Sprints title sponsor. A major improvement at the track was the construction of a tunnel under the track on the south side between turns one and three. This tunnel would serve several purposes. First of all it would give access to the inside area of the track between turns one-three and the south paddock, opening up a new spectator area. Secondly, it was built high enough to allow the big transporters to get through, thus allowing movement of the big rigs while

The field powers up the hill as the Texaco Havoline 200 restarts following a yellow flag period. The cones at the left mark the line where timing and scoring clocked each lap.

the track was hot. Until now they had to cross the track between turns 13 and 14 and could do so only when the track was cold. Coupled with this was the creation of an exit from the paddock on the south end, in order to use the tunnel. The project was sponsored by Briggs & Stratton, and their name is on the tunnel, as well as an arch spanning the track at this point.

The track also received attention with the entire four miles being repaved. This was the first new surface since the track last was repaved in 1976. Speeds were expected to jump now that the track had a new coat of sticky asphalt. The asphalt mix was a special concoction, designed to hold up over a wide range of temperatures. It was hoped that it not only would withstand the harsh Wisconsin winters but also the effects of hot racing tires.

Change also was evident with the sanctioning bodies. The SCCA and USAC separate FF2000 series were merged to form the U.S. FF2000 Championship. The pro Sports 2000 series, which had its birth 12 years earlier at RA, folded. IMSA continued to struggle with its World Sports Car concept, and it was safe to say that it had survived 1994 only through the presence of the Ferrari WSC. IMSA's healthiest series, the Barber Saab Series, switched to the SCCA. Further, the spec car, arrive and drive series now was known as the Barber Dodge Series as Dodge contracted with Skip Barber to sponsor all his activities. On the other hand, IMSA's Firestone Firehawk Series became known as the IMSA Street Stock Series as Firestone withdrew its sponsorship after 10 years to concentrate on Indy cars.

The Cousins June Sprints was again held the last weekend in June. This was the 40th running of this premier event and 533 cars were running in the eight races held covering the 25 SCCA club racing classes. Something new this year was the running of a round of the Dodge/Shelby Pro Series—the first time that a pro race was scheduled on the June Sprints weekend. The weather was delightful, and a crowd of 15,000 fans turned out to enjoy the fun.

Two class winners this weekend exemplified the spirit of SCCA club racing. Steve Pommer backed his HP Austin-Healey Sprite into the barriers in morning practice. He pounded it out as best he could, then drove his truncated car to the HP win in the afternoon. Mark Weber was a crew of one on his Sprite. He had nothing but trouble in practice and labored long and hard doing all the work trying to get his car to run right. He almost missed the race as he was under the car trying to fix his brakes as the grid was forming, but he made it and won FP.

The Formula Fords again did their best to entertain with 13 laps of constant lead swapping. Tom Dalrymple won after passing Dan Rinehart going up the hill for the last time. Keith Brown finished third. The three all had a chance at winning as they came out of turn 14 but it was Dalrymple who made the right move. The Spec Racer event started 89 cars, making the track look like rush hour on the Dan Ryan Expressway. Tony Buffomante, Chris Funk and John Collier Jr. inched ahead of the bunch and traded the lead several times before Collier took advantage of a missed shift by Buffomante on the last lap to win.

The Formula feature was won by Tony Ave who had an untroubled run in Olsson Engineering's Swift DB-4. Robert Sollenskog was second with Dan Carmichael third, both in Ralt RT-40s. FC was won once again by Dave Weitzenhof, which was fitting since he was awarded the Governor's Cup this year. Weitzenhof scored his 11th class victory at the Sprints, second only to Jerry Hansen. It took him a few laps to get past Tony Stefanelli's Piper, but once by he cruised to the checker.

The Formula Vee race was led at various points by Bill Noble, Eric Tremayne, Jeff Salcedo, Brian McCarthy and Tom Stephani. Not once each, but many times as the lead changed constantly. Into the last lap the order was Salcedo, McCarthy, Jacques Lazier and Bill Noble. At the checker the leader was Bob Lybarger! Again, FV provided the best cut-and-thrust, rock 'em, sock 'em racing.

The sports racing event was led early by Jeff Miller, but not late. Miller had seemingly exorcised his demons by winning the previous two years, but not so. On lap four Miller's engine failed, putting him out. Tom Jagemann went on to win in his CSR Lola-Olds, while Al Beasley Jr. finished second overall and first in DSR in his LeGrand-AMW. Alan Andrea was the S2000 winner, taking the class lead on the second last lap when leader Webb Bassick retired with a flat tire sustained in a collision while defending his position from Andrea.

The Dodge/Shelby Pro Series wound up the weekend with a 52 mile race. It was a perfect weekend for Augie Pabst III. Driving on his home track, not far from his Oconomowoc, WI, home, young Pabst started from the pole and led every lap on the way to his first pro win, a storybook weekend. Mike Davies finished second after starting ninth, coming through the field in fine fashion. Bennett Dorrance, Gary Tiller and Jerry Gillis rounded out the top five.

The Texaco-Havoline 200 was blessed with a fine summer weekend, running the first weekend in July. A great turnout of approximately 75,000 fans viewed the Indy car race, making this the largest weekend in Wisconsin sports history. Weather was very warm and humid, but nobody seemed to mind, as this is what all were waiting for.

The SCCA Trans-Am race had a full field with several multi-car teams battling for supremacy. Roush had two Mustangs for Tom Kendall and Jon

Gooding, while Gloy had three for Dorsey Schroeder, Boris Said and Brian Simo. On the Chevrolet side were the Buz McCall team with Ron Fellows and Jamie Galles; Pickett Racing with Greg Pickett, Brian Till and R.J. Valentine; and Rocketsports with Paul Gentilozzi, Price Cobb, Bill Saunders and Tim McAdam. In all, 29 cars started the 100 mile race.

It would be nice to say that the race was an artistic success, but to be honest it was a bit ugly. There were far too many cases of contact, leading to several crashes and many hard feelings. Jamie Galles started his Camaro from the pole, due to SCCA's inversion of the Fast Five qualifiers, but was passed almost immediately by Said and Schroeder. After things shook out, Said was the leader with Schroeder, Cobb, Till, Kendall, Fellows, Pickett, Gooding and Gentilozzi. Schroeder found his handling going off and dropped back in the pack with Kendall advancing, only to make contact with Cobb and spin back to 17th place. Till pressured Cobb for third, but then made contact with Cobb. Price went off in his Rocketsports Camaro, only to come back on right into the side of Till. As if Till hadn't had enough excitement, he collided with his team owner Pickett on the next lap, ending his day.

Meanwhile, Schroeder was moving again, and when he tried to take Galles on lap 18 he hit him from behind, spinning Galles off. For his troubles Schroeder was hit with a stop and go penalty. Said still led, with Schroeder (before his stop) and Fellows between him and Kendall in fourth. Then, Kendall tried to take Fellows going into one, and there was contact. Kendall hit the back of Fellows' Camaro, sending it into the barriers hard. Fellows was not amused.

Two laps from the end Kendall caught and passed Said in Canada Corner for the lead, holding it to the finish. But it wasn't the finish. SCCA officials assessed Kendall and Cobb the time equivalents of stop and go penalties. This meant that Boris Said was the winner, Brian Simo second and Kendall third. Rob Rizzo, Ford Mustang, was fourth, followed by Schroeder and Tony Ave, Camaro. It was an unsatisfactory ending to what could have been a great race between a fine group of drivers. Kendall was embarrassed by the penalty, but he didn't let it bother him, as he went on to win his second Trans-Am championship.

A one hour World Challenge race followed which was taken by David Murry in the Rohr Racing Porsche 911 Turbo. Victor Sifton in the Canaska Camaro led the opening laps of the one hour race with John Heinricy next in the Morrison Corvette. Murry used all of his Porsche's turbo power to move past both by the third lap and was unchallenged for the balance of the 80 miles thereafter. Sifton retired and Heinricy slowed with a fluid leak, putting Stephan Dinan in second in his BMW 540i and Jochen Rohr third in the second Rohr Porsche 911 Turbo. Heinricy came in fourth with teammate Jim Minneker fifth. Sixth went to comedian Tim Allen, making his pro racing debut in the Saleen Mustang entered by the team he co-owned with Steve Saleen.

The final race on Saturday and the first on Sunday were two separate Barber-Dodge events. Both were won by Jaki Scheckter with Fredrik Larsson second on Saturday and Thomas Schie in the runner up spot Sunday.

RA was round 10 of the 1995 PPG Cup Series. The previous year Penske Racing had dominated, winning 12 races. This year was more competitive as five drivers had won the first nine events. Jacques Villeneuve II was the points leader. The new pavement had the expected effect on qualifying times and 24 cars broke Paul Tracy's one year old track mark of 1:45.415. Villeneuve was fastest at 1:41.261, 142.206 mph in his Team Green/Player's Ltd. Reynard 95I-Ford. He took the pole in the final seconds of qualifying, knocking rookie Gil de Ferran from the top spot. De Ferran was in Jim Hall's Pennzoil Reynard 95I-Mercedes Ilmor. Michael Andretti, now back with Newman-Haas, was third in the K-Mart/Texaco Lola T-95/00-

Ford. Alongside Michael was Raul Boesel, running very fast indeed in the Rahal-Hogan Duracell Lola T-95/00-Mercedes. The third row comprised Al Unser Jr. in the Marlboro Penske PC-24-Mercedes and Bobby Rahal in the second Rahal-Hogan Lola, sponsored by Miller Genuine Draft. The seventh starter was Scott Pruett driving the Patrick Racing Lola T-95/00-Ford. This car marked the return of Firestone to Indy car racing after an absence of over 20 years. Firestone had not won yet on its return, but they were competitive and it was only a matter of time. Teo Fabi was next, driving the Combustion Engineering Reynard 95I-Ford for Forsythe Racing. Forsythe and Green had amicably split after the '94 season and were fielding separate teams. Rounding out the top ten qualifiers were Christian Fittipaldi, Emerson's nephew running Indy cars after three years in Formula 1, in the Walker/Chapeco Reynard 95I-Ford and Bryan Herta in the Ganassi/Target Reynard 95I-Ford.

The large bore production car race saw a very large field of Cobras compete. Here Bob Bondurant leads the pack into turn 3.

Villeneuve handled the start superbly and led de Ferran around the first lap. The field fell into place much as they had qualified, except for Paul Tracy who moved from 11th to sixth. Tracy was driving for Newman-Haas this year, Penske having gone back to a two car team. He was driving his K-Mart/Budweiser Lola T-95/00-Ford in pain, as he had broken his foot earlier in the week go-karting. On the second lap two of the biggest names were out. Going down the Moraine Sweep Michael Andretti and Al Unser Jr. contrived to come together and both retired. Following a full course yellow to clean the mess, Villeneuve led, followed by de Ferran, Boesel, Tracy, C. Fittipaldi, Fabi, Rahal, Herta, Jimmy Vasser in the second Ganassi/Target Reynard 95I-Ford and Stefan Johansson in the Bettenhausen/Alumax Penske PC-23-Mercedes. There were two Honda engined cars in the race. The highest running was the Comptech/Motorola Reynard 95I of Parker Johnstone, which was 11th.

The first round of pit stops came with Villeneuve retaining the lead. Tracy stalled, his foot giving him a great deal of pain, and dropped to sixth. He was driving marvelously though and soon passed Herta for fifth on lap 21. Two laps later Christian Fittipaldi and Boesel became preoccupied with disputing third and Tracy slipped past Boesel for fourth. Lap 30 saw one of those embarrassing moments. Mauricio Gugelmin tried to take his PacWest/Hollywood Reynard 95I-Ford past the Galles/Quaker State/Tecate Lola T-95/00-Mercedes of Adrian Fernandez, only to spin and collect his teammate Danny Sullivan. Explain that to the boss.

That incident set off the second round of pit stops and the Jim Hall team gambled, leaving de Ferran out on the track until the end of the caution period. The hope was that de Ferran could go the rest of the way without pitting again, while all the others would. De Ferran duly led until his delayed stop which dropped him back to 15th. Unfortunately, not only did a subsequent full course yellow allow the rest to go the distance without another fuel stop, but de Ferran spun off the track on lap 46 and retired with gearbox trouble.

Villeneuve continued to lead with Tracy now up to second. Rahal, Boesel and Fabi all had off course excursions which dropped them from potential podium finishes. Jacques Villeneuve II was the dominant winner, leading all but the four laps that were led by de Ferran. Paul Tracy came in second, a very courageous drive with a foot that was throbbing unmercifully. Indeed, Tracy had to be helped from his car and a chair was provided for him on the podium. Jimmy Vasser took the final step on the podium, com-

ing in an uneventful third. Andre Ribeiro was delighted with the Honda engine and Firestone tires as he steadily moved from 12th on the grid to a fourth place finish in the Tasman Motorsports LCI Reynard 95I-Honda. Rahal was fifth, followed by Fernandez, Pruett, C. Fittipaldi, Fabi and rounding out the top ten, Johansson. Villeneuve took a big step towards the 1995 PPG Indy car championship, which he would win in only his second season of Indy car racing.

The day concluded with 53 Dodge/Plymouth Neons racing for 48 miles. The Chrysler-sponsored race was won by Ian Phillips who took the lead on the last lap from Monte Cowles.

On July 22-23 it was time for the Historic Races, or to give them their jaw-breaking formal name, the Merrill Lynch/Brian Redman International Challenge Presented by the Chicago Historic Races. This year again had a Grand Marshal, and grand he was indeed. America's first World Champion, Phil Hill, was on hand to preside over matters and to spend a couple hours at the autograph table in the midway.

The feature this year was the Cobra vs. Ferrari Challenge, in recognition of the 30th anniversary of Cobra's World GT Championship. Among the two dozen Cobras present were two of the Daytona coupes plus the one-off Daytona Super Coupe. The race itself had 29 cars of which were 16 Cobras. Six Ferraris ran along with some contemporary competitors such as a couple Jaguar XKEs and an Aston Martin DB-4GT Zagato, which was driven by Brian Redman. Cobras won again, and it was fitting that the lead Cobra was driven by Bob Bondurant.

The Can-Am field was down to 15 cars this year, but they were interesting and they were loud. Besides the usual McLaren and Lola entries, there also was one of the '74 all-conquering Shadow DN-4s, two McKees, two Porsche 908s, a Ferrari 512M, a Shadow Mk. III and a Lola T-73B coupe. Charlie Gibson won in his McLaren M6B.

Other sights to see included Augie Pabst's two Scarabs, the Ford Mk. IIs that finished 1st and 3rd at Le Mans in 1966, all three Echidnas and in an aural, as well as visual treat, a Ferrari 641. This Ferrari, a 1990 F-1 car, did not race (there are certain restrictions Ferrari puts on the sale of its old F-1 cars) but did some exhibition laps. The sound of its 3.5 liter 750hp V-12 engine was worth the price of admission alone!

That concluded the car portion of RA's 1995 spectator season. However, mention must be made of the Fall Vintage Festival in late September. The VSCDA had an Elva festival, with 41 Elvas present; surely the biggest assembly of Elvas anywhere at any time. To top it off, Elva founder, Frank Nicholls, was the Grand Marshal.

149

1996

The 1996 Chicago Historic races celebrated the 30th Anniversary of the Can-Am and an incredible field of over fifty cars took the green. Here the field enters turn 14 on lap one.

1996 witnessed the CART vs. IRL hostilities breaking out into full war. Tony George's IRL ran five races including the Indy 500, all on ovals. CART ran 16 events spread between ovals, true road courses and street circuits. RA, of course, cast its lot with CART and the mid-August CART date produced an all time record crowd. Clearly, the fans in Wisconsin and the surrounding states voted with their feet and voted for CART and RA.

The 1996 schedule was one of great interest. The June Sprints celebrated its 40th Anniversary, promising full fields as usual. The Historic Race weekend celebrated the 30th Anniversary of the start of the Can-Am, and word was spreading that this would be the greatest assemblage of Can-Am cars since the series folded after 1974. Indeed, the English-based Super Sports group, which runs historic sports racers in Europe, had committed to attend this event. Finally, the CART/Trans-Am weekend was now in mid-August, one week after Mid Ohio, giving fans a great midwest road racing one-two.

Capital improvements continued at the track with the construction of a paddock lavatory facility. To say that this was long needed is a major understatement. The track toilets, upgraded from wood enclosures to cinder block in the mid '70s, were an embarrassment to such a big league track.

The new facility featured all modern amenities, such as flush toilets and showers.

June 22-23 brought the June Sprints, now sponsored by the *Chicago Tribune,* back for its 40th Anniversary celebration. Unfortunately, the weather was not in too much of a celebratory mood and Sunday saw a big rainstorm hit in the afternoon. Nonetheless, an entry of 415 cars and a spectator turnout of 15,000 had a good, if wet, time.

The Formula Ford race was very different from past years. First place was a runaway, not the usual dog fight. Jon Horgas had the field measured and led all the way in his Van Dieman. The fight was for second with Dan Rinehart and John LaRue flipping the place back and forth until joined by Steve Kelly and Max Spector who made it a four-way fight. Kelly wound up second with Spector third, then Rinehart and LaRue. If the fight for first in FF was a runaway, FV made up for it as could be expected. Bill Wallschlaeger, Andres Sorrano, Peter Guillan, Bill Noble, Brad Stout and Mike Kochanski ran as one for the entire race. Stout led going into the last lap, Wallschlaeger led coming out of turn 14, but Guillan won! Typical June Sprints FV!

The Spec Racer mob (there were 84 starters!) filled the track with start to finish action. Warren Stilwell and Lee Fleming spent the first part of the race locked in tight embrace. At half distance Robert Mumm and Tony Buffomante caught up with them and made it a four way duel. The last lap was a scramble; all four shuffled constantly, trying to get the proper position for the run to the flag. They came across the S/F line almost four abreast with Fleming's nose just a mite ahead of Mumm's, exciting indeed!

The formula feature was taken by Robert Sollenskog in his Ralt RT-40. Most unfortunately, his closest pursuer, Tony Ave, crashed heavily trying to retake first from Sollenskog, suffering severe leg injuries that would sideline him for the balance of the year. John Schaller and Brian French, both in Ralts, followed Sollenskog. In FC Dave Weitzenhof picked up his 12th Sprints class victory.

The sports racing event once again saw Jeff Miller lead the opening rounds in his Lola-Kohler. However, once again Miller's luck was not good. This time it wasn't the engine that failed, but rather the tires. The race started on a wet track and Miller chose rain tires. This was a bad choice because the track dried and the tires overheated. Miller drifted back to seventh place after leading the first five laps. Dan Doyle in an ex-Olds Pro Series Lola-Olds CSR picked up first. The top three in Sports 2000, Webb Bassick, Andrea Kasiewicz and David Downey followed.

The Historic weekend this year was the best yet. The biggest field, foreign participation and the biggest crowd, combined with fine weather made for a great time. The Grand Marshal this year was Sir Jack Brabham, three time World Champion. Sir Jack not only spent a couple hours signing autographs and greeting fans in the midway but also drove a Brabham BT-6 Formula Junior in the formula event, finishing third in class and twelfth overall.

The talking point, however, was the 30th Anniversary of the Can-Am. The word was out that this was *the* event and an astounding 84 Can-Am cars appeared. They covered the gamut from the early Lola T-70s through the big block McLarens to the last of the line Shadows. All manner of Lolas were there: T-70, T-73B, T-163, T-163B, T-165, T-222, T-310. McLarens? McLaren Elvas Mk I, II, & III; M6A, M6B, M8B, M8C, M8D, M8E, M8F, M12, M20. Shadow Mk. IIIs, DN-2 & DN-4. March 707. McKee Mk. II, VI, VII, IX and XIV. Porsche 917-8 Spyders. Plus Genies, a Kincraft, a rare BRM, the Burnett, the Shelby King Cobra, the Honker II, Porsche 908s, Matichs and Ferraris. Yes, one could get a sore neck with all the head swiveling trying to see everything. A dozen of these cars were from Europe as the International Super Sports Association, which runs historic sports car racing in Europe, came over *en masse.*

Of course, it took a keen eye to really know what one was viewing. Over the years many McLarens have been rebodied as M8Ds and M8Fs. As *AutoWeek* put it, "all 15 of the world's nine M8Fs were here." Further, there were a few instances of more than one car claiming to be a certain car from the '70s. But that is more of a case of *caveat emptor* than anything else and did not diminish from the spectating pleasure.

The 10 lap, 40 mile race started over 50 cars, larger than any actual Can-Am field ever was. Bill Auberlen won in a McLaren M20, leading most of the way. His closest pursuer was George Follmer in the McLaren M8F semi-replica *McLaren from Hell.* Follmer was out early when a wing nut flew back through his radiator. The Europeans filled the next several places with Charlie Agg second in a McLaren M8F followed by Chris Chiles in a March 707 and Jost Kalisch fourth in a BRM P-154. The race was a spectacle in many ways, not the least being the Can-Am Thunder; the noise from over 50 big unmuffled V-8s was truly ground shaking.

The Can-Am event overshadowed the other cars that were there which was a bit unfortunate, because there were mouth-watering cars everywhere. Cobras, many Ferraris, a couple Mirages, two Scarabs, a Maserati 200-S, Alfa Romeo Disco Volante, Cooper and Lotus Juniors, Aston Martins, spe-cials, Listers, Jaguars and so on. Two days were not enough to see everything that was there!

The weekend of August 16-18 brought the Indy cars and Trans-Am to RA, along with some support races. The weather was glorious, and record crowds streamed through the gates all three days. Saturday's first race was the 100 mile Trans-Am and again this year it was dominated by the Ford Mustangs. Tom Kendall and Dorsey Schroeder were at the top of the point standings, locked in a close battle for the crown. Kendall once again was the fast qualifier in his Roush Mustang and started fifth with SCCA's inversion of the Fast Five. Jamie Galles started first in the Buz McCall Camaro, but third starting Boris Said was ahead by the end of lap one. Said's Roush Mustang got Schroeder's Gloy Mustang at turn five and nicked past Galles at turn 12. By lap three Kendall was into second and it was a Roush one-two as they led Schroeder, Galles, Ron Fellows in the second McCall Camaro and Brian Simo in the second Gloy Mustang. Further back Greg Pickett in his own Camaro and Paul Gentilozzi and Eric Van de Poele in Rocketsports Camaros battled among themselves.

A full course yellow ensued when Dale Phelon hit the turn 13 bridge, destroying his Mustang and breaking several ribs. At the mid point of the race team orders came into play as Kendall was anxious to get the maximum amount of points. Said moved over in turn five and waved Kendall past into a lead he would hold for the balance of the race. Said ran shotgun for Kendall, protecting his rear. Schroeder was a lonely third, but fourth almost changed hands when Galles got under Simo in turn 14. Galles spun, Simo got away, and a close following Pickett hit Galles, putting both out. Simo finished in fourth with Fellows fifth and Max Lagod sixth, first of the *independents.* In the one race remaining this season, Kendall finished fourth while Schroeder dnf'd, making Kendall the champion for the second year in succession and third time overall.

Saturday's other race was the SCCA World Challenge. Due to many extended delays in Indy car practice and qualifying, the race got underway some two hours late, after 6:00 PM. Fortunately it was a sunny day and enough daylight remained to get all 22 laps completed. Martin Snow got a great start in his Porsche 911 Turbo and came by the first time with a substantial lead over Steve Saleen's Mustang. Almo Coppelli in the fierce Callaway Corvette entered by the Italian Agusta Racing Team, Andy Pilgrim in the Rohr Racing Porsche 911 Turbo and Shane Lewis in the boxy Mosler Intruder soon demoted Saleen to fifth and took out after Snow. They reeled him in, but disaster struck for Coppelli, as he collided with Snow while passing him, taking both out. Pilgrim moved into the lead and held it for the balance of the 88 miles. Saleen passed Lewis for second, but Lewis repassed at turn eight on the last lap to finish in that spot. Coppelli had run up a large point lead by winning the first three races of the season, but that was being eroded race by race. However, the Italian was able to score enough points in the two races remaining to take the championship.

Sunday morning it paid one to get to the track early. An absolutely monstrous crowd turned out, in excess of 75,000 people, and by late morning the highways were backed up all the way into Plymouth. The Sheboygan County Sheriff's Department finally had to block off the roads as there was no room left in the track, all the parking areas filled to overflowing. The track has never had a crowd like this, but it was a good problem to have.

As the crowds were still making their way into the track, the Barber Dodge Series ran a 14 lap, 56 mile race. Norway's Thomas Schie beat pole sitter Tony Rena off the line and led all 14 laps for an easy victory. Rino Mastronardi and Derek Hill (son of Phil Hill) swapped second before Rino prevailed, Hill coming in third.

The Formula Atlantic cars returned to RA for the first time since 1990.

Christian Fittipaldi was the surprise early leader in the 1996 CART race. He held it until late in the race when he suffered engine failure.

The '96 version of the Player's/Toyota Atlantic Championship was all Patrick Carpentier. He had led every race since mid-June, five in all, flag-to-flag, starting from the pole each time! This weekend would be no different. Carpentier needed only one point to clinch the title and he got that in qualifying, taking the pole again. Then he led every lap in the race, as simple as that. To top off his season, he took his Lynx Racing Ralt RT-41 to wins in the last two races, making it eight straight wins and nine in the season, both records. It was no surprise that he moved up to Indy cars in 1997.

Despite Carpentier's utter dominance, there were other people in the race. Carpentier's Lynx teammate, Jeret Schroeder, ran second early but went out with a broken gearbox. Lee Bentham, Paul Jasper and Chuck West traded places a few times before West came out second with Bentham and Jasper next.

That cleared the table for the CART Indy cars. This year's hot team and combination belonged to Chip Ganassi. He used his Target sponsorship dollars wisely and had Jimmy Vasser and former F-1 driver Italian Alex Zanardi in Firestone-shod Reynard 96Is powered by very powerful Honda engines. It was the setup to have. Vasser won four of the season's first six races, including the U.S. 500 and was the points leader. Zanardi came on strong the second half of the year and had already notched two wins in his rookie year. While Vasser did not win again after May, his early lead—plus Zanardi taking points from the opposition—held up for the 1996 PPG Cup championship.

The other teams using Honda engines also were meeting with various levels of success. Tasman Motorsports had won three times with its Lola T-96/00s. Andre Ribeiro had two big wins in the LCI Lola, before his countrymen in Rio, at the first ever Indy car race in Brazil and the Marlboro 500 at Michigan. Adrian Fernandez had scored one win in the Quaker State/Tecate car. Jim Hall's Pennzoil team had one win with Gil de Ferran, but should have had more as de Ferran's Reynard had dropped out a couple times with victory in sight. As the season wound down it was bittersweet for Hall, who had already announced his retirement at the end of the year, ending a spectacular career as driver, engineer, designer, innovator and team owner. The sixth Honda runner was Parker Johnstone in the Brix/Comptech Motorola Reynard. Johnstone had no wins, but did have a second. He was handicapped in relation to the other Honda runners in that his team was running to a much smaller budget.

The closest pursuers of the Ganassi team were Penske Racing and Newman/Haas. Penske was in the process of having a winless season, a startling development for what arguably has been Indy car racing's top team over the past 20 plus years. The problem seemed to lie in the chassis. The Penske PC-25 just did not get it right this year. It was reasonably good on short ovals but on superspeedways and road circuits it simply did not handle. Penske was running three cars, all Marlboro sponsored. Al Unser Jr. and Paul Tracy were in the main Penske entry, while Emerson Fittipaldi ran an all red Marlboro-Latin America car for the satellite Hogan-Penske team. Fittipaldi would not be present at RA as he had a serious crash two races earlier at Michigan, suffering a broken neck that was expected to keep him out of racing for over a year, if not cause his retirement. Young Danish sensation Jan Magnussen was deputized into Fittipaldi's car. The Penskes, of course, were all running Mercedes engines.

The Newman-Haas team was the *works* Lola entry as usual, but that arrangement was coming to an end. At the end of the season Lola and Haas would split, ending Carl's 29 years as U.S. Lola distributor. The team had already announced that it would use the American-built Swift chassis in 1997. Swift, owned by driver Hiro Matsushita, had never built an Indy car before, but had a long record of success in lesser formulas. Michael Andretti, who had three wins this year, and Christian Fittipaldi would drive the team's Lola T-96/00s, Andretti's sponsored by K-Mart/Texaco Havoline and Fittipaldi's by K-Mart/Budweiser. Both cars were powered by the Ford XD engine.

Toyota entered Indy car racing this year with its turbo V-8. A long learning curve was in prospect, but hopefully Toyota learned from the failures of Porsche and Alfa Romeo, and the success of Honda. Dan Gurney's All American Racers, long the Toyota entrant in American road racing, built new Eagle Mk. V cars for Juan Fangio II and P.J. Jones. The Eagle returned to Indy car racing after a 10 year absence. It was the first American built chassis in Indy car racing since the Truesports of the early '90s. The Arciero team, now co-owned by Toyota's off-road entrant, Cal Wells, was running an MCI sponsored Reynard 96I-Toyota for Italian sensation Max Papis who had taken over for Jeff Krosnoff who had regrettably lost his life in a terrible crash earlier at Toronto.

Paul Tracy, Scott Pruett and Jimmy Vasser fight for position in turn three during the Texaco Havoline 200.

The lap record remained intact as Alex Zanardi fell short of equaling Jacques Villeneuve's one year old mark. Zanardi took the pole at 1:41.998, 141.179 mph. De Ferran was alongside him in the first row while the Newman-Haas pair, Andretti and Fittipaldi shared row two. Mauricio Gugelmin turned in a good time in the PacWest/Hollywood Reynard 96I-Ford to take the fifth spot, with Bryan Herta alongside in the Team Rahal/Shell Reynard 96I-Mercedes. Vasser and Tracy were next; then came Bobby Rahal in his Team Rahal/Miller Reynard 96I-Mercedes and Magnussen. Starting eleventh was another sensational rookie, Greg Moore in the Forsythe/Players Reynard 96I-Mercedes. Moore had entered Indy car racing this year after a dominating '95 Indy Lights year in which he won 10 of 12 races. The 21 year old Canadian had led some races this year and was unlucky not to have at least one win under his belt.

The Texaco Havoline 200 began with a bang-literally. Coming into turn three on the first lap, Zanardi and de Ferran managed to get mixed up, putting de Ferran out on the spot and Zanardi back in 11th. Jan Magnussen also got involved in the melee and was out. After the dust settled Christian Fittipaldi was in the lead followed by Gugelmin, Andretti and Herta. Tracy dropped from the lead group when he spun into the gravel trap, losing a lap in the process.

Fittipaldi continued to lead while Herta moved up to second, followed by Gugelmin, Rahal and Andretti. Moore exited the race spectacularly as Ribeiro moved over on him while being passed, putting Moore into the guard rail in Kettle Bottoms at almost 200 mph. Moore bounced along the rail, shedding parts most of the way, winding up in the turn 12 sand trap. Mercifully, the livid Moore was uninjured. At the same time this was happening, Davy Jones somehow contrived to get his Galles/Delco Lola upside down in a one car incident at turn 13. He too escaped injury. All this action naturally brought out a full course yellow.

This was on lap 15 and was the leading edge of the first pit stop window. Most came in for service except Zanardi and Papis, who were first and second as the race entered its middle portion. Both had stopped earlier and were out of sequence. Zanardi opened a bit of a lead while Unser Jr., Andretti and Fittipaldi all got around Papis. Fittipaldi shortly passed Andretti

for third, and then Ribeiro struck again. His Lola-Honda stuttered exiting Canada Corner and Mark Blundell, PacWest/Visa Reynard-Mercedes, moved past on the inside. Blundell's teammate, Gugelmin, was right behind and following Blundell past Ribeiro. The only problem was that Ribeiro turned right into Gugelmin, spinning him into Blundell. All three were out and another full course yellow was called. Incredibly, this was the second straight year that both PacWest cars went out in the same crash!

Zanardi pitted during this caution and Unser assumed the lead, holding it through the second round of pit stops. Once everyone was fueled for the duration, Unser led Fittipaldi, Andretti, Zanardi, Rahal, Stefan Johansson in the Bettenhausen/Alumax Reynard 96I-Mercedes, Herta, Johnstone, Scott Pruett in the Patrick Lola T-96/00-Ford, Vasser, Fangio, Raul Boesel in Team Green's Brahma Reynard 96I-Ford and Papis. They were all on the lead lap. On lap 45 of 50 Fittipaldi's engine expired, robbing him of second. He got out of the smoking car and bent over the guardrail, distraught at the cruel turn of fate. But fate was not done. Things seemed set for the finish and for the first win of the year for Penske and Unser. Then, when least expected, heartbreak. Unser was entering Canada Corner, less than one mile from taking the checkered flag, when his engine erupted in a huge cloud of smoke. Unser was out, deprived of a sure win. Michael Andretti flew under the waving checker, a very surprised and delighted winner. Bobby Rahal followed him, scoring a fine second place finish. Zanardi took the final podium spot, third being far more than he expected following his first lap adventures. Johansson, Herta, Vasser, Pruett, Fangio and Papis followed. Parker Johnstone would have been in that group, but as the race ended he was getting out of his car which was upside down in the gravel trap at turn one. Paul Tracy, who was a lap down, tried to pass Johnstone when such a move just wasn't on and hit him, sending Johnstone into a frightening series of barrel rolls. Fortunately, the likable Johnstone was uninjured, if very unamused. CART took a dim view of all these shenanigans and fined Ribeiro and Tracy $40,000 each. The race was not pretty.

Those fans who chose not to battle the traffic immediately stayed to watch 75 Plymouth and Dodge Neons race for 48 miles. Jeff Altenburg triumphed over the rush hour crush.

1997

The schedule was the same as 1996, with the same three spectator weekends. More capital improvements took place, enhancing spectating.

Most of the improvement took place in the turns 12-13 area. The hill on the outside of Canada Corner, while providing a fine view of one of the best turns on the track, had become virtually unusable in the past decade due to erosion and plant growth. Those who risked the tricky descent to the fence found little to see due to an overabundance of shrubbery. The track cleared the shrubbery and built a wide wooden staircase, then installed a goodly sized grandstand, thus returning a fine viewing area to the fans. The outside of the turn itself was given a large gravel trap, a welcome addition coming as it is at the end of a 200 mph straightaway. The Bill Mitchell Bridge at turn 13 was replaced by a wider structure which allowed a freer flow of traffic, both motorized and pedestrian. Also, since it was now roofless, transporters had another way of leaving the track while the track was hot.

Grand Marshall of the 1997 Historic weekend was the old snake himself, Carroll Shelby. Shelby delighted the crowd with some demonstration laps in one of his *new* Cobras.

Off track the political wars now involved the SCCA vs. IMSA for control of U.S. road racing. While the two sanctioning bodies had coexisted (albeit somewhat uneasily) for many years, things were changing. Charles Slater, who had owned IMSA for three years, put it up for sale, apparently his fun done. A group of IMSA entrants, led by Rob Dyson, Charles Morgan, Henry Camferdam and a few others, negotiated to buy it from Slater. Their idea was to then combine it with SCCA Pro Racing in a loose alliance that would have the effect of unifying U.S. road racing. Unfortunately, at the last moment Slater sold the sanctioning body to Andy Evans, the owner of Scandia Racing and a very wealthy financial broker. Evans' ideas were almost 180 degrees from those of the jilted owners' group. Evans renamed IMSA Professional Sportscar Racing (PSR), bought the Mosport track in Ontario and purchased the rights to Sebring. He then undertook a campaign both at home and in Europe that was designed to make his group the preeminent group in sports car racing. The ensuing clash with not only the SCCA, but also other sanctioning groups and the PSR entrants would culminate by the end of the season in cataclysmic change in U.S. road racing.

The CART vs. Indianapolis Motor Speedway split widened, as the IRL introduced a *spec* car chassis powered by 4.0 liter non-turbocharged stock-block engines. With the exception of Galles Racing, which had been uncompetitive in CART for the last couple years, no CART teams went to the IRL, while the Della Penna IRL team stepped up to CART. The IRL ran its own series again, but clearly the top drivers and teams were in CART. It appeared for the foreseeable future that there would be no reconciliation between the two series, with CART continuing to strengthen itself as the premier U.S. open wheel series and the IRL filling the role of a form of *Indy Lights*.

The June Sprints, this year sponsored by the nearby Kohler Company, ran the weekend of June 20-22. This turned out to be a very bad choice as torrential rains hit most of Wisconsin, producing flash flooding. The track had such heavy rain overnight on Friday that it was impossible to race on Saturday. The lower lying portions of the track were underwater and access roads were flooded. For the first time in RA's 43 seasons, a day's events were canceled.

Sunday morning dawned dry and fair. Qualifying and seven races (shortened to 30 minutes each) were squeezed into the now one day event. Attendance was down significantly due to many fans having to stay home and deal with flooded basements. Then the most horrible event in a jinxed weekend happened. During early morning qualifying, Mary Wollensen spun her Mini-Cooper in the kink and was hit broadside by a Camaro. She had

154

no chance and succumbed to her injuries.

The Governor's Cup presentation went to Tony Ave, who was honored for his comeback from the serious injuries he sustained in last year's Sprints. Also honored was Bud Seaverns, who had been active at RA from the start, first as a driver and later as an official.

The Formula Vee event again was a scramble. Five cars swapped the lead many times before Brad Stout won in a Protoform, just nipping Tom Stephani and Mike Kochanski at the line. Formula Ford was an emotional win for Dan Rinehart, who was driving his last race for the foreseeable future. Dan had lost his job, and the last of his money was going into this weekend. He fought hard with Jon Horgas, and the two came together a lap from the finish, Horgas going off course and Rinehart prevailing to the win.

The Formula feature went to Steve Forrer's Ralt RT-40, but the real action was in FC. Dave Weitzenhoff led in his Citation with Scott Rubenzer and Steve Thomson trading second back and forth in their Van Diemens. On the last lap Weitzenhoff got trapped behind one of the slower FA cars and Rubenzer saw the opening. He dove inside and managed to stave off Weitzenhoff's counter attack to win.

Tom Jagemann won the sports racing feature in his Lola T-89/90-Olds, and once again Jeff Miller's luck was sour. Miller started way down the field after trouble in qualifying, but thrilled the large Kohler Company contingent on had by knifing through the field. He was up to second and closing on Jagemann when he bounced over a curbing. A piece of body work flew off his 6 cylinder Kohler powered Lola, pierced his radiator and put him out. The Sports 2000 category went to Martin Ryba, Lola, while Mike Reupert was the winner in DSR in a Lola-AMW.

The Historic weekend had undergone a change as it was no longer the Chicago Historic Races. The event had grown so much from its start that the track felt that Joe Marchetti's organization was too small to run what was now a major event. Hence the track exercised its option in the contract with Marchetti, gave the sanction to the Vintage Sports Car Drivers Association (which ran the non-spectator Fall Vintage Festival) and took the promotion of the event in-house. Marchetti was extremely unhappy with this and sued the track to get the decision reversed; however, the text of the contract was very clear, and the court quickly ruled in the track's favor.

The featured *marque* this year was anything to do with Carroll Shelby. Cobras, Mustang GT-350s and Ford GT-40s were out in force. Carroll Shelby was the Grand Marshall, and it was a grand sight to see the legendary Texan drive exhibition laps around the four miles in a 427 Cobra. He also spent a good deal of time signing autographs in the Shelby Owners' Club tent.

A number of interesting cars were on the ground including three Scarabs. Augie Pabst had his usual two and Ali Lugo had a Formula 1 Scarab, this being rebuilt from the remains of the car crashed by Chuck Daigh at Silverstone in 1961. Rob Walton (of the Wal-Mart family) brought an ex-Jim Hall birdcage Maserati T-61, a Cobra Daytona coupe and a Ferrari GTO for his amusement. There also were Listers, a Lotus 40, the only center-seat Porsche RSK F-2 car in existence, a Cunningham C2R, the McKee Howmet turbine, 20 Can Am cars and the usual gaggle of Formula Juniors, Porsches, Elvas, Triumphs, MGs and the like.

Bob Brown, who had driven at RA as far back as 1962, won the large formula event in a Lola T-332. The Can-Am race was only a third as large as 1996's Can-Am Reunion. This year Juan Gonzalez won in a Shadow DN-4 over the 1966 McLaren Elva of Tom Grunnah.

The big CART weekend was August 15-17. Unfortunately, it was a weekend plagued by rain with the only difference between days being a degree of just how hard it was raining. On one hand, everyone grumbles about being wet and uncomfortable, but on the other a slick track often times brings out some sterling performances.

Saturday's 100 mile Trans-Am race was a case in point. Tom Kendall gave all a lesson of virtuoso driving on a changing track. This was round 10 of the 1997 Trans-Am season, and Kendall had won all nine preceding races! Kendall was enjoying a dream season, winning with ease at every race so far. His Roush Racing Ford Mustang was superbly prepared by the Dan Binks-led crew, and the bleached blond Kendall was on such a roll that he probably had the competition psyched-out as soon as his black and green All Sport car rolled off the trailer.

At the green flag the track was wet, with a light rain falling. Dorsey Schroeder qualified on the pole and led away in his Gloy Racing Raybestos Ford Mustang. He led Kendall until the Carousel where Tom calmly and decisively passed *on the outside!* Schroeder's Mustang was wagging fiercely, but Kendall's car was as if on rails. Superb driving indeed. Kendall opened up a comfortable lead, but the weather had another card to play. As the race passed half distance, the sun broke through the clouds and the track dried. The rain tires were fast overheating. Kendall led Paul Gentilozzi, Camaro; Jon Gooding, Schroeder, Brian Simo and Mike Borkowski, all Mustangs as the pit stops started.

Schroeder pitted first, but a faulty jack shot his efforts at getting an edge. On lap 19 Kendall pitted for four slicks. He reentered the race 45 seconds behind Simo's Gloy Valvoline Mustang and waited for Simo to pit. Only problem was that Simo had decided to try to go non-stop, gambling that his lead was big enough to hold off the speed advantage of Kendall's slick shod car for five laps. He couldn't. Once Kendall cranked it up, he took 15 seconds a lap off Simo's lead and sailed past into first on lap 24 of 25, winning the race and the season championship, his fourth. Simo held on for second, but his tires were well and truly shot. Gentilozzi took the third podium spot.

Kendall went on to win 11 in a row before Borkowski snapped his streak. Nonetheless, he set a book full of records, including most consecutive wins in a major race series and the most Trans-Am wins in a season. In addition, his fourth Trans-Am title and third in a row, are series records.

Saturday's other event was a 36 mile race for Neons, won by Eric Heuschele. He would finish second in Sunday's second race taking the season crown.

Sunday was a miserable, wet day. Dark, dank, the kind of day that grows moss on anything that stands still for over a minute. Unfortunately, the bad weather was felt at the gate, with many casual fans apparently deciding to roll over and go back to sleep as soon as they looked outside. The gate was about 50,000, down over 20,000 from the previous few years, all due to the weather.

The Kool/Toyota Formula Atlantic series was Sunday morning's first race. Sadly, the weather was so atrocious that spin outs and crashes were almost too frequent to record. As a result of all the full course yellows only three laps were run under green. Quality showed in that brief time, though, as Alex Baron put his Lynx Racing Ralt into first and held it. Joao Barbosa was second and Steve Knapp third. Baron went on to win five of the year's 12 races, taking the championship. His Lynx teammate, Memo Gidley, won two more events and was second.

The heavens opened at this time, flooding the track. Everything was put on hold as high water rendered the track unusable. The 2:30 race start time came and went. For a good time it appeared that the CART race would be postponed to the following Saturday. Fortunately for the water logged fans who huddled in their cars for hours, the rain stopped around 3:30 and optimism arose. It was decided to run the second Neon race at this time, hoping that over 50 of the little sedans would clear up some of the water that the jet blower didn't get. After the 24 mile race, won by John Phillips, CART decided that it was a go. The race finally started at 4:50, almost 2 1/2 hours late, and well after the time it should have ended!

Qualifying, of course, had taken place in two sessions on Friday and Saturday. When all was done, PacWest Racing Group had further established itself as a force in Indy car racing. Mauricio Gugelmin took the pole in his Hollywood cigarettes sponsored Reynard-Mercedes at 1:42.379, 142.242 mph. His teammate, Mark Blundell, who had already won twice this year, was second, a tick behind at 1:42.542. The third fastest qualifier was Alex Zanardi in the Target/Chip Ganassi Reynard-Honda. Zanardi, who had taken the season by the throat, was coming off three wins and a second in the past four races and was leading the points standings. Fourth fastest qualifier was rookie sensation Dario Franchitti, driving a Reynard-Mercedes for Carl Hogan. Michael Andretti was fifth in the Newman-Haas K-Mart/Texaco Swift 07.i. Swift had entered Indy car racing this year, and Carl Haas was its distributor. Andretti had won one race so far in the Swift, but was unlucky not to have more wins. The top ten was filled out by Scott Pruett, Patrick Racing/Brahma Reynard-Ford, Gil De Ferran, Walker/Valvoline Reynard-Honda, Bryan Herta, Rahal/Shell Reynard-Ford, Raul Boesel, Patrick/Brahma Reynard-Ford and Greg Moore, a winner twice this year, Forsythe/Players Reynard-Mercedes. In all, 28 cars would start.

Early in the Texaco Havoline 200 the lead was narrowly held by pole sitter Mauricio Gugelmin. His teammate Mark Blundell and Alex Zanardi follow him through turn five.

After the long rain delay, the field finally headed out at ten minutes to five, long after most spectators figured they would already be headed for home. Because of the fact that the track was still very wet, all started on rain tires, and the start was taken in single file order rather than two abreast. However, the yellow was out before the field even got to turn three. Gualter Salles spun in his Davis Racing Reynard, Paul Tracy went off course in avoidance and did a slow, lazy roll after hitting the tire wall. Tracy was OK, but scratch a former winner before the race was even 10 seconds old.

After everything was cleared the race started in earnest, with *Big Mo* Gugelmin leading, followed by Blundell, Zanardi, Franchitti and Andretti. This lasted until lap nine, when Blundell passed his teammate to take the lead. All had started on rain tires, but a dry line was appearing and the question now was when would slicks be in order. The first of the front runners to pit for slicks was Michael Andretti, who came in a bit early on lap 15 for fuel and a switch to slick tires. Michael's strategy was sound, but the execution was faulty. His first lap out of the pits saw him lose it on the approach to Canada Corner and slide off into the gravel, putting him out. His misfortune was to everyone else's advantage, as the pace car came out, and they all pitted under yellow for refueling and to switch to slick tires. Bryan Herta stayed out on rains and led the next few laps. Franchitti came out behind Blundell but he inexplicably forgot that the track was under yellow, tried to pass Blundell coming out of turn one, slid off course and crashed. A rookie mistake, which may have cost him the race. Herta finally pitted and when the green waved, Blundell led Zanardi, Gugelmin, De Ferran, Pruett, Andre Ribeiro (Tasman/LCI Reynard-Honda), Moore, Christian Fittipaldi (Newman-Haas/K-Mart Budweiser Swift-Ford), Raul Boesel (Patrick/Brahma Reynard-Ford) and Bobby Rahal (Team Rahal/Miller Reynard-Ford). After another yellow when Boesel and Ribeiro collided at turn one, the race settled down with Blundell leading Zanardi, with Gugelmin chasing.

This went on for several laps until the next round of pit stops when Zanardi's Ganassi crew got him in and out of the pits ahead of Blundell.

Zanardi then led Blundell, the margin very close. Blundell challenged, but Zanardi had his measure. Finally, just two laps from the end, the motor in Blundell's car blew in a big way. Zanardi came home the winner, with Gugelmin second, followed by De Ferran, Fittipaldi, Pruett and Rahal. This was Zanardi's fifth win of the year, and as the season went through its last three races his lead was such that he won the PPG Cup with one race to go. Zanardi became the first Italian to win the U.S. national championship.

A Barber Dodge race, originally scheduled for 11:30 in the morning, wound up the day's activities, taking the green flag at 7:30 at night! Rino Mastronardi and Derek Hill passed the lead back and forth countless times in a very intense duel for first until Hill slid off into the gravel at turn 12 with just two laps left. Mastrondardi came home the winner, but Hill would recover to take the series title.

A few weeks later, a meeting of the SCCA, Bill France Jr., Rob Dyson and a number of other promoters, entrants and television personnel saw the formation of a new racing series, largely in reaction to the excess of Andy Evans. This took the name United States Road Racing Championship. The USRRC, nominally an independent body, but actually under the control of SCCA Pro Racing, would run events for both GT cars and a newly constructed Can-Am series. These cars would for all intents and purposes be cars that run in PSR's World Sports Car series. At the end of 1997 it appeared that the SCCA would take over all professional sports car racing, with PSR fading away. However, as 1998 began, Don Panoz, who had made a fortune in pharmaceuticals, became interested in racing and in essence whipped out his checkbook and rescued PSR, now owned by a foursome of its executives. Thus, 1998 would see two parallel professional sports racing series exist, each competing for the same small pool of entrants. Not a healthy situation.

As racing ended at RA, construction began on a new pedestrian/vehicular bridge. Snap-On Tools was the sponsor of the bridge, which will cross the track at the entrance to the Carousel. The intent is to open up the inside of the Carousel as a major spectator area. It had not been in use for many years due to the presence of the off-road course. The track had discontinued that experiment, however, and the need for spectator space, especially on the CART weekend, was strong.